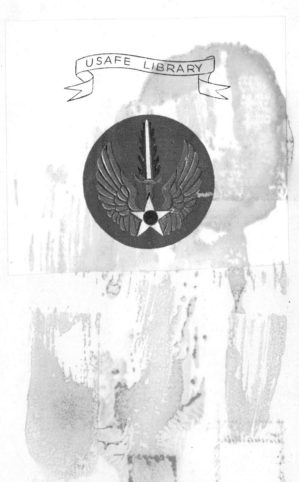

THE CRITIC AT THE

OPERA

The Royal Opera Arcade, Pall Mall, built by Nash
in 1819 at the rear of the late-eighteenth century
King's Theatre, Haymarket

THE CRITIC AT THE
OPERA

By

DENNIS ARUNDELL

The breath of music, brother lutenist,
Is sound, which into points of time art breaks:
But poetry is the language music speaks.
(*The Slighted Maid*) Act III

LONDON
ERNEST BENN LIMITED

First Published 1957 by Ernest Benn Limited
Bouverie House · Fleet Street · London · EC4
© Dennis Arundell 1957
Printed in Great Britain

TO
the Memory of
Edward J. Dent

Contents

Foreword   page xi

PART ONE

UP TO 1700 – SIGHT

I   The Start of Opera   17
II   Inigo Jones and Ben Jonson   23
III   Davenant and Opera   37
IV   Opera at Rutland House   49
V   Opera at the Cockpit, Drury Lane   60
VI   The Duke's Theatre and *The Slighted Maid*   73
VII   Davenant and Killegrew   88
VIII Dramatic Opera and Shadwell   99
IX   French Opera in London   107
X   Locke's *Psyche*   114
XI   Dryden and Opera   129
XII   Purcell and Opera   144

PART TWO

UP TO 1800 – SOUND

I   Italian Opera Introduced   157
II   Italian Singers Introduced   169
III   A Critical Discourse upon Operas   180
IV   Steele and Addison   193
V   The Royal Academy   216
VI   The Touchstone   241
VII   Handel and his Rivals   250
VIII Comedy Operas Triumph   252

CONTENTS

PART THREE

UP TO 1914 - SENSE

I Mozart Operas Introduced   *page* 283
II *Figaro, Don Giovanni, The Barber*   292
III Lord Mount-Edgcumbe's Reminiscences   303
IV *Freischütz* to *The Bohemian Girl*   313
V *Ernani* to *Faust*   329
VI *The Flying Dutchman* to *Carmen*   348
VII *The Ring, Meistersinger, Tristan*   361
VIII *Otello* to *Butterfly*   372
IX *Samson and Delilah* to *Prince Igor*   387

Bibliography   404
Indexes   407
   I   Composers and Conductors   407
   II Masques, Operas, and other Theatre Enter-
       tainments   409
   III Singers   414
   IV Theatres and other places for Masques,
       Operas, etc.   416
   V   General Index   417

Illustrations

The Royal Opera Arcade, Pall Mall, today   *frontispiece*
(By courtesy of the *National Buildings Record*)

Interior of the Duke's Theatre, Dorset Garden   *page* 16

Interior of the King's Theatre, Haymarket   *page* 156

Interior of the Royal Italian Opera, Covent Garden   *page* 282

(These three by courtesy of the *Raymond Mander and Joe Mitchenson Theatre Collection*)

Foreword

WHEN, some years ago, I gave a series of operatic record programmes on the air under the title *First Time in This Country*, I introduced each record with comments from the London papers on the occasion of the first performance of the work in London. To prepare for this I haunted the Newspaper section of the British Museum at Colindale, and during my search through the opera critiques from 1800 to 1914 was fascinated to see not only how fundamentally right most of the critics were, in spite of prejudiced mistakes due to the taste of the day, but also how that taste changed through the years: it is a commonplace to laugh at past criticisms for not conforming with what later generations think, and we forget that in their day the critics were not necessarily wrong, though even in their own time everyone might not agree with them.

I at first thought it would be interesting to opera-lovers to make these nineteenth-century opinions available in a readable form, but I soon realised that I could not start with the nineteenth-century regime of the tenor hero without looking back to the eighteenth-century regime of the *castrato*, whose passing was so regretted by opera enthusiasts like Lord Mount-Edgcumbe: I then found that I could not start with the unsuccessful invasion of the public theatre by Handel and the Italian opera without giving some picture of what it was ousting, so in the end I had to begin—not unreasonably, I think—at the beginning.

Although, like other readers of the evidence, I cannot help drawing my own conclusions, I have tried to let the contemporaries speak for themselves—in the seventeenth century chiefly the gossips, in the eighteenth the professional rivals, in the nineteenth the recognised critics: for that reason this book is full of quotations, for it is surely better to give the actual contemporary words rather than a modern précis which might leave the reader dubious as to whether a sentence represents contemporary opinion or my wishful reading of it. The only liberty I have taken with the quotations is to modernise the spelling and punctuation and to disregard the fashionable capital letters of the earlier periods which

xi

appear to give such a charming olde-worlde atmosphere, but which in fact not only confuse the issue but also soon become unreadable.

I do not claim to have made any startling discoveries—though I was fascinated to find evidence concerning the performances of the first *Dido and Aeneas* and the really first London *Zauberflöte*, and surprised to learn that the great Italian opera invasion of the London stage in the eighteenth century was by no means the success the casual reader of musical history might imagine: first introduced in 1705, Italian opera may roughly be said to have failed to hold the stage (however crazily it bobbed up again) in 1708, 1713, 1718, constantly between 1720 and 1728, 1732, 1737, 1740, 1748, 1756, 1757, 1763 and 1782.

At the same time it is interesting that some fashionable scenic artists have always been ready to ignore composer or author for the sake of their design, that some would-be knowledgeables have always been ready to pretend equality with true experts by preferring sung words to be in a language in which they are not proficient, that committees—especially of financial representatives—are not always the best organisers of artistic ventures, and finally—whatever else is said—that the public only flocks to operas that are conceived and presented in terms of theatre, which should include first and foremost the best music and the best singing, combined with the truest emotion and presented in the sincerest way.

If operas should not be so presented, then all opera-composers have wasted their time in writing for theatres: they should all have waited for the microphone, which can record and reproduce the human voice without the full warmth of the human personality that can magnetise a theatre audience. Records are often said to give pure music (though it more often turns out to be a mechanically improved version of the natural sounds), but, excellent as the best records are, their pure music often is diminished into pure notes—well worth the study of the intellectual musician, but without the power to sway an opera audience to the hisses or cheers that keep the theatre and music alive.

I have of course not attempted to include comments on all operas that have been produced in London, and so must inevitably have left out several of somebody's favourites, but though I have occasionally mentioned some opera productions without com-

xii

ment, merely for the sake of indicating some sort of continuity—
and I hope I have not avoided at least mentioning any important
work—I have concentrated mainly on the early developments in
the seventeenth century, when the opera theatre was chiefly ruled
by sight, on the controversies of the eighteenth century, when it
was ruled by sound, and on the more lasting of the operas produced in the nineteenth century, when professional critics did their
best to judge with sense.

Finally, apart from acknowledgments that are made in the text
—most prominently to Professor Dent, Löwenberg and Allardyce
Nicoll *passim*—I must thank especially the many people I have
worked with in the musical theatre: conductors, singers, designers,
stage and lighting staffs, for having interested me so instructively
in the whole problem of opera.

PART ONE

Up to 1700

SIGHT

Interior of the Duke's Theatre, Dorset Garden, in
the reign of Charles II. The apparent depth of the
stage is due to the use of perspective scenery

CHAPTER ONE

The Start of Opera

ONE of the most misleading statements ever made on the subject of opera, and one which is repeated again and again, is that opera, both in its origins and in its practice through the centuries, has always been essentially a product of an intellectual aristocracy. That great opera enthusiast, Edward Dent, to whom I owe more than I can say for having many years ago encouraged me to combine academic research with theatrical practice, goes so far as to say that 'it is a historical fact that opera, ever since it came into being, has flourished most conspicuously when it was under the patronage of a court and an aristocracy' and, after pointing out that the 'first operas ever put together were the creation of a small set of aristocratic intellectuals in what was then the most intellectual city of Europe—Florence', he claims that in 'music, and in drama as well, there was a wide gulf between the art of the "intellectuals" and that of "the people", just as there is at the present day', apparently implying that intellectual art is superior. However on the very next page of the same book,[1] when pointing out that the earliest operas were composed for single performances to celebrate a wedding or other grand social occasion, he somewhat negatives the artistry of the aristocracy, for, after remarking that the 'undisguised "intellectualism" of such performances' (and who ever heard of an intellectual wedding celebration?) 'would limit their appreciation to a comparatively small circle', he points out that 'naturally there were plenty of people . . . who enjoyed the show as an expensive spectacle and went there to be seen as well as to see'.

Of course it is true that encouragement for opera—as for all the arts—came at first from royalty and the nobility, but apart from a few outstanding patrons who were themselves composers, flautists or harpsichordists, most of these society leaders were chiefly interested in putting on a better show than their neighbours, and so poured out their money to obtain the best artists available and to prevent those artists leaving their employment to serve some other patron. Naturally those patrons who had a true love of art would tend to employ the better artists and would be able to provide those artists with better, or at least richer, materials: but even up to the time of Mozart at least the artist was merely a paid servant of the patron and kept his job by pleasing the patron's whims, while at the same time satisfying his own artistic sense as far as he could. In fact it was the aristocratic patron's money that made opera possible, not his intellectual artistry.

But this is not all. No aristocratic patronage, whether of a princely individual, a noble committee or a civic body, has been able to make an opera successful without public approval. Wherever the funds for the original performance have come from, it has invariably been the public that have made the popularity and success—artistic and commercial—of the Mozarts, the Rossinis, the Verdis, the Wagners, the Puccinis, while the patrons who have made the performances possible have merely been the backers behind the scenes, like the backers behind any stage enterprise: and it must not be forgotten that most failures of operatic managements have been the result of ignorant artistic interference on the part of those who held the purse-strings.

Naturally there are instances where a long purse has been able to nurse a work of art until the public has been able to assimilate, and so appreciate it—and this holds good not only in the history of opera, but also in the history of the theatre, which also, it should not be forgotten, depended for many years on royal or noble patronage: but such royal or noble patronage for both opera and theatre was valuable only in so far as the patrons had long purses—long enough at least to allow the public to be wooed and the author or composer to write. Many years after the King's or the Duke's company of actors in seventeenth-century England had ceased to exist, playwrights dedicated their works to noble patrons, partly in the hope of a large subscription towards the production or an attendance in person that would glamorise the performance for the public at least as much as a Hollywood sprinkling does in the stalls of to-day. But all such patronage never helped the theatre except with money or glamour, and opera has achieved success only when it has broken away from the control of the noble patron or when it has been able to be so exciting that it has included the noble patron among its ordinary public: at random, for example, *The Beggar's Opera* for over two hundred years, the great touring companies of the late nineteenth century, some of which carried on into the twentieth, the Old Vic, Sadler's Wells, the great Beecham seasons, which combined fine singing with artistic integrity—the 'grand' society-patronised seasons of round 1900 could only provide fine singing, which pleased the public when it was good enough but not when the finest voice was wasted on a poor work, whatever patronage a Lady de Grey might give.

The public, in fact, no matter how much it is lectured to or encouraged, invariably ends by wanting an entertainment to be the best possible of its kind, whether it is the exciting magic of *Freischütz*, the tunes of Puccini or voices that can sing the great operas of the mid-nineteenth century. The public decides: as Sir Thomas Beecham once said to a young tenor who felt he couldn't sing another encore, 'They'll tell you if you can or not': 'they' are the final arbiters, not the connoisseurs of art.

Would opera ever have grown if it had remained in the hands of Count Bardi and his young friends in Florence? I suspect that the enthusiasts who in the sixteenth century developed the idea of telling a story to music were very much the same as the undergraduates at Cambridge who worked with Dent on the historic revival of *The Magic Flute* in 1911. And would their work have been so valuable if they had stayed in the rarefied atmosphere of Cambridge, instead of coming, as they did, to the Old Vic to work untiringly on opera for ordinary people to enjoy? To do that—unsupported by noble patronage or, for that matter, any financial backing to speak of—they had to make both ends meet, making do and mending: in fact, though both they and Lilian Baylis were working at opera because they loved it and believed in it, they were at the same time dealing with it from a truly commercial angle, balancing cost and public appeal against potential and actual receipts, though it meant cutting their cloth very carefully.

To entertain an audience has always been a tricky undertaking, and the first 'undertakers' of opera (as they were later called) were spoiled by having enough backing from the noble patrons to let them waste their cloth—even when it was cloth of gold—right from the days when the first opera, *La Dafne* by Peri, was produced in Florence at the end of the sixteenth century. In England at that time—just after *A Midsummer Night's Dream*—public theatres were well established, and theatre managers and shareholders were so experienced in box-office economics that it was soon possible for Shakespeare to retire to Stratford-on-Avon and for Alleyn to found Dulwich School out of their ventures. They had also realised that music added considerable attraction to their plays.

It must also be stressed—what is little known—that though the idea behind operatic invention was the telling of a tale with music, the chief interest in opera at the time was the gorgeous decoration with which it was dressed. Those who think that opera was primarily a musical entertainment presume from the earliest scores that it began in a very tentative way. Musically that may be true (though what seems tentative to our ears probably sounded most revolutionary to sixteenth-century ears), but all festivities are usually presented lavishly, and the earliest opera of which the score has survived—*Euridice* by Peri—commissioned in 1600 by Grand Duke Ferdinand of Tuscany for the marriage of his niece Maria de' Medici to King Henri IV of France—was no exception.

In his book *The First Night of Twelfth Night*, Leslie Hotson quotes what two eye-witnesses said of *Euridice*: one said (in Hotson's translation) that the

representation recited in music especially succeeded most famously, through the great diversity of the exquisite inventions which appeared in it, by the singular beauty of the main scene, frequently most miraculously transformed into many scenes, as also by the excellence of the intermezzi—of machines, of songs, of music, and a thousand other entertainments which continually swept the audience into admiration. And certainly one could not be sure whether these should be marvels of fancy or realities; or which at that time were greater: the *gusto* which the stage created with such rare and well-accompanied shows, or the delight which was born in the theatre, through so lofty and so majestic an assemblage of spectators.

The other said that 'its scenic arrangements and its intermezzi deserved much praise. But the manner of singing it grew easily displeasing, and moreover the moving of the stage-machines was not always successful'. Anyway, the scenic arrangements were ambitious.

Even on the London public stage of the day scenery cannot have been as non-existent as many Shakespearean purists pretend: there had been scenes and effects of sorts even in the old Moralities and Mysteries and, as Allardyce Nicoll and I remarked many years ago, while Shakespeare constantly describes imaginary lighting effects in words, he never describes the scenery, which many experts think was equally imaginary. In any event, theatrical effect, which at the time was one of the first essentials of opera—and should be still—became more and more one of the first essentials of entertainment in England.

In the next forty years, during which Ben Jonson was Shakespeare's chief successor in the public theatres, the aristocracy in England enlarged the fashionable entertainment of the private masque by emulating the extravagant splendour of the new Italian operas, the fame of which had spread at least to France, Germany, Poland and England: they had been admired by visitors to Italy for the weddings of Henri IV of France with Maria de' Medici and of the Prince of Mantua with the Princess of Savoy, for celebrations of the election of the Emperor Ferdinand II of Germany, for a visit of the Prince of Poland and later for the King of Poland's brother.

After putting on spectacular operas for weddings or receptions, the Italian 'undertakers' realised there might be a large public outside the palaces ready to pay for novel entertainment, and in 1637, the year of Jonson's death, the first public opera-house was built in Venice—though performances were only given, like those of the masques, at times of annual celebration, such as New Year or Easter, or on special occasions. In 1638 a Venetian opera was dedicated to the British Ambassador Extraordinary, and the following year London very nearly had a public opera-house, as will be seen.

If this had been built, it is probable that the London audience would have been more ready than Venice to understand the new kind of theatre entertainment, for the paying public in London had for many years been used to an increasing amount of music in the theatre, and on occasion had been allowed to catch a glimpse of spectacular masquers in procession through the streets and once or twice in performance in some civic hall. As long ago, too, as 1611 Shakespeare had introduced into *The Tempest* not only some nine songs or snatches and some six instrumental pieces of music for dances or entries, but also the long musical scene of Iris, Ceres and Juno, called up by Prospero's magic with dancing Naiads and Sicklemen to celebrate the betrothal of Ferdinand and Miranda. This allegorical *scena*, beginning with soft music and

21

including speeches, a dialogue duet and a graceful dance, had been for the ordinary theatre-goer a miniature version of the grand masques expensively staged in private by the nobility for special occasions, exactly as the contemporary Italian operas were— Twelfth Night, Shrove-tide or any occasion of special social significance.

[1] *Opera*, Penguin Books.

CHAPTER TWO

Inigo Jones and Ben Jonson

IT is difficult nowadays to get any true picture of what the masques were like, for there are very few contemporary descriptions of them—apart from the printed explanations made by the 'inventors'; that is, the author and the designer of the scenes and costumes. Their versions are magnificent enough, and in one respect must often have surpassed even the most stupendous modern production (even of the most impressive three-dimensional cinemascope or cinerama film), considering that the masques were mostly performed not only in magnificent costumes, loaded with real jewels that the present-day impresario could not afford, but also in intricately solid and movable scenery aided by the new technique of trick-perspective realism, both of shape and of painting. Perspective designs became quite a craze in the second half of the seventeenth century. Pepys often admired the many realistic paintings of false distance in the house of his friend, Mr. Povy, and on the wall of his garden,

being strange things to think how they do delude one's eye, that methinks it would make a man doubtful of swearing that ever he saw anything.

He even bought one of Christopher Wren's instruments for drawing in perspective and much enjoyed using one of the new 'perspective-glasses' (what would now be called field-glasses or operaglasses) at St. Margaret's, Westminster, 'seeing and gazing at a great many very fine women' during the service.

At the beginning of the century, on Twelfth Night, 1605, elaborate perspective painting was seen in *The Masque of Blackness*, by Ben Jonson, which was performed in the Banqueting House at Whitehall, with the Queen and her Ladies appearing as negresses:

First, for the scene, was drawn a landscape consisting of small woods and here and there a void place filled with huntings, which falling—

(this obviously means that scene was a front curtain)

—an artificial sea was seen to shoot forth, as if it flowed to the land, raised with waves which seemed to move, and in some places the billows to break, as imitating that orderly disorder, which is common in nature. . . .

23

The masquers were placed in a great concave shell, like mother of pearl, curiously made to move on those waters and rise with the billow: the top thereof was stuck with a chevron of lights, which, indented to the proportion of the shell, struck a glorious beam upon them as they were seated one above another, so that they were all seen, but in an extravagant order.

The masquers were all in azure and silver, with feathers and jewels interlaced with ropes of pearl, which must have looked well against the black of their faces, and at the sides of their shells six huge sea-monsters swam, carrying on their backs twelve torch-bearers in sea-green 'waved about the skirts with gold and silver', with garlands of coral and sea-grass on their heads, holding shells out of which the torches burned.

These thus presented, the scene behind seemed a vast sea (and united with this that flowed forth) from the termination or horizon of which . . . was drawn by the lines of perspective—the whole work shooting downwards from the eye.

The whole scene was well set-off by a background of dark clouds, though Sir Dudley Carleton, who saw it, said 'there was all fish and no water' and thought the blackfaced ladies 'a very loathsome sight'.

This was the earliest stage-work in England by Inigo Jones, who had come back from studying architecture in Italy, full of enthusiasm for the elaborate scenes that were staged there in the newly invented operas and other spectacles. How the spotlights 'struck a glorious beam' on the masquers may not be known exactly, but Inigo Jones must have seen the seven books on architecture by Sebastiano Serlio written in Italian some fifty years earlier: they were translated into English a few years after *The Masque of Blackness*, and in them are descriptions, not only of perspective scenery and the construction of it, but also of how to throw a beam of coloured light by placing a torch behind a bottle of watered colours or even of wine, with a reflector made of a polished basin. Nearly a hundred years before it had been even possible to make a rising and setting sun

in the form of a ball of crystal filled with distilled water, behind which were two lighted torches, which rendered the sky of the scenery and prospect-view so luminous, that it had the appearance of the real and natural sun.
This sun, which had around it an ornament of golden rays that covered the curtain, was drawn little by little by means of a small windlass that was there,

24

in such a manner that at the beginning of the performance the sun appeared to be rising, and then, having climbed to the centre of the arch, it so descended that at the end of the piece it was setting and sinking below the horizon.[1]

I am stressing the ingenuity and realism of the effects in the masques because it is so easy to think of all printed descriptions of scenery as being merely the author's fanciful description of what he imagined, and we forget that the theatrical devices of the seventeenth century were far from being makeshift and that they encouraged audiences to expect bigger and better spectacles. *The Masque of Blackness* did not, of course, include such complicated machines as those Inigo Jones later used—trees that sank out of sight, stairs descending from the heavens, or clouds making palaces in the air, all of which might have singers and dancers on them: but it does give some idea of the grandeur to which the noble audiences became accustomed.

Naturally as well as such ingenious stage mechanics some devices were used that seem to us ingenuous: for instance, scene-changes in the masques, where there was not often a front curtain, were sometimes made while the attention of the audience was distracted by such things as blinding lights or some movement that diverted the eye, and on one occasion the noise of breaking wood made the spectators think that the stand on which they were sitting was collapsing, so that they not unreasonably took their eyes off the stage while the transformation took place.[2]

Inigo Jones in the following year, 1606, did the designs for Ben Jonson's masque, *Hymenaei*, in honour of the marriage of the fourteen-year-old Earl of Essex: on this occasion his work was rather more elaborate, as can be seen from a contemporary letter describing the masque, in which it was said that at one moment eight ladies sitting on the two horns of a cloud

descended upon the stage, not after the stale downright perpendicular fashion, like a bucket into a well, but came gently sloping down.

It also quotes the gossip of the day that the titled performers

hired and borrowed all the principal jewels and ropes of pearl bothi n court and city. The Spanish Ambassador seemed but poor to the meanest of them.

Finally it sums up the performance by saying that

both Inigo, Ben, and the actors, men and women, did their parts with great commendation.

It is perhaps significant that Inigo is mentioned before Ben, for Jonson definitely felt that the spectacle was getting more attention than his poetry, and he put his scorn into words in his introduction to this same masque: after implying that thoughts put into words are of more lasting value than spurious decorations which only appeal momentarily to those who have 'little or—let me not wrong 'em—no brain', he goes on to say:—

I am contented these fastidious stomachs should leave my full tables and enjoy at home their clean empty trenchers, fittest for such airy tastes, where perhaps a few Italian herbs, picked up and made into a salad, may find sweeter acceptance than all the most nourishing and sound meats in the world.

So, at the first hint of importing anything from the new musical entertainment of Italy, the time-honoured argument of Sense versus Senses flared up—the argument that is always at the back of any discussion on opera. Jonson certainly had some justification for his fears, because though opera had started in Italy with the object of telling a story, it soon developed, or rather degenerated—through its rich, noble patrons—into a display of spectacle, and it was this side of opera that Jones was introducing into England.

Jonson must, however, have known that it was not the poetic image or the intellectual allegory that appealed to a festive audience: but if he was really in any doubt on the matter, it must have been brought home to him a few months later when in the summer of 1606 King Christian IV of Denmark visited England and was entertained by James I with a fine masque at Theobalds: the contemporary description of the performance definitely refutes the fond belief that masques were for scholastically minded audiences:—

One day a great feast was held, and after dinner the representation of Solomon his Temple and the coming of the Queen of Sheba was made, or, as I may better say, was meant to have been made before Their Majesties by device of the Earl of Salisbury and others. But alas!, as all earthly things do fail to poor mortals in enjoyment, so did prove our presentment hereof.

The lady who did play the Queen's part did carry most precious gifts to both their majesties; but, forgetting the steps arising to the canopy, overset her caskets into his Danish majesty's lap and fell at his feet, though I rather think it was in his face. Much was the hurry and confusion: cloths and napkins were at hand to make all clean.

His Majesty then got up and would dance with the Queen of Sheba, but he fell down and humbled himself before her and was carried to an inner chamber and laid upon a bed of state, which was not a little defiled with the presents of the Queen which had been bestowed on his garments, such as wine, cream, jelly, beverage, cakes, spices, and other good matters.

The entertainment and show went forward—and most of the presenters went backward, or fell down, wine did so occupy their upper chambers.

Now did appear in rich dresses Hope, Faith and Charity. Hope did essay to speak, but wine rendered her endeavours so feeble that she withdrew and *hoped* the king would excuse her brevity. Faith was then left all alone, for I am certain she was not joined with good works, and left the court in a staggering condition. Charity came to the King's feet and seemed to cover the multitude of sins her sisters had committed: in some sort she made obeisance and brought gifts, but said she would return home again, as there was no gift which heaven had not already given his majesty. She then returned to Hope and Faith, who were both sick in the lower hall.

Next came Victory in bright armour and presented a sword to the King (who did not accept it, but put it by with his hand) and by a strange medley of versification did endeavour to make suit to the King. But Victory did not triumph long, for, after much lamentable utterance, she was led away like a silly captive and laid to sleep on the outer steps of the antechamber.

Now did Peace make entry and strove to get foremost to the King: but I grieve to tell how great wrath she did discover unto those of her attendants and, much contrary to her semblance, most rudely made war with her olive-branch and laid on the pates of those who did oppose her coming.

I have much marvelled at these strange pageantries: and they do bring to my remembrance what part of this sort in our Queen's days, of which I was sometime a humble presenter and assistant, but I ne'er did see such lack of good order, discretion and sobriety as I have now done.

The writer, Sir John Harington, who was at the time forty-five years old, and therefore well able to compare the past days of his godmother, Queen Elizabeth, with those of James I, ends as follows:—

I will now in good sooth declare to you, who will not blab, that the gunpowder fright is got out of all our heads and we are going on hereabout as if the devil was contriving every man should blow up himself by wild riot, excess and devastation of time and temperance.

This vivid account does more to create the atmosphere (and what an atmosphere!) of an actual performance of a masque than all the other meagre contemporary accounts put together; and though this performance was possibly more exceptionally licentious—anyway as far as the performers were concerned—than most that were given in the seventeenth century, it is well worth remembering, not only in contrast with the perhaps less obviously riotous Elizabethan shows, but also as a counterblast to the belief that has been so firmly planted by most books on the history of opera—that the philosophical idea behind the masque, like the theoretical idea that germinated opera, either demanded or got an intellectual presentation before an intellectual audience. (After all, how many have ever been primarily interested—if at all—in the 'redemption through woman' idea, when they go to Wagner's early operas ?)

The spectacle was certainly the most important ingredient, whether considered from the point of view of the noble audience or from that of the noble amateur performers in their jewels and feathers: the words and the theme were merely pegs on which to hang the decorations, while the music at first was merely a necessary background for dances or an occasional song.

But six months after the disastrous *Solomon and the Queen of Sheba*, Campion, being a composer as well as a poet, made the music more important in a Twelfth Night masque in honour of the wedding of the Lord Hayes on January 6, 1607, and performed before the King: he seems to have used an exceptionally large number of musicians, to judge from the unusually meticulous details he gives of the music in his printed description—twenty-eight instrumentalists divided into three sections to the right and left and in front of the stage, four on the stage, five singers to the right and five to the left, six picked Royal Chapel voices for a special motet, as well as soloists on the stage. For the singers he wrote words not only for the usual part-songs, some of which were danced to, but in this masque alone he also introduced a 'song in form of a dialogue' in which a soprano and tenor Silvan discuss

> Who is the happier of the two,
>   A maid or wife?
> Which is more to be desired,
>   Peace or strife?
>   What strife can be where two are one,
>   Or what delight to pine alone?

They are then answered by a bass (Zephyrus):

> None such true friends, none so sweet life,
> As that between the man and wife.

A second 'dialogue for four voices', in which, however, they seem to sing in couples, bids farewell to Hesperus, the star 'which is kindest to a loving bride', in words which consist of shorter questions and answers; but a third dialogue, sung by a tenor Silvan and a bass Hour, is even more conversational, for all that it is in rhyme:—

> Silvan. Tell me, gentle hour of night,
> Wherein doest thou most delight?
> Hour. Not in sleep.
> Silvan.   Wherein then?
> Hour. In the frolic view of men.
> Silvan. Lovest thou music?
> Hour.   O 'tis sweet.
> Silvan. What's dancing?
> Hour.   Ev'n the mirth of feet.

the very shape of such a dialogue—and indeed the word 'dialogue' —seems to suggest that it was sung to notes that somehow echoed natural speech, but how far it resembled the new Italian recitative must remain uncertain until or unless the original music is ever discovered. As this may have been the earliest occasion when recitative was used in an English work, it is tantalising that Campion only published the five songs that were sung in this masque, together with the music by himself, Thomas Giles, and one of the musical family from Milan named Lupo.

Was Campion perhaps introduced to the style of the first Italian operas by Lupo? He certainly cannot have heard such music himself when he was in France in 1591 as a volunteer under Robert, Earl of Essex, for the first opera was not given for another six years. He probably was told about it by Inigo Jones, but not in much detail, for Jones seems to have thought of music as a mere adjunct to his scenic effects—useful when played loud to cover the the noise of a scene-change,[3] as can be seen from this description from the 1610 masque, *Tethys' Festival*,[4] by Ben Jonson's rival, Samuel Daniel and Inigo Jones:—

> Suddenly, at the sound of a loud and fuller music, Tethys and her nymphs appear with another scene, which I will likewise describe in the language of the architector who contrived it and speaks in his own metier to such as are understanding and lovers of that design.

(This is, of course, a hit at those who were not, such as Ben Jonson.)

> First, at the opening of the heavens, appeared three circles of lights and glasses, one within another, and came down in a straight motion five foot and then began to move circularly: which lights and motion so occupied the eyes of the

spectators that the manner of altering the scene was scarcely discerned, for in a moment the whole face of it was changed, the port vanished, and Tethys and her nymphs appeared in their several caverns gloriously adorned.

Obviously the 'lights and glasses', however they were manipulated, were considered more important than the loud music—at any rate by Inigo Jones and his supporter, Daniel.

But though Ben Jonson objected to the introduction of such 'Italian herbs' of decoration into a solid English pie, from this time on he followed Campion's example and accepted the Italian idea of sung dialogue—after all, it did at least include words, which were all-important to him, and he had heard the method faintly pre-echoed in some madrigals. So from 1611, when King James heard Shakespeare use it in *The Tempest*, Ben Jonson included sung dialogue in almost all his masques (and he wrote some twenty-five in as many years). Whether he saw sense in this new musical conversation when he could see none in trick scenery, or whether this novel music so attracted the noble audiences that he had to include it, hardly matters: include it he did—and not always in semi-philosophical or eloquent verses.

His first attempt—in *Oberon, the Fairy Prince* (January 1, 1611) —was a rather dully mechanical questionnaire by two Fays on the virtues of the young Prince (Prince Henry of Wales):—

> Seek you Majesty, to strike?
> Bid the World produce his like.
> Seek you glory, to amaze?
> Here let all eyes stand at gaze.

However, even this was not ineffective in performance, to judge from a contemporary comment [5] on this

very stately Masque, in which was an excellent scene, ingenious speeches, rare songs, and great varieties of most delicate music in the beautiful room at Whitehall.

It is tantalising that the writer fails to mention if the new 'recitativo' type of music was used, but he at least seems to have considered the music more worth mentioning than most of his contemporaries.

Musical experiments were bound to be tentative, in spite of the poets, for the nobility went to the masques to see and be seen in an aura of splendour both in the audience and in the entertainment, in which the audience—or at least the leaders—took part in the final dance. When three sumptuous masques were given for the marriage of the lovely Princess Elizabeth to the Elector Palatine in 1613, competitive fashion had to be curbed by a royal order stating that

> no lady or gentleman should be admitted to any of these sights with a vardingale, which was to gain the more room, and I hope may serve to make them quite left off in time.

During these celebrations the gorgeously and fantastically caparisoned masquers made a grand procession through the streets with decoratively harnessed horses, and a new hall was specially built for dining and dancing in. A year later one of the masques for the wedding of James I's bounced-up favourite, now the Earl of Somerset, with the Countess of Essex—both scandalously released from their previous mates by a convenient divorce—was financed for its single performance by Sir Francis Bacon to the tune of £2,000.

In the meantime Inigo Jones, after his contribution to Princess Elizabeth's wedding celebrations, spent a further two years in Italy, and on his return was made the King's Surveyor of Works, which must have enhanced his importance: but for the moment Ben Jonson did not rebel, and his Twelfth Night masque for January 1617, *The Vision of Delight*, which James I saw twice in a fortnight, owed a great deal to Italian example, for not only was it largely taken from a grand musical spectacle called *Notte d'Amore* ('Night of Love'), part of the wedding celebrations of the Grand Duke Cosimo de' Medici, Prince of Tuscany, and Maria Maddalena, Archduchess of Austria, nine years before,[6] but it also seems to have introduced to England the Italian phrase for sung dialogue.

At the very opening of this masque Delight appeared and, in Ben Jonson's own words, 'spake in song (*stilo recitativo*)' the following lines, which incidentally seem to lay down the essentials of a masque:—

> Let us play, and dance, and sing,
>   Let us now turn every sort
> O' the pleasures of the spring
>   To the graces of a Court—
>   From air, from cloud, from dreams, from toys,
>   To sounds, to sense, to love, to joys.

Let your shows be new as strange,
Let them oft and sweetly vary:
Let them haste so to their change,
As the seers may not tarry:
Too long t' expect the pleasing sight
Doth take away from the delight.

In *The Vision of Delight* Ben Jonson mixed recitative with song and speech, but four weeks later, when his next masque [7] was given by the Lord Hay for the French Ambassador, 'the whole Masque', in Jonson's words,

'was sung (after the Italian manner) stylo recitativo, by Master Nicholas Lanier, who ordered and made both the scene and the music.'

As a rule the sung words in the masques were at least graceful, if not philosophical, but in 1618 Jonson tried a bold experiment. His Twelfth Night masque with the unpromising title of *Pleasure Reconciled to Virtue* was so popular with James I that it was repeated six weeks later with an extra scene entitled *For the Honour of Wales*: in this the scene was changed from Mount Atlas to the mountain Craig-Eriri, and instead of classical characters there appeared Griffith, Jenkin, Evan (an attorney), Howell and Rheese—the last three being singers as well as actors—and a dialogue-song in very down-to-earth language was sung in the dialect which is indicated by the original spelling:

1. Aw, God bless is our good King S'ames,
   His Wife, and his Sildren, and aull his Reams,
2. And aull his 'ursipful S'istice of peace about him,
1. And send that his Court be never without him.
2. Ow, that her would come down into Wales,
1. Her s'ud be very welcom to Welse Ales.
2. I have a Cow.
1.   And I have a Hen;
2. S'all give it Milk,
1.   And Eggs for aull his Men.
Chorus. It self s'all have Venison, and other Seere,
   And may it be starved, that steal him his Deere,
   there, there, and every where.

I do not suggest that this seventeenth-century Welsh Calypso was sung in Italian recitative, but I do suggest that it shows not only that dialogue to music was very soon accepted as a natural ingredient in a musical entertainment, and also that a sung dialogue might well be in colloquial language, anticipating Purcell's later country dialogues, though Jonson left this as an isolated experiment.

In 1619 Ben Jonson was made Poet Laureate, and as such must have begun to feel that he was in a better position to stand up to the Surveyor of Works and champion sense against scenery—it would be interesting to know Jonson's comment on the disaster which was caused this year by a fire lit to melt some glue for mending some masque scenery that was to be used a second time: the firebrick got so hot that the deal board on which it was standing,

suddenly conceiving flame, gave fire to the device of the masque, all of oiled paper and dry fir,

and so started a conflagration that burned most of the papers in the offices of the Signet, Privy Seal and Council Chamber in Whitehall.

Ben Jonson's first outspoken attack on Inigo Jones seems to have been his satirical picture of him as a know-all in his 1622 Twelfth Night masque, *The Masque of Augurs*. Ben Jonson in this masque called him Van-goose, a rare artist and a projector of masques, who, though English, talks with an accent to show how travelled he is, and claims that in his next masque he will introduce Turkish Pashas, thirty thousand janissaries with all their houris and eunuchs, the Persian Sophy, the Cham of Tartary and the King of Mogul, and that he will

make deir men, and deir horse, and deir elephanten be seen fight in de ayr, and be all killen, and aliven, and no such ting. And all dis . . . by de refleshie van de glassen.

He says he will place the glasses

as it be two, dree, veir, vife towsand mile off: Ick sall multipliren de vizioun, met an ander secret dat Ick heb.

In spite of the obvious satirical exaggeration, Inigo Jones must at least have known of the principle of reflecting mirrors and of the need for some screen or other mirror on which to project a multiple picture, which we are inclined to think was a fairly recent invention, and which certainly may make intriguing scenic effects, whether a simple magic lantern, an effects lantern or a film back-projection is used.

Inigo Jones was not alone in thinking the effects important. In

B

1625—the year Charles I came to the throne—Bacon's essay on *Masques and Triumphs* praised good settings:—

It is true, the alteration of scenes, so it be quietly and without noise, are things of great beauty and pleasure, for they feed and relieve the eye, before it be full of the same object. Let the scenes abound with light, specially coloured and varied.

But when Ben Jonson wrote his first masque for Charles I, *Love's Triumph through Callipolis* (1631), not only did he, I think, have the whole of this, his third masque with a sea background, set to music—even the lines that are not expressly marked to be sung are so shaped that they call for music and are at once followed by a chorus—but he also boldly put his name before that of Inigo Jones. A month later they again collaborated in a Shrove-tide masque, *Chloridia*, again, I think, entirely set to music, apart from one long comedy speech in the middle, and again Ben Jonson put his name first.

The result was that, though his plays were still performed at Court and elsewhere, Ben Jonson was never asked to write another masque: as one Mr. Pory wrote on January 12, 1632, the Twelfth Night masque for that year was written by Aurelian Townshend,[8]

Ben Jonson being for this time discarded, by reason of the predominant power of his protagonist, Inigo Jones, who this time twelvemonth was angry with him for putting his own name before his in the titlepage, which Ben Jonson made the subject of a bitter satire or two against Inigo.

His bitterest attack against scenic effects and their now triumphant champion, who dominated the masques for some years to come, was in his *Expostulation with Inigo Jones*. In this he asks the 'Master Surveyor':

> What is the cause you pomp it so, I ask?
> And all men echo, you have made a masque?
> I chime that too, and I have met with those
> That do cry up the machine and the shows;
> The majesty of Juno in the clouds,
> And peering forth of Iris in the shrouds;
> The ascent of Lady Fame, which none could spy . . .

(which shows that Inigo's clever machines and mathematical calculations did not always work).

He goes on to point out that many such wonders are provided

> In the mere perspective of an inch-board,

and that colours, to those that understand them, are supposed to

> reveal
> Mythology, there painted on slit deal.
> Or to make boards to speak! There is a task!
> Painting and carpentry are the soul of masque.
> Pack with your peddling poetry to the stage!
> This is the money-got, mechanic age.

(And we thought the mechanic age was three hundred years later
—now!) He stresses that when the painter places the orchestra out
of earshot and makes performers wear unsuitable costumes, he
will always excuse himself (as many still do to-day) on the ground
of what is called by him 'design.'

> But in the practised truth, destruction is
> Of any art beside what he calls his.

Jones, he says, now wants not only to be in charge of all stage
properties, scenery and effects, but to supervise even the music
(does this mean that it really was Jones who introduced recitative
to this country from the Italian opera?). In any event, his stuff is
only second-hand from Italy and grossly overpaid: and yet everyone is expected to

> . . . fall down before it, and confess
> Almighty Architecture, who no less
> A goddess is than painted cloth, deal board,
> Vermilion, lake, or crimson can afford
> Expression for, with that unbounded line
> Aimed at in thy omnipotent design!

But in spite of this attack and a faint echo of it in his play of two
years later, *Tale of a Tub*, Ben Jonson nearly lost favour at Court
completely, and Inigo Jones with his scenic effects went from
strength to strength, dominating all his later collaborators. Among
these, however, was a young man who not only became Poet
Laureate when Jonson died six years after his last collaboration
with Inigo Jones, but who also determined to introduce the comparatively new art-form of opera into England—not for the
society audiences that admired and were admired in the fantastic
masques, but for a paying public that would rush to see and hear

(and especially to see, if Inigo Jones was right) glories they had not dreamed of.

¹ Vasari, *Lives of the Most Eminent Painters* (trans. S. du C. De Vere) as quoted by Lily B. Campbell, *Scenes and Machines on the English Stage.*

² Simple as such tricks seem on paper, their fundamental principles are sound: when the curtain fell on the Paris prologue of *The Scarlet Pimpernel*, Fred Terry had red lights blaze into the eyes of the audience from the front of the stage— theatrically exciting as well as helping to mask the time of the scene-change: in Gielgud's production of *Dear Brutus* the Puckish host, Lob, walked from his chair through the fireplace in view of the audience, but invisibly because at that moment other characters left in a group into a brighter light on the opposite side of the stage: I used the same trick in *Faust*, changing from Valentine's death in the street to the Cathedral, to the Brocken, to the Prison, without lowering the curtain. The collapsing auditorium, I imagine, has not been used recently.

³ This must not be taken to imply that stage-mechanism was then more clumsy than now, as anyone will realise who goes to the theatre or opera much or who looks in at some television shows.

⁴ Tethys is usually called Thetis.

⁵ Quoted by Mary Susan Steele, Ph.D., in *Plays and Masques at Court.*

⁶ *The Court Masque*, Enid Welsford.

⁷ Sometimes called *Lovers made Men* and sometimes *The Masque of Lethe*. The 1692 edition of Jonson's works gives no title.

⁸ As quoted by Mary Susan Steele, Ph.D., in *Plays and Masques at Court.*

CHAPTER THREE

Davenant and Opera

THE two spiritual fathers or godfathers of opera in England might well be said to be Inigo Jones and Shakespeare, because Jones, who had surely seen the new operas of Italy, was chiefly responsible for introducing their great characteristic of scenery into this country, and Shakespeare by artistic instinct knew from the start and later developed his belief that music could be of the greatest importance in an acted story. But it is more than possible that one of them was in a way even more directly responsible than that.

There is every reason to suppose that in the year 1605, after he had finished *Othello* and perhaps while he was working on *Macbeth* and *Lear*, Shakespeare used often to go to Oxford, where he often visited the Crown Inn, because the owner and his wife were friends of his through their absorbing love for all kinds of stage plays. The wife was a very beautiful woman, and according to rumour Shakespeare was more than a godfather to her son who was born the following year and given the name William to put before the family surname of D'Avenant. In later years a pointed allusion was made to the fact that 'D'Avenant' might easily have been derived from 'Avon', and when he grew up the boy never seems to have taken offence at the implied suggestion.

Certainly he did his best to follow in the footsteps of the famous family friend, who died when the boy was ten, for two years later he is said to have written his ode '*In remembrance of Master William Shakespeare*' (though it was not published till much later), and his first play dates from his twentieth year, to be followed the next year by another—both tragedies and both in the sort of prose that might easily be turned into blank verse. And in 1630 in a tragi-comedy, *The Just Italian*, he introduced music for the first time—a short dialogue sung by two boys.

When he was about twenty-seven Davenant had his first comedy, *The Wits*, performed at the Blackfriars Theatre, and in January 1634 it was played at Court before Charles I and Queen Henrietta Maria. This play, strangely enough, although a comedy, was almost entirely written in blank verse, and in it Davenant includes a burlesque of recitative singing.

Shore, a constable, meets a musician, and, after a piece of imitation Shakespearean badinage, on learning that the musician has just come from a wedding, and knowing that 'where there are weddings there will be music', invites the musician to sing 'The Constable's Catch' with him, whereupon:

the second catch is sung and acted by them in recitative burlesque.

The words of this catch have no bearing on the burlesque, but it is interesting to notice that recitative must have been fairly well known by this time—even to the general public—if a play could include a burlesque of it, though probably the young author would think it smart to satirise something which might only be known to his society friends among the audience,[1] while the subtlety of a catch in recitative would intrigue a musician.

Five days after the royal command performance of this play, one of the finest masques was presented before the King by the gentlemen of the Inns of Court: this was *The Triumph of Peace* by James Shirley, who was able to relegate Inigo Jones's name to a footnote at the end of the printed masque together with those of the composers of the music, Simon Ives and William Lawes. These musicians, together with the instrumentalists and singers, were chosen by Bulstrode Whitelocke, an enthusiastic amateur musician who later became indirectly one of the factors that made opera possible in England. Before the masque there was a procession of the sixteen masquers 'in cloth of tissue and wrought as thick with silver spangles as they could be placed', in four chariots each drawn by six horses attended by a hundred of the most handsome young men of the Inns of Court, and followed by a comic procession of beggars on the poorest-looking horses that could be found, together with animal imitators on horseback, 'northern music' on bagpipes, gods and goddesses, and various 'devices'. The masque itself was very ornate in a variety of scenes—it was in this masque that the cracking of scaffolding was heard to distract the audience from the scene change: the whole show

was incomparably performed, in the dancing, speeches, music and scenes: the dances, figures, properties, the voices, instruments, songs, airs, composures, the words and actions, were all of them exact; none failed in their parts, and the scenes were most curious and costly.

Costly it was indeed, for the music cost about £1,000, the clothes for the horsemen averaged out at £100 a suit—that is, £10,000 in all—and the cost of the rest of the masque came to over £20,000. Even without considering the difference in value of the pound between that day and this, that was a colossal expense for one performance, as was planned—though it was repeated at the Queen's request eight days later in Merchant Taylors' Hall, which gave ordinary citizens a rare chance to see one of these noble entertainments, and it certainly pleased them, 'especially those of the younger sort and of the female sex'.

But in the history of opera this masque is of considerable importance, because some of William Lawes's music to the many dialogues in it still exists—the most interesting being the long scene in dramatic recitative between Irene (Peace) and Eunomia (Law) with the chorus: this is reprinted in E. J. Dent's *Foundations of English Opera*, and should certainly be studied together with the Lawes music to Milton's private masque *Comus* of the same year by all who are interested in the musical development of opera in England. In style it varies between elementary recitative, according to the natural accentuation and intonation of the words—in spite of constant musical stops or cadences, and choral writing, both reminiscent of contrapuntal madrigals and experimental in the new block harmony style: the singing is interspersed with short instrumental interludes suggesting entries or dances. However, that all belongs to the artistic development of opera rather than the popular development of opera. From the audience point of view, on the other hand, it is intriguing to know that the part of Irene was sung by a tenor and that the singer was Nicholas Lanier, who had composed the music for and sung in Ben Jonson's masque *The Vision of Delight* seventeen years before—so he must have been a fairly mature goddess, as he was forty-six when he sang Irene.

The Triumph of Peace was regarded as a practical answer to a recently published diatribe against actors by William Prynne: this *Histrio-Mastix: The Players' Scourge* was popular with the growing sect of Puritans, but it led to the author's being indicted for libel because in the list of contents the phrase 'Women actors notorious whores' was taken to reflect on Queen Henrietta Maria, as she often took part in the Court shows. So Prynne was pilloried, had his ears cut off, was fined £5,000 and imprisoned for life, and for the time being masques were still produced.

A year later, 1635, young Davenant had his first masque, *The Temple of Love*, performed at Whitehall by the unabashed Queen and her ladies, with wonderful decorations by the Surveyor of His Majesty's Works, Inigo Jones, whose name unquestionably preceded that of the new poet, 'Her Majesty's Servant'.[2] The printed text says that this masque,

for the newness of the invention, variety of scenes, apparitions, and richness of habits was generally approved to be one of the most magnificent that hath been done in England.

Some of the designs Inigo Jones had taken from a triumphal tournament given in Italy nineteen years before, from which he also got the idea of introducing Brahmin priests, and from which the names of the central character, Indamore, Queen of Narsinga, were derived, according to Enid Welsford in *The Court Masque*.

One costume-description from this masque is, I think, worth quoting here, as it is worded much nearer to the instructions given by a costume-designer to a costume-maker than usual. It is the design for the costumes worn by nine Persian youths who are in quest of the Temple of Love, led by the twenty-three-year-old Duke of Lennox, nephew of Davenant's patroness, Frances, Duchess of Richmond, who herself had appeared in Jonson's *Masque of Blackness* thirty years before. The Persian youths made their entry

apparelled in Asian coats of sea-green embroidered, that reached down above their knees, with buttons and loops before, and cut up square to their hips, and returned down with two short skirts: the sleeves of his coat were large without seam and cut short to the bending of the arm and hanging down long behind, trimmed with buttons as those of the breast: out of this came a sleeve of white satin embroidered, and the basis answerable to the sleeve, hung down in gathering underneath the shortest part of their coat: on their heads they wore Persian turbans silvered underneath and wound about with white cypress and one fall of a white feather before.

It seems quite possible that this was the first time the Persian style of coat was seen in England—the style that became generally fashionable under Charles II and that finally deteriorated into the English and Victorian frock-coat.

The masque that Davenant wrote in the following year for the

Middle Temple, with Mr. Corseilles making the designs instead of Inigo Jones, who seems only to have designed the Court masques, was *The Triumphs of the Prince d'Amour*, hastily 'devised and written in three days' to welcome the King's cousin, the Elector Palatine. Apart from the introductory speech it was all set to music by the Lawes brothers, and some of this music can still be seen in the Bodleian Library.

On August 6 of the following year, 1637, Ben Jonson, the Poet Laureate, died, and a few months later Davenant wrote at least one more masque, *Britannia Triumphans*, which was presented in January 1638 by Charles I and his Lords in a hall that was specially built between the Guard-Chamber and the Banqueting House for this masque and for the Queen's masque *Luminalia* which was given a month later.[3] In a letter written on November 9, 1637, by George Garrard to the Earl of Strafford, he says they had already started on this 'Masquing House'

of fir, only weather-boarded and slightly covered. At the marriage of the Queen of Bohemia I saw one set up there,[4] but not of the vastness that this is, which will cost too much money to be pulled down, and yet down it must when the masques are over.

As it turned out, it was not pulled down till eight years later.

By the end of the year 1638, two days after the Court had seen another of his plays, *The Fair Favourite*, for the second time in less than a month, Davenant was made Poet Laureate, at the special request of the Queen, and three months later, on March 26, 1639, he was granted a Royal Patent giving him permission not only to build a playhouse 'behind the Three Kings Ordinary in Fleet Street'

wherein plays, musical entertainments, scenes, or other like presentments may be presented,

but also

to act plays in such house so to be by him or them erected: and exercise music, musical presentments, scenes, dancing, or other the like.

The patent also gave him *carte blanche* to put on his shows at any time, whether the performances clashed with those of other houses or not, and specifically allowed him, his heirs, executors, administrators and assigns to take and receive of such our subjects as shall resort to see or hear any such plays, scenes and entertainments whatsoever, such sum or sums of money as is, are, or hereafter from time to time shall be accustomed to be given or taken in other playhouses and places for the like plays, scenes, presentments, and entertainments.

I have made these quotations from the patent rather than state that the patent gave him permission to build an opera-house, because, as the word 'opera' is not used in the patent, it might be thought that I was guilty of a misrepresentation—especially in view of the history of opera in England in the next few years and of Dryden's explanation of how Davenant came to put on musical works.[5] But in spite of other experts on the theatre, W. J. Lawrence in *The Elizabethan Playhouse* was confident that the wording of the patent meant that Davenant had in mind the production, among other shows, of operas and concerts, and, as E. J. Dent carefully wrote in *Foundations of English Opera*, 'there seems every reason to suppose' that this interpretation is correct.

Davenant obviously planned giving performances of dramatic masques tricked out with all the extraneous attractions of music, dancing, singing both of songs and of recitative, and the novelty of changeable scenery that had been gradually grafted from Italian opera on to the performances he knew so well and in which he had taken considerable part. These spectacular productions had seldom been glimpsed by the ordinary citizens of London, but when they were—either in the form of the preliminary processions which often preceded the actual masque or in their entirety—they were always hailed with ecstasy, as the recent *Triumph of Peace* had shown. No wonder, then, that Davenant saw in the public presenting of such shows a possible gold-mine, for he was a natural theatrical showman: not only had he inherited from his two fathers—actual and artistic, or legal and literal—an instinct for the theatre in all its ramifications, but he had also absorbed from them a doubly strong business sense: the one had made an inn pay, while the other had made theatrical shares valuable. Whatever critical artists might say, Davenant knew that the public would probably flock indiscriminately to a novel form of entertainment, as they have always done (at least while the craze lasts).

If Davenant had had his way in 1639, England would have been the first country outside Italy to see public opera, and that only two years after the building of the first Italian public opera-house.

It is interesting to realise that those two years' experience of public shows with scenes and recitative music might easily have been caught up in England, for, apart from the fact that the English masque had learned a lot from the Italian shows, as far as stage machinery and sung dialogue were concerned, the Italian stage was certainly not so much in advance of the English: in fact in 1611—nearly thirty years before Davenant made his operatic plans —an English visitor to Venice thought the playhouse he visited there was

very beggarly and base in comparison of our stately playhouses in England: neither can their actors compare with us for apparel, shows, and music.[6]

Whether or not after thirty years the new Venetian opera-houses had advanced any further than the wooden pillars painted like marble of the London playhouse called the Swan, which in 1611 had been seventeen years old, the English had shown that they were ready to appreciate the new Italian craze for staging and sung dialogue, and Davenant must have felt on pretty sure ground when he planned building a new theatre for such novel entertainment for the ordinary citizens of London in the very bounds of the City itself.

In the summer of the same year (1639), three months after he was granted his patent, he was appointed Governor of the King and Queen's Company of Actors who appeared at the Cockpit Theatre just outside the City itself in Drury Lane. I imagine that this was done to give him professional standing and—what was more important—professional experience. He was only thirty-three, and up to now it was only as an author that he had been concerned with dramatic shows: his masques had been performed at Court and he had had a few plays performed publicly, both at the old Burbage-Shakespeare theatre at Blackfriars and at the Drury Lane Cockpit (as it was still colloquially called, in spite of its new name, the Phoenix) among their usual daytime shows and by royal command as evening entertainments even further outside the City boundaries, either at the other Cockpit Theatre in the old Palace of Whitehall at the edge of the country or at Hampton Court in the country itself.

But Davenant's plans received some severe check, for by October 1639—only seven months after he had been granted his building contract—he gave up his right to the site he had in mind.

Although no specific reason has been found to explain his change of plan, it must have been that the general trend of political uneasiness affected the business interests of the City and the artistic interests of the nobility. Prynne's attack on the stage had merely been a preliminary sign of the growing strength of the Puritans, and in their antagonism to the King and all he stood for they began to clamp down on all the things he enjoyed, including the presentation of stage-plays.

After the production of one more masque—Inigo Jones's last also—in 1640, Davenant, by nature and environment an ardent Royalist, suffered the usual experiences of that party: accused of marshalling the army for the King in 1641, he twice escaped arrest and fled to France, but later was knighted for valour at the siege of Gloucester: again he went to France, and became a Catholic, but returned to beg Charles, at the request of the Queen, to give up the Church for the sake of peace: a third time he went to France, but was captured when he tried to get over to America and was imprisoned in Cowes Castle. When in France he must have seen the Italian operas introduced by Cardinal Mazarin to that country in 1645 and 1647.

While in prison he still thought of the new opera technique, and began a lengthy poem of rhymed alternate lines—six thousand four hundred and sixty in all—called *Gondibert*, in the Preface to which he explained 'to his much honoured friend, Mr. Hobbs' that alternate rhymes are suitable for setting to music and that short stanzas are easier for both composer and singer, 'which in stilo recitativo, when the story is long, is chiefly requisite'. He evidently thought, theoretically at least, that this interminable poem might be sung, and his friend, Mr. Hobbs, in his Answer to the Preface clearly realises that the art of recitative had recently been revived in Italy.

Even when Davenant was brought up to London and tried for his life, the means by which his inevitable death sentence was commuted and his resultant imprisonment in the Tower of London came to an end are further proofs, though indirect, of his love of music. He escaped the death penalty chiefly through the intercession of the Foreign Secretary, the poet Milton, himself the son of a composer who had sung the praises of Elizabeth in the famous collection of Oriana madrigals, and he was ultimately freed from prison through the efforts of Bulstrode Whitelocke, the Keeper of the Tower, who had organised the music for the famous *Triumph of Peace* masque [7] and who himself was an enthusiastic amateur composer, proud of having written (with assistance) one popular dance-tune known as Whitelocke's Coranto.

Music, after all, was not outlawed by the Cromwell Government: Cromwell himself enjoyed it privately (even on an organ he had saved from what was officially considered an idolatrous building), and he allowed more books of music and books on the composition of music to be published year after year. Certainly such 'prophane and licentious entertainments' as maypole dancing and stage plays had been clamped down on officially, just as had any music that was part of religious services in which saints were worshipped in the form of idols; but stage-plays had by no means died out. Frequent performances were given in London in first one and then another theatre or hall which certainly ran the risk of being stopped, and even might lead to the wholesale arrest of the actors and their parade through the streets in their costumes to be fined a nominal small amount before they were released: but still the stage-plays went on, rather like the mushroom growth of ill-run night-clubs or bottle-parties that sprang up after the Defence of the Realm Act came in, and lasted right through the nineteen-twenties and nineteen-thirties; and, like them, theatres during the Commonwealth were winked at by the authorities, until it was felt that the time had come to send soldiers to break them up and amuse the crowd by making a female-impersonating boy in his black stage gown splash his white shoes and stockings with mud on the way to the court.

But at the same time that these public shows were being given surreptitiously, a school was openly started to teach the very things that were banned officially. By 1649 many Royalists had come back to London and were at least tolerated by their influential friends of the other side, such as Whitelocke, who himself had once been a King's man; and for the young men of society, as Leslie Hotson pointed out in his book *The Commonwealth and Restoration Stage*, one Sir Balthazar Gerbier started an academy at the village outside London called Bethnal Green, where they might learn languages, history, mathematics, music, playing on instruments, dancing, and art, including architecture, drawing, painting and 'the secret motions of scenes'. They also studied military sciences, and Gerbier taught by special request 'the operations of several sciences' by representing them in scenes.

At about the same time there was a troupe of English strolling players going round Europe under their leader, George Jolly, who soon found they were being surpassed at the Great Fair at Frankfort by the Prince of Orange's players, who performed with music, songs and scenes in the French manner. That was in 1651, the year before Davenant was released from the Tower: three years later Jolly showed that he had learned a new trick of entertainment, for he wrote to Basle offering his company and pointed out that he now had Italian decorations and actresses as well: in 1655 he was back at Frankfort for the Fair, and there his all-singing all-acting, all-scenic performances were seen by the young Charles, Prince of Wales.

That was the year in which Davenant went over to France again, during which visit he was able, as he had just been made a widower, to marry a rich Frenchwoman of an old family. Whether or not she brought him enough money to start him on his operatic venture, he invited shareholders to join him in a scheme 'to build a structure for representations and shows' of which he was to be the author. It seems, as Hotson says, that the scheme was started but the theatre was not built. However, Davenant was not discouraged: he evidently started a company of actors some time before April 1656 which performed in various theatres in London—Hotson believes, I think rightly, that he rang the changes on the theatres, judging from a satirical poem called 'How Daphne Pays his Debts' (Daphne being a sort of anagram of his name and an allusion to his laureateship). Davenant was evidently very elusive to his creditors, of whom he had many after coming out of prison almost penniless. The following verses allude to those creditors:

> At the month's end they come again,
>   Molesting him like devils.
> 'Well, now I'll pay ye all,' quoth he,
>   'I must be Master o' th' Revels.
>
> The State hath promised this to me,
>   As the Clerk of the Parliament saith,
> And I hope that you will do as I do,
>   Believe the Public Faith.

Already I have hired a house,
    Wherein to sing and dance:
And now the ladies shall have masques
    Made à la mode de France.'

So far the allusions might merely be to his plans and promises, but the next verses show this is not so:

This house was Pothecaries' Hall,
    I tell to him that asks,
Because of a meeting that was there,
    Which he said was one of his masques.

If there you find him not, come to St. Jones's,
    Where his next house is hiring,
And if you come quickly, you shall see
    The players themselves attiring.

For surely he doth play, but must
    Be watched like Bacon's head,
'Time is, Time was', but still you come
    When the 'Time past' is said.

I can tell y'of more of's houses, one
    In fields of Lincoln's Inn,
Another in Drury Lane: and thus
    Daphne will never lin——.

Whether or not he, a Royalist, did in fact become Master of the Revels to Cromwell, or whether he merely hoped for the post, he certainly was later accused of having held that appointment. As for the various places where the poem says he performed his 'masques' the Apothecaries' Hall was definitely used by him for rehearsing after the Restoration, so it probably was suitable for stage performances. 'St. Jones's', as Hotson says, must be near the dissolved priory of St. John's, Clerkenwell—either the great house that had belonged to the Office of the Revels (it is tempting to think that he would have had that house had he been Master of the Revels) or the house nearby in Charterhouse Yard called Rutland House, where Davenant lived on returning from France; the Lincoln's Inn Fields house was the Gibbons's Tennis Court (a building for real tennis, it should be remembered, not a grass lawn) where a play had been performed at least three years before this, while the Drury Lane house was probably the old Cockpit Theatre. The verse about 'Bacon's head', alluding to the powers of divination attributed to the supposed mechanical invention of the fourteenth century alchemist-philosopher Roger Bacon, seems to make it quite certain that these theatres were used in turn, as Hotson, who first pointed out the importance of this poem, says. A later verse runs:

> Now in these houses he hath men
> And clothes to make them trim;
> For six good friends of his laid out
> Six thousand pounds for him.

but it seems unlikely that in the circumstances Davenant had four theatrical companies at the same time—more probably he had a skeleton staff and a wardrobe at each house to make quick and unobtrusive transference possible: as for the money, Hotson could only find that Davenant had definitely collected under a thousand pounds, though his shareholders later claimed he had had up to nearly three thousand in all.

It seems quite clear that, relying on the blind eye of authority and the unconcealed enthusiasm of the Londoners—especially the society youth—for entertainment, Davenant had given some sort of theatrical shows more or less surreptitiously early in 1656: but in May he openly distributed handbills announcing an 'Entertainment in declamation and music, after the manner of the ancients' to take place in Rutland House, Charterhouse Yard, Aldersgate Street, where he was living. Although therefore this was a private house, the public were allowed to be admitted at five shillings a head, and the entertainment, by its very description, was in some accord with the aims of Count Bardi and his circle, the originators of opera.

---

[1] By this time he had been a page in two of the smart London houses, Lady Richmond's and Lord Brooke's, so probably his jokes pleased the knowledgeable set as much as the 'Ivy' jokes in the *Sweet and Low* revues failed to amuse or be intelligible to, say, North-Country factory hands up to London by the coachload in recent years—this will itself call for a footnote of explanation in years to come!

[2] The 1634 masque, *Coelum Britannicum*, printed among Davenant's works by his widow in 1673, was apparently by Thomas Carew.

[3] Miss Welsford in *The Court Masque* thinks that if Davenant wrote any of the *Luminalia*, it was merely the songs and prose descriptions, not the whole masque, as Professor Brotanek in *Beiblatt zur Anglia* and Mr. Simpson in *Designs by Inigo Jones* thought.

[4] See p. 31.   [5] See pp. 51 and 99.

[6] Coryat, *Crudities*.   [7] See p. 38.

CHAPTER FOUR

Opera at Rutland House

FOR twenty years now musicians in England had known of the principles of opera and a large number of the older society people had already heard recitative in the masques of the old days, while the younger ones probably studied it, and certainly experimented with perspective scenes at the Bethnal Green Academy, which had by now transferred to Whitefriars. Apart from this, quite a number of English travellers had of course seen opera actually performed in Italy. Milton himself, only four days after Davenant had got his first and abortive opera-house patent in 1639, had written of the grand musical entertainment given by Cardinal Barberini in Rome, which was, according to Löwenberg, a performance of the first comic opera ever written, *Chi Soffre, Speri*, by Mazzochi and Marazzoli; and Milton was so greatly impressed by the singing of Leonora Baroni, and by the accompaniment played by her mother, Adriana Baroni, herself once a famous singer, that he certainly wrote Latin verses in praise of her, even if the story that she was the unknown beauty he fell in love with is not true.

The twenty-four-year-old diarist Evelyn in 1644 had written with admiration of the Florentine Bernini—sculptor, architect, painter and poet—who,

a little before my coming to the City, gave a public opera (for so they call shows of that kind) wherein he painted the scenes, cut the statues, invented the engines, composed the music, writ the comedy, and built the theatre.

The next year he saw another 'magnificent opera' in Rome, and at Venice he wrote that

we went to the Opera where comedies and other plays are represented in recitative music by the most excellent musicians vocal and instrumental, with variety of scenes painted and contrived with no less art of perspective, and machines for flying in the air, and other wonderful motions: taken together it is one of the most magnificent and expensive diversions the wit of man can invent. The History was *Hercules in Lydia*: the scenes changed thirteen times. The famous voices, Anna Rencia, a Roman, and reputed the best treble of women: but there was an eunuch who in my opinion surpassed her: also a

Genoese that sung an incomparable bass. This held us by the eyes and ears till two in the morning.

Evelyn pointed out that the opera-houses were only open in Venice during special occasions such as Carnival time, and at Shrove-tide 1646 in Venice he recorded that the

diversion which chiefly took me up was three noble operas, where were excellent voices and music,

and he was pleased to escort the celebrated Anna Rencia to a fish dinner after the performance, when she sang for him with the *castrato*, and later at the English Consul's he heard again 'the Genoese, the most celebrated bass in Italy, who was one of the late opera band'.

Some years later (1651) he saw in Paris 'the royal masque or opera' with fine voices, impressive scenery and a string orchestra of twenty-nine. But although Evelyn had so much admired the music, it is quite obvious that he was almost more impressed by the magnificent scenery, the ingenious machines and the fact that there were so many changes on the stage to take the eye—it will be noticed that he puts 'eyes' before 'ears'. Sir John Reresby, too, writing of the carnival in Venice about the time that Davenant gave his first tentative operatic performance, says that operas

are usually tragedies, sung in music, and much advantaged by variety of scenes and machines.

No wonder, then, that Davenant, now fifty years old in 1656, anticipated an interested audience at his first boldly public show, which he called *The First Day's Entertainment*. He expected four hundred, but only a hundred and fifty people came—not, I think, because he had miscalculated the interest the show would cause among both artists and society, but because of the natural feeling among those who wanted to go that they had better let others go first, just in case there was any trouble.

There was no trouble: Davenant would not have openly handed out bills advertising the show if there had been any risk, and so on Friday, May 23, 1656, after a flourish of music, the great purple-and-gold curtains parted and the Prologue entered to apologise for the narrowness of the room (it was only twenty-two feet wide), the cramped seats for the audience facing each other on each side of the room so that they were not able to face the stage, and the smallness of the stage (it was only about twelve feet deep in acting-space)

> . . . You cannot front our cupboard-scene,
> Nor sit so easily as to stretch and lean.

—though he pointed out that they would all like to see each other and be seen as in the old days of the masque and in what was to be true opera fashion.

He went on to ask the audience to think of the passage that the room so much resembled as a passage (both literal and meta-phorical) leading

> To our Elysian Field, the Opera,

at which, the Prologue said, Davenant had aimed for so long and which he soon hoped to achieve, though he was now grown old and could not help regretting the promise of past times by com-parison with the present. He even dared to say that the day would come when the powers-that-be would do more than boast of their physical success and think of setting an example to future generations (through such higher things as literature, music and opera, no doubt), and the Prologue ended with an apology for the actors who were to make the declamations, as they had been out of practice in public for so long.

Davenant himself quite clearly regarded this entertainment as a step towards opera, and so gives the lie to Dryden, who fourteen years later (1670), two years after the death of Davenant, whom he did not know very well, wrote that because he had not been allowed to present plays during the Commonwealth.

he was forced to turn his thoughts another way and to introduce the examples of moral virtue, writ in verse, and performed in recitative music.

This idea, that Davenant only introduced opera technique to get round the banning of spoken plays, does not fit all the implications of his early patent and of all his writings, especially this prologue: it has, however, been repeated many times by learned scholars who have failed to notice that though *The First Day's Entertain-ment* is no opera and though Davenant may have later produced a spoken version of his next real operatic venture at Rutland House, they came into being because the loophole in the law forbidding stage plays allowed music to be used in a costumed entertainment, thereby giving Davenant the chance to try out the very thing he had had in mind for at least seventeen years.

Dryden later thought that Davenant's experiments fore-shadowed heroic poetic plays with their rhyming lines: Davenant intended them as imitations of operas: and ultimately the two met in the Dryden type of dramatic opera towards the end of the seventeenth century when Dryden himself wrote lines for the type of music and scenes for the type of staging that he himself says Davenant borrowed from Italian opera.

The First Day's Entertainment consists of two long scenes—the first between Diogenes the Cynic and Aristophanes the Poet, who declaim against and for 'Public Entertainment by Moral Repre-sentations', the second between a Parisian and a Londoner, who declaim 'concerning the pre-eminence of Paris and London'. The four long speeches that make up these two scenes are introduced by instrumental music that prepares the atmosphere for each speaker—sullen music for Diogenes, pleasant for Aristophanes, French for the Parisian and 'music imitating the Waits of London' for the Londoner; they are ended by a song—or, as I think from the printed text, a dialogue—summing up the arguments: the whole entertainment finished with 'a flourish of loud music'—all the music written by four composers—Dr. Charles Coleman, who had written masque-music and was made a Doctor of Music at Cambridge in 1651; Henry Cooke, who at that time taught singing after having apparently been to Italy for study and who always retained the military title of Captain which rank he reached in the Royal army before the end of hostilities; Henry Lawes, who with or without his brother had great experience of writing recitative music not only in masques for the Court in the old days but also for Milton's masque *Comus*, which had been produced privately at Ludlow in 1634; and George Hudson, of whose career at this time nothing is known, though later he was favoured by an appointment from Charles II, as were also Coleman and Cooke.

Unfortunately none of the music to this entertainment has sur-vived: but in the declamatory speeches there are some comments which obviously reflect the views of the day on the new sort of operatic entertainment that as yet had not been properly seen in England. Diogenes, who stands for the Puritan, and so disap-proves, anticipates that Aristophanes may try to defend operas because of their polish, when it is nothing more than posing and formal singing.

Would he prescribe you a certain comely posture in your sleep, and not to wake without a long complement to your chamber-grooms? Would he not have you cough but when alone, or, if in public, then with a musical concordance to the rest that have taken cold?

He seems to suggest that even in those days operatic acting was bound to mean over-exuberance of gesture:—

Would he have you at table carve with your arm a little extended, as if you were nicely to finish a touch in painting—or more at a stretch, as if you were to fence for your meat?

One can almost see the grandiosity of the ham acting when he suggests that in opera a greeting is made

as if when you met you were always treating to reconcile empires

and a parting is as fulsome as if the characters were

Kings that depart from their daughters when they are married by proxy and embarking for another climate.

Diogenes thinks that music is morally wrong (as the fanatical Puritans did), but he makes one remark which links Ben Jonson's fears with all future operatic arguments:—

Does not ecstasy of music transport us beyond the regions of reason?

—sense against the senses again. Scenes, he points out, are nothing but deception:—

You gaze on imaginary woods and meadows where you can neither fell nor mow, on seas where you have no ships, and on rivers where you catch no fish.

—anticipating the old Cambridge musical don who, unable to swallow the modernities of the new Wagner, stopped a rhapsody by a young enthusiast on *Tristan and Isolde* with the words, 'I say no more, if you can take pleasure in vicarious adultery.' Only poetry, Diogenes thinks, can be

the subtle engine by which the wonderful body of the opera must move.

and here it is Davenant who has slipped in the word 'wonderful'.

Aristophanes defends the graceful manners in opera by comparing them with the slovenly, off-hand rudeness of ordinary people such as Diogenes, and music he defends against such un-harmonious people: as for scenes, why not

see vast seas and provinces, fleets, armies and forts without the hazards of a voyage or pains of a long march?

and anyway there is no deception 'where we are prepared and consent to be deceived'—Diogenes might just as well stop up the bunghole in his tub because he cannot have what he sees through it: he agrees, however, that the 'several beauties' of poetry 'make up the shape of the opera'. The argument between the Parisian and the Londoner has no bearing on opera, comparing as it does such things as the fog and football of London with the noisy families and culinary contemplation of Paris.

The singers in this entertainment were Captain Cooke, Edward Coleman (the son of the composer) and his wife (who thereby became the first woman to appear on the public stage), another woman and 'other inconsiderable voices'. The show lasted an hour and a half, and it was announced that other declamations would follow: but there seems to be no record of these having been performed.

In the autumn of the same year, however, Davenant brought out, also at Rutland House, not only the first true opera to be seen in England, but the first English opera, *The Siege of Rhodes*.

Even now Davenant did not call his new work an opera, but

a representation by the art of perspective in scenes and the story sung in recitative music

—so ingrained was the habit from the masques, if not from the practice in Italy, that the scenes come before the music: and as the years go on, it seems fairly obvious that for some the chief interest in operas, whether of the Dryden–Purcell play with music kind or of the all-sung kind, was first and foremost the spectacular.

Davenant's preface to the 1656 edition of *The Siege of Rhodes* is addressed to the reader and apologises, like the Prologue to *The First Day's Entertainment*, for the smallness of the room, but practically promises larger premises if there is enough public support:

the defects which I intend to excuse are chiefly such as you cannot reform but only with your purse—that is, by building us a larger room.

The small stage limited the cast to only seven, and as this meant that the changeable scenes—five in all—at the back of the stage were only some nine feet high and seven feet wide, Davenant commented:

This is so narrow an allowance for the fleet of Solyman the Magnificent, his army, the Island of Rhodes, and the varieties attending the siege of the city, that I fear you will think we invite you to such a contracted trifle as that of the Caesars carved upon a nut.

However, no skill was lacking in the designs for the scenes, as Davenant pointed out,

which will not be doubted by those who can judge the kind of illustration and know the excellence of Mr. John Webb, who designed and ordered it.

The designs of all the scenes by John Webb, the nephew and pupil of Inigo Jones, like many designs by Inigo Jones for the earlier masques, are in the collection of the Duke of Devonshire at Chatsworth: some of the Inigo Jones designs for Ben Jonson's and Davenant's masques have been reproduced in Vol. XII of the Walpole Society, and some of *The Siege of Rhodes* designs have been reproduced in the *Burlington Magazine*, Vol. XXV, so that though the music (by the same composers that were connected with *The First Day's Entertainment*, with young Matthew Locke in addition) has been lost, the words and the scenes—the two chief ingredients according to the taste of the day—do still exist.

It is surprising to us nowadays that Webb thought it natural to paint human beings in action in his scenery, maybe for the first time in a public theatre, but Dent has pointed out that even to-day scenery is only naturalistic in so far as the audience can accept it in accordance with an agreed convention, and anyway Webb was concerned in trying to reproduce atmosphere, not realism. So the first scene shows the Turkish fleet in the distance approaching the island of Rhodes, the second shows the city 'beleaguered at sea and land', with the guns of the Turkish army actually firing: the third scene, the royal pavilion of Solyman, shows the officers' quarters through practical arches, the fourth scene is a view of Mount Philermus,

artificers appearing at work about that castle which was there, with wonderful expedition, erected by Solyman. His great army is discovered in the plain below drawn up in battalia, as if it were prepared for a general assault,

and the final scene is

a representation of a general assault given to the town, the greatest fury of the army being discerned at the English station.

Incidentally, although there were only five scenes, Davenant rang the changes on them so that there were in fact ten scenes in all.

As the size of the stage prevented the use of complicated machinery to change the scenes such as Inigo Jones had used in the great halls where the masques had been given, the changes in *The Siege of Rhodes* were effected by the simple method of dividing each picture down the middle and sliding each half on or off to disclose or hide the next scene—the first movable scenes in the London theatre, and a method which was used for many years after. It is also worth noting that it is in this work that the stage-direction expressly indicates the drawing up of the front curtain for the first time, unlike the drawing apart of the curtains in *The First Day's Entertainment*.

Among Davenant's other innovations must be included, I think, the placing of the orchestra in front of the stage for the first time in a public theatre. I believe this has not been pointed out before, because Dent in *Foundations of English Opera* thinks the players either were squeezed in behind the scenes, as in the French theatres of the day, or were placed above the stage in accordance with the Elizabethan custom, which certainly prevailed in the London theatre long after this—especially as the musicians for *The First Day's Entertainment* had definitely been high up, as the contemporary account of the performance seems to make quite clear. Allardyce Nicoll also in his *Restoration Drama* thinks the orchestra in Davenant's theatre was either above or at the side of the stage.

But surely the orchestra cannot have been anywhere high up in the room at Rutland House for *The Siege of Rhodes* if, as I suspect from the measurements in Davenant's description and Webb's elevation of the stage, the frieze at the top of what was to all intents the proscenium joined the ceiling of the room about thirteen feet from the floor. No doubt there was still the 'loover-hole' (lantern or small balcony, specially built or otherwise) which the musicians had used in *The First Day's Entertainment*, but Davenant definitely states that the stage was only about fifteen feet in depth,

including the places of passage reserved for the music,

and if taken in conjunction with Webb's measured ground plan, that must mean that the 'places of passage' were in front of the stage, for they could not have been at the back, as Dent thinks possible, if there was to be any synchronisation between the singers and the accompaniment. In a play with only an occasional song, or a work like *The First Day's Entertainment*, it has always been practicable (though not invariably satisfactory) to conceal the orchestra behind, over or under the stage; but for a work that is entirely sung, the first rehearsal would show that visual as well as aural contact must be made between the singers and the orchestra.[1]

No doubt, as Nicoll says, music must have been played either in front of or above the stage, in accordance with the play's requirements, even after Killegrew tried out the orchestra in front in 1663—just as it has been played in various positions even in the present day; but I think it is fairly clear that, whatever Davenant did in his own theatre later, the narrow room in Rutland House would not have allowed the orchestra to be above or at the side of the stage, and so, as the operatic requirement of synchronisation made a position behind the scenes undesirable—quite apart from the fact that Webb's ground plan seems to give no room for it there—Davenant almost certainly experimented for the first time in a public theatre with the orchestra in the position which Killegrew adopted and which later became the standard position.

There is one curious thing about *The Siege of Rhodes* that Dent has pointed out: that is, that in no respect is it in any way like any Italian opera of the time, which invariably took the story from antiquity, if not from mythology. Davenant's story was comparatively modern—only just over a hundred years old, for the siege had taken place in 1522. Nor is the libretto laid out according to the Italian arrangement of songs and choruses.

Dent presumes that this clearly proves that Davenant's real aim was to get theatres reopened and his plays performed, and believes that he first wrote the work as a straight play and only adapted it for music as a means to an end. There can be no doubt, however, that he always had in mind the idea of performing opera publicly and, for whatever reason he produced the musical version, he certainly took infinite trouble. He showed in his preface that he well understood the principle of writing words for music, for he points out that singing dialogue takes longer than spoken dialogue, and so his lines of varying lengths are usually far shorter than the more normal blank verse of a spoken play because shorter lines are better for setting to music, as the hearer can soon tell—the same comment that Dryden made later.[2]

The story itself, full of heroics, misunderstandings and reconciliations, is of no operatic interest, but it is interesting that the lilt of the musical short lines often forces Davenant to become banally colloquial (though such lines often lose their banality when set to music), and starts him off writing ingenious rhymes such as are more usually associated with the eighteenth century, though they are of course found in the popular and ribald songs of the seventeenth century. He obviously was not afraid of mixing serious language with lighter phrases.

Here are some examples of Davenant's words for recitative music in *The Siege of Rhodes*: the first straightforward, but in the uneven lines that are so suitable for setting to music:

> Arm, arm, Villerius, arm!
> Thou has no leisure to grow old:
> Those now must feel thy courage, warm,
> Who think thy blood is cold.

Later simplicity becomes ingenuous, as when Ianthe in a nightgown is brought in in a chair and is addressed as follows:—

> Fair virtue, we have found
> No danger in your wound.
> Securely live
> And credit give
> To us and to the surgeon's art—

to which she replies:

> Alas, my wound is in the heart.

The final lines of the opera, sung by a Chorus of Soldiers, run like this:

> You began the assault
> With a very long halt,
> And, as halting ye came,
> So ye went off as lame
> And have left our Alphonso to scoff ye.
> To himself, as a dainty,
> He keeps his Ianthe,
> Whilst we drink good wine and you drink but coffee.

Evidently Davenant believed in ending on the jolly note and sending the audience away happy.

Two of the composers of the music, Captain Henry Cooke and young Matthew Locke, also sang in the performance: they took the parts of Solyman the Magnificent and the Admiral of Rhodes respectively, while the Pasha (Bassa) Mustapha was Henry Purcell, the father of the great composer.[3] The parts of Alphonso, a Sicilian Duke, and his greatly misunderstood wife, Ianthe, were sung by Edward Coleman and his wife, so Mrs. Coleman, who already was the first woman to appear on the public stage in London in *The First Day's Entertainment*, now became the first woman opera-singer in London: the show itself was the first public entertainment in England to be all sung, the first with movable scenery and the first with a rising front curtain.

[1] When Rinuccini's libretto for the first opera, *Dafne* (Peri 1597), was re-set by Marco da Gagliano in 1608, the composer insisted that the instruments should be placed where they could see the soloists and so ensure synchronisation.

[2] See p. 151.

[3] I am not persuaded that my friend Professor Westrup is right in claiming that Thomas was the father, for his conviction is based on a letter once in the possession of W. H. Cummings (who never made such an assertion), which apparently has not been examined or even seen since it was said to have been sent to a Japanese library: besides, thirty years ago both Barclay Squire and Geoffrey Arkwright gave me outspoken reasons why they could not think the letter authoritative. It seems a pity that the latest edition of *Grove's Dictionary* ignores the views of these two scholars and says that Professor Westrup's researches seem to have established Thomas as the composer's father. The letter can still not be seen, I understand, although it is now said to be in America. However, it is an academic point: whatever relation he may have been to the composer, Henry Purcell the elder did play Mustapha in *The Siege of Rhodes*.

CHAPTER FIVE

Opera at the Cockpit, Drury Lane

IT was very clever of Davenant, as Hotson says, to have avoided trouble with the authorities by having the characters in *The Siege of Rhodes* played by singers instead of actors, for the former had never been officially suppressed, as the latter had. He evidently felt on fairly safe ground, for the following January he wrote to Secretary Thurloe urging the usefulness of public entertainments both in keeping up morale and so avoiding mob-dissatisfaction, encouraging the trade that results through the spending of a happy crowd, and giving employment. He suggested that as Parliament was shortly to vote £400,000 for war with Spain, it would be good propaganda if he gave a representation with scenes of the cruelty of that nation in the West Indies, especially to natives of the British Isles.

Evidently the reply, after due consideration, was favourable, for in the early summer of the next year, 1658, Davenant had the very work he proposed produced in a recognised public theatre. Years later the accusation was made by Sir Henry Herbert, the Master of the Revels for Charles II, that Davenant had held that post for 'Oliver the Tyrant', and had only been able to present his new show through Cromwell's favour. Whether this was so or not, Cromwell cannot have disapproved of the piece politically. Only the year before this Admiral Blake had defeated the Spaniards in his last great battle at Santa Cruz, and this may well have encouraged the Council to permit this theatrical perfor- mance, which not only attacked Catholic Spain, but also made England out to be the only hope of the world, both civilised and uncivilised.

This propaganda show was called:

The Cruelty of the Spaniards in Peru; expressed by instrumental and vocal music and by the art of perspective in scenes, etc.

It was, according to the libretto,

represented daily at the Cockpit in Drury Lane at three afternoon punctually, and attention was called to the fact that

notwithstanding the great expense necessary to scenes and other ornaments in
the entertainment, there is good provision of places made for a shilling. And it
shall begin certainly at three afternoon.

Davenant planned this entertainment, perhaps cautiously, more
like a masque than even such an opera as *The Siege of Rhodes*, but
the effect of the music, the speeches (all spoken by the Priest of the
Sun), the songs or dialogues, the dances and painted scenes, seems
more dramatic—or anyway more theatrically exciting—than the
more naturalistic work. It is all full of atmosphere.

The opening symphony is 'a wild air suitable to the region':
the first painted scene shows a West Indian landscape with a wood
of

cocoa-trees, pines and palmitos, and on the boughs of other trees are seen
monkeys, apes, and parrots, and at farther distance valleys of sugar-canes,

while on the shores of the rivers are natives carrying ingots of gold
and wedges of silver and happily hunting and fishing. The first
speech and the first song stress their native innocence, after which

a rope descends out of the clouds and is stretched to a stiffness by an engine,
whilst a rustic air is played, to which two apes from opposite sides of the wood
come out, listen, return, and coming out again begin to dance. Then after a
while one of them leaps up to the rope and there dances to the same air, whilst
the other moves to his measures below. Then both retire into the wood. The
rope ascends.

The next scene, of the invading fleet with the flags of the
Austrian eagle, is introduced by a trumpet air, and the Peruvians
painted on the scene are shown in amazement at such things as
ships that they had never seen before and mourning that the prophecy of disaster from a bearded people out of the sea is coming
true: after the same has been stressed in speech and song, two
Indians enter and mime the same idea.

The third scene, preceded by 'a symphony consisting of four
tunes', evidently to suggest a clash of ideas, is concerned with the
civil war between the two Royal brothers which weakened Peru
at the arrival of the Spanish invader.

The fourth scene—again preceded by a conglomeration of four
tunes—shows the defeat of the great Peruvian army by a small
body of Spaniards 'by the noise and fire of their guns' and by the

armour 'defensive and offensive too'. This scene ends with a triumphant saraband danced by two Spaniards 'exactly clothed and armed according to the custom of their nation', with the accompaniment of castanets.

The fifth painted scene is described as follows:

> A doleful pavan is played to prepare the change of scene, which represents a dark prison at great distance: and farther to the view are discerned racks and other engines of torment with which the Spaniards are tormenting the natives and English mariners, which may be supposed to be lately landed there to discover the coast.
>
> Two Spaniards are likewise discovered sitting in their cloaks and appearing more solemn in ruffs, with rapiers and daggers by their sides, the one turning a spit, whilst the other is basting an Indian Prince, which is roasted at an artificial fire.

This is the scene, no doubt, that may have won Cromwell's approval, as the speech in it so closely touches on religious propaganda, spoken as it is by the innocent Priest of the Sun:—

> What race is this, who for our punishment
> Pretend that they to haste from Heav'n were sent
> As just destroyers of idolatry?
> Yet will they not permit
> We should our idols quit,
> Because the Christian law makes converts free.
>
> Or if, to please their priests some chief permits
> A few of us to be their proselytes,
> Yet all our freedom then is but deceit.
> They ease us from our chains
> To make us take more pains,
> Light'ning our legs to give our shoulders weight.
>
> And other Christian strangers landing here
> Straight to their jealous sight as spies appear,
> And those they so much worse than heathens deem
> That they must tortured die.
> The world still waste must lie,
> Or else a prison be to all but them.

Then follows the complementary song and a mime ballet showing 'an insulting Spaniard' beating three Peruvians with his truncheon as they limp in silver fetters into a wood to collect gold and silver, and then, when they collapse under the weight, beating them on again.

The sixth scene—like all propaganda, whether in a Cromwellian masque-opera or a Hollywood war-film—shows hope of liberation by the one altruistic nation:—

An army is discerned at distance, consisting of English and Peruvians: the van is led by the English

(of course)

who are distinguished by the engines of England and their red-coats

(which must surprise all who think of the Parliamentary soldiery as buff and brown and grey and black):

The rear is brought up by the Peruvians, who are known by their feathered habits, glaives and spears. There is likewise discerned a body of armed Spaniards, their backs turned and their rear scattered as if put to flight.

(Again that was to be expected, but—unlike the producers of a celebrated Burma film of recent years, in which success was won by one heroic member of an expeditionary force which was not in fact as prominently present as others—Davenant now makes a naïve confession.)

These imaginary English forces may seem improper, because the English had made no discovery of Peru in the time of the Spaniards' first invasion there: but yet in poetical representations of this nature it may pass as a vision discerned by the Priest of the Sun before the matter was extant in order to his prophecy.

This last scene is longer than the others, because after the usual speech there comes a comedy-ballet of a Spaniard who, laden with gold and silver, falls asleep 'with his basket for his pillow', only to be woken by two apes and a great baboon which drive him into the wood. The final song 'foretells the subversion of the Spaniards by the English':

> We shall no longer fear
> The Spanish Eagle darkly hov'ring here,
>   For though from farthest climes he hither fled
>   And spaciously his wings has spread,
>   Yet th' English Lion now
>   Does still victorious grow
>   And does delight
>   To make his walks as far
>   As th' other e'er did dare
>   To make his flight.

The show ends with a Grand Dance in which a Spaniard who is proud and sullen to the Indians

pays a lowly homage to the English, who often salute him with their feet, which salutation he returns with a more lowly gravity: whilst the English and the Indians, as they encounter, salute and shake hands in sign of their future amity.

The Cruelty of the Spaniards in Peru was obviously more varied than the more conventional domestic heroism of *The Siege of Rhodes*, and even in description achieves something of the condensed drama of the well-written propaganda film or radio feature-script of to-day.

Davenant, I feel sure, wrote it in this style of a sung-and-mimed lecture-recital in costume in order not to antagonise the more fanatical Puritans excessively: it was not so obviously a dramatic show as *The Siege of Rhodes* had been, but that had been given in a private house, whereas *The Cruelty* was for a public theatre, and it was therefore tactful to repeat the tentative experiment of an illustrated debate or talk with which Rutland House was first opened to the public—if that got by the authorities, a more dramatic and more correct form of opera could soon be given.

If rumour was true, Cromwell at least tolerated musical stage works, for according to Anthony Wood he had sanctioned the Rutland House performances

because, being in an unknown tongue, it could not corrupt the morals of the people

—whether the unknown tongue was music, or whether Wood thought that, being in stilo recitativo, it was sung in Italian, hardly matters: but while semi-private performances had been given by permission or at least without objection from Cromwell or the authorities, it was a different matter to give fully public performances of stage works of any kind.

Not that Davenant relied on his history-lesson to draw the public: that was only the façade to hoodwink or appease objectors. As can be seen from even the brief summary of the work, *The Cruelty of the Spaniards in Peru* was tricked out with every device to entertain the audience—music for the highbrows, dances for the lowbrows, scenery for the novelty-seekers, bloodthirsty horrors for the enthusiasts for bear-baiting by dogs, and even tight-rope walkers to make up variety. Rope-dancing, by the way, was very popular in London at that time: the rip-roaring theatre, the Red Bull in Clerkenwell, employed several rope-dancers during the Commonwealth (all with good English names, such as Whitehead, Montford, Peadle, Spencer, Capon and Cox), and in 1654 another had appeared who was said to be 'an Albion Blackamoor', alluding to the rumour that he really was a Black-friars waterman whose mother lived at Bankside. This rope-dancer, also known as the Turk, quite possibly was engaged by Davenant for the dancing apes scene—to judge by Evelyn's de-scription of his performance the year before:

I saw even to astonishment the agility with which he performed; he walked barefooted taking hold by his toes only of a rope almost perpendicularly, and without so much as touching it with his hands; he danced blindfold on the high rope and with a boy of twelve years old tied to one of his feet about twenty foot beneath him, dangling as he danced, yet he moved as nimbly as if it had been but a feather. Lastly he stood on his head on the top of a very high mast, danced on a small rope that was very slack, and finally flew down the per-pendicular on his breast, his head foremost, his legs and arms extended.

The perpendicular rope could have descended from the clouds in the Davenant show and been 'stretched to a stiffness', and the boy dangling from the Turk's foot might well be described as 'moving to his measures below'.

But though Davenant's variety show attracted a large public, it was not universally approved: the Puritans certainly would not have approved on principle, and the Cavaliers might well have disapproved the attack on Catholic Spain, while self-styled serious artists probably objected because Davenant was sufficiently com-mercially minded to make use of topical enthusiasms—out of which have often emerged artistic achievements never attained by consciously high-flown idealists—and were jealous because he was successful.

Shades of all three types of disapproval can be sensed in a satirical ballad of the time which I here print in its entirety because, although it gives a clear hint as to the sort of show *The Cruelty of the Spaniards* was and how it struck some members of the audience, it has, I think, never been even mentioned in any book on opera (though Leslie Hotson quotes from it) and has only been reprinted by H. E. Rollins in a *Contribution to the History of the English Commonwealth Drama* from *Studies in Philology*.

Dryden had printed his version of it in *Miscellany Poems* 1716. It is entitled

Peru : or, a new ballad.

and is here given in modern spelling and punctuation in accordance with my practice all through this book.

> Now God preserve the realm
> And him that sits at helm!
>   I will tell you of a new story
> Of Sir William and his apes,
> With full many merry japes,
>   Much after the rate of *John Dory.*

(*John Dory* was an old narrative ballad of the capture of a mediaeval Frenchman of that name by one Nicholas of Fowey in Cornwall.)

> This sight is to be seen
> Near the street that's called Queen,
>   And the people have named it the Opera;
> But the Devil take my wife,
> If all the days of my life
>   I did ever see such a foppery!
>
> Where first there's one begins
> With a trip and a cringe
>   And a face set in starch to accost 'em;
> Ay, and with a speech to boot,
> That hath neither head nor foot,
>   Might have served for a Charterhouse rostrum.

(That alludes to *The First Day's Entertainment.*)

> Oh, he looked so like a Jew
> 'Twould have made a man to spue,
>   When he told 'em 'Here was this', 'Here was that',
> Just like him that shows the tombs,
> For, when the total comes,
>   Tis two hours of the Lord knows what!

(The guide to the tombs in Westminster Abbey always drooled on and on, and so merely deserved, according to one reference, one penny, for all the use his information was.)

66

Nor must I here forget
Oh, the music! how 'twas set
   But for [1] two airs and a half: and, by Jove,
All the rest was such a jig,
Like the squeaking of a pig,
   Or cats when they're making their love.

(So the music was 'modern'!)

The next thing was the scene,
And that—oh, 'twas lain
   Now the Lord he knows where, in Peru:
With a story for the nonce
Of raw head and bloody bones—
   But the devil a word on't was true!

(Everybody did not believe the propaganda.)

There you might have seen an ape
With his fellow for to gape,
   Now dancing, and then turning o'er.
What cannot poets do?
They can find out in Peru
   Things no man ever saw before!

When presently the Spaniard
Struts in with his long whinyard—[2]
   Now, Lord of Thy mercy, how grim!
Who'ld ha' thought that Christian men
Would have eaten up children,
   Had we not seen 'em do it limb by limb?

Oh, more cruelty yet!
Like a pig upon a spit
   Here lies one: there's another boiled to jelly:
Just so the people stare
At an ox in the fair
   Roasted whole with a pudding in 's belly.

Troth, I durst have lain my head
That the King he had been dead,
   When I saw how they basted and carved him,
Had he not come up again
On the stage for to complain
   How scurvily the rogues they had served him.

(There are no lines for the revived king, so I suppose this means
that the same actor appeared again later on—unless he came on in
a ballet as a ghost: it seems clear, anyway—if we can take these

lines as factual and not merely as satirical—that the basted prince
was an actor and not a painted figure on the scene.)

> A little farther in
> Hangs a third by the chin
>   And a fourth cut out into quarters.
> Oh, that Foxe had then been living!
> They had been sure of Heaven,
>   Or at least been some of his Martyrs.

(John Foxe, who wrote the *Book of Martyrs*, had died in 1587.)

> But—which was strange again—
> The Indians they had slain
>   Came dancing in all in a troop:
> But oh, give me the last,
> For as often as he passed
>   He still trembled like a dog in a hoop.

(This seems to prove that all the tortured figures were realistically
mimed instead of being painted on the backcloth, as in the later
play, *The Empress of Morocco*.)

> And now, my Signior Shrug,
> In good faith, you may go jog,
>   For Sir William will have somewhat to brag on:
> Oh, the English boys are come
> With the fife and the drum
>   And the Knight must still conquer the Dragon!

> And so my story's done,
> And I'll end as I begun
>   With a word—and I care not who knows it—
> God keep us great and small
> And bless us some and all
>   From every such a pitiful poet.

(That last verse seems to suggest that the anonymous author may
well have been a disgruntled rival to Davenant.)

   After the production of *The Cruelty of the Spaniards* Cromwell
died—on September 3, 1658, and the following month Davenant
renewed his licence with the new Protector, Richard Cromwell.
This allowed him to put on shows, and he may even have thought
of refitting the derelict Fortune Theatre to that end. He now felt
freer, and so decided to spread his wings and produce a work that
was really much more akin to opera—this is, I think, the only
chronology that explains the events, though I have never seen it

suggested by experts on the period: they unfortunately remain vague on the matter.[3]

He therefore presented an entirely novel work at the Cockpit, the sequel as it were to *The Cruelty of the Spaniards*, though in fact the events of the new show had preceded those of the earlier. He called the new show *The History of Sir Francis Drake*, and this with its predecessor was an even more modern subject than *The Siege of Rhodes* had been. It was also on a large scale, for while *The Siege of Rhodes* had had only seven singers and *The Cruelty of the Spaniards* merely two or three in addition to one declaiming actor and some dancers, this new work had no less than fifteen soloists, of whom five were principals, as well as a male chorus and the usual dancers.

The action of the new opera was more peacefully romantic than that of either of its predecessors, not only because Drake rescues

a beautiful lady tied to a tree, adorned with ornaments of a bride, with her hair dishevelled, and complaining with her hands toward heaven,

but because the good-hearted English mariners are always so ready to make friends with the poor natives—a kindness that is rewarded at the end when they capture all the gold and silver the Spaniards have loaded on to ninety mules (though Drake nobly says that 'this attempt is not for gold, but fame')—incidentally there is a realistic touch when the bells of the mules are heard approaching.

The actual story is not as exciting as the previous opera—even the fighting takes place off stage, but the characters are, it seems to me, far more real than those in *The Siege of Rhodes*, the dances are more naturally brought in, and there is hardly any political propaganda, apart from the obvious praise of British courage and the naval patriotism that comes to a climax in the final Grand Chorus, which is first sung by Drake himself:

> Our course let's to victorious England steer,
> Where, when our sails shall on the coast appear,
>   Those who from rocks and steeples spy
>   Our streamers out and colours fly
>   Will cause the bells to ring,
>   While cheerfully they sing
>   Our story, which shall their example be
>   And make succession cry 'To sea! To sea!'

This, then, with its large cast and its sung dialogue, is quite definitely an opera on the grand scale and it is a great pity that none of the music to any of Davenant's works seems to exist. But no doubt the audience—many of whom well remembered the stage-plays and masques of twenty odd years before—would not have bothered so much about the recitative, but were quite content to find both these operas more exciting theatrically than edifying politically, especially *Sir Francis Drake*, which, apart from the singing, was as like a good old play as two peas.

In fact this was exactly what the authorities thought about it too, for in December one Rachel Newport wrote to her brother saying that

it is thought the opera will speedily go down, the godly party are so much discontented with it,

and nine days later the Council under Richard Cromwell were so worried as to how it was possible that 'the opera in Drury Lane is shown in imitation of a play' that an order was made summoning Davenant and the actors to attend and explain not only how the production came about but also how far they went.

Nothing drastic seems to have resulted for the time being: no doubt it would have been tricky to press a charge if the rumours were in fact true that Oliver Cromwell had himself sanctioned musical performances in costume, for that would be equivalent to criticising his sanctions: apart from that, Davenant had been scrupulously careful not to follow up his innovation of presenting a woman on the public stage, which might have led to a charge of licentiousness—there is no woman in either *The Cruelty of the Spaniards* or *Sir Francis Drake*, apart from the rescued bride, who was only painted on the scenery.

Two months later, in February 1659, it is true that the House of Lords set up an examining committee because

there are stage-plays, interludes, and things of the like nature called opera acted to the scandal of religion and the Government,

but Davenant and his opera seem to have been saved by the very thing that had prevented the realisation of his operatic ambitions twenty years before—the political situation. In March a correspondent wrote to one of the Government's secretaries pointing out that although Parliament had recently not imposed on the three thousand Cavaliers still in London an order that they should be banished to twenty miles outside, that order would certainly be enforced to prevent any trouble,

unless the consideration of Sir Wm. Davenant and his opera, which goes up again next week, prevail to the contrary.

Presumably the potential audience of Cavaliers was not sent out of London, for Davenant's operas continued, and on May 6 Evelyn noted in his diary how surprised he was that at such a time of political unrest it was permitted to give the performance of an opera 'after the Italian way in recitative music and scenes' and that it drew an audience. All the same, although he felt guilty, he could not help going to it with a party of friends, but was disappointed that it was not as good as the operas he had seen in Italy.

In all probability this was one of Davenant's operas, though about the same time there was a performance in 'the military ground of Leicester Fields'—about where the London Hippodrome now stands—of James Shirley's opera-like masque, *Cupid and Death*. It had been given privately before the Portuguese Ambassador six years before, but now had its first public performance with extra music by Matthew Locke.

The story of this show, how the arrows of Cupid got exchanged with those of Death, with dire results, while they stayed the night at an inn, was presented with the usual entries, speeches and dances that were so typical of the old masques, as well as the now fashionable sung dialogue scenes which in their dramatic characterisation approximate far closer to operatic scenes than the earlier masque-dialogues. The music, too, is freer, more emotional and more florid than the music William Lawes wrote a quarter of a century before for Shirley's earlier masque, *The Triumph of Peace*. I am stressing this gap of time because, as Lawes and Locke are usually mentioned only a page or two apart in books on music or opera, it is so easy to forget that Locke was about forty years younger than the Lawes brothers. As the music to both these works still exists, the change of style can be appreciated (though unscholarly musicians can hardly see any difference). But this is not the place to enlarge on a description of *Cupid and Death*, for it contains nothing new either in treatment or popular appeal: to the musical historians of opera it is of immense value, as it is the one surviving example of a late Commonwealth near-opera, but *Sir Francis Drake*, which was presumably set to the same sort of music, was in general more advanced—not only in its modern historical background as compared with the other's allegorical story, but also in its essentially and entirely operatic treatment.

[1] 'Bate' in the original.
[2] i.e. dagger.
[3] Allardyce Nicoll in *Restoration Drama* on p. 29 gives as the date of both *The Cruelty* and *Sir Francis Drake* as 'towards the close of 1658', but on p. 358 he dates them 'c. June 1658'.

CHAPTER SIX

The Duke's Theatre and 'The Slighted Maid'

IN 1659 opera or near-opera was by now attracting the public, for that same summer the question was asked in *Endless Queries: or An End to Queries*:

Whether the stage-players being turned out of doors cannot—to get their livings—in imitation of the opera, set up dumb music.

At the same time the political situation was insecure, and in August Davenant was arrested as having been concerned in an abortive Cavalier rising, only to be released twelve days later.

By March 1660, however, Davenant must have been feeling pretty secure, for after writing a panegyric to General Monk, who was now for inviting the refugee Charles II back to England, he not only obtained a passport for France but also took the lease of a tennis-court near Lincoln's Inn Fields which had been built by Thomas Lisle, with a view to converting it into a public theatre.

Davenant indeed must have had good reason to feel confident, because only a month after Charles II landed in June 1660 he roughed out on paper a draft order giving himself and Thomas Killegrew (who already had a royal warrant) a theatre monopoly and the right to build two theatres

with all convenient rooms and other necessaries thereto appertaining for the representations of tragedies, comedies, plays, operas, and all other entertainments of that nature.

Sir Henry Herbert, Charles's Master of the Revels, protested on the grounds that Davenant was a turncoat, but to no avail: Davenant roughed out a further order suppressing all other theatres in London—and this, as Hotson points out, before he had even got his own licence, and the following day he got his patent, allowing him also to take money from the public, even if it meant increasing the usual prices of admission

in regard of the great expenses of scenes, music and such new decorations as have not been formerly used.

Charles II was obviously quite determined to have entertainments in the theatre, especially if there was music in them, for in October he granted a patent to one Giulio Gentileschi to give musical shows with machines and scenes and artists to be imported from Italy: that came to nothing, but two months later, no doubt remembering the musical scenic shows he had seen George Jolly give at the Frankfort Fair, and conveniently forgetting that he had just given Davenant and Killegrew a theatrical monopoly, he gave Jolly a patent to build another theatre and to perform there, provided no 'play, interlude or opera' was profane, scurrilous or obscene. Jolly then started at the Cockpit, while Davenant presented plays at the last theatre to have been built in Elizabeth's reign, the Salisbury Court, on the site of the old granary of Dorset House near Fleet Street.

Here, however, there were no facilities for scenery, which he regarded as so important, and which is carefully stressed in all his patents: on the other hand, he did manage to have music, which cost him up to thirty shillings a night. He started building his new theatre on the site of Lisle's tennis-court by Lincoln's Inn Fields, and in January 1661 got a lease of a garden behind it on which to build a scene-dock, so that in the summer his 'new theatre with scenes' (as he called it in his preliminary contract with the actors he engaged) was opened. It was named the Duke's Theatre, as his actors were officially known as the Duke of York's servants, but it soon became popularly known as the Opera.

Like Killegrew's rival company, the King's servants, at the Theatre Royal, or the King's, in Vere Street, Davenant's company included women, as expressly authorised, the four chief actresses being lodged at Davenant's house, which was another extension at the back of the theatre. The opening show in the presence of Charles II—his first appearance at a public theatre—was *The Siege of Rhodes* altered and enlarged: it ran twelve days with great applause.

Pepys saw the fourth performance, when the audience had to wait for the King and Queen of Bohemia to arrive: he thought it 'very fine and magnificent, and well acted', except for the actor playing the Eunuch, who was hissed for being so bad. That actor, by the way, at the first performance had been petrified at appearing before royalty and anyway was not used to being on the stage, for he was merely the prompter who attended rehearsals each morning and the performances each afternoon: his name was Downes, and he later became the first English stage historian by his account of plays and operas from this time up to the turn of the century.

Evidently the town flocked to Davenant's new theatre, for two days after his visit to the Opera, Pepys went to the King's, which had opened before the Duke's, and commented on how he thought it

strange to see this house, that used to be so thronged, now empty since the Opera begun: and so will continue for a while, I believe.

It was probably the novelty of changing scenery that chiefly attracted the public there, for both houses had the new interest of women acting and not all the shows at the Duke's, Lincoln's Inn Fields, were musical—though the new and enlarged version of *The Siege of Rhodes* was certainly not all spoken, as has been presumed, for Evelyn, who saw it in 1662, definitely states that it was in recitative music, and Pepys some years later was so fond of the music to it that he asked one of the fiddlers at the Opera about it,

which he tells me, he can get me, which I am mightily glad of.

Davenant justified his belief that novelty in the theatre pays—as long as the public is interested—and he was always ready to enlarge his theatre interests, even by not altogether scrupulous means: he tried to get the right to build a new theatre in Dublin and to hold it in a monopoly, although at that very time the only theatre there (the first in Ireland) was being helped to recover from the bad days in which it had fallen—as it turned out, it was the Dublin manager who succeeded in getting the patent to build a new theatre there for all kinds of entertainment, including operas. In 1663 Davenant and Killegrew took over Jolly's licence on royalty terms, while Jolly got permission to tour the country, which perhaps was more to the taste of that strolling player: at the same time it suited the patentees' book, for by trickily letting the King think they had bought Jolly out, they were able to use his licence to plan the setting up of a nursery theatre for actors.

On February 23, 1663 Pepys saw a play at the Duke's Theatre which he did not think much of and which merits only an occasional reference in books on the theatre—not very surprising, as it is of little literary interest: but it is surprising that books on opera ignore it,[1] because not only does it make a great feature of music but it also is obviously the forerunner of the kind of dramatic opera that was later copied and developed by Shadwell and Purcell. But the most interesting thing about it is that it is the missing link between dramas, masques, and operas: the masques and entertainments that are introduced are not mere excrescences, but are integral parts of the drama: while at the end a musical scene directly brings about the denouement. It was, in fact, far in advance of its time in construction and, being so, might have been thought worthy of more than a couple of lines in even a book on Restoration Drama. To make up for this negligence on the part of both dramatic and musical scholars, here is a descriptive examination of it.

The play in question was *The Slighted Maid* by Sir Robert Stapylton and 'the instrumental, vocal and recitative music was composed by Mr. Banister'.[2] The collaboration was in accordance with Davenant's encouragement of young musicians, for the composer John Banister, who had been sent to study the violin in France by Charles II and in 1662 was made leader of the King's band, was barely thirty-three, while the author was getting on for sixty: but, apart from the clever dovetailing of music and play, there is reason to think they thought alike, for Banister was go-ahead and outspoken by nature, and so was Sir Robert, who had been a Benedictine monk as a young man, realised he was 'too gay and poetical to be confined within a cloister' (as Anthony Wood said), became a Protestant, attended the future Charles II when Prince of Wales and, after being knighted at Nottingham in 1642 and taking his D.C.L. at Oxford, became one of the Gentlemen Ushers of the Privy Chamber at the Restoration.

The story of the play shows the unravelling of four intersecting paths of true lovers, complicated by the interference of a comically villainous couple; it takes place in Naples. Diacelia, Princess of Bulgaria, though loved by Prince Salerno, is betrothed to his cousin, young Lugo, who, however, has fallen in love with a girl who seems no better than she should be—Leandra, apparently the daughter of a Greek hag called Menanthe. Salerno, philosophically accepting his dismissal by Diacelia, has decided to console himself with other ladies' favours—unlike his friend Iberio, who is still madly in love with one Pyramena, unfortunately married to a youth named Decio. This Decio, it seems, believing that his sister

Ericina had died after her affections had been betrayed by Iberio, has tried to bribe a young man, Arviedo, to poison him, though Pyramena declares her husband is

> The goodest man, nothing but innocent mirth,
> His whole delight is to make songs and masques.

If only Iberio had not been so jealous, Pyramena would have kept her promise to marry him: but now she is married to Decio, they can still be friends, as Salerno and Diacelia also decide to be, though the Prince expresses his doubt of her chastity in a song:—

> Thy love is chaste—they tell me so.
> But how, young soldier, shalt thou know?

The first act ends with Diacelia's betrothed, Lugo, making an excuse to postpone his wedding and Arviedo bringing an invitation to Iberio to visit Decio at his house in full confidence that he never intended to poison him.

The second act begins with a comedy scene between two of Decio's servants, drinking and singing

> Drink to me, boy!
> Here's to thee, boy!
> A health to our master!
> A nobler never obeyed I:
> Couple him with my lady—
> Never man had a chaster!

They are interrupted by the arrival of Salerno and Iberio, who is prepared to risk anything in Decio's house for the sight of Decio's wife, Pyramena, with whom he tries to flirt. Salerno warns him the house is guarded by 'mariners out of the Turkey ship', and they draw their swords when the sailors rush in—only to be surprised when the sailors (and their wives) proceed to start a dance as a welcome arranged by Decio, who now appears for the first time and astounds Iberio (and the audience) by hospitably promising him Pyramena's affection, as becomes an altruistic, unselfish host. Decio now takes Arviedo away for a talk, leaving the guests with his wife, although refreshment is served—as Pyramena said before, he thinks of nothing but theatre:

> I cannot get my husband to the banquet;
> He's so pleased with your cousin Arviedo,
> His brother lutenist, he has carried him
> To see his new scenes.

Salerno tactfully refuses supper and goes to bed, whereupon Iberio tries to force Pyramena to be unfaithful to her husband, but refrains when she takes a knife from the dinner-table to kill herself and is persuaded to sit down and play cards till her husband gets back!

At the beginning of the third act Decio has brought Arviedo 'to see his new scenes', which are introduced by the following theorising on art in front of a laurel-tree near which are set three stage-properties—a shepherd's crook, a musical pipe and a laurel wreath:—

Decio.   The breath of music, brother lutenist,
          Is sound, which into points of time art breaks:
          But poetry's the language music speaks.
          Poetry's that divinity of numbers
          By which Pythagoras transformed himself
          Into the sev'ral shapes of men an gods:
          And thou or I may do 't as well as he.
Arviedo. I think we may.
Decio.   Behold th' experiment!
          I'm Decio now: but now that I take up
          This shepherd's hook, pipe and poetic laurel,
          I am Apollo, shepherd to Admetus,
          Not herdsman: I have left his royal droves
          In Thessaly to keep his flocks in Naples.
          Will Arviedo be my favourite,
          My Hyacinthus?
Arviedo.   What must transform me?
Decio.   Poetry—a new ode which I've composed:
          Sit down and hear it: 'tis Apollo's song.

              Here I pipe: here I keep
              King Admetus's sheep:
          Here I gather laurel for my wreath.
              But, Apollo, where
              Dost thou live? Oh, not here!
        Absent loves live not where they breathe.
              But my spirit is
              In a place of bliss,
      Wheresoe'er that blessed place may be—
            In a garden, or a grove,
            In a grot, or an alcove:
        Ever where my love is, there am I.
              Uncircumscribed thus acts the mind:
              Why should the body be confined?
            Swift as thought can move,
            Little God of Love,

> Carry me upon thy nimble wings
>> To the top of yonder tow'r,
>> Where precisely at this hour
> Hyacinthus strikes his lute and sings.
>> We are met, sweet boy!
>> What I now enjoy
> Not a god besides myself shall know.
>> Cupid, thou hast leave to play.
>> To thy mother fly and say
> That Apollo has a heav'n below.

Arviedo. You have feasted mine ear.
Decio.   I'll treat thy eye.
The sweetest prospect Naples has I'll show thee—
The pasture where Apollo feeds his flock.

> *The scene is discovered over which in capital letters is writ* CAMPI
> ELYSII. *Decio describes it thus.*

Th' Elysian Fields my Hyacinthus sees.
Those walks are jessamine and orange trees:
Beneath a crystal river cuts the plain,
Wherein you see those fair trees o'er again:
Close by the flow'ry bank a flock of sheep
Feeds in a mead—the shepherds fast asleep,
The shepherdesses lying arm in arm.

Arviedo. Is't life? Or art?
Decio.   Art-magic! Hear the charm!
Rise, dull sleepers! Fie, how coldly
You move! Shepherds, come on boldly!
No wolf shall your flocks endanger.
Dance and welcome this young stranger!

> *The Shepherds dance and go off.*

Decio then convinces Arviedo that he only offered him a bribe
to test him and gives him a ring of his dead sister Ericina. Arviedo
vows he will repay Decio, who replies:—

> I'll show thee how to pay this debt and leave
> Me in arrear—get dancers, and this evening
> Make me a serenade: tis only a round
> Well danced and a short song or two. Let's see
> Thy poetry.

Arviedo.   I never studied it,
Yet naturally I'm a ballet-maker.

He goes to get it ready while Decio, learning that Iberio is alone
with Pyramena, is content not to interfere.

Later in the act Decio, being assured of Pyramena's good

behaviour, would like to celebrate, if only the masque were
ready. At that moment the porter announces:—

> Sir, a kind of masque
> Is brought you: (these hard words stick in my throat)
> They call't a serenade. Here's the presenter.

Arviedo steps forward and the masque begins.

> *Enter the Evening—in a crown of shadowed stars and a cloudy veil*
> *with some small stars upon it—brought in by two Winds.*

After a little dialogue '*Flageolets play afar off*' and then this dialogue
is sung:—

Evening.	I am an Evening dark as night.
	Jack-with-a-lantern, bring a light!
Jack.	(*within*) Whither? Whither? Whither?
Evening.	Hither! Hither! Hither!
Jack.	Thou art some prattling echo of my making.
Evening.	Thou art a foolish fire by thy mistaking.
	I am the Evening that creates thee.

> *Enter Jack in a black suit bordered with glowworms, a coronet of*
> *shaded beams on his head, over it a paper lantern with a candle in't.*

Jack.	My lantern and my candle waits thee.
Evening.	Those flageolets that we heard play
	Are reapers who have lost their way:
	They play, they sing, they dance around:
	Lead them up! Here's fairy-ground.
Chorus.	Let the men ware the ditches!
	Maids, look to your breeches!
	We'll scratch them with briars and thistles.
	When the flageolets cry,
	We are a-dry:
	Pond-water shall wet their whistles.

> *Exeunt Evening, the Winds and Jack.*

Decio.	Does Pyramena know this dancing lantern?
Pyramena.	The Ignis Fatuus, I suppose: some call it
	Jack-with-the-lantern, some Will-with-the-wisp.
	'Tis th' evening's false light, which leads stumbling clowns
	O'er moors and marshes into bogs and pits.

> *The violins and flageolets play.*
> *Jack leads in the reapers, the men in their half-shirts and linen drawers,*
> *the maids in straw hats; they stumble and their sickles fall into the*
> *scene.*

(This must mean that they fall through trap-doors in the stage.)

They dance in figures.
At the end of the first dance Jack leads them out and once or twice they
thread the doors after him

(That is they follow-my-leader in and out of the permanent doors
on each side of the stage.)

then they take hands, compass in Jack, dance a round, and sing.

Buff's a fine sport
And so's course o' park:
But both come short
Of a dance in the dark.
We trip it completely:
The pipe sounds so neatly:
But that which surpasses
Is the breath of the lasses.
Oh, the pretty rogues kiss featly!

Jack runs away and leaves them to stumble out in the dark.

A few spoken lines with thanks from the guests and the act
ends.

In the fourth act Decio tells Pyramena he only married her out
of spite, so as to be revenged for his sister's death in the way that
will hurt her faithless lover, Iberio, far more than his death—the
loss of his beloved Pyramena. Having made this announcement,
Decio arranges to be called away, certain that Pyramena will seize
the opportunity to send for Iberio. This she does: but when Iberio
arrives, he no sooner learns from Pyramena that she has been
Decio's wife in name only and is willing to run away with Iberio
till she can be divorced, than they are captured and bound (together with Arviedo) by Decio's servants.

The fifth act begins with the satisfactory unravelling of the sub-
plot, which has carried on all through the first four acts—Lugo
finds he loves Princess Diacelia after all, his cousin Prince Salerno
falls in love with Leandra, who turns out to be Diacelia's innocent
younger sister, and when the comic villains Peralta, a pirate turned
crook, and the Greek bawd, Menanthe, a laundress who kid-
napped Leandra, have been punished and married, the reconciled
pairs all go to see a special masque devised by Decio and the released Arviedo, after Iberio and Pyramena have been forced to
drink an opiate.

This final masque is based on the story of how, when the lame
God Vulcan caught his wife Venus and her lover Mars together,

he threw a net over them to make them a laughing-stock for all the gods. The scene is Vulcan's Court, and over it is the inscription 'Foro del Volcane'—in the tradition of the old masques and in the language of the birthplace of such spectacles: soft music is played, and Aurora, the Goddess of Dawn, enters in a black veil. In sung dialogue she summons the sun-god Phoebus to rise, who first answers her from behind the scenes, then he enters 'with his beams on' and objects that if the day should start too soon it would disclose Mars and Venus to Vulcan.

So far the recitative poetry is little different from the usual lines given to allegorical deities such as were used in most masques both before and after the scene of Iris, Ceres and Juno in *The Tempest*: but now the style changes and becomes more down to earth and vigorous, and even on the printed page the words give a lively theatrical impression of the actual performance—it is not good literature, but it is well calculated for the stage and culminates in a surprising denouement.

Aurora.   I'm sorry Mars and Venus had
          Such privacy: but I am glad
          That Phoebus does at last appear
          To shine away Aurora's fear.
Phoebus. What frighted thee?
Aurora.   I know not what:
          But thou know'st all.

          Within Vulcan roars out 'No work, rogues?'

                              What noise is that?
Phoebus. Tis Vulcan in a greater heat
          Than th'irons by his Cyclops beat:
          He makes the horror of that noise,
          Teaching and knocking his great boys
          From hammering out Jove's thunder, set
          To file and polish Vulcan's net
          Which he'll catch Mars and Venus in.

          Laughing within.

Aurora.   What now?
Phoebus.   To laugh the smiths begin.
          At furious Vulcan, halting off
          To measure his wife's bed, they scoff.
Aurora.   I'll leave the place: I can no more
          Endure the laughter than the roar.

          Tuning within.

Phoebus.   Hark, they record! They'll sing anon.
        Tis time for Phoebus to be gone,
        For when such lyric asses bray,
        The God of Music cannot stay.
          Exeunt Phoebus and Aurora.

There now follows 'The Cyclops Song', which surprisingly is entirely sung behind the scenes, but of course although the stage of the masque might be empty, the characters watching it were still on the stage of the theatre, so that there was still something to hold the eyes of the theatre-audience. The song (the first to be sung by stage-strikers?) goes as follows:—

        Cry our ware, sooty fellows
        Of the forge and the bellows!
          Has Jove any oaks to rend?
          Has Ceres sickles to mend?
          Wants Neptune a water-fork?
          All these are the Cyclops' work.
        But to wire-drawn iron-rods,
        To file nets to catch the Gods,
        What can make our singers so fine?
        Drink, drink, wine, Lippari-wine!
Chorus.   Smoke, smoke breeds the tysick! [3]
        Wine, wine's the best physic!
          For every Cyclop a full can!
        Our terms run thus—
        Some wine for us,
          Or no net for our master, Vulcan!

        Enter Vulcan with iron links in his hand and a horseshoe reversed on his head: he drives before him the four Cyclops drunk, wearing half-vizards with one eye in the forehead.

Vulcan.   Drink fire, you lazy monsters! Lippari-wine?
        No liquor down with you but mine?
Cyclops 1. We make a shift.
Vulcan.   It seems so, for you reel.
        Is this my cobweb weaved in steel?
        How horridly it looks—
Cyclops 2. *(he points with two fingers at Vulcan)* But not so horrid
        As Vulcan does, who shoes his forehead!

(Alluding, of course, to the cuckold horns of the inverted horseshoe.)

Vulcan.   With gaping loopholes and wrought all awry!
        My wife's pox put out thy one eye!
Cyclops 3. He means her smallpox, and that seldom misses
        The eye, for tis a small Ulysses!

(As all classical schoolchildren know, Ulysses escaped from the Cyclops' leader, Polyphemus, by putting out his one eye.)

Cyclops 4. I'll dance my eye out!

Vulcan.   Let who dare, advance
             A step! No, rogues, you shall not dance.
             I'll lay your legs fast: your heels you may shake
             In th' iron stocks: those you can make!

> *Enter two Cupids, a white and a black, with bows and forked arrows, with which they point at Vulcan.*

Cyclops 1. Not dance? Cow'rds? Here come cocks that are no dastards.
             Two Cupids? Y'have a charge of bastards.

Cyclops 2. One for the white men!

Cyclops 3.   For the black another!

Cyclops 4. (*to Vulcan*) Your wife's a very fruitful mother!
             These Cupids shoot in crossbows sure, for they
             Have forked arrows.

Cyclops 1.   Sa, sa, sa!
             We have our forks too, and though drunk yet hearty
             We'll join with the malignant party!

(i.e. the anti-Puritans—the term given by the Roundheads to the pleasure-loving Royalists.)

> *Exeunt the Cyclops, and after Vulcan and the Cupids have begun the dance, the Cyclops return with cans [4] in their hands : they dance and drink. When the antic's done, all cry 'Ware Horns!' and they run away: only the white Cupid stays.*

Vulcan.   My hammer! Dogs, your legs have saved your brains.
             Still the European brat remains
             Upon the place—Venus's only joy.
             Come hither, my wife's fine white boy!
             You just change colours, sirrah, get a robe
             As black as midnight makes the globe!
             Mourn at thy mother's funeral! If thou stay'st,
             Thine shall be first—

Cupid.   Hold, I'm in haste!

> *Exit white Cupid.*

Vulcan.   I am so too: my net I cannot make.
             Tis now Venus's time to wake.

> *Vulcan pulls out a steel watch.*

             Time Vulcan measures by exacter trial
             Than Phoebus does on his sun-dial.
             A master in my art I'm known to be,
             Though not in th' art of poetry:
             My verse halts like myself, but day and night
             My workmanship, this watch, goes right.

The scene then opens and discovers Mars and Venus 'lying on a bed; at the bed's feet sits Cupid weeping', but to the surprise of both the stage and real audience the sleeping lovers are seen to be Iberio and Pyramena. Decio now enters, dressed in a nightgown (for reasons that will soon be obvious) and with a drawn sword in his hand stops the masque: he wakes the couple and announces this as his final revenge for the death of his sister Ericina. Iberio, however, makes it clear that he was not faithless to her, for it was his father who had forced him to be betrothed to her, though he had always loved Pyramena. Convinced that this is true, Decio now undoes his nightgown and discloses that he really is the slighted maid Ericina herself, who took over the personality of her dead brother Decio for revenge: now all is explained, Pyramena's marriage is null and void, she can wed Iberio, Decio-Ericina can marry Arviedo (who turns out to be Giulio, 'the young heir to the family, honour and valour of the great captain Gonsalvo') and so the play ends with four happy couples.

From the literary-dramatic point of view *The Slighted Maid* may be unimportant, though Dryden was quite inaccurate in the criticism of the play's construction that he made some fifteen years later in the preface to his version of Shakespeare's *Troilus and Cressida*: he deprecated the lack of logical progression of events in

all plays after the new model of Spanish plots, where accident is heaped upon accident, and that which is first might as reasonably be last—an inconvenience not to be remedied but by making one accident naturally produce another, otherwise 'tis a farce and not a play.

To prove his point he went on:—

Of this nature is the *Slighted Maid*, where there is no scene in the first act which might not with as good reason be in the fifth.

The play is certainly not a farce, literally or dramatically, and, as far as I can see, Stapylton's order could not be changed at all without entirely spoiling the intricate structure he built up brick by brick. Unfortunately he made it too complicated, and because the complications are only possible by making most of the characters false to their own natures, the general effect, in spite of the excessively varied incidents, is dramatically unsatisfying. Pepys saw it three times, first on February 23, 1663, when he thought it well acted, though the play hath little good in it, being most pleased to see the little girl dance in boy's apparel, she having very fine legs, only bends in the hams, as I perceive all women do.

Incidentally, Decio must be one of the earliest male impersonation parts.[5] Three months later Pepys saw it again, on May 29, and was pleased to see a former attractive stage-struck maid of his wife's as Pyramena:—

a great part, and did it very well, and I believe will do it better and better, and prove a good actor. The play is not very excellent, but is well acted, and in general the actors in all particulars are better than at the other house.

Only the day before he had been surprised to see her merely walk on in *Hamlet*. Presumably this ex-maid, Gosnell, who never seems to have qualified for any mention as an actress except by Pepys, was taken on at the Duke's house as a performer ready 'to play as cast', whether it was as one of a crowd or as understudy to a leading actress, for Pyramena was one of Mrs. Betterton's parts.

But though *The Slighted Maid* in Pepys's opinion had little good in it and was not very excellent as a play, the acting was good enough to justify the statement on the title-page of the printed version that it was 'acted with great applause', and the proof of this is that it survived its first production and Pepys saw it for the third time five years later—on July 28, 1668—when he still thought it 'a mean play' and remarked that Gosnell

is become very homely, and sings meanly, I think, to what I thought she did.

Granting, then, that in spite of its intricacies the play was dramatically ingenuous—a copy in the British Museum contains at the beginning and the end a seventeenth-century manuscript comment 'simple play'—it still was good enough to be revived five years after its first production (if it was not kept in the repertoire till then). That may have been chiefly due to the acting— and all the parts are well calculated to show off the actors' abilities, but the chief interest to us nowadays—if not to the contemporary audience—is in the musical scenes, the attempt to make them naturally spring from the characters of Decio and Arviedo, and the ingenious use of the last masque to bring about the dramatic denouement.

Later musical dramas or dramatic operas included ingredients of the masque form, just as earlier masques included ingredients of both plays and operas, but *The Slighted Maid* is indeed the missing link—the neglected link—between masque and opera, because it includes three whole masques dovetailed into the structure of a play. Stapylton in fact seems to have thought along the same lines as Davenant and in some ways surpassed him, so deserving recognition in any account of the history of opera in England.

[1] Dent, in *Foundations of English Opera*, only alludes to it as having a scene parodied in Buckingham's *Rehearsal*.

[2] Not Locke, as Dent says.

[3] 'Phthisic'—consumption.

[4] For those who are interested, this word is spelt 'kans' all through.

[5] Of course many Elizabethan female characters, such as Rosalind in *As You Like It*, disguised themselves as boys, but they were acted by boys: Decio was played by an actress.

CHAPTER SEVEN

Davenant and Killegrew

By May 1663 Killegrew with the King's company had left his old theatre in Vere Street and opened his new Theatre Royal in Bridges Street, the first Drury Lane Theatre, as it is sometimes called. Davenant at once showed his genius for novelty by putting on at the Duke's Theatre what is to all intents and purposes a topical revue, called *The Playhouse to be Let*. The thread on which it is hung is the interviewing by an actor and the theatre manager of possible lessees for a theatre during the long vacation.

The first is a Frenchman with a troupe of French comedians, then comes a musician who is only encouraged to stay when he threatens to go to the other theatre that 'is to let in Vere Street'. The actor cannot understand why the musician is so certain of getting a theatre till he explains there is money in novelty and his novelty is 'heroic story in stilo recitativo': this starts a discussion.[1]

Player.   In stilo recitativo? Tis well: I understand you, sir. But do you think that natural?

Musician. Because tis not in custom, you therefore think, sir, it is out of nature?

Player.   It seems so, sir, to me—unless you would metamorphose men into birds. Suppose I should not ask but sing you now a question and you should instantly sing me an answer—would you not think it strange?

Musician. Well, sir, as how?

The actor now starts singing:—

Player.   'Take out your watch—and tell me, sir, the hour!'
           Then you reply—
           'My watch, sir, is at pawn—but tis past four!'

I am not scholar enough to know whether that rhyme was in those days natural or whether, as it would be now, amusingly forced: but the singing of ordinary conversation has been a stock joke ever since this early example of it. The musician, then, after a naturally rude comment on the actor's singing voice, explains one of the principles of recitative, as it was then understood.

Recitative music [he says] is not composed of matter so familiar as may serve for every low occasion of discourse. In tragedy the language of the stage is raised above the common dialect—our passions rising with the height of verse— and vocal music adds new wings to all the flights of poetry.

The musician is asked to wait a bit, while other candidates for the theatre arrive (not all appear, intriguing unseen visitors are 'the new motion-men of Norwich, Opera-Puppets'): a dancing-master offers to put on narrative ballets, explained by rhymed speeches—as Davenant had done in *The Cruelty of the Spaniards*, and, as he boasts here through the mouth of the actor, 'If these be not novelties, I'll to sea.' Finally a poet comes to suggest burlesque shows in verse. The actor then gets each of the applicants to give a sample, after he has carefully planted a few friends in the upper gallery, where, as he says, the clapping always starts.

The Frenchman has a broken English version of Molière's *Sganarelle* performed—no doubt a riotous satire on the French comedians that Pepys had seen play at the Drury Lane Cockpit that August, who had given a performance that he thought

was so ill done, and the scenes and company and everything else so nasty and out of order and poor, that I was sick all the while in my mind to be there.

For the musician's 'stilo recitativo' example Davenant included *The History of Sir Francis Drake*, which is preceded by putting his belief in the popular appeal of such works into the mouth of the theatre manager:—

Now we shall be in *Stilo Recitativo*. I'm in a trance when I hear vocal music: and in that trance inclined to prophesy that 'twill bring us inundations of shillings.

To this the actor replies:—

Thou understandest recitative music as much as a dray-horse does Greek.

To illustrate narrative ballet *The Cruelty of the Spaniards in Peru* is then performed, and finally there is a ribald burlesque of *Antony and Cleopatra* in slang with excruciating rhymes such as lasted through the eighteenth century up to the grand pantomimes of the great period of such shows. Davenant ends the epilogue to his entertainment with the lines:—

> The title at the doors was that which drew
> You hither by the charm of being new.
> You'll spoil the jest unless the play succeed,
> For then we may e'en let our house indeed.

That brought to an end the newest of all his new shows. He had, of course, produced other plays as well—many of them Shakespeare (and there again he was an innovator, for he tried to dress his production of *Henry VIII* in correct period costume) but his great claim to theatrical fame is surely his brilliant showmanship, which realised the drawing-power of novelty, and so led him to present to the ordinary London public the first movable scenery, the first actress, the first all-sung dramatic story, the first narrative ballet, the first revue, and maybe the first burlesque, together with the first orchestra to sit in front of the stage—and almost all these derived from or were part of the new kind of dramatic entertainment, opera.

Davenant soon followed up his revue with another musical play by Stapylton—this time a tragi-comedy with the title *The Stepmother*. It was not only given at the Duke's Theatre in Lincoln's Inn Fields, but also before the King at the Cockpit Theatre in Whitehall. Though more direct than *The Slighted Maid*, it is dully unreal and certainly deserves the comment at the beginning and end of the British Museum copy in the seventeenth-century writing and spelling—'Badd'.

Nor is it saved by the musical scenes: the first masque is merely a dialogue about the love of one of the couples, sung by a standing Cupid and a kneeling Flamen perched on two pedestals: a comic 'antic' is danced by a mock conjurer and a mock witch, with 'another conjurer and another witch, and from under his coat and her gown drop out two little familiars, an he and a she', but this only leads to a singing Bard in his cave and the discovery of a murder plot: the second masque muddles up four classical legends —and leads nowhere: while the third masque of Philomela and Procne, the nightingale and the swallow, miscalled Diana's masque, ends with some of the characters in the play dancing, but though the chief characters all appear as actors in the masques, that fails to make them an integral part of the play, as the masques in *The Slighted Maid* had been. The style of writing, too, does not compare with the more direct and actable language of *The Slighted Maid*, so that it is tempting to imagine that Davenant helped with the former play and left Stapylton to cope with the latter on his own—but that is mere surmise: and there would be no point in doing more than mention *The Stepmother*, were it not for the fact that 'the instrumental, vocal and recitative music was composed by Mr. Locke'—the first stage work, in fact, with music entirely by him, as is recorded in *Grove's Dictionary*, but not, I think, in any book on opera, except Dent's *Foundations of English Opera*—and there only in a footnote.

Neither *The Slighted Maid* nor *The Stepmother* contains detailed descriptions of the scenery, but Davenant made such a feature of finely painted and changing scenes that Killegrew in the rival Theatre Royal in Bridges Street or Drury Lane began to adopt them and compete with the Duke's Theatre, where Davenant put up the prices of admission, according to Dennis's *Remarks on a Play* (*The Conscious Lovers*) 1723, by more than a third to cover the cost of scenery.[2]

In both theatres the scenery was much admired not only by London playgoers but also by visitors from France, such as M. de Monconys, who was very impressed by the changing of the scenes and the machines in both the Duke's and the King's houses; though one Frenchman, however—M. de Sorbières—thought too much stress was laid on the decorations. This brought a swift reply from a Dr. Sprat, who defended the variety of scenes against the monotony of the French theatre, which seemed to depend on words alone, though another English writer, Richard Flecknoe, however, published with a play of his in 1664 his belief that although scenes 'are excellent helps of imagination, most grateful deceptions of the sight, and graceful and becoming ornaments of the stage', the tendency recently had been for the stage to appeal to the eye rather than to the ear—and anyway the English, with their lack of knowledge of lighting and indeed of anything more than bare painting, could not even approach the proficiency of the French, far less the genius of the Italians.

The opera-lover who reads this book will by now be chafing at so much stressing of scenic innovations, but this is a book on opera, not a book on music, and at this time opera primarily depended on scenery. Not that music was ever far from the thoughts of the theatre showmen who were trying these new experiments. In this same year 1664 Pepys heard from Killegrew that he intended to put on four operas a year to run for six weeks at a time in such a way that

we shall have the best scenes and machines, the best music, and everything as magnificent as is in Christendom: and to that end hath sent for voices and painters and other persons from Italy.

Killegrew in his new theatre in Bridges Street had even placed the orchestra in front of the stage, in imitation, I think, of Davenant's arrangement for *The Siege of Rhodes* at Rutland House: [3] Pepys disliked this new position, as he found most of the music sounded under the stage, while

there is no hearing of the basses at all, nor very well of the trebles, which sure must be mended.

All the same, Davenant's example had forced the rival theatre to realise the necessity of using not only scenes but also musical shows on occasion.

It was about this time that Davenant sent the chief machinist of his theatre with some actors over to Paris to study and bring back, if possible, the latest stage devices for improving the presentations. This certainly bore fruit, because, after the next two years, during which the theatres were largely closed owing to first the Great Plague and then the Great Fire, a French visitor of 1666, M. Chappuzeau, considered that, to judge by the scenes and machines he saw at the Duke's Theatre, the English would soon equal the Italians. Evelyn in 1664 had commented on the production of *The Indian Queen*, a play by Sir Robert Howard and his brother-in-law Dryden, that it was

beautified with rich scenes as the like had never been seen here or haply (except rarely) elsewhere on a mercenary theatre,

though two years later he seldom went to the public theatre because of the 'foul and undecent women' who were allowed to act there.

In 1667 Evelyn heard three excellent Italian singers, two *castrati* and one woman, no doubt brought over by Killegrew, who thought the time was now ripe for him to go ahead with his programme of three years before, which had come to nothing. He thought that London was now ready for Italian opera in Italian, and so he got the Italian composer Baptista Draghi, who was living in London, to write a special work, part of which Pepys heard the composer play through on February 12th, when he went

by and by with Lord Brouncker to his house, there to hear some Italian music: and here we met Tom Killegrew, Sir Robert Murray and the Italian Signor Baptista, who hath composed a play in Italian for the Opera, which T. Killegrew do intend to have up: and here he did sing one of the acts.

It is worth noting that Pepys anyway thought of this musical composition as a play first and foremost: he also recorded that Draghi, who was both librettist and composer, sang it all from memory, accompanying himself at the harpsichord 'most admirably'. He was very impressed with the work, but, bothered at only understanding the music, makes a shrewd comment:—

The words I did not understand, and so know not how they are fitted, but believe very well, and all in the recitativo very fine. But I perceive there is a proper accent in every country's discourse, and that do reach in their setting of notes to words, which therefore cannot be natural to anybody else but them: so that I am not so much smitten with it as, it may be, I should be, if I were acquainted with their accent.

Pepys gathered from Killegrew and Moray (Murray), who understood Italian, that the text was excellent. Killegrew told him that theatre business was half what it had been before the fire, and that therefore he was doing everything he could to improve the standard, increasing salaries, using wax instead of tallow candles, employing nine or ten good instrumentalists instead of two or three mere fiddlers, and making the whole theatre decent enough for even the King to come to regularly and not only on state occasions:[4] he had been many times to Rome to hear the music, though he was unable to sing or play himself, and he had brought over many Italian musicians, to whom he was paying £200 a year each out of the money set aside by the King for the upkeep of the 'four ridiculous gondolas' and their gondoliers dressed in ostentatiously huge costumes of crimson satin that had been sent by the Doge of Venice six years before. Killegrew made it quite clear to Pepys that he intended to have operas performed at both the Duke's and the King's theatres, as he had not been able to build another training-theatre for such shows.

Although Pepys was full of admiration for Draghi's musical memory, he realised that

in recitativo the sense much helps him, for there is but one proper way of discoursing and giving the accents.

The party then went on to hear Draghi coach one of Killegrew's English actresses in singing Italian, Pepys looking forward to hearing the Italian musicians in four days time and comparing them with such English musicians as Captain Cooke, whom he would see the following day.

When he did meet Cooke the next day, Pepys was furious with him for having

the arrogance to say that he was fain to direct Sir. W. Davenant in the breaking of his verses into such and such lengths, according as would be fit for music, and how he used to swear at Davenant and command him that way, when W. Davenant would be angry and find fault with this or that note—but a vain coxcomb I perceive he is, though he sings and composes so well.

After dinner Cooke and two of his boys from the Chapel Royal sang

but it was indeed both in performance and composition most plainly below what I heard last night, which I could not have believed.

Pepys by looking at the music was surprised that Cooke had so disregarded the feeling behind the words, and though he admitted that Cooke as a singer was excellent, he could never forgive him for

bragging that he do understand tones and sounds as well as any man in the world, and better than Sir W. Davenant or anybody else.

Three days later Pepys went as arranged to Lord Brouncker's, where Killegrew brought the Italian musicians, including a woman (whom Pepys was disappointed to learn from Killegrew 'would not be kissed'—how different from the English stage-singers of the day!) and two tall male sopranos—presumably the same Evelyn had heard earlier. The music he liked, but thought English singing was better—certainly than that of the *castrati*:—

they sing indeed pretty high and have a mellow kind of sound, but yet I have been as well satisfied with several women's voices and men also. . . .

Again Pepys comments on the self-evident fact that is so often disregarded by music-lovers even to-day—that singing must be understood as well as enjoyed:—

The women sung well, but that which distinguishes all is this, that in singing the words are to be considered and how they are fitted with notes—and then the common accent of the country is to be known and understood by the hearer, or he will never be a good judge of the vocal music of another country. So that I was not taken with this at all, neither understanding the first, nor by practice reconciled to the latter—so that their motions, and risings and fallings, though it may be pleasing to an Italian or one that understands the tongue, yet to me it did not.

So sure of the truth of this criticism was he that he added:—

(I) do from my heart believe that I could set words in English and make music of them more agreeable to any Englishman's ear (the most judicious) than any Italian music set for the voice and performed before the same man, unless he be acquainted with the Italian accent of speech.

He liked the actual music and admitted that the Italians' sense of rhythm was far better than anything in England ('unless it be a good band of practised fiddlers'), but he felt so out of touch that he was glad to slip away, 'leaving them at it', even though it meant being given a lift by Captain Cooke!

So home and to supper, not at all smitten with the music tonight, which I did expect should have been so extraordinary, Tom Killegrew crying it up, and so all the world, above all things in the world, and so to bed.

Nothing seems to have come of Killegrew's plans for Italian opera for the time being, and I suspect the reason might be that though he and Davenant had started their nursery theatre in Hatton Garden[5] (cleverly engaging Jolly to run it to keep him quiet), they were still rivals. Davenant, anyway, had yet another new idea for intriguing the public in 1667—or at least those who shared Pepys's desire to understand what was being sung: this new idea, which made Italian opera take a back seat for the time being, was to collaborate with a younger writer in adapting Shakespeare's *Tempest* in accordance with the new operatic trend. Davenant was now sixty-one, with some forty years experience of stage-writing and producing on and off, while John Dryden, aged thirty-six, had only had his first play produced four years before.

When he published their new version of *The Tempest* two years later, Dryden (or, as he then called it Driden) tactfully paid great tribute to the memory of Davenant, whom he found imaginative, quick-witted, original, helpful and most self-critical. It was Davenant who had opened Dryden's eyes to the greatness of Shakespeare, for whom Davenant 'had particularly a high veneration', and it was Davenant who had what Dryden considered the excellent idea of introducing into *The Tempest*, as a counterpart to Miranda, who had never seen a man, a man who had never seen a woman: he also wrote the comic scenes for the sailors.

But I think it is obvious that, while Dryden may have been responsible for following Davenant's example of adding to the cast by giving Caliban a sister and Ariel a sweetheart, Milcha (who is just brought in to perform a saraband as a speciality at the end), only Davenant could have thought of including two sung dia-logue scenes—in spite of Captain Cooke's depreciation of him.

The first is nothing less than a miniature masque or operatic scena: the villainous shipwrecked royalty who have just landed on Prospero's island hear music behind the scenes, and two devils sing of the sins of ambition, tyranny and usurpation, and so prick the consciences of Alonzo and Antonio: the devils now appear and call up the personifications of Pride, Fraud, Rapine and Mur-der, who all dance round Alonzo singing before they vanish.

The second dialogue scene is more truly operatic in the usual sense of the word, because it is sung by actual characters in the play and it does carry on the action. In the original *Tempest* Ferdinand first enters following Ariel, who sings, 'Come unto these yellow sands' and, after 'Full fathom five' has reminded him of his drowned father, he and Miranda meet. As altered by Davenant, Ferdinand follows Ariel off the stage after 'Full fathom five', and some scenes later they re-enter, Ariel having become an echo, which by repeating Ferdinand's last words gives him advice and encouragement. Ferdinand, however, is afraid it may be an evil spirit tempting him to disaster, so he decides to test it.

Ferdinand. I'll try if it will answer when I sing
My sorrows to the murmurs of this brook.

He sings.

Go thy way!
Ariel.   Go thy way!
Ferdinand. Why shouldst thou stay?
Ariel.   Why shouldst thou stay?
Ferdinand. Where the winds whistle and where the streams creep,
Under yond willow-tree fain would I sleep.
Then let me alone,
For tis time to be gone.
Ariel.   For tis time to be gone.
Ferdinand. What cares or pleasures can be in this isle?
Within this desert place
There lives no human race:
Fate cannot frown here, nor kind fortune smile.
Ariel.   Kind fortune smiles, and she
Has yet in store for thee
Some strange felicity.
Follow me, follow me,
And thou shalt see.

Ferdinand then speaks:—

> I'll take thy word for once: lead on, musician,

and meets Miranda and Prospero.

This was the 'curious piece of music' that Pepys found 'mighty pretty' when he saw the first performance on November 7, 1667, in such a crowded house including Charles II and the Court that Pepys was forced to sit in the side-balcony 'over against the music-room' (which Allardyce Nicoll quotes as proving that Davenant had his orchestra above the stage, while Killegrew first placed it in front—forgetting that while an occasional song or short sung scene such as these two interpolations in *The Tempest* can, like all incidental music, be performed without special contact between orchestra and singers, a longer sung work such as *The Siege of Rhodes* or *Sir Francis Drake* is sure to suffer in such conditions).

Apart from these two scenes the collaborators kept the other Shakespeare songs and snatches and added a couple more. These Dryden might have written, for he had included the usual odd song or dance in his five earlier plays, but up to now he had no great sympathy with the new 'operatic' invasion of the drama and he never did change his opinions easily. In the prologue to his first play (1663) he had made an astrologer prophesy that it would be a failure because it was not in the fashion:—

> Your play is ill designed:
> It should have been but one continued song,
> Or at the least a dance of three hours long.

After that hit at presumably—or anyway possibly—the 1663 revivals of *Sir Francis Drake* and *The Cruelty of the Spaniards* he sarcastically and boastfully apologised in another prologue that

> We neither promise you one dance or show

and in the epilogue sneered at authors

> Who write new songs and trust in tune and rhyme.

I think there can be no doubt that it was Davenant who invented the two sung scenes in *The Tempest*, but after that time Dryden began to include sung dialogues in his plays with great effect, having been lucky enough to have been shown how to use operatic effects by one of the few Englishmen who understood the method and who had practised it more than most.

The great success of *The Tempest* (Pepys saw it many times and

D   97

invariably enjoyed it) seems, as I say, to have discouraged Killegrew from presenting the Italian opera by Draghi because it
proved that English singers—with effective scenery—could draw
an audience even to a fifty-year-old play, suitably doctored. Some
five weeks before it opened, Killegrew's rival company at the
Theatre Royal had put on Beaumont and Fletcher's version of the
same Shakespeare play, called *The Sea-Voyage* or *The Storm*,
which was obviously an attempt to scotch the new version before
it appeared (this is surely more in accordance with theatre practice
than to imagine that *The Storm* gave the inventive Davenant
the idea to dash off a new and much-altered version and get it
on in five weeks): however, the public preferred the new work,
agreeing with Pepys that *The Storm* was 'but a mean play compared with *The Tempest*', which remained one of the sure successes at the Duke's Theatre in Lincoln's Fields for some time.

Davenant's extended use of musical scenes in straight plays, as
Evelyn said, started the fashion to the extent that in February
1668 Mrs. Phillips' play *Horace* had a masque and an antic dance
interpolated between the acts, and Davenant planned for future
musical spectacles by engaging Christopher Wren to build him a
fine new theatre in Dorset Garden, but before it was started on
Davenant died, on April 8, 1668, his *Tempest* being played before
the King both three weeks before and a week after.

His best epitaph was perhaps written by Beaconsfield's father,
Isaac d'Israeli, in his book *Calamities and Quarrels of Authors*:—

D'Avenant was a man who had viewed human life in all its shapes, and had
himself taken them. A poet and a wit, the creator of the English stage with the
music of Italy and the scenery of France; a soldier, an emigrant, a courtier, and
a politician:—he was, too, a state-prisoner, awaiting death with his immortal
poem in his hand; and at all times a philosopher!

[1] The scene is in blank verse, but so colloquial that I think the points are
better made if printed as prose. The scholar can read it (and probably has done
so) in its original form.

[2]

	Old Price	New Price
Pit	1s. 6d.	2s. 6d.
Box	2s. 6d.	4s.
1st Gallery	1s.	1s. 6d.
Upper Gallery	6d.	1s.

[3] See p. 56.

[4] A boldly wise example to present-day theatre managers, most of whom
in times of bad business are more inclined to cheesepare.

[5] See p. 75.

CHAPTER EIGHT

Dramatic Opera and Shadwell

Two years later, in his essay on *Heroic Plays* that he printed with his play *Almanzor and Almahide*, Dryden started the false presumption that Davenant never really intended to introduce opera to England:—

> it being forbidden him in the Rebellion times to act tragedies and comedies, because they contained some matter of scandal to those good people who could more easily dispossess their lawful sovereign than endure a wanton jest, he was forced to turn his thoughts another way and to introduce the examples of moral virtue writ in verse and performed in recitative music. The original of this music and of the scenes which adorned this work he had from the Italian operas, but he heightened his characters (as I may properly imagine) from the example of Corneille and some French poets.
>
> In this condition did this part of poetry remain at His Majesty's return, when, growing bolder, as being now owned by a public authority, he reviewed his *Siege of Rhodes* and caused it to be acted as a just drama.[1]

Dryden fails to notice that Davenant had welcomed the necessity that forced him to use recitative music, but then he was trying to give a historical reason for his own rhymed verse-plays—and not without justice. It must not be forgotten, too, that to Dryden a 'just drama' might well include music of all kinds—even in *Almanzor and Almahide* he has two long solo songs, one of them being a Zambra Dance (that is, a sung dance at a royal feast of the Spanish Moors): at this stage of his career he probably thought of the sung dialogue to which Davenant introduced him as merely another musical number, though he modified his views later.

It is interesting that Dryden should mention Corneille, for apart from the fact that his rhymed lines may well have influenced English heroic poetry, there can be little doubt that Davenant first came in touch with at least the reflection of Italian opera during his visits to Paris, whether or not, as Dent thinks, Corneille's treatment of the story of Andromeda with music and machines on top of the spoken lines suggested to Davenant how to modernise *The Tempest*. Certainly he got a great deal from France—machines, ballet and heroic rhymed couplets—and now French musicians and performers were trooping over to England in the wake of Charles II, who preferred the lilting light tunes of Paris to the more formal, if more polished, Italian sonatas.

At last, on November 9, 1671, the great Duke's Theatre or opera-house that Davenant had planned was opened in Dorset Garden by his widow. Christopher Wren had certainly spared no expense: although it was said to have cost about £5,000, it did in fact cost nearly twice as much—no wonder, when one thinks of the great gilt proscenium and the ornate decorations carved by Grinling Gibbons with busts and pictures of the great dramatic poets of the past. Dryden several times gibes at the grandeur of this theatre, for his own plays, performed by the rival King's company, had to be given, when their own theatre was burnt down in 1672, in the Lincoln's Inn Fields theatre that Davenant used to have and which was only a makeshift compared with Wren's building.

One of the first 'operas' produced at the Duke's was another Davenant–Shakespeare adaptation—*Macbeth*, which was tricked out with all the latest inventions of French stagecraft and long sung scenes complete with dancing. The old prompter, Downes (though according to him it was played at the Lincoln's Inn Fields theatre in 1671, which date is now disputed) recorded that it was

dressed in all its finery, as new clothes, new scenes, machines—as flyings for the witches, with all the singing and dancing in it, the first composed by Mr. Locke, the other by Mr. Channell and Mr. Joseph [2] Priest. It being all excellently performed, being in the nature of an opera, it recompenced double the expense.

To musicians the interest of *Macbeth* is that the music seems far more rhythmic and tentatively melodic than earlier settings of sung scenes: to scholars it is the fascinating problem whether the *Macbeth* music that has survived is by Locke, Purcell or whom: to audiences of the day it must have been the thrilling novelty of seeing the witches 'in the machine hanging in the air' and finally flying over the stage.

A month after the new Duke's house opened, the rival Theatre Royal endeavoured to ridicule the Davenant-inspired quasi-operatic productions by presenting an up-to-date version of the Duke of Buckingham's eight-year-old *Rehearsal*, which had never been performed before. It burlesqued several plays chiefly by Davenant or Dryden, but especially scenes that followed the growing craze for introducing music, whether dances or dialogues—the conventional battle between the General and the Lieutenant-General, satirising *The Siege of Rhodes*, epitomises—though in a ribald way—the static technique of operatic convention: in the words of Mr. Bayes (Davenant–Dryden):—

I make 'em, sir, play the battle in *recitativo*. And here's the concept:—just as the very same instant that one sings the other, sir, recovers you his sword and puts himself in a warlike posture, so that you have at once your ear entertained with music and good language and your eye satisfied with the garb and accoutrements of war.

But musical scenes were not laughed off the stage. By 1672 the Duke's house in Dorset Garden was run by the actors Betterton and Harris on behalf of Davenant's son, Charles, aged seventeen, now made. manager by Lady Davenant, and the following autumn it became known that it was planning an even grander operatic production than any that had been seen before: not only were there to be 'great machines', but dancers were being imported from France. In view of the practical complications of installing new machinery in the theatre, to say nothing of negotiations with foreign artists, it seems likely that these preparations were made some six months in advance, for the letter giving that news was written in August and the opera to which it possibly referred may have been yet another adaptation of *The Tempest* which was eventually produced some time in the early spring of 1674.[3]

This new version was really an adaptation by Thomas Shadwell of the earlier Davenant–Dryden adaptation of the Shakespeare play: but such a jigsaw puzzle, complicated by further emendations by the actor Betterton, is only of academic interest to literary scholars. As far as the public went, what mattered was that this dramatic opera version was an enormous success. Downes recorded it as follows:—

The Tempest, or *The Enchanted Island*, made into an opera by Mr. Shadwell, having all new in it, as scenes, machines,—particularly one scene painted with myriads of aerial spirits, and another flying away with a table furnished out with fruits, sweetmeats and all sorts of viands, just when Duke Trinculo and his companions were going to dinner. All things were performed in it so admirably well, that not any succeeding opera got more money.

So expensive was the production, as the Prologue said, that explanations were given in the Epilogue as to why double prices had to be charged for seats:—

When you of wit and sense were weary grown,
Romantic, rhyming, fustian plays were shown,
We then to flying witches did advance,
And for your pleasure trafficked into France.
From thence new arts to please you we have sought:
We have machines to some perfection brought
And above thirty warbling voices got.
Many a god and goddess you will hear,
And we have singing, dancing devils here—
Such devils and such gods are very dear.

Obviously Charles Davenant through his advisers was determined to follow his father's practice of giving the public novelty
at any cost to both the management and the public too. Here are
a few examples of how Shadwell added to the Dryden–Davenant
version—no doubt under instruction. The shipwreck scene used to
end with the passengers and the sailors merely leaving the stage,
and was straightway followed by the entrance of Prospero and
Miranda; now the Dorset Garden theatre regaled the audience—
perhaps for the first time in a public musical show—with ingenious lighting effects that were far more advanced than had been
seen in London before:

when the ship is sinking, the whole house is darkened and a shower of fire falls
upon 'em. This is accompanied by lightning and several claps of thunder to the
end of the storm.

In the midst of the shower of fire the scene changes. The cloudy sky, rocks
and sea vanish, and, when the lights return, discover that beautiful part of the
island, which was the habitation of Prospero: tis composed of three walks of
cypress-trees, each sidewalk leads to a cave, in one of which Prospero keeps his
daughters, in the other Hippolito: the middle walk is of a great depth and leads
to an open part of the island.

In the new and longer version of the scene when the devils come
to threaten the consciences of Alonzo and Antonio they rise from
below through trap-doors, and where the earlier version merely
introduces 'eight fat spirits with cornucopia in their hands' dancing an invitation to the villains to feast, and makes Alonzo and his
party exit to a table off-stage, Shadwell first has a dance of fantastic spirits, then makes two spirits bring on a table covered with
'meat and fruit', and finally, as Downes said, has two spirits
descend and fly away with the table. At the end, when all the
parties are reconciled, in the new version Prospero uses his magic
to transform the scene and calls up the Gods and Goddesses of the
sea to entertain his guests:—

Neptune and your fair Amphitrite, rise!
Oceanus with your Thetis too, appear!
All ye Sea-gods and Goddesses, appear!
Come, all ye Tritons, all ye Nereids, come,
And each your saucy element to obey:
  For you have princes now to entertain,
And unspoiled beauties, with fresh youthful lovers.

> *Neptune, Amphitrite, Oceanus and Thetis appear in a chariot drawn with sea-horses: on each side of the chariot Sea-gods and Goddesses, Tritons and Nereids.*

Then follows a completely sung masque in which Amphitrite begs Neptune to let her order Aeolus, the wind-god, to control the four winds, who fly down on to the stage: the Tritons sound their trumpets made of shells, and Oceanus promises the company a safe voyage home, while twelve Tritons dance as they 'mingle with the singers'.

The old songs were retained (though perhaps the echo duet that Pepys liked so much was reset and Ariel's consoling song now became a duet with his sweetheart Milcha), and a long new song for one of the devils was introduced which was set by the Italian composer Reggio and began with the vigorous words 'Arise, ye subterranean winds'. The music was obviously regarded as of considerable importance, for the men and boys of the Chapel Royal who sang in the production were given special leave to stay in London for that purpose when the King went to Windsor, provided they attended him at week-ends, and the usual orchestra of about twelve was increased—there were twenty-four stringed instruments 'with the harpsical and theorboes which accompany the voices', and it expressly states at the beginning of the printed play that the orchestra was placed between the pit and the stage. There was a specially painted false proscenium-arch, with the figures of Fame, the Lion and the Unicorn, and Angels supporting the Royal Arms. No wonder that all this grandeur and novelty drew the audience even at double prices—Nell Gwynn, by now no longer in a position to bother about the pennies, came four times with a party in her side-box to see it between September and December and, what is more, paid, according to Treasury Orders quoted by Montague Summers in his book *The Restoration Theatre*.

Soon after the production of *The Tempest* [4] the new Theatre Royal in Bridges Street (Drury Lane) was opened and Dryden's prologue on that occasion bitterly scoffs at the clap-trap glitter of the Dorset Garden Theatre while apologising for the comparative simplicity of the new building:—

> A plain-built house, after so long a stay,
> Will send you half-unsatisfied away;
> When, fall'n from your expected pomp, you find
> A bare convenience only is designed.
> You, who each day can theatres behold,
> Like Nero's Palace, shining all with gold,
> Our mean ungilded stage will scorn, we fear,
> And for the homely room disdain the cheer.

He goes on to complain that there was no point in competing with such magnificence as long as the public have lost the taste for witty comedies or serious drama:—

> Twere folly now a stately pile to raise,
> To build a playhouse, while you throw down plays,
> Whilst scenes, machines, and empty operas reign,
> And for the pencil you the pen disdain,
> While troops of famished Frenchmen hither drive,
> And laugh at those upon whose alms they live.

Dryden had always resented the performances of the occasional French companies that had come to London, but this year, 1674, they had become more frequent and the French stage-machinery that had been installed at the Dorset Garden Theatre was drawing the public away from the rival company:—

> Well, please yourselves: but sure tis understood
> That French machines have ne'er done England good.
> I would not prophesy our house's fate,
> But, while vain shows and scenes you overrate,
> Tis to be feared—
> That, as a fire the former house o'erthrew,
> Machines and Tempests will destroy the new.[5]

Dryden then felt that the home of what he considered worthwhile drama had a serious rival in the Dorset Garden theatre with its operatised Shakespeare and its catch-penny stage tricks: but that was not its only rival. Among the Frenchmen who had come over to England, no doubt to escape the fear of secret arrest recently exploited by the ambitious and ruthless Louis XIV with his sealed *lettres de cachet*, were two musicians—Robert Cambert and Louis Grabu.

The latter, considered by his English rivals an inferior composer, had come to England in 1665 and a year later, to the fury of John Banister, who had written the Echo-song in *The Tempest*, managed to acquire a court appointment and became the Master of the King's Music in 1667. Cambert had started opera-experiments in France about the time of Davenant's *Cruelty of the Spaniards*, and, under a licence from Louis XIV in 1669 to the author Pierre Perrin, composed operas in French after the Italian model, only to be tricked out of it by the Italian Lully in 1672, with the result that he came to live in England. One result of these two examples of the infiltration or usurpation by foreign musicans—no doubt through the specious sales-talk usually employed by the lesser of such people—was that Grabu gave performances in French of Cambert's opera *Ariane* about the same time that *The Tempest* was produced, and so made Dryden refer bitterly to the French rivals as well as the Dorset Garden management.

It is not surprising that the French opera attracted an audience: it is always tempting to mistake the unusual for the excellent— whether it is natural views or native customs or food of the country which we are not used to at home: one of the stage-shows that has always remained in my memory is a performance of Strindberg's *Miss Julie* in Copenhagen, not one word of which could I understand and the story of which was at that time unknown to me: it may have been good, it certainly was different. When to that strangeness there is added a slight superficial knowledge of the foreign language, there is a warm glow of superiority that gives a spurious enjoyment, as it did many years ago in the mind of a former Prime Minister, whom I saw laugh heartily at the Latin play at Westminster School when he recognised the one word 'mensa'.

This quasi-intellectual appreciation, which is even further enhanced by a superficial acquaintance with any technical terms, was well pilloried by Dryden in the same prologue, when he alluded to the society knowledgeables who knew something of the new operatic jargon, and so were ready to patronise the opera performed by foreigners:—

> Mark when they play, how our fine fops advance
> The mighty merits of these men of France,
> Keep time, cry 'Bien!' and honour the cadence!

Notice the delicious affectation of the French pronunciation of the word 'cadence' with the accent on the second syllable! No doubt some of the audience could appreciate the rhythms or the cadenzas, but a large number obviously had caught hold of a phrase or two like those opera-frequenters of to-day who through sheer and often genuine enthusiasm ostentatiously call out 'Brava!' or 'Bis!', though the only foreign phrases they really know come off gramophone labels. Still, they are the chief supporters of operas in foreign languages just as they were in Dryden's day.

¹ See p. 51.   ² Or Josias.   ³ See p. 95.

⁴ I am quite aware that theatre-historians now accept W. J. Lawrence's dating of the Shadwell *Tempest* as after the opening of the new Theatre Royal, on the grounds that the manuscript *Tempest* Prologue in the British Museum seems to answer the accusations in the Dryden Prologue, though they do disregard his presumption that 'Machines and tempests' alludes to *Macbeth*. I find it difficult to believe that Dryden would give a free advertisement to a rival show that was only in rehearsal—certainly with such anticipatory fear—and think either the MS. prologue was introduced into the already running *Tempest* or— and this is far more likely—that it was answering the general gossip criticisms of the Theatre Royal supporters and that these criticisms were made official, as it were, by Dryden later. The matter is only of academic interest, but when the scholars are so eager to discriminate the facts they can find to fit their theories it is only fair that their theories are from time to time re-examined.

⁵ A MS. copy (not, as Nicoll seems to imply, a different prologue) in the Huntington Library gives 'Tempests and Operas'.

CHAPTER NINE

French Opera in London

CAMBERT'S opera on the story of Ariadne, the wife of Theseus who was deserted on an island where she was consoled by Bacchus, had been rehearsed in France some five years before, but had never been performed owing to the death of the great opera-patron Cardinal Mazarin. Grabu evidently organised a performance in London at the Court Theatre in Whitehall, and by arrangement with the composer or otherwise made musical alterations or additions, to judge from the printed libretto in which it says the opera was 'Now put into music by Monsieur Grabu'. This change-over of composer is a musical puzzle which has not yet been solved, but W. J. Lawrence established[1] that it was certainly performed at Whitehall because when it was later transferred to the new Theatre Royal—how this must have infuriated Dryden!—Grabu was allowed by the Lord Chamberlain to borrow scenery from the Whitehall Theatre for a fortnight, and the frontispiece to the English libretto which was printed before the transfer shows a picture of an actual performance of the first scene.

In spite then, of Dryden's anti-French prologue at the opening of the new Drury Lane Theatre on March 26, 1674, which must have been spoken with the management's approval, Killegrew has already arranged for the French opera to play at Drury Lane. The very next day Grabu got permission to borrow the scenery, the libretto was already printed, and three days later, on March 30, the King attended a performance[2]—a strange state of affairs indeed, but no doubt Killegrew felt he must try to do two antagonistic things at once: appeal to those who might prefer drama to spectacle and attract those who preferred spectacle by putting on a rival kind of spectacle. At least it is clear that opera, in one form or another, was taking the town with a vengeance.—Evelyn records that in January of this year he saw

an Italian opera in music, the first that had been in England of this kind,

and some hold that it must have been the French opera *Ariane* which was all sung in the Italian way, though it can only be called the first, in that it was sung in a foreign language (such are the theoretical contortions scholars can get into when data are in-sufficient, inexact and apparently contradictory). It is even more extraordinary when one knows that this opera of the deserted wife was put on in London with a new prologue expressly to greet Mary of Modena, the new wife of James, Duke of York, the King's brother and heir apparent.

The title-page of the English libretto says that it was 'acted by the Royal Academy of Music', and the preface to Charles II, after fulsomely praising Britain for welcoming refugees

whilst all Europe besides lies now groaning under the weight of a cruel war and sees on every side her cities sacked and spoiled,

and for having been chosen by heaven

to prove a new Ark, a most safe harbour still ready to receive and shelter all the shattered remains of the wrecked universe,

goes on to praise the King for wanting to

complete the splendour and magnificence of Your Imperial seat by establish-ing within her stately walls Your Academy of Operas, the fairest and most charming of all public shows.

An apology is made for any deficiencies:—

Your Majesty will doubtless find these first representations of Your opera very defective: but, Sir, it dares flatter itself with hopes that You will pardon its faults and consider that the Academy that executes the same is yet an infant, a new-born beauty, whose features and lineaments are scarce come to their shape and proportion, but cannot fail growing to perfection in her due time and age, provided you deign own her for your creature and afford her Your Royal care and protection.

This last provision makes it quite clear that Grabu was jumping the starting-gun: no doubt Charles had given him every en-couragement, even some verbal guarantee that he would approve a Royal Academy, but evidently he had not so far granted Grabu a patent. This is probably the first time this has been pointed out: most authorities on theatre or opera merely say that this Royal Academy was short-lived and—unless I have missed it—none have quoted any evidence of its foundation: short-lived it certainly was, for the simple reason, I think, that it never existed except as a dream-child of Grabu's wishful-thinking mind. The preface was signed

Your Majesty's most humble, most obedient and most faithful servant and subject, Your Royal Academy of Music,

thereby trying to make it an accomplished fact, while at the same time enabling Grabu to shelter behind anonymity in case of trouble, or at least to suggest that the performers had once been members of the opera company Cambert composed for in France which went by the name of the 'Académie des Opéras'.

The libretto also contains an address to the Reader explaining the reason for the printed translation:—

The Reader is desired in perusing this book to consider two things: first, that it is a mere translation and nothing else, and that, the original itself being neither a strain of wit, nor yet the style of it puffed up, but only a bare collection of phrases and expressions made fit for sound and harmony, the author, who is well enough fixed in his reputation, would have thought himself wronged, had the translator turned the sense of his work out of its right channel.

It is thus made clear that the English text was not meant to be sung and was only a translation of the sense of the original, and also that, like Davenant, the author, Pierre Perrin, intended his words to be sung, not read (an important distinction which should always be borne in mind by readers of librettos, but which is often forgotten even by the translators themselves, who are inclined at times to modify what would sound well in singing so as to make it look better in print—this was once admitted to me by one of the best recognised translators of opera librettos).

The writer goes on to support the same belief as Ben Jonson's— that a musical work should appeal to sense as well as to the senses —in the second point he puts forward for the reader's consideration:—

Secondly, that this traduction was thought absolutely necessary for the satisfaction of those who, being unacquainted with the French tongue, and who, being spectators, would find themselves necessitated to see the most pressing of the senses go away from the theatre ungratified by their not understanding the subject that brought them thither.

He cannot help a hit at the self-imagined omniscience of the critics of the audience, though his lack of tact would not have had such serious repercussions as it would two centuries later, when critics were professional writers with a possibly vitriolic pen and certainly the last word in an argument.

For the English it will doubtless seem flat and too much a stranger to please the critics of the time, whose nice palate can scarce relish the finest and most natural things their own country can produce.

He finishes, however, with the current belief that the spectacle can fill the theatre.

But, let it run what fortune it will, it can fare no worse than a thousand far better things have done: and, worse than they are, the pomp and magnificence of its representations will alone prove sufficient to plead their excuse.

The production was certainly magnificent—possibly even more magnificent than the Dorset Garden shows, for, while they borrowed certain devices from the French theatre, *Ariane* naturally includes all the grandeur of the French court theatre for which it was planned—especially the great variety of spectacular dance-scenes which were the chief ingredient of the French court ballets (apart from the introductory praise of the King—which was also reproduced in this opera for England): French dancers had been brought over for the Duke's Theatre and for court entertainment at Whitehall, and now they could be seen in real French ballets—no wonder the fops went mad about them.

Davenant had long ago introduced mimed dances by two or three performers, and Dorset Garden had shown expensive scenery, flying effects and ingenious lighting, but *Ariane* seems to have been the first opera shown in England in which the action is as closely described as in the earlier masques, and as this set the fashion for all succeeding operas, I am including these most vivid descriptions, which have not all, I think, been reproduced before: they give a clear picture of the lively production, which in only a few instances was surpassed in the later Purcell operas which are constantly being described and quoted in all books on early opera.

There was a huge cast—on paper, at least—though there probably was a lot of doubling by the performers; and although the English operas that followed had often even larger casts, the majority of the principal performers in those shows were actors, whereas in *Ariane* there were some fifteen solo-singers and some twelve different sets of dancers or decorative supers.

In London the opera began with a congratulatory Prologue in a scene showing a prospect of Thames opposite to London, on the waves of which is seen floating a great shell, as it were of mother of pearl, bearing three nymphs, representing three rivers, Thames, Tiber, and Seine.

The three rivers, to judge from their omission in the cast list, were introduced into the London production expressly to greet the new royal bride, which they did together with the river Po in front of a realistic picture of London from the Surrey side, with its churches, houses, and even the traitors' heads stuck up on poles on London Bridge, as is shown in the frontispiece to the libretto. The great shell on the water with cupids above is not realistic, but the gondola-like boat that can be seen is (was this one of the presentation gondolas, funds for which had been raided by Killegrew for theatre musicians?).

After the formal prologue the story of the successful wooing by Bacchus, god of wine, of Ariadne, deserted by Theseus, is romantically told and extended by much bucolic realism and theatrical spectacle, as can be seen by the Interludes that are attached to each scene—the similarity with the practice of the earlier masques is underlined by the use of the word 'masque' itself all through.

The first interlude has two 'Masque-entries': the first:—

Indian Kings, slaves to Bacchus, glad to see themselves subdued by so charming a god, dance round about his statue erected upon an altar in the middle of the theatre.

(I presume this means 'in the middle of the stage', though it is tempting to imagine that in the Court performance the auditorium might have been arranged as for a masque with the statue in the middle of it.) The second entry is as follows:—

Whilst the Indian Kings are dancing, enter Saliens,[3] Priests of Bacchus, who, joining dance with them, do skip and leap both upon the altar and round the same.

Soon after this, at the end of her scene, Megaera, the Fury,

with her burning torch in her hand, flies up into the air with dragons following her.

In the first Masque-entry of the second interlude

The Bacchants, abhorring the falsity of Theseus, run Furies-like, their burning torches in their hands, to burn him in his ship, as they see him sail on the sea: but the waves and billows do force them back to the shore. During the conflict Thetis, the Goddess of the sea, who is of kin to Bacchus and sees their bold attempt, surges up out of the water and strives to oppose their rage. The Bacchants persisting in their design, the Sea-Gods enter.

The second entry must have been a fine scene:—

A huge sea-monster, swimming near the shore where the Bacchants are still striving against the waves, enters combat with them: the Bacchants leave their torches and with darts wound the monster, whereupon he vomits out of his jaws several Sea-Gods and plunges into the sea.

These fall a-wrestling with the Bacchants and do form a regular fight, after which they grasp each other fast in their arms and precipitate themselves all into the sea.

Bacchus now falls in love with Ariadne,

little Cupids fluttering about Bacchus do charm him with chains of flowers,

and presently there is danced

a warlike dance of several Ensigns or Foot-colours

(no doubt with a military band on the stage—one of the 'symphonies' mentioned in the cast-list).

One of the surprising results on Bacchus of his love for Ariadne is that he gives up drink (unlike what I suspect to be the ribald truth that I have long wanted to see on the operatic stage—that she took to it when her husband left her), and this leads to the next 'Intermede', which is called 'A Masque of Satyrs':—

These Satyrs, covered with mourning crêpe, in dancing take the bottle out of Silenus's hands and, joining lamentations with him, do bury the same in a tomb covered over with Cypress-branches and sing at its funeral a mournful ditty.

But a little later it is quite clear that Bacchus's abstinence, which his followers so much deprecated, was only short-lived while Ariadne was refusing him, and the fourth interlude brings back gaiety:—

A company of Satyrs, having their heads crowned with ivy, the leaves of which are gilded, their horns twisted about with chains of flowers, a cup in their hands, bring the bottle which they buried before triumphantly out of the tomb where it lay. They set the same, dancing, on a little throne made of green turf, strewed with flowers, whilst other Satyrs are singing.

The triumph ending, a small cloud comes down from above that steals away their bottle up into heaven, leaving the Satyrs gazing with admiration.

When Bacchus and Ariadne are married:—

Enter Clowns who, being all drunk, fall a-dancing after their manner. These rustics come to dance at Bacchus's wedding, bringing with them presents of such things as their village affords—some bring in their baskets sausages, others eggs dyed in several colours, and others truffles. Old Silenus, while they are dancing, changes their baskets and gives them others, where instead of sausages they find live eels, instead of eggs frogs, and for truffles live rats.

Were the animals really alive, as the text seems to imply, or were they trick animals? If they were alive, the actors must have been glad to finish with this embryo-harlequinade scene and get on to the finale—though that meant entrusting themselves to a large stage-machine:—

A glittering palace comes down from heaven, on the middle of which is seen a royal throne: over the throne hangs a crown made of seven precious stones, the crown suspended by four little Cupids flying. Venus with the three Graces sits on the throne with bands of symphonists about her.

During the symphony the palace and throne descend slowly upon the theatre, where, being fixt, Venus and the Graces come down from the throne and, taking the new married pair, lead them by the hand and place them on the same—Bacchus in the middle, Ariadne on his right, Venus on his left hand, and the Graces at their feet.

Later, at the words

> Place on her head that glittering crown!
> She has deserved it! It's her own!

there is a grand transformation:—

The seven gems which composed her crown are enflamed of a sudden and changed into so many bright stars, known in heaven by the name of Ariadne's Hair.

At the end comes an exhortation in true party spirit:—

> Let's drink, let's love and sing all day!
> Let love, and Bacchus live alway!

and finally:—

The Clowns dance to the sound of voices and instruments all the while the palace is drawing up.

---

[1] *Times Lit. Supp.* 26 September 1929.

[2] This must have been at Whitehall, if the date April 9 for the date of the first Drury Lane performance is right, as claimed by Allardyce Nicoll and accepted by Löwenberg.

[3] Is this a mistake by the translator, muddling the Sileni (the fat old men who followed Bacchus) with the Salii (the jumping priests of Mars)?

CHAPTER TEN

Locke's 'Psyche'

WHATEVER the fops may have thought of *Ariane*, it seems to have led to trouble for Grabu. He evidently did not return the scenery to Whitehall by April 10, which was the end of the authorised loan period, for over a fortnight later Killegrew had a letter from Court demanding the scenery back, and at the beginning of May there was trouble between four French dancers who claimed they were under contract to dance only for Grabu, and Killegrew, who claimed to have a contract with them which Grabu must have known, as he was at the Theatre Royal rehearsals. The result of this was that the dancers were ordered to keep to the terms of the Killegrew contract and appear at the Theatre Royal when wanted at 10s. a day when dancing, at 5s. a day when not. Grabu's insolent claim on the title-page of the libretto to have written or rewritten the music of *Ariane* without any acknowledgment of Cambert, the original composer,[1] cannot have been welcomed by Cambert, especially as Grabu had acknowledged the original librettist, Pierre Perrin, though only by initials: but his most tactless mistake was surely to presume that Charles II would authorise the Royal Academy of Music for the presentation of French operas duly altered by Grabu for his own self-aggrandisement.

In any event he lost his post as Master of the King's Music the following year, and no other French opera seems to have been given in London for over ten years. The French influence, however, was irresistible and about this time [2] an English opera was produced which was admittedly borrowed and copied from a play by Molière, Corneille and Quinault which included musical interludes. This was *Psyche*, by Thomas Shadwell, with vocal music by Matthew Locke and instrumental music by G. B. Draghi.

Downes recorded the production as follows:—

The long expected opera of *Psyche* came forth in all her ornaments:—new scenes, new machines, new clothes, new French dances. This opera was splendidly set out, especially in scenes, the charge of which amounted to above £800. It had a continuance of performance about eight days together: it proved very beneficial to the company, yet the *Tempest* got them more money.

Montague Summers thought that 'long expected' implied careful advertisement by organised gossip: there is nothing to show that it was organised, but rumours must have flown about between September 1673, when Shadwell was working on the text, and the date of its production.

Psyche is, as Dent wrote in his *Foundations of English Opera*,

an important landmark in our musical history, because it is the first systematic attempt at a musical and dramatic scheme which for a long period was characteristic of English opera. The principal characters do not sing at all, but there is a continual attempt to bring them into contact with music, and to employ music as often as possible to heighten dramatic effect.

But this is hardly fair to Shadwell, who, as Dent admitted, had at least the makings of a good librettist: it implies that the drama was of the first importance and that music was introduced wherever possible to heighten the dramatic effect. The opposite was really the case, as Shadwell wrote in his Preface: it was his first attempt at rhyme, and he was quite aware he would be accused of borrowing the play from the French *Psyche*, though in fact the story was as old as Apuleius: he is quite frank about his debt to Molière and the others:— •

For several things concerning the decoration of the play I am obliged to the French and for the design of two of the only moving scenes in the French, which I may say without vanity are very much improved, being wrought up with more art in this than in the French play, without borrowing any of the thoughts from them.

Dent agrees that in at least one scene he has improved on the Molière, and includes a most fascinating literary-dramatic comparison of the two plays in his account of *Psyche*: but that is only of academic interest, for Shadwell makes it quite clear what was the practical difference between them after explaining that he had not bothered to revise his early rushed version—not, as literary historians have said, because he was slapdash and lazy, but because the drama was not of great importance: he wrote:—

The candid reader will forgive the faults when he considers that the great design was to entertain the town with variety of music, curious dancing, splendid scenes and machines.

Those entertainments in fact were not there to improve the play: the play was there merely to introduce the entertainments. He goes on to show that he, too, like Jonson and Davenant before him, fully realised that good lyrics for music should be far slighter than great poetry, which is complete in itself and needs no music to enhance it:—

In all the words which are sung I did not so much take care of the wit or fancy of 'em as the making 'em proper for music, in which I cannot but have some little knowledge, having been bred for many years of my youth to some performance of it.

Far from being slapdash he showed a practical knowledge of the problem, for he added:—

I chalked out the way to the composer in all but the song of Furies and Devils in the fifth act, having designed which line I would have sung by one, which by two, which by three, which by four voices, etc. and what manner of humour I would have in all the vocal music.

I shall show later how meticulous he was at times in indicating the colour of music he wanted.

Like Davenant Shadwell was not concerned with art but with commercial theatre, and so he tried to please as wide an audience as possible:—

I believe the unskilful in music will not like the more solemn part of it—as the music in the Temple of Apollo and the song of the Despairing Lovers in the second act, both which are proper and admirable in their kinds and are recommended to the judgement of able musicians: for those who are not so, there are light and airy things to please them.

He also fully realised that a musical entertainment depends on several experts and that it was not for him as author to claim chief credit, as it is with a dramatist or as it later became with an opera-composer: he tactfully—but I think genuinely—praises his fellow-artists:—

by his excellent composition that long known, able, and approved master of music, Mr. Locke, Composer to His Majesty and Organist to the Queen, has done me a great deal of right. All the instrumental music which is not mingled with the vocal was composed by that great master, Signor Gio: Baptista Draghi, Master of the Italian Music to the King. The dances were made by the most famous master of France, Monsieur St. Andrée. The scenes were painted by the ingenious artist, Mr. Stephenson. In those things that concern the ornament or decoration of the play the great industry and care of Mr. Betterton ought to be remembered, at whose desire I wrote upon this subject.

That is probably one of the earliest records of an author's gratitude to his producer or director. Shadwell's modest disclaimer of
special praise as poet is stressed again in the prologue:—

> His business now is to show splendid scenes,
> T' interpret twixt the audience and machines.

From the literary-dramatic point of view, apart from Dent's
comparison with the French play, *Psyche* has often been dealt
with—and dismissed—by scholars, and Locke's music has similarly
been quoted and commented on usually by comparison with
Purcell's music of about fifteen years later. As, however, it is the
prototype of the English dramatic opera—combining the best
qualities of, say, *The Cruelty of the Spaniards in Peru*, *The Slighted
Maid* and the two musical adaptations of *The Tempest*, with a bit
of French ballet-opera thrown in, here is a short account of it
which, by avoiding any academically anatomical examination,
may to some extent recreate the sort of entertainment the audience
at the Dorset Garden Theatre saw and came to expect.

At the start of the first act Psyche's conversation with two ladies
on the contentment of rural life is gently broken by 'a symphony
of recorders and soft music', and after the great nature-god Pan
has sung her praises in recitative with a tuneful chorus there is 'a
short symphony of rustic music, representing the cries and notes
of birds: that introduces a dance by four Sylvans and four Dryads,
which is followed by a single voice singing with double echo:—

Voice 1. Great Psyche shall find no such pleasure as here!
Echo 1.   No such pleasure as here!
Echo 2.   As here!

Two voices now sing, then three, then four, until at last all join
in the chorus. This is the first example of Shadwell's lay-out for
voices that he alluded to in the preface, but here, too, he shows his
appreciation of orchestral colour—which I have not seen alluded
to elsewhere: he says that this chorus should be accompanied by
flageolets, violins, cornets, sackbuts and oboes.[3]

Psyche is now visited by the allegorical figures of Ambition,
Power, Plenty and Peace, whose speeches invite her to go out
into the great world: Envy foretells her future woes, supported
by a singing chorus of Furies. Two princes, rivals for her hand,
are rejected by Psyche but made friends by her, and yet her sisters
are still jealous of her charms and invoke Venus to aid them.

Venus appears in her chariot 'hovering in the air' and sings her promise that Psyche shall suffer, whose father, the King, brings the act to an end by summoning all to the Temple of Apollo to learn who shall be her husband.

That act, like most first acts, is mostly taken up with preparing the threads of the story—the Cinderella-like simplicity of Psyche, her rejected but faithful suitors, her jealous sisters, and the hint of coming trouble: at the same time it does contain the rustic scene of Pan, birds, dancing woodland deities and echoes, a chorus of Furies and a singing goddess in the air.

The second act, however, builds on that preparation and starts with a blaze of white and gold—the Temple of Apollo, with a great procession of priests and boys, men and women, including a stage-orchestra of wind instruments, the men in surplices, the women veiled, and all in white to set off the gold. The Chief Priest starts the ceremony by singing and, after a dance of the priests with cymbals, bells and torches, he leads the crowd of worshippers in a litany:—

Chief Priest.	Jupiter, Juno, Minerva, Saturn, Cibele—
The Response.	Be propitious to our vows and prayers!
Chief Priest.	Mars, Bellona, Venus, Cupids, Vulcan—
The Response.	Be propitious to our vows and prayers!
Chief Priest.	Bacchus, Pan, Neptune, Sylvanus, Faunus, Vertumnus, Palaemon—
The Response.	Be propitious to our vows and prayers!
Chief Priest.	All ye gods, goddesses and all the powers—
The Response.	Be propitious to our vows and prayers!

After a chorus and some sentences from three priests:—

> *Chief Priest turns and kneels at the altar again. The boys run out and fetch, one a flambeau, the others little faggots of cedar, juniper, etc. The Priest rises and lays them on the altar. All but the Chief Priest and boys are kneeling, intent upon the altar without speech or motion. As soon as the fire is kindled, which the Priest does himself with the flambeau,*

Chief Priest.   (*with a loud voice*) Behold the fire!

> *All but the Chief Priest fall flat on their faces, then rise again.*

After this fine piece of production by Betterton, with its impressive silent stillness of the white crowd broken by the Chief Priest's cry and the sudden abasement of the worshippers, the ceremony continues and at last the oracle of Apollo speaks 'with a very loud and hollow voice' and pronounces Psyche's fate to find her future husband, a poisonous serpent, when she is left alone on Venus's rock—a fate that Psyche accepts.

The scene now changes to 'a rocky desert full of dreadful caves, cliffs and precipices with a high rock looking down into the sea,' where two despairing lovers are joined by two more pairs who sing:—

> Break, break, distracted heart! There is no cure for love.

and after they have killed themselves, Psyche appears, deserted by all but her two faithful princes: they, however, are driven away by infernal spirits and Psyche is borne aloft into the clouds by Zephyrs, while Cupid watches.

The third act begins with Vulcan and the Cyclops (left over from *The Slighted Maid*?) richly dressed, singing, drinking and dancing as they work in Cupid's glittering palace of gold forging great silver vases, among Corinthian columns festooned with Cupids and roses all of gold. When they have gone, Cupid tells Psyche of his love, while invisible singers sing, and then sends Zephyrs to invite her sisters to visit her.

Back in the city now, the Priests of Mars celebrate the reputed victory of the two princes over the poisonous serpent with a warriors' dance, striking their shields with their swords, 'kettle-drums beating and trumpets sounding'—a vigorous ballet that by its mere description seems more akin to the *Prince Igor* dances than to the unexceptionable taste of the traditional British musical. Venus again appears, and in sung dialogue makes Mars summon the Furies to bring all to confusion by breaking the altar. The act ends with Psyche's sisters, rejected as brides by the princes, who sense that Psyche is alive, planning her murder.

In the fourth act Psyche entertains her sisters in her golden palace with music and dancing—ten golden statues leaping from their pedestals to dance and ten cupids rising from the empty pedestals, strewing the stage with flowers and flying off in different directions. The Zephyrs prevent Psyche from being murdered by her sisters, but when she is abandoned by Cupid for asking the forbidden question who he is,

> *the garden and palace vanish and Psyche is left alone in a vast desert*
> *upon the brink of a river in marsh, full of willows, flags, bullrushes and*
> *waterflowers, beyond which is seen a great open desert.*

There she learns that her father has killed himself for grief, and she is only stopped from following his example when the God of the River suddenly rises with his Nymphs, singing their prophecy of her future happiness. The princes find her, but when she is carried off from them by Furies at Venus's order, they first beat off the soldiers sent by her sisters and then drown themselves, hoping to meet her in the other world: Cupid has the sisters taken down to Hell by the Furies.

The first scene of the last act was utterly unlike anything that had gone before, for it represented Hell itself with burning ruins on each side of the stage: in the nearest of these to the audience were the figures of Prometheus, no doubt with the eagle tearing at his liver as he lay chained to the rock, Sisyphus with the huge marble block that rolled downhill despite his constant effort to push it to the top, Ixion, chained hand and foot to the wheel that whirled perpetually in the air, and Tantalus, starving and thirsty, reaching out for ever-receding water and fruit under the over-hanging rock that threatened to fall and crush him. Towards the back of the stage on each side were Furies and Devils tormenting the damned, while in the centre of the stage there rose up from below the great throne of Pluto, the God of Hades, made of pillars of fire, with Proserpina, his queen, at his side, and at their feet the three judges of the dead, Minos, Aeacus and Rhada-manthus. As the fiery throne rose, numbers of Devils and Furies came up through trap-doors all over the stage. Through the pillars of flame the Gate of Hell could be seen at a distance and through that again a lake of fire, while in the far distance at the other side of the lake were vast crowds of the dead waiting for Charon to ferry them over the ghostly water.

There is singing and dancing for the devils in Hell, where Psyche's sisters gloat over her misfortunes: but, singing kindly, Pluto and Proserpina console Psyche and give her a magic casket of beauty as an offering to Venus. They and all Hell then vanish, and Psyche, after meeting the princes' ghosts, finds herself once again by the marshy desert. She opens the casket and faints, but though spurned by Venus, is revived by Jupiter and reunited with Cupid.

Now comes the grand transformation scene. Apollo summons the heavenly choir, which arrives to music by flageolets and re-corders, six pairs of royal lovers from Elysium with a symphony of pipes, Bacchus with his wild followers to music of oboes, and finally to a symphony of recorders the spirits of the skies, and gods and goddesses who appear 'hanging in the skies' in chariots and clouds. Three of the Elysian lovers—three sopranos—now sing 'to the recorder, organ and harpsicals'; Jupiter descends to a symphony of soft music of all the instruments with Cupid and Psyche on each side of him: six Elysian princes, 'gloriously habited', dance: Mars and a chorus sing with trumpets, kettledrums and flutes: Bacchus and his rout sing with oboes and rustic music: finally all the voices, all the instruments and all the dancers join together wishing

> All joy to this celestial pair,
> Who thus by Heav'n united are.
> Tis a great thing, worth Heaven's design,
> To make love's pow'r with beauty's join.

The final dance by the Elysian princes winds in and out through festooned and garlanded arbours which are brought on the stage by their attendants and moved about in varying positions as they dance through them and the opera ends with six spoken lines from Jupiter claiming that

> Love's the most glorious object of the mind.

The Epilogue points out that, whether the play be good or bad, the performers, designers and orchestra have done their best, while the management have staked everything on this spectacular production:—

> We in one vessel have adventured all:
> The loss, should we be shipwrecked, were not small.
> But, if it be decreed that we must fall,
> We fall with honour. Gallants, you can tell—
> No foreign stage can ours in pomp excel
> And here none e'er shall treat you half so well.

After that not unnatural exultation that the Duke's Theatre put on better shows than the King's the Epilogue goes on to show that later historians would be wrong in claiming that opera could only succeed when supported by the nobility: the two rival theatres got no State subsidy, but in the Duke's Theatre production of *Psyche*

> Poor players have this day that splendour shown,
> Which yet but by great monarchs has been done.
> Whilst our rich neighbours mock us for't, we know
> Already th' utmost they intend to do.

The King's Theatre may have got rich by investing in land and houses, but they put on dirty, bawdy farces, at which it is surprising to see so many ladies—

> What is become of former modesty?
> Yet—
> Best judges will our ornaments allow,
> Though they the wrong side of the arras show.
> But oh, a long farewell to all this sort
> Of plays, which this vast town cannot support!
> If you could be content th' expense to bear,
> We would improve and treat you better ev'ry year.[4]

Some time in 1675, after Shadwell had the words printed, Locke published the vocal score of *Psyche* (together with the music to *The Tempest*), but he had no time to praise Shadwell, as he had so much to say about the music.

He expected criticism from other musicians,

it being become a kind of fashionable wit to peck and carp at other men's conceptions, how mean soever their own are.

Expecting therefore to fall under the lash of some softheaded or hardhearted composer (for there are too many better at finding of faults than mending them), I shall endeavour to remove those few blocks which perhaps they may take occasion to stumble at.

The first may be the title, *opera*.

(He had entitled the publication 'The English Opera, or the vocal music in *Psyche* . . . etc.')

To this I must answer that the word is borrowed of the Italians, who by it distinguish their comedies from their operas—those, a short plot being laid, the comedians according to their different themes given speak and act *extempore*; [5] but these after much consideration, industry and machines to illustrate the grand design,—

(as usual the spectacle is mentioned first)

—with art are composed in such kinds of music as the subject requires, and accordingly are performed.

He goes on to boost his own skill and refers the reader to the printed page for particular excellencies:—

their nature for the most part being soft, easy, and—as far as my ability could reach—agreeable to the design of the author: for in them you have from ballad to single air, counterpoint, recitative, fugue, canon, and chromatic music, which variety (without vanity be it said) was never in court or theatre till now presented in this nation—

(true enough)

though I must confess there has been something done (and more by me than any other) of this kind, and therefore it may justly wear the title, though all the tragedy be not in music.

He gives credit to Shadwell for modifying the all-sung opera of the Italians:—

for the author prudently considered that, though Italy was and is the great academy of the world for that science, England is not, and therefore mixed it with interlocutions as more proper to our genius.

Evidently criticisms were made—as always with 'modern' music—that it was a strain on the voice to sing Locke's music— for he points out the next stumbling-block for cavillers:—

The extreme compass of some of the parts. To which the idols of their own imagination may be pleased, if possible, to know that he who composes for voices, not considering their extent, is like a botching stult who, being obliged to make habits for men, cuts them out for children. I suppose it needs no explication.

He claimed he wrote then for singers whose ability he knew. The old-fashioned academics he expected would find some of the harmonies 'modern' and object to

the extravagances in some parts of the composition, wherein—as among slender grammarians—they may think fixed rules are broken: but they may be satisfied that, whatever appears so, is only by way of transition from time or half-time concords and covered by extreme parts, or to suspend the ear and judgment for satisfying both in the cadence.

(That is, they should not be bothered by the discords, but should notice how they lead on to their final resolution.)
Some expert musicians evidently criticised some of the singers for singing out of tune,

to which with modesty it may be answered 'He or she that is without fault may cast the first stone'.

He did not deny that some of the singers may not have sung im- peccably, but remarks that most of the performers were not musicians, and so should be praised for their good qualities rather than blamed for their faults: his actual words are:—

for those seldom defects (the major part of the vocal performers being ignorant of music) their excellencies when they do well (which generally are so) rather ought to be admired than their accidental mistakes upbraided.

Locke here hits on a fundamental truth which is constantly borne out by the history of operatic singers and which is nowadays as constantly disregarded by those who judge from the mechanically selected perfection of a gramophone record—that, as Toscanini once said, musicianship is less important to stage singers than a feeling for music and consequently many stage singers (provided they are sensitive to music) have achieved brilliance by employing other gifts, such as beauty, personality, sincerity, characterisation, integrity, or a sense of the stage to compensate for an occasional or general vocal inadequacy—gifts which mostly are of less value in the concert-room or on a gramophone record, where a mere technical ability and physical power may serve.

Locke ends by dealing with what he hoped would be the last cavilling question:—

Why, after so long exposed, is it now printed?

(This of course implies that the opera had been given publicly for a long time before the vocal score was printed—and on this hangs a doubt about the accepted date of the first production of *Psyche*.) His answer is fourfold:—

First, to manifest my duty to several persons of honour who expected it.
Secondly, to satisfy those lovers and understanders of music, whose business or distance prevented their seeing and hearing it.
Thirdly,—

(and this is a little difficult to understand)

—that those for whom it was composed, though perchance ignorant of the quality, by the quantity may be convinced the composing and teaching it was not in a dream, and consequently that, if the expense they have been at do not answer their big expectation, the fault's their own, not mine.

(I take that to mean that the great mass of music was what the management asked for, and so it was their responsibility: this is borne out by his last answer—that it was published to show future composers how much managements might demand and managements how much composers had to labour.)

Finally, by way of caution, to prevent what differences may happen between them and whoever they may have occasion to employ for the future, that on either side there be no dependence on good words or generosity.

Dent considers this preface 'rather peevish', though he adds

Any musician will sympathize with Locke in his resentment of ignorant criticism; but in these days we should consider it both undignified and useless to express it in print.

Surely we ought to be glad then that Locke did express it on behalf of musicians of all time, though some of us may think that he
displayed restraint rather than peevishness. Is gentlemanly silence
better than outspoken truth?

Shadwell, as Dent says, had the skill to conceive the work as
combining the play, the music and the staging—

all three arts uniting to produce an effect such as none could achieve by itself

—an interesting combination that was seldom met with afterwards until the Wolf's Glen scene of the *Freischütz* paved the way
for Wagner. Shadwell was quite justified in praising his fellow
craftsmen, for no expense was spared on the production: even the
Cyclops were dressed in shining satin, as we know from the
epilogue to a play of 1675 called *Love in the Dark*, gibing, as
Dryden had done before, at the new taste for opera:—

> As charms are nonsense, nonsense seems a charm
> Which hearers of all judgement does disarm:
> For songs and scenes a double audience bring,
> And doggrel takes, which smiths in satin sing.
> Now to machines and a dull mash you run,
> We find that wit's the monster you would shun,
> And by my troth 'tis most discreetly done.

The 'monster' obviously alludes to Psyche's threatened husband,
and I suspect that the following three lines:—

> Players turn puppets now at your desire:
> In their mouth's nonsense, in their tail's a wire,
> They fly through clouds of clouts and showers of fire,

allude to the Furies and Devils in Hell flying about by means of a
wire attached to their backs.

So spectacular was the production that it is surprising the scenery
did not cost more than £800 (especially when we know that for
one scene only in another work an artist was paid £300): it is not
surprising, however, that the prices of admission were trebled this
time, nor that the audience was entreated to make such shows
possible in the future.

So successful was *Psyche* that not only was it revived more than
once in the next twenty-five years, but it also merited being
burlesqued at the rival Drury Lane Theatre soon after its first
production under the title *Psyche Debauched*. The author, Thomas

Duffett, who also wrote the burlesque *Mock-Tempest*, ridiculed everything in *Psyche*: he made fun of the self-praising preface:—

You like not this solemn music 'Fiddle, fiddle, hey down diddle'. I value not myself upon the wit, but the fitness of the words for air and melody:—

> 'Faddle, fiddle, hey down diddle,
> Faith, let's be merry!'

I have skill though I say't that shouldn't. . . . I'll turn my back to none, though some have been bred up many year to't; I myself chalked out the way to the tune-maker; I know I have many foes that say I make not what I own, but mum for that: this rare opera is all mine, I'll swear; but for the dress and trim, give the Devil his due, I am beholding to the most serene and clear Monsieur Stephen the King's corn-cutter; and so are you all, for he put me upon't.

He satirised the music with its 'reci-tantivy', its bird-music and echo-music:—

We'll make an echo of our own. . . . One must be Voice and another must be Air, and another must be Rock: then Voice must talk soundly to Air and beat her against Rock, and Rock must beat her back again: and then Air must cry out and scold with Voice—and that's Echo.

The litany to the deities in the Temple scene was turned into:—

Two Priests.   James Naylor, Pope Joan, Wat Tyler, Moll Cutpurse, Choco-
               relly—
All answer.   Help our opera, because 'tis very silly!
Two Priests.   Masaniello, Mosely, Jack-straw, Jantredisco, Pimponelli—
All answer.   Help our opera, because 'tis very silly! *etc.*

The Cyclops became paviors, the magic casket a bottle of brandy that made the burlesque Psyche drunk and the very names of the characters were imitated either colloquially (Nicholas for Nicander) or comically (Wouldhamore and Sweetlips for Aglaura and Cidippe). To add to the fun the two princes were played by actresses, while the heroine was acted by the low comedian Joe Haines, all anticipating the later pantomime. But the remarkable thing was that the burlesque was so detailed—a convincing proof that *Psyche* in particular and opera in general of the Shadwell kind was becoming the chief popular form of entertainment.

---

[1] He also produced an altered version of Cambert's *Pomone* about now.

[2] Possibly earlier than the now accepted date.

The date of *Psyche* is probably more debatable than the date or authorship of the operatic *Tempest*.

Allardyce Nicoll's discovery of the entry 'Psyche first Acting' against the date February 27 of the year (apparently) 1674, old style, i.e. 1675 in our reckoning would seem to be conclusive and Löwenberg (whose March 9 is the same in accordance with his post-dating seventeenth century dates by ten days to conform with the new style) thinks this is supported by the fact that both the text and the vocal score were published in 1675 also.

The date of the vocal score is, however, against the belief, for in it Locke asks the rhetorical question, 'Why, after so long exposed, is it now printed?'—'so long exposed' obviously meaning 'having been so long before the public'. What does 'so long' mean?

Now even to-day, when show-music is usually published either in printed form or as gramophone records more or less simultaneously with the first night, I find theatre-people agree with me that 'so long' after the first night would more likely mean two or three years than seven or eight months: but eight months would be the longest time between February and preparation for engraving even if the score was published in December: besides, even if eight months was a long time nowadays compared with the usual custom of simultaneous publication, it could not be compared with the usual custom of 1675 because there was none—*Psyche* was the first English vocal score to be printed.

It must be remembered, too, that Vernon's letter telling how the Duke's House was 'preparing an opera and great machines. They will have dancers out of France, and St. André comes over with them' was written at the end of August 1673, the very time Shadwell was working at *Psyche*, as can be calculated from his printed preface, so that he probably was alluding to *Psyche*. This is borne out by the fact that his allusions more closely fit that opera than *The Tempest*, quite apart from Downes's express mention of 'new French Dances' and the statement that St. André danced in *Psyche* according to Nicoll and Summers.

Now of course if *Psyche* was preparing in autumn 1673 and was ready enough for St. André to be named, spring 1675 would indeed make the opera 'long-expected', as Downes recorded: but if Downes's date of February 1674 (in our reckoning) were correct (which would make Locke's 'so long' more plausible), the opera might still be considered 'long expected' by an eager audience, though in fact it would not be an excessive time to spend on preparation for such a spectacle.

Flimsy as these theories will seem to literal-minded scholars, they are, I believe, logically accumulative, and show that Downes may have been right with his date of February 1674 after all (1673 O.S.). I do not produce as further argument (though it is worth noting) that Draghi, who had in 1667 been preparing an Italian opera for Killegrew, was one of the composers of *Psyche*, which might conceivably have been his original opera, never produced for years until adopted by a different management and largely rewritten by other writers—as has often happened in the theatre: that would have made it 'long expected' for seven years (by no means out of the question, as I know to my cost).

The three things that I find difficult to believe, if 1675 is presumed the year of production, are that Locke should consider 'so long' to mean less than a year, that Vernon's letter should not refer to *Psyche*, and if it did, that the production did not take place for eighteen months.

If Downes was right, there remains the difficulty of the Lord Chamberlain's entry, but it should not be forgotten that 'first acting' may not mean 'first performance': after all, if one accepted Pepys as a literal authority, it could be maintained that Ford's *Tis Pity She's a Whore* 'was acted the first time' on September 9, 1661; Shirley's *Hyde Park*, 'an old play', on July 11, 1668, 'the first day acted'; Fletcher's *The Coxcomb* on March 17, 1669, 'the first time acted, but an old play'; Webster's *Appius and Virginia* on May 12, 1669, 'a new play, the first day acted . . . an old play'. 'First acting' therefore can mean 'first performance this season'.

Psyche may have been first produced on February 27, 1675, but the Lord Chamberlain's record does not prove it (quite apart from mistakes in dating in other references): if, then, Downes's date of a year earlier were correct after all, it would fit the other facts better, and incidentally would give even stronger point to Dryden's objection to French influence and operatic attractions in his prologue on the opening of the new Drury Lane Theatre on March 26, 1674.

[3] For those who do not know, 'flageolets' were more like penny whistles than recorders, violins included all string instruments, cornets were like hunting horns but made of wood or ivory and if curved were bound with leather, sackbuts were early trombones.

[4] The last four lines are presumed to mean that spectacular opera was proving impossible, but this does not join up with the hopeful confidence of the earlier lines comparing the splendour at the Duke's with the sordid, cheap fare at the King's. I believe the meaning to be 'Good riddance to this sort of cheap play that a rich town like London cannot put up with, for the Duke's management will put on bigger and better shows each year if the audience will put up with increased prices for seats'—prices were trebled for *Psyche*.

[5] i.e. the *Commedia dell'arte*.

CHAPTER ELEVEN

Dryden and Opera

At the end of 1675 there arrived in England the lovely Hortense Mancini, the favourite niece of the late Cardinal Mazarin. Charles II, who had wanted to marry her sixteen years before, installed her in St. James's Palace and settled a pension on her, which enabled her to indulge her fancies for parties and gambling—pastimes of which her uncle had disapproved—and musical and dramatic entertainments, of which he certainly approved, having introduced Italian opera into France thirty years before. Later it will be seen that the Duchess de Mazarin, as she was known, did her best to introduce Italian opera to London: she was not immediately successful, for during the last twenty-five years of the seventeenth century there was roughly no change in the type of musical stage-work that was accepted by the London audience.

The Davenant–Shadwell type of opera, adding musical scenes to a spoken play in the style of *Psyche*, remained fashionable and—with two professional and two semi-amateur exceptions—was the only type to be seen, though some might be better than others, with better music or more spectacular scenes.

Davenant's son, Charles, now twenty-two, was the first to follow and help set the fashion: he wrote an opera on the subject of Iphigenia in Tauris, misleadingly called *Circe*, with music by John Banister: it was produced in 1677 and, as Downes recorded, 'being well performed, it answered the expectations of the company'. It contained the usual musical priests, furies, winds, gods, dragon-drawn chariots and masque-like visions (which in this opera are rather machine-made—though the Frightful Dreams in a 'Place of Horror' bring some operatic drama into the work by introducing the ghost of Clytemnestra, slain by her son Orestes). Its chief interest is that it is the first tragic English opera, ending with the killing by Orestes of the evil queen Circe and himself, and, spattered with thunder and lightning and 'horrid music' leading to a final conflagration of the whole city.

In the same year as *Circe*, however, something happened that led to a great improvement in English operatic methods, though

E   129

at the same time it was the smallest of small clouds hinting at a danger that would lead to the suffocating of English opera—at least as was being developed at that time. The danger was that the public were beginning to get a little taste for Italian opera tricks—not that any Italian opera was performed, but the Duchess de Mazarin and the Italian musicians resident in London naturally introduced the newest Italian music, and one of the growing fashions in Italian opera was the song that usually began by expressing some more or less general emotion, then became more particularly dramatic and perhaps more apposite to the drama, and finally repeated the passages on general emotion by starting again from the beginning—in Italian 'da capo'—the 'da capo' aria, in fact. That it must have become known to at least quite a number of people who belonged to artistic circles can be seen from the fact that Dryden, who, as will be shown, was notorious for having no ear for music, wrote a song in the 'da capo' form for his play *The Kind Keeper: or, Mr. Limberham*—the first four lines are not exactly repeated at the end, but the intention is clear and he called it 'A Song from the Italian':—

> By a dismal cypress lying
> Damon cried, all pale and dying,
> 'Kind is death that ends my pain,
> But cruel she I loved in vain!
> The mossy fountains
>   Murmur my trouble,
> And hollow mountains
>   My groans redouble:
> Every nymph mourns me,
>   Thus while I languish:
> She only scorns me,
>   Who caused my anguish.
> No love returning me, but all hope denying.'
> By a dismal cypress lying,
> Like a swan so sung he dying,
> 'Kind is death that ends my pain,
> But cruel she I loved in vain!'

Dryden was evidently beginning to eat his words, as he was often forced to do by expediency—certainly where opera and music were concerned: he was always vehemently opinionated, but quite ready to change if it was to his advantage—he had been glad to be taken up by the great man of the theatre Davenant and to be shown how to mix music with drama, but after Davenant's

death, when it seemed to him he was well in with the rival theatre
manager Killegrew and had had six plays performed, Dryden was
very ready to sneer at the Duke's Theatre for performing operas:
but seeing that they were drawing the public away from the
Theatre Royal, to which he was under contract, he began to think
there was something in them, after all, so he not only deserted to
the Duke's Theatre, but set about writing an opera himself and in
1678 published *The State of Innocence and Fall of Man, an opera.*

This long poem in dramatic form taken from *Paradise Lost* with,
it was said, Milton's consent before he died, was never performed
and is nothing like an opera of any kind as printed, for it includes
only one lyrical scene—a dream that Eve has, seeing herself and
what the future holds for her, just as the heroine of the recent
American *Oklahoma* saw herself in a dream, except that Eve's
double sings while mock-angels tempt her to eat of the tree.
It is not correct, however, to say that it was conceived by Dryden
as an opera of the Shadwell type, for although there was only this
one lyrical scene printed, the music indicated through the whole
work was not, as Hogarth wrote in his *Memoirs of the Musical
Drama*, entirely instrumental: the opening of the first scene of
Chaos, after a symphony of warlike music for the fall of the
rebellious angels who were to be seen 'wheeling in the air and
seeming transfixed with thunderbolts', contained tunes of victory
and a hymn and ended with 'a tune of horror and lamentation'
for the fallen angels in their lake of brimstone, from which
Lucifer rose and spoke: between the first and second acts after the
devils had flown and danced they were to sing

> *a song expressing the change of their condition—what they enjoyed be-*
> *fore, and how they fell bravely in battle, having deserved victory by*
> *their valour, and what they would have done, if they had conquered.*

In the second act, the newly created Adam, as he is taken by the
angel Raphael to see the glories of the world, says

> . . . let earth and heav'n above
> Sound our Great Maker's pow'r and greater love,

and a song is sung, while just before the end of the whole show

> *a heaven descends full of angels and blessed spirits, with soft music: a*
> *song and chorus.*

The words of these musical scenes, however, were not printed, if
indeed they were written, but it does show that Dryden was

already thinking—however inadequately—of taking an active part in developing the new fashion of dramatic opera, which he later did most successfully.

In 1681 Shadwell tried his hand again with a musical entertainment—*The Lancashire Witches*, 'being a kind of opera', as Downes said: but the chief attraction in this was the various complicated flying effects which were certainly not danger-proof to the actors concerned but made a lot of money both for the author and the Duke's Theatre.

Two years later Betterton went to Paris for Charles II to try to get French opera-singers to come over to London, but he seems only to have succeeded in bringing back the wretched Grabu who, as the English Ambassador in France, Lord Preston, wrote to the Duke of York, would

endeavour to represent something at least like an opera in England for his Majesty's diversion.

The collaboration then started between Grabu, the French opera hack, and Dryden, the hater of both opera and the French invasion of the London theatre: the desire to get in with Charles II, by giving him the opera he wanted, resulted in Dryden's completely reversing his previously unalterable opinions—as he was always ready to do when it suited his book—while Grabu, hoping to recover the royal favour he had forfeited ten years before, no doubt gladly welcomed, like all refugee second-raters, the idea of a patriotic subject for the opera, and was more than willing to show Dryden how to write a prologue to it that would be, after the custom of the French theatre, crammed with fulsome flattery of the King.

The opera—planned for 1685—was to be on the story of the great British King, Arthur, while the prologue should sing the praises of Charles and—luckily, as it turned out—of his brother James, Duke of York, under the allegorical names of Albion and Albanius. Dryden as usual prepared a lengthy preface, which on this occasion gave an explanation and history of opera in general, and of this one in particular. His definition of opera has constantly been quoted, but he makes other statements that I quote here as well, not because he was expert on the subject, but because, being known to be absolutely tone-deaf to music (as will be seen),[1] and therefore by no means an expert on that part of opera at least, his opinions more probably echo those of his contemporaries in an attempt to justify his championing a cause he had previously sneered at.

If wit has truly been defined a propriety of thoughts and words, then that definition will extend to all sorts of poetry, and, among the rest, to this present entertainment of an opera: propriety of thought is that fancy which arises naturally from the subject or which the poet adapts to it, propriety of words is the clothing of those thoughts with such expressions as are naturally proper to them—and from both these, if they are judiciously performed, the delight of poetry results.

An opera is a poetical tale, or fiction, represented by vocal and instrumental music, adorned with scenes, machines, and dancing.

Scenes and machines, which used to be of the first importance, have now been put second to the story and the music by Dryden, the dramatist, and an examination of English operas after this time seems to support this new order of precedence between comparatively equal ingredients.

The supposed persons of this musical drama are generally supernatural, as Gods and Goddesses, and Heroes, which at least are descended from them, and are in due time to be adopted into their number. The subject therefore, being extended beyond the limits of human nature, admits of that sort of marvellous and surprising conduct, which is rejected in other plays.

He goes on to explain that even so the deities must never act out of character, though their actions and language should be grander than that of ordinary people.

If the persons represented were to speak upon the stage, it would follow of necessity that the expressions should be lofty, figurative and majestical: but the nature of an opera denies the frequent use of those poetical ornaments—

(a shrewd point that is often forgotten by inferior librettists and composers, who think that words for music should be high-flown and flowery—a misconception that Weber later pointed out to Planché, when writing *Oberon*: Dryden goes on to elaborate this point:)

for vocal music, though it often admits a loftiness of sound, yet always exacts an harmonious sweetness—or, to distinguish yet more justly, the recitative part of the opera requires a more masculine beauty of expression and sound, the other—which for want of a proper English word I must call the 'songish' part—must abound in the softness and variety of numbers, its principal intention being to please the hearing rather than to gratify the understanding.

133

This greater importance of sound than of sense (though not, if I understand him correctly, implying a disregard of sense) is accepted by Dryden, because, as he says, like all laws of art or science, it derived from its first inventors—in the case of opera, the Italians, who brought it to perfection, though they may have got the idea from the entertainments of the Spanish Moors at their Zambras, or royal feasts. With Italians the first operas

seem to have been intended for the celebration of the marriages of their princes, or for the magnificence of some general time of joy. Accordingly the expenses of them were from the purse of the Sovereign, or of the republic, as they are still practised at Venice, Rome, and other places at their carnivals.

The French style of Prologue,

which is a compliment to the sovereign power by some God or Goddess, so that it looks no less than a kind of embassy from heaven to earth,

he thinks came from the pastoral opera *Il Pastor Fido* by Guarini [2] written for a ducal marriage, and this reference makes him correct himself on his dictum that all opera characters must be divine or near-divine:—

meaner persons may sometimes gracefully be introduced, especially if they have relation to those first times which poets call the Golden Age wherein by reason of their innocence those happy mortals were supposed to have had a more familiar intercourse with superior beings: and therefore shepherds might reasonably be admitted as of all callings the most innocent, the most happy, and—

(this, I think, shows charming common sense:—)

—who, by reason of the spare time they had in their almost idle employment, had most leisure to make verses and to be in love—without somewhat of which passion no opera can possibly subsist.

Dryden then praises Italian as the softest, sweetest, most harmonious of all past and present languages:—

it seems indeed to have been invented for the sake of poetry and music: the vowels are so abounding in all words, especially in the terminations of them that—excepting a few monosyllables—the whole language ends in them.

He now compares it to the disadvantage of other languages: the French have tried to simplify theirs by 'throwing off unnecessary consonants, which made their spelling tedious and their pronunciation harsh', but, after all, as an ill voice, though never so throughly instructed in the rules of music, can never be brought to sing harmoniously, nor many an honest critic ever arrive to be a good poet, so neither can the natural harshness of the French or their perpetual ill accent be ever refined into perfect harmony like the Italian.

His comment on English is interesting. He points out that it has more natural disadvantages than French through its Teutonic monosyllables and excess of consonants, though it is relieved by other words derived from Latin, French, Greek, Italian and Spanish: it therefore is pre-eminent in great poetry, thanks to 'our English genius' but, because it is pronounced with as soft an effeminacy as Danish and yet has few feminine rhymes, it is not as good as French for songs, though it certainly is better for recitative. At first sight this may seem a surprising opinion, but it is surely true that while a melodic flow is broken by excessive consonants (which Purcell was, always, careful to avoid) dramatic narrative is unintelligible unless consonants attract the attention of the ear.

Through these difficulties [he says] I have made shift to struggle in my part of the performance of the opera, which, as mean as it is, deserves at least a pardon, because it has attempted a discovery beyond any former undertaker of our nation.

He conveniently forgets his former instructor, Davenant, and thinks that if this original opera fails it will not be his fault but because of the nature of the beast—though he is sure a lot of it will please both eye and ear.

After so ungraciously having claimed praise as an innovator and disclaimed any responsibility for flaws, he goes on to say that he has not much fear of failure:—

for I may without vanity own some advantages which are not common to every writer, such as are the knowledge of the Italian and French languages, and the being conversant with some of their best performances in this kind,

(had he only read them, or had he seen Italian and French operas?)

which have furnished me with such variety of measures as have given the composer, M. Grabu, what occasions he could wish to show his extraordinary talent in diversifying the recitative, the lyrical part, and the chorus—in all which (not to attribute anything to my own opinion) the best judges (and those too of the best quality) who have honoured his rehearsals with their presence have no less commended the happiness of his genius than his skill.

This must not be taken as true, for in the first place it is a flattering compliment to Charles II who heard some of the rehearsals, in the second place the best judges in Dryden's opinion were those who said they liked the work—as will be shown later on—and in the third place—as will also be shown—no good judge could possibly have praised Grabu's work (certainly not Charles who liked good common sense no less than a good tune) and no good good judge did.

That however could never have prevented Dryden riding a horse to death once he had backed it: he went on:—

And let me have the liberty to add one thing—that he has so exactly expressed my sense in all places where I intended to move the passions that he seems to have entered into my thoughts and to have been the poet as well as the composer. This I say not to flatter him, but to do him right, because amongst some English musicians—

(Banister being one)

—and their scholars, who are sure to judge after them, the imputation of being a Frenchman is enough to make a party who maliciously endeavour to decry him.

(Dryden had a short memory when it suited him.)

But the knowledge of Latin and Italian poets, both which he possesses, besides his skill in music and his being acquainted with all the performances of the French operas, adding to these the good sense to which he is born, having raised him to a degree above any man who shall pretend to be his rival on our stage. When any of our countrymen excel him, I shall be glad for the sake of old England to be shown my error: in the meantime let virtue be commended, though in the person of a stranger.

Time and again in the history of opera, in this country at least, the second-rater from abroad arrives as the romantic refugee with a reputation for knowledge and experience (as Grabu was 'acquainted with all the performances of the French operas') which he builds up with a mass of ultra-technical terms to impress the non-expert but influential enthusiast—often with a skilful flattery that would be obvious except to the delighted recipient (Grabu evidently pleased Dryden by 'happening' to know Latin and Italian poetry, in both of which Dryden fancied himself a connoisseur).

Sometimes the pretensions of a plausible foreigner are blown sky-high on the arrival of a real authority from the same town, but more often the tales from the Vienna woods are accepted as gospel, and we shall now never know if Grabu really had only

been a secondary *répétiteur* under Cambert in Paris: the acceptance of such fresh pretenders, however, will always rankle.

After his eulogy of Grabu, Dryden proceeds to excuse himself if
critics find lack of thought or invention, on the grounds that in an
opera those are not so important:—

The necessity of double rhymes and ordering of the words and numbers for the
sweetness of the voice are the main hinges on which an opera must move—

he thinks therefore that such words can only be written by a poet

with that nicety of hearing that the discord of sounds in words shall as much
offend him as a seventh in music would a good composer.

Was this a hit at Locke, who certainly used sevenths and practically
consecutive sevenths (as Purcell later approved) in *Psyche*? Dryden
anyway must have got the simile from some old-fashioned
musician, unless it was one of the musical terms he happened to
know.

He goes on to say that thought is not as important in opera
as the choice of words, not meaning 'elegancy of expression,
but propriety of sound, to be varied according to the nature of the
subject', and he further points out that writing words for music
entails great ingenuity, if not invention, to make them fit: he
evidently had to write some of the words to existing music

as if I had not served out my time in poetry, but was bound prentice to some
doggerel rhymer who makes songs to tunes and sings them for a livelihood.
Tis true I have not been often put to this drudgery, but where I have, the words
will sufficiently show that I was then a slave to the composition—which I will
never be again: 'tis my part to invent and the musician's to humour that invention. I may be counselled and will always follow my friend's advice where
I find it reasonable, but will never part with the power of the militia.

The words, in fact, were really of the first importance in
Dryden's opinion. He then explains that this opera-prologue to
which he prefixed this long preface was intended to introduce

a play of the nature of the *Tempest*, which is a tragedy mixed with opera or a
drama written in blank verse, adorned with scenes, machines, songs and dances,
so that the fable of it is all spoken and acted by the best of the comedians, the
other part of the entertainment to be performed by the same singers and
dancers who are introduced in this present opera. It cannot properly be called a
play, because the action of it is supposed to be conducted sometimes by supernatural means or magic, nor an opera, because the story of it is not sung.

Unfortunately 'some intervening accidents' stopped the original
plan, so Dryden extended the original one-act operatic prologue

by two more acts, and made it one long allegorical opera with scenes described as planned by Betterton. The preface ended with a final boost for the music and for Grabu, who obviously needed it badly:—

To conclude, though the enemies of the composer are not few and that there is a party formed against him of his own profession, I hope and am persuaded that this prejudice will turn in the end to his advantage, for the greatest part of an audience is always uninterested (?), though seldom knowing, and if the music be well composed and well performed they who find themselves pleased will be so wise as not to be imposed upon and fooled out of their satisfaction. The newness of the undertaking is all the hazard. When operas were first set up in France, they were not followed over-eagerly, but they gained daily upon their hearers till they grew to that height of reputation which they now enjoy. The English, I confess, are not altogether so musical as the French, and yet they have been pleased already with the *Tempest* and some pieces that followed, which were neither much better written nor so well composed as this. If it finds encouragement, I dare promise myself to mend my hand by making a more pleasing fable: in the meantime every loyal Englishman cannot but be satisfied with the moral of this, which so plainly represents the double restoration of his sacred Majesty.

(The double restoration, by the way, was Charles's return to the throne and the saving of his life by the discovery of the Rye House plot.)

This allegorical all-sung prologue, blown up into a three-act opera utterly unlike the *Psyche* model, was heard in rehearsal by Charles II, and according to Dryden much admired by him, but its production had to be postponed when the King died in February 1685. But this failed to daunt the author and composer: they went ahead with the production merely adding a grand assumption of Albion (Charles II) in an oval chariot into the clouds of heaven

shining with gold, abundance of Angels and Cherubims flying about 'em and playing in 'em: in the midst of its sits Apollo on a throne of gold,

and when Neptune has suggested that the new royal star should be near Orion, as he was so connected with the sea, Apollo overrules him and very appositely—but rather tactlessly—suggests he should shine 'Betwixt the Balance and the Maid'.

The long version of the opera already pilloried the Protestant adherents of handsome young James, Duke of Monmouth, Charles's beloved illegitimate son, and his self-seeking Svengali, the Earl of Shaftesbury, for they had been concerned in the Rye House plot against Charles: but, now that he was dead, they were still more revolutionary minded against his brother, the new Catholic King, James II—in fact, as soon as *Albion and Albanius* opened, Shaftesbury's dupe, Monmouth, landed at Lyme Regis and started marching on London with an ever-increasing army of West-country men: news of this caused such consternation that the opera only lasted six performances with a result that the management failed to cover half its costs and so landed into great debt.[3]

In *Wit and Mirth, or Pills to purge Melancholy*, a famous collection of ballads and songs put together by Thomas D'Urfey and published in 1720, there are these verses ridiculing both Dryden and Grabu. The very title—'The Raree-show, from Father Hopkins', alluding to the author, who, with Sternhold, had made an uncouth metrical version of the Psalms which was published complete in 1562—is a hit at Dryden's awkward lyrics which is doubled in the actual verses that hit at him under the nickname of Bays (alluding to his laureateship): Grabu is pilloried under his own name, and the words fit the rather jerky rhythmic tune printed above them as awkwardly as Dryden's fitted his music.

> From Father Hopkins, whose vein did inspire him
>   Bays sends this raree-show public to view:
> Prentices, fops and their footmen admire him,
>   Thanks patron, painter and Monsieur Grabu.

> Each actor on the stage his luck bewailing
>   Finds that his loss is infallibly true:
> Smith, Nokes and Leigh in a fever with railing
>   Curse poet, painter and Monsieur Grabu.

(These three leading actors of Betterton's company might well curse the management's loss through the expense of this incompetent work which only drew the cheaper audience and a few dilettante fops.)

> Betterton, Betterton, thy decorations
>   And the machines were well written, we knew:
> But all the words were such stuff we want patience—
>   And little better is Monsieur Grabu.

(So the words were considered the worst part of it.)

'Damn me,' says Underhill, 'I'm out two hundred,
  Hoping that rainbows and peacocks would do:
Who thought infallible Tom could have blundered?
  A plague upon him and Monsieur Grabu!'

(Evidently Cave Underhill, who with Nokes had both acted at the Cockpit in 1660 and joined Davenant three years later, was on the managerial side with Tom Betterton, who this time over-trusted the effect of his machines, spectacular though they were—the tail of the peacock drawing Juno's chariot spread out as it came down to a width of nearly thirty feet ('it almost fills the opening of the stage from scene to scene'), while Iris's rainbow is described in the text as follows:—

> *Iris appears on a very large machine. This was really seen the 18th of March 1684 by Capt. Christopher Gunman on board his R.H. Yacht then in Calais Pier: he drew it as it then appeared and gave a draught of it to us. We have only added the cloud where the person of Iris sits.*

The intriguing lack of description almost tempts a belief that it must have been a flying saucer, but even if it was, the audience was not attracted either by that or by the dancing, which the ballad implies was the least bad part of the show.)

Lane, thou hast no applause for thy capers,
  Tho' all without thee would make a man spue:
And a month hence will not pay for the tapers,
  Spite of Jack Laureate and Monsieur Grabu.

Bays, thou wouldst have thy skill thought universal,
  Tho' thy dull ear be to music untrue:
Then, whilst we strive to confute the *Rehearsal*,
  Prithee learn thrashing of Monsieur Grabu!

(So there it is in plain English—Dryden had no ear for music, and I presume the last two lines mean that, in spite of all attempts to prove Buckingham's play *The Rehearsal* wrong in pillorying the poet as a conceited incompetent,[4] Dryden was bettered even by the third-rate Grabu. The author of the ballad now forgets Grabu to concentrate on deflating the self-satisfied conceit of Dryden with his advertising prefaces, his unmusical lyrics, his toadying flattery and a prophecy that *Albion and Albanius* would certainly not draw the money.)

With thy dull prefaces still thou wouldst treat us,
  Striving to make thy dull bauble look fair:
So the horned herd of the city do cheat us,
  Still most commending the worst of their ware.

> Leave making operas and writing lyrics
>   Till thou hast ears and canst alter thy strain:
> Stick to thy talent of bold panegyrics
>   And still remember the breathing the vein.
>
> Yet, if thou thinkest the town will extol 'em,
>   Print thy dull notes, but be thrifty and wise—
> Instead of angels subscribed for the volume,
>   Take a round shilling, and thank my advice.

(An angel was worth ten shillings.)

> In imitating thee this may be charming,
>   Gleaning from Laureates is no shame at all:
> And let this song be sung the next performing,
>   Else ten to one but the prices will fall.

The author was obviously no friend of Dryden's (was it
D'Urfey himself?), but that his accusation of Dryden's lack of a
musical ear—twice stated—was true can be proved even without
knowing anything of music, Grabu's or anyone else's, if Dryden's
praise for Grabu's setting of his words is remembered when the
Frenchman's accentuation of English is glanced at. As an example, here are some lines sung by Juno and then repeated by
other voices with the accented syllables in italics—the music by
the way is a straightforward rhythmic tune in triple time with
'laugh' ornamented

> *Why* stay we then on *earth*
>   When mortals *laugh* . . . and *love*?
> *Tis* time to *mount* above
>   And send *Astrea down*,
> The ruler of his *birth*
>   And guardian of his *crown*.
> Tis time *to* mount above
>   And send *Astrea down*.

Seeing how often Dryden's definition of an opera is quoted—
and it is quite right it should be—it is as well to bear in mind his
unmusical ear: in fact, I am not sure that he did not go so far as
to hate music as much as he misunderstood it (though that did
not stop him trying to cash in on it). If he did not hate it, he must
have been very stupid on this one point for all his brilliance in
other directions, for his Prologue to this very opera (which he
wanted to be a success with the throne) sneers at such entertainments: after starting by lamenting that for twenty years audiences

have only liked rubbish and no longer can stomach worthwhile dramatic fare, he goes on:—

> We now prescribe, like doctors in despair,
> The diet your weak appetites can bear.
> Since heavy beef and mutton will not do,
> Here's julep dance, tisane of song and show:

('tisane' being a French infusion of herbs)

> Give you strong sense, the liquor is too heady:
> You're come to farce—that's asses' milk—already.

He says that for callow youths sound may be good enough till they are old enough to appreciate sense—if they are lucky enough to live so long—while England can congratulate herself for being tricked more recently than France by show, which the Italians invented: constant variety and change—especially for the worse—always pleases and is derived from France,

> without whose rules
> None must presume to set up here for fools.
> In France the oldest man is always young,
> Sees operas daily, learns the tunes so long
> Till foot, hand, head keep time with ev'ry song.
> Each sings his part, echoing from pit and box
> With his hoarse voice, half harmony, half pox.
> 'Le plus grand Roi du monde' is always ringing—
> They show themselves good subjects by their singing.

After which tactless sneer at French fools for their stupidity at singing the praises of the King, he shows his muddled thinking by recommending such behaviour by bidding the Londoners,

> Cits and Citesses, raise a joyful strain!
> Tis a good omen to begin a reign:
> Voices may help your charter to restoring,
> And get by singing what you lost by roaring.

The full score of the opera was published in 1687, and in the preface to James II Grabu again put his foot in it with a tactlessness that only a second-rate alien can show: after pointing out that Charles II had liked it at rehearsal, he goes on:—

The only displeasure which remains with me is that I neither was nor could possibly be furnished with variety of excellent voices to present it to Your Majesty in its full perfection. Notwithstanding which you have been pleased to pardon this defect as not proceeding from any fault of mine, but only from the scarcity of singers in this island.

James may not have minded the insulting excuse, but English musicans, both composers and executants, must have resented such conceited rudeness being printed and only waited for the chance to hit back.

[1] See p. 140.

[2] Löwenberg dates Guarini's *play* 1585, six years earlier than the supposed first opera, though it was not printed till 1590.

[3] Nicoll says the opera opened on June 3 according to a MS. note by Luttrell and an entry in the Lord Chamberlain's records recording a visit by the King and Queen and the Maids of Honour on that date to 'the Opera': he also says the news reached London on the sixth night it was performed. Writers on Monmouth give June 11 as the date of his landing—how long did it take to reach London from Lyme Regis then?

[4] See p. 100.

CHAPTER TWELVE

Purcell and Opera

THE second exception to the *Psyche* type of dramatic opera was probably performed at Court when Dryden was working on *Albion and Albanius*: it was Blow's all-sung opera of *Venus and Adonis*, in which the part of Cupid was sung by Lady Mary Tudor, then perhaps eleven years old, while her mother, Mary Davis, one of Davenant's original company, who was a fine singer and a most light and graceful dancer, sang Venus, and her father, Charles II, was a proud member of the audience. Historically this little three-act opera is most important, both from the musical and the operatic point of view—especially with regard to the skill with which by the simplest means Blow colours the emotion of each scene, whether domestically amusing, as in the spelling-lesson scene, or poignantly tragic, as after Adonis's death; in that respect it has been dealt with by Dent and others, but as it seems only to have been written for a private family performance, it naturally had no noticeable effect either on the London audience's attitude to opera or on the development of sung drama—except in so far as it may have suggested the second and more famous amateur experiment in operatic form: certainly Blow himself never tried again.

The year after *Albion and Albanius*, London did see the public performance of another non-Shadwell type of opera: this was *Cadmus et Hermione* by Lully, the first French grand opera of a serious character, which had been produced in France in 1673. Incidentally no other Lully opera was ever produced in England until his *Amadis* was given in London by amateurs in 1938, and even this 1686 production of *Cadmus* had, I think, escaped the notice of opera historians until W. J. Lawrence in *The Times Literary Supplement* of September 26, 1929, solved a riddle: it was known that there had been some French opera performed in London in February 1686, because in the Rutland papers there is a letter from Peregrine Bertie to the Countess of Rutland saying that 'next week begins the French Opera', five days later he wrote 'The French Opera will begin the week after next', and on Feb-

ruary 11—the date when the Lord Chamberlain's records show
that the King and Queen and the Maids of Honour were at the
French opera—he wrote:

Today was the French Opera. The King and Queen were there, the music was
indeed very fine, but all the dresses the most wretched I ever saw: twas acted
by none but French.

The riddle that W. J. Lawrence solved, after quoting the Rutland
papers, was an allusion to it in the prologue to a farce by Thomas
Jevon called *The Devil of a Wife*: here are the apposite lines:—

> Be favourable to this same piece at hand,
> And d'ye hear, friends, don't shall-I, shall-I stand.
> If I in pocket find you dive for cat-call,
> I'll let down curtain, I'll tell ye that all.
> Catcalls well-tuned might do we in operas—
> They'd serve for hoboys [oboes] to fill up a chorus,
> Or in a French love-song—observe you now—
> > (*He sings*)
> 'A Cadmeus pur qua mene vou'
> Begar, Monsieur, it be de pretty whyne,
> 'Ki la dance de Meneway?' Oh it be very fine!
> > (*He dances*)
> Dances you have, and various here tonight,
> But they are English all, all English quite:
> Throughout English songs, farce English too—
> That's French scene—
> All nonsense without any more ado.

The first words that I have given in inverted commas (italics in
the original) are phonetically spelled versions of the words of the
song identified by Lawrence as sung by Hermione in Act II,
Scene 4, when Cadmus is bidding her farewell before going to
fight the Dragon of Mars—in the French it reads:—

> Ah, Cadmus, pourquoi m'aimez vous?

The second passage in inverted commas (obviously meaning
'Who is dancing the Minuet?') alludes to the Minuet danced by
Comus and Hamadryads.

The prologue is worth quoting here, not only because of the
ingenious identifications and because most books on opera in
England fail to mention it, but also because nothing could have
been burlesqued in the prologue to a popular type of play unless
the allusion was recognisable by most of the audience, and this

shows that this French opera and those two tunes at least must have attracted quite a number of people.

There is still the problem to be solved of what singers performed the opera: as Lawrence said, it is unlikely they were acting members of the French Académie Royale, because on February 15, four days later, the Académie produced Lully's new *Armide*, but he queried whether the harsh Edict of Nantes against the Protestants of France might not have sent a flood of refugee singers and dancers to England, as it certainly sent Lully's chief scene-painter, Jacques Rousseau. It seems to me that behind this obviously shoddy and, as Jevon seems to imply, laughable production Grabu must have been pulling his ineffective little strings —if his grand patriotically English opera had not made his mark with James II, he would certainly have been ready to rush to the other extreme and try to prove that only foreigners knew anything about music.

Unfortunately for him, this theory was at that very moment showing signs of being proved false by Blow's pupil, Henry Purcell, who in 1679 had not only become organist of Westminster Abbey at the age of twenty when Blow resigned, it is said, in his favour, but had also written his first stage-music for a play called *Theodosius*: in the next eight years he was only asked to write occasional music for some six other plays, but the turning point in his theatrical career came in 1689, after, if not partly because of, the crowning of the Protestant William and Mary in place of the Catholic James II and his Italian wife.

One of the results of this change-over was that many Italians left England, and Purcell celebrated—or at least commemorated— the departure of a well-known Italian *castrato*, who had been singing in the Whitehall Catholic Chapel, with a harpsichord piece entitled 'Sefauchi's Farewell', alluding in English phonetics to the singer's nickname from his most famous operatic role, Siface, by which he was better known than by his real name of Giovanni Francesco Grossi. He had sung the part of Siface when he was twenty-five in Cavalli's opera *Scipione Africano* in Venice in 1678–9—which has not, I think, been noticed before.

Of course many Italians did not leave London, the Duchess de Mazarin among them, though she had by now moved from St. James's Palace to the village of Chelsea: but whether or not popular favour turned towards home-grown music, Purcell's star was in the ascendant. At first, however, it showed rather faintly in an experimental way with the fourth exception to the *Psyche* type of opera.

Josias Priest, who arranged dances for Betterton, and so must have met Purcell during his earlier theatre engagements, also ran a school for young ladies at Gorges House in Chelsea, and it was here that Purcell's one all-sung opera, *Dido and Aeneas*, the libretto by Nahum Tate, was performed. This was possibly in 1689, but more probably, I think, in the summer of 1690, when D'Urfey, who wrote the Epilogue, was staying at the school.[1]

There is a further indication that it was performed in the summer is a fact which has, I think, never been pointed out before and which makes *Dido* even more of an exception—it was almost certainly played in the open air, for, apart from the first scene, which is non-committal, every scene is an exterior. Outdoor scenes are always difficult to put on indoor stages, especially for amateurs, and Tate, the librettist, must have had good reason for calling attention to the fact that the witches were outside the cave in 'this open air', and for not putting the hunting party in some sheltering nook, the sailors inside a tavern or the dying Dido indoors.

Without here examining the evidence in detail, it is worth pointing out that in the famous Kip's map of Chelsea at the time neither the house nor the gardens of Gorges House seem to provide the necessary space for staging *Dido*, but at the end of the garden, according to a water-colour map of apparently 1706 in Chelsea Library, there was the Wood Yard belonging to Lindsey House, which still exists between the river and where Gorges House stood. If Mr. Priest had permission to use the Wood Yard for his opera, not only would he have had a building for Dido's Palace, open fields on the right, a view of the river for Aeneas's ships, beyond the Wood Yard the Stable Yard for the rough sailors boosing, and for the witches probably the entrance to one of the underground tunnels that enabled provisions to be brought from the river to the houses without marking the lawns on the river side of the houses; but also an excellent echo effect would be got by a few voices in one of the entrances to what could literally be called a 'deep vaulted cell' (an odd phrase to use for a romantic witches' cave), to judge from the Roman arched tunnel-passage of which there is a water-colour in the Chelsea Library.

With all this necessary scenery ready made (even the flying of the witches specified in the printed libretto might have been done with pulleys in the lofts of the Wood Yard), the setting seems probable, and it seems even more likely when we find in Hawkins that the great lover of musical dramatic entertainments, the Duchess de Mazarin, at one time lived in Lindsey House. We know that she got the chief singers of the day to sing for her when she was in Chelsea, which would explain why Purcell wrote Belinda's part as he did—not really suitable for a schoolgirl—and as at the time she was trying to make both ends meet, having no longer the entrée to Court, may she not have tried to add to her income from her society gambling parties at Basset by being the patroness of the girls' school behind her house?

I have only given my new deductions briefly here, but even if the link between Mazarin, Chelsea and *Dido* were weaker than it is, I am sure that *Dido*, instead of being a freak experiment, was in fact a spearhead of the forces for opera in England. But however much it may have pleased the proud parents of the schoolgirl chorus and ballet, there seem to be no contemporary accounts of it, nor did it have any immediate effect on opera form, for its style was not followed up by Purcell or anyone else at the time. All the same, even if he had no other evidence, it must have convinced Priest at least that here at last was an English dramatic composer worthy to succeed and surpass both Banister and Locke, both of whom had died some ten years before. By word of mouth, then, the theatre-men must have woken up to Purcell's possibilities, even if Betterton himself did not go talent-spotting at Chelsea among the pupils of his dancing-colleague.

If my date of 1690 for *Dido* is correct, Purcell was already working in the professional theatre; if it should be 1689, then possibly *Dido* induced collaboration with Priest and Betterton. In any event, Betterton's dramatic opera *The Prophetess or the History of Dioclesian* was produced at Dorset Garden in the summer of 1690,[2]

set out with costly scenes, machines, and clothes, the vocal and instrumental music done by Mr. Purcell, dances by Mr. Priest: it gratified the expectation of Court and City, and got the author great reputation,

as Downes said.

This is a fine example of the *Psyche*-type Shadwell sort of dramatic opera, but apart from having better music, it is no different from others of the kind, though the scenes and machines were finer than had been seen before—'*a dreadful monster comes from the farther end of the scenes and moves slowly forward*' to break up into dancing Furies, a quadruple palace of deities descends '*so large it fills all the space from the frontispiece of the stage to the farther end of the house and fixes itself by two ladders of clouds to the floor*', while at the same time a garden with fountains and orange-trees and the view of a distant palace rises from under the stage: the dances included one for Cane Chairs and another for Butterflies, apart from the more usual Bacchanal and rustic dances.

One thing it did do, however: it established Purcell in the theatre, and in October incidental music by him was performed with the play *Amphitryon* by Dryden, who in his preface again shows his opportunism by praising Purcell almost as if he, the poor scribbler, had discovered the new genius:—

But what has been wanting on my part has been abundantly supplied by the excellent composition of Mr. Purcell, in whose person we have at length found an Englishman equal with the best abroad—at least my opinion of him has been such since his happy and judicious performances in the late Opera and the experience I have had of him in the setting my three songs for this *Amphitryon*, to all which—and particularly to the composition of the Pastoral Dialogue—the numerous quire of fair ladies gave so just an applause on the third day.

The Pastoral Dialogue—which is not quite so innocent as Dryden's phraseology would seem to suggest—was printed with the other songs in 1690, but by March 1691 Purcell's music to *Dioclesian* was printed complete together with a dedicatory preface which included Purcell's views on the state of music in England at the time which must certainly be quoted here:—

Music and poetry have ever been acknowledged sisters which, walking hand in hand, support each other: as poetry is the harmony of words, so music is that of notes, and as poetry is a rise above prose and oratory, so is music the exaltation of poetry. Both of them may excel apart, but sure they are most excellent when they are joined, because nothing is then wanting to either of their perfections, for thus they appear like wit and beauty in the same person.

Poetry and painting have arrived to their perfection in our own country, music is yet but in its nonage, a forward child which gives hope of what it may be hereafter, in England, when the masters of it shall find more encouragement.

(So the foreign influence was still strong.)

'Tis now learning Italian, which is its best master, and studying a little of the French air to give it somewhat more of gaiety and fashion. Thus being farther from the sun, we are of later growth than our neighbour countries and must be content to shake off our barbarity by degrees. The present age seems already disposed to be refined and to distinguish betwixt wild fancy and a just, numerous composition.

He goes on to point out that the Duke of Somerset, to whom he was dedicating the score, was a great patron of music and to hope that English poets would soon

begin to grow ashamed of their harsh and broken numbers and promise to file our uncouth language into smoother words.

Purcell soon showed what he meant by that, for when he collaborated with Dryden again in the summer of 1691 in the dramatic opera *King Arthur* that had originally been planned to follow the prologue version of *Albion and Albanius*, he had no hesitation in altering the poet's words, as he always did, to make them more singable. One of Purcell's chief aims in simplifying the lyrics he was given to set was to avoid an excessive splutter of consonants: his skill in setting English words naturally and musically is of course well known, but as this sensitiveness to a musical balance of consonants and vowels has not, I think, been pointed out before, here are a few examples from *King Arthur* of how he always altered words that read well to words that sound better and fit the movements of the singer's mouth easier.

In the evil spirit Grimbald's song against the good spirit Phildel, Dryden's line

Too far, alas, he has betrayed ye

became

To fear, alas, he has betrayed ye

so avoiding the ugly-sounding repetition of the open-mouthed 'ah' in 'far' and 'alas'. In the famous Frost Scene Dryden made Cupid sing:

What! dost thou dream of freezing here?

which Purcell made easier to sing and understand as

What dost thou mean by freezing here?

In the praise of Britain in the final masque the sibilants are weeded out of the line

Foreign lands thy fishes tasting

by making it

Foreign lands thy fish are tasting:

Finally the first lines of Venus's lovely song, which, as Burney said, 'time has not the power to injure. It is of all ages and countries', were simply changed for the better from Dryden's version

> Fairest isle, all isles excelling,
>   Seat of pleasures and of loves,
>   Venus here will choose her dwelling
>   And forsake her Cyprian groves.

which reads perfectly well, to

> Fairest isle, all isles excelling,
>   Seat of pleasure and of love,
>   Venus here will choose her dwelling
>   And forsake her Cyprian grove.[3]

Dryden evidently was forced to realise that Purcell was right in asking for changes in the words—perhaps in manuscript even more changes were made than can be seen by comparing the printed text with the musical versions, for in his preface, after alluding to the alterations he had made for political reasons since he first wrote it 'seven years ago' and praising the composer, he first writes:—

There is nothing better than what I intended but the music, which has since arrived to a greater perfection in England than ever formerly—especially passing through the artful hands of Mr. Purcell, who has composed it with so great a genius that he has nothing to fear but an ignorant, ill-judging audience.

Then he goes on to explain why it may not read as well as it sounded—

But the numbers of poetry and vocal music are sometimes so contrary that in many places I have been obliged to cramp my verses and make them rugged to the reader that they may be harmonious to the hearer—of which I have no reason to repent me, because these sorts of entertainment are principally designed for the ear and eye, and therefore in reason my art on this occasion ought to be subservient to his.

(though he has to finish by implying that Purcell's demands were ludicrous in the face of his own poetic skill).

And besides I flatter myself with an imagination that a judicious audience will easily distinguish betwixt the songs wherein I have complied with him and those in which I have followed the rules of poetry in the sound and cadence of the words. Notwithstanding all these disadvantages there is somewhat still remaining of the first spirit with which I wrote it.

So Dryden had no ear for the difference between the words for speaking and the words for reading. It was Purcell's genius for making English words sound natural when sung to better tunes than those of Lawes or Locke that made music and play into an organic whole in his three great dramatic operas—*Dioclesian*, *King Arthur*, and the 1692 musicalisation of *A Midsummer Night's Dream* called *The Fairy Queen*, in which the whole Shakespeare play was ornamented with a variety of entertainments, grand, charming or comic, far in excess of a limited dancing version recently given at Covent Garden.

Downes recorded that *King Arthur*, in which Josias Priest was also concerned, 'pleased the court and city, and being well performed was very gainful to the company': his comment on *The Fairy Queen* is illuminating:—

This in ornamentation was superior to the other two, especially in clothes, for all the singers and dancers, scenes, machines and decorations, all most profusely set off, and excellently performed, chiefly the instrumental and vocal part composed by the said Mr. Purcell, and dances by Mr. Priest. The court and town were wonderfully satisfied with it, but the expenses in setting it out being so great, the company got very little by it.

The great expense of ever more dazzlingly sumptuous scenery and costumes for such works landed Betterton in financial difficulties—even *Dioclesian* and *King Arthur* seem to have been not as profitable as Downes suggests, if we are to believe what Colley Cibber wrote in 1740. After all, he was nineteen when *Dioclesian* was produced, and no doubt heard, as he recorded, that 'the singers and dancers were better paid and embroidered' than the actors. All the dramatic operas, he said, were

set off with the most expensive decorations of scenes and habits, with the best voices and dancers. This sensual supply of sight and sound, coming in to the assistance of the weaker party, it was no wonder they should grow too hard for sense and simple nature, when it is considered how many more people there are that can see and hear than think or judge.

Possibly Purcell's great and growing popularity might eventually have drawn audiences even with less spectacular presentation, but he died in 1695, and no other English composer had his ability in setting English words tunefully—the last big dramatic work that is always attributed to him, new incidental music to the Davenant–Dryden–Shadwell *Tempest*, was, I am convinced, finished by someone else, for in some of the numbers there are false accentuations and over-elongated weak syllables that are entirely alien to Purcell's instinct and practice, quite apart from the fact that the Dance of the Winds is almost note for note the same as the Storm music for Envy's entrance in Lully's *Cadmus et Hermione*, which we know had been played in London nearly ten years before: [4] obviously someone else put the 'Purcell' *Tempest* score together and, to judge from the French addition, it is not impossible that the arranger was Grabu himself, who was still in London and gave a concert in the winter of 1694.

Other foreigners had begun to give concerts in London—an Italian lady twice in January 1692 and a fine singer named Giuseppe Felice Tosi twice in 1693—and some sections of fashionable society had begun to take them up, as can be seen from the conversation at a music meeting in a play to which Purcell wrote music in 1691, *The Wives' Excuse*:—

Friendall.	Ladies and gentlemen, how do you like the music?
Mrs. Sightly.	Oh, very fine, sure, sir!
Mrs. Witwoud.	What say you to 't, young gentleman?
Springame.	. . . the music's extremely fine.
Wellvile.	Especially the vocal part. For I did not understand a word on 't.
Friendall.	Nor I, faith, Wellvile, but the words were Italian, they sung well, and that's enough for the pleasure of the ear. . . . Wilding, thou hast been so busy about that young girl there, thou know'st nothing of the matter.
Wilding.	O sir, you are mistaken, I am a great admirer—
Friendall.	—of everything in petticoats!
Wilding.	—of these musical entertainments: I am very musical, and love any call that brings the women together.

He certainly gives an honest reason for liking music, and admits he knows nothing about it, but thought that sonatas and chaconnes were Italian violinists.

So the fops at whom Dryden had sneered over twenty years before for patronising French operas they could not understand, were now taking up Italian singers who were as unintelligible as they had been to Pepys twenty-five years before. But with the death of Purcell at the age of thirty-six in 1695, the foreigners had no serious opposition, and society began to encourage the invasion of foreign artists, with the result that at the turn of the century fashionable London was ready for Italian opera.

[1] It certainly must have been after the 1689 Coronation of the Protestant William III, as the Epilogue boasts that the girls are Protestants and scoffs at Rome allowing 'strange tricks to please her sons'—which may have referred to the rumour of the warming-pan that was said to have smuggled a fake son

and heir into the Palace: neither boast nor scoff would have been so spoken when Catholic James was King. D'Urfey in his preface to *Love for Money: or The Boarding School* (published 1691) states that he wrote that play 'in June last' and that he had been accused of ungraciously using it to expose the 'Boarding School near London' where he had stayed 'all last summer': he certainly denies that he ever had more than common courtesies from them, 'which I may fairly say I have equally returned', and says the scene of his play 'might have been York as well as Chelsea'—the latter place having been chosen by him for its beauty—but D'Urfey protests too hard, and I think that, as gossip said, it was at Chelsea that he stayed, and that he returned their courtesies to him by writing the *Dido* Epilogue, which also negatively refers to the scurrilous scandals that he put into the play.

[2] Nicoll says November, but the London Gazette for June 12–16 advertises the first edition of the text and for July 3–7 announces that the music will be printed.

[3] Merely for amusement—unless the information is one day proved true—here is a personal experience connected with 'Fairest Isle'. As all musicians know, it is quite uncertain whether the last note of the phrase to which 'isles' is sung should be A natural or A flat—Professor Westrup logically criticises me as the editor of the Purcell Society Edition of *King Arthur* for 'sitting on the fence with a vengeance' by printing A flat in the sung version which was collated from various MSS. and A natural in the instrumental version which was taken from the printed (but not always correct) *Ayres for the Theatre*. Many years ago, at a time when I was so tied up in the straight theatre that I had no time to think of music, I dreamed—although I have never had any premonitions or any pretensions to psychic experiences—that Mrs. Purcell told me the mistake lay, not in the A—which was natural, but in the note on the first syllable of the following word 'excelling' which should be B flat not G. Without claiming this 'evidence' to be irrefutable, I would point out—before other professors laugh—that, apart from this reading avoiding the tritone which the A natural makes, contrary to Purcell's usual practice, a carelessly written B flat without a clear leger-line could easily, as Professor Dent agreed, be copied as a G. The higher note gives a more grateful phrase to sing and admirably suits the words: it is true that the voice-part would then make consecutive fifths with the bass, but these would be mitigated by the contrary motion and it seems to me so good that I hope the Mrs. Purcell of my dream was not pulling my leg!

[4] Mlle. M. L. Pereyra, Assistant Secretary to the Société Française, first pointed this out to me in 1931 and remarked that 'Arise, ye subterranean winds' (with its false roulade on 'sub-') seems to be similarly Lullian: whether the song is an isolated imitation of Lully by Purcell or not, there are no grounds for suspecting, as M. Prunières did in a concert-programme including parts of *Cadmus* on October 27, 1931, that Purcell passed off the Lully storm-music as his. This, coupled with the many false accentuations, shows that Purcell only wrote some of the music in the *Tempest* score as we know it from the Purcell Society Edition collated from non-contemporary manuscripts.

PART TWO

Up to 1800

SOUND

Interior of the King's Theatre, Haymarket, 1791.
This is the second theatre on the site and forms a link
between Handel's Opera and Her Majesty's of the
nineteenth century

CHAPTER ONE

Italian Opera Introduced

THE casual reader of the average book on the history of music or opera in England can hardly be blamed for thinking that Italian operas successfully flooded the London theatres in the eighteenth century, and that for the first fifty years at least Handel was the only opera-composer accepted by the audiences. There is also a strong impression that although there were controversies and rivalries in the opera-world at the time of Handel, they were merely fostered by jealous enemies, and so are not worth recalling.

Handel was certainly put on an operatic pedestral by his society friends, but they hardly succeeded in keeping him there, and his adverse critics, who refused to be swayed by fashion, by no means consisted of unsuccessful musicians: nor, though Italian opera became a society craze for short lengths of time and really at one theatre only, did it either monopolise the London stage or prove a great success artistically or financially, except when it attracted the man in the street with exceptionally fine singers, coupled on occasion with some startling theatrical device or intriguing story. Most Italian operas that were performed in London in the eighteenth century are now merely names in books and seldom-looked-at scores in libraries, while many of the more numerous English musical works [1] were, and even still are, often revived for the sake of tunes that were more generally attractive than the sometimes better written music of the Italians.

The very first real opera to be performed in London in the eighteenth century was English, and was the first public production of Purcell's *Dido and Aeneas*: this was given at the old Lincoln's Inn Fields Theatre in 1700, most unsuitably as an addition to Charles Gildon's alteration of Shakespeare's *Measure for Measure*. At Drury Lane a dramatic opera of the Shadwell type, *The Grove, or Love's Paradise*, with music by Henry Purcell's brother, Daniel, appeared in the same year, and two other dramatic operas, *The Island Princess* and *The Virgin Prophetess*, in 1701, with a revival of Purcell's *Tempest* at Dorset Garden.

By 1703, however, foreign singers began to be fashionable, and society leaders attended subscription-concerts 'to hear a parcel of Italian eunuchs, like so may cats, squall out somewhat you don't understand', as one of the characters in Thomas Baker's *Tunbridge-Walks* says, and in 1704, as quoted in Corey's *The Metamorphosis*, an Italian concert singer won great popularity with 'a squall somewhat like singing'. It is true that in those two years there were revivals of Purcell's *Circe*, *Timon*, *The Libertine* and *Dido and Aeneas*, as well as the prototype of English dramatic opera, Locke's *Psyche*, but the trend towards Italian opera was so strong that on December 14, 1704, the architect John Vanbrugh and his fellow dramatist William Congreve, both about thirty-five, were granted a licence to perform all kinds of theatre entertainments, including operas, 'at any convenient place'.

The patentee of both Drury Lane and Dorset Garden theatres, Christopher Rich, evidently had the same idea, for on December 30 he engaged the lovely English singer, Catherine Tofts, who seems to have made her debut in a concert the year before, to sing for one year from January 5, 1705, and on January 16 she appeared at Drury Lane in the first Italian opera to be seen in London. This was *Arsinoe, Queen of Cyprus*, originally produced at Bologna with music by Franceschini in 1676.

For England, however—partly, no doubt, because a full evening's entertainment with continuous music was a novelty—the Italian libretto by Stanzani was translated, and, when first printed, attention was drawn to the fact that it was not like the English dramatic opera in the description, 'An opera after the Italian manner. All sung.' The music was put together—whether arranged or composed is not known—by Thomas Clayton, a former member of William III's band who had just been studying in Italy, and it was sung in English by an all-English cast—Leveridge, Cook and Mrs. Cross (these three had sung in some seven stage works by Purcell during his lifetime), Hughes, Mrs. Lindsey and Mrs. Tofts—while between the acts Italian songs were sung by Mrs. Tofts's foreign rival, Margarita de l'Epine,[2] who had been in London since 1692.

These were perhaps the first prima donnas in London whose partisans fostered operatic rivalry, for one Saturday night the foreign singer was greeted with hisses and 'throwing of oranges' from a former servant of Mrs. Tofts, who, after her maid's arrest, published a letter she had written to Rich, the manager of Drury Lane Theatre, saying:—

I hope no one will think it was in the least with my privity, as I assure you it was not. I abhor such practices, and I hope you will cause her to be prosecuted, that she may be punished as she deserves.

Leaders of society, whether swayed by patriotism or by love of music, took sides for or against the two fine singers: as was written by John Hughes at the time:—

> Music has learned the discords of the State
> And concerts jar with Whig or Tory hate.
> Here Somerset and Devonshire attend
> The British Tofts and every note commend,
> To native merit just, and pleased to see
> We've Roman hearts from Roman bondage free.
> There famed l'Epine does equal skill employ,
> While listening peers crowd to the ecstatic joy:
> Bedford to hear her song his dice forsakes,
> And Nottingham is raptured when she shakes:
> Lulled statesmen melt away their drowsy cares
> Of England's safety in Italian airs.

The appearance of the two singers the same evening must have drawn a large audience of rival partisans, and *Arsinoe* was a great success, being played over twenty times in its first year. Not everyone who saw it thought it was good, however: the anonymous author of *A Critical Discourse upon Operas in England, and a means proposed for their Improvement* (1709) [3]—Mr. X I shall call him, as I shall often refer to him, wrote of *Arsinoe*:—

There is nothing in it but a few sketches of antiquated Italian airs, so mangled and sophisticated that instead of *Arsinoe* it ought to be called the Hospital of the old, decrepit Italian Operas.

As it was the first of its kind, however, it was, he said, received with applause.

It certainly looks as if Clayton, whatever his merits as a musician, knew what he was about, for he definitely succeeded in his aim that he advertised in his preface to the published translation:—

The design of this entertainment being to introduce the Italian manner of singing to the English stage, which has not been before attempted, I was obliged to have an Italian opera translated, in which the words, however mean in some places, suited much better with that manner of music than others more poetical would do. The style of this music is to express the passions, which is the soul of music: and though the voices are not equal to the Italian, yet I have engaged the best that were to be found in England, and I have not been wanting—to the utmost of my diligence—in the instructing them. The music, being recitative, may not at first meet with that general acceptation as is to be hoped for, from the audience's being better acquainted with it: but if this attempt shall be a means of bringing this manner of music to be used in my native country, I shall think my study and pains very well employed.

The words undoubtedly were mean in some places, as for example in the aria quoted in George Hogarth's *Memoirs of the Musical Drama* (1838):—

Recit.   Queen of Darkness, sable Night,
                            Ease a wandering lover's pain!
Aria.   Guide me, lead me
                            Where the nymph whom I adore—

(So ends the first section quite definitely and unintelligibly: then comes the middle section:—)

                            Sleeping, dreaming,
                            Thinks of love and me no more.

Then come the first two lines again *da capo* making complete nonsense:—

                            Guide me, lead me
                            Where the nymph whom I adore.

But though the words might be 'mean', Clayton certainly helped to introduce Italian all-sung opera. In the meantime Vanbrugh and Congreve had found a 'convenient place' for their theatre in the 'second stableyard going up the Hay Market', which they bought for £2,000, and, three months after the Drury Lane *Arsinoe*, their newly built theatre, the Queen's, opened on Easter Monday, April 9, 1705.

Their first operatic production, obviously intended to outshine the Englished Italian opera of the rival house, was an Italian pastoral opera performed in Italian, *The Loves of Ergasto*.[4] It was composed by Giacomo Greber, who had come to England with Mrs. Tofts's rival, de l'Epine, his pupil and known as 'Greber's Peg'. This opera was, as Downes said,

performed by a new set of singers arrived from Italy—the worst that ever came from thence, for it lasted but five days [5] and, they being liked but indifferently by the gentry, they in a little time marched back to their own country.

At one time, as Downes called it a 'foreign opera' and as Cibber later called it a 'translated opera, to Italian music', there was uncertainty as to what language it was performed in, but in 1921 W. J. Lawrence proved that Downes, who had given the right date, was also right about the Italian singers (Burney in his *History of Music* only mentioned the 'Italian boy') by finding the Epilogue by Congreve that was spoken

at the opening of the Queen's Theatre in the Haymarket with an Italian Pastoral

in which it is made quite clear:—

> To novelty we know you can be true,
> But what, alas! or who is always new?
> This day without presumption we pretend
> With novelty entire you're entertained,
> For not alone our house and scenes are new,
> Our song and dance, but ev'n our actors too.
> Our play itself has something in't uncommon—
> Two faithful lovers and one constant woman.
> In sweet Italian strains our shepherds sing:
> Of harmless loves our painted forests ring
> In notes perhaps less foreign than the thing.
> To sound and show at first we make pretence:
> In time we may regale you with some sense—
> But that at present were too great expense.

(Still the stress on sound—which now comes first—and show, with a vague hope of sense in the future!)

The Loves of Ergasto was therefore the first Italian opera sung in Italian in London, though in 1703, as Burney recorded, Italian 'interludes and mimical entertainments of singing and dancing' had been given in London, which, however, could not have been, as he thought, 'the first attempt at dramatic music in action perhaps in the kingdom'. The anonymous critic of 1709, Mr. X, said that this, the first pastoral opera to be seen in London, was such a failure 'that the undertakers of the opera ought to tremble at the very name of "pastoral" '. It must be remembered at the same time that *The Loves of Ergasto* was an isolated experiment at a theatre which presented a repertoire of English plays.

Christopher Rich at once seized the opportunity to sneer professionally at the Italian performances at the new theatre with all the British patriotism the Theatre Royal, Drury Lane, could justifiably show. On April 23—St. George's Day—only a fortnight after the *Ergasto* first night, the Epilogue to *The Tender Husband* by Sir Richard Steele at Drury Lane pleaded:—

F   161

Britons, who constant war with factious rage
For liberty against each other wage,
From foreign insult save the English stage!
No more th'Italian squalling tribe admit
In tongue unknown! 'Tis Popery in wit!

There was even more justification of this protest from Drury Lane, where English was considered the right language for the English theatre, for at the Queen's foreign artists shared the stage with Congreve and many fine English actors who had appeared in his plays at Lincoln's Inn Fields—the remains, Cibber said, 'of the best set of actors that I believe were ever known at once in England by time, death, and the satiety of their hearers mouldering to decay'. They were headed by Betterton, now past seventy, the introducer of many foreign theatre tricks in the past, and they were now content to tolerate foreign artists because for the first time they were guaranteed salaries instead of being on share terms.

Not that Rich at Drury Lane was against novelty in the theatre, even when it came from abroad—after all, to the jealous fury of his dancers, he would have introduced an elephant on the Dorset Garden stage if the theatre could have stood up to a wider entrance in the walls, and only Cibber's outspoken public protest had cut short the engagement of rope-dancers—he had even given *Arsinoe*, the first Italian opera in London, though it is true he had given it in English.

Nor were the two theatres in fact as rival as they publicly pretended, for Christopher Rich controlled not only Drury Lane, of which he was patentee, but the Queen's also, as managed by his factotum Owen Swiney or McSwiney. Vanbrugh probably was too busy working on Blenheim Palace, which he started on in April.

The new Queen's Theatre, Cibber wrote, was, however, built too expensively far out among the green fields and though 'a vast, triumphal piece of architecture', was not so good for the straight actors as the old plain Lincoln's Inn Fields Theatre.

For what could their vast columns, their gilded cornices, their immoderate high roofs avail, when scarce one word in ten could be distinctly heard in it?

The fifteen-foot-high vaulted roof was chiefly at fault:—

This extraordinary and superfluous space occasioned such an undulation from the voice of every actor that generally what they said sounded like the gabbling of so many people in the lofty aisles in a cathedral.

The tone of a trumpet or the swell of an eunuch's holding note, 'tis true, might be sweetened by it, but the articulate sounds of a speaking voice were drowned by the hollow reverberations of one word upon another.

How often, even up to recent times, have architects constructed ingenious buildings as theatres that failed from the theatrical or acoustical point of view! An example of curved surfaces causing the undulation of the speaking voice can be seen at the present Sadler's Wells Theatre, where some years ago plays were discontinued in favour of operas partly because of the multiple blur resulting from speaking towards the curved side walls joining the proscenium.

Obviously by 1705 singers were beginning to realise their scarcity value during this new craze for opera, for a singer known as the Baroness, who had sung for Vanbrugh and Congreve up to November of this year, soon claimed money due for breach of a verbal contract made at the Sign of the Cock in Bow Street. At the same time Mrs. Tofts refused to sing again for Rich, because he withheld money from her for not singing when she had lost her voice—entirely, she claimed (like many singers before and since), through his making her sing three times in one week, though the weather was too hot for any audience and the town was empty (no doubt her real reason for losing her voice).

The rival managements were forced to meet the claims of the rival singers—ten guineas a performance for the Baroness at the Queen's, and for Mrs. Tofts £16 13s. 4d. a performance, the practice-room to dress in, two women dressers and for the gentlemen who rehearsed with her at Drury Lane two bottles of wine per rehearsal. Incidentally the opera-singers were better paid than the actors—Vanbrugh paid Mrs. Bracegirdle only £5 per performance if receipts allowed, with a guarantee of £3, which worked out at £100 per annum for two performances a week.[6]

So the occasional opera was still given among the plays at both houses, the first being a revival of *Arsinoe* at Drury Lane in January 1706. In the same month Rich contracted with the German–Italian violoncellist, Nicolo Haym, who had been in London just a year, to prepare another opera for him, and engaged one Mr. Northman to translate it. It had been produced first in Naples in 1696 as *Il Trionfo di Camilla, Regina de Volsci*. Rich stipulated that Haym should continue playing in the orchestra at Drury Lane, though he generously allowed him to accompany his pupil,

Joanna Maria, when she sang at the Queen's—the singer usually known, Allardyce Nicoll thinks, as the Baroness.

At the Queen's a new English dramatic opera was given in February—*The British Enchanters: or, No Magic like Love*, by Granville, Lord Lansdowne. This opera, Downes said, was

very exquisitely done, especially the singing part—making love the acme of all terrestrial bliss, which infinitely arrided both sexes and pleased the town as well as any English modern opera.

Incidentally in the preface the author expressly says the dialogue is not to be treated as recitative, but this production did not mean that the Queen's had dropped Italian opera, for in March another was given, called *The Temple of Love*, by a double-bass player, Giuseppe Saggione—Mr. Sidgeon, as Downes Anglicised him. But the first round of the fight between Italian and English as the best operatic language in London theatres was lost by Italy, for this opera was sung in English and the whole cast was English, except for some French dancers and the composer's wife, Maria Gallia—yet another name, Allardyce Nicoll thinks, for Joanna Maria, the Baroness.

The Temple of Love lasted only six days, however, and did not come up to expectations—indeed even the Epilogue to it sneers at the new craze :—

> Get some famed opera, anyhow translated,
> No matter, so the tother house don't get it!
> Get clothes, though the actors with halfpay dispense!
> Get whims, get anything . . . but sense!

Later, Mr. X said this opera was

so poor and trivial (indeed the author and the work seem to be both of a piece) that probably it might have passed muster in the Indies or some other barbarous countries where music was hardly ever heard of, but 'twas impossible it should take in London, where nothing but what is excellent in its kind is secure of applause.

In contrast to this, Drury Lane revived *King Arthur*, and at the beginning of April the Queen's also returned to English dramatic opera with D'Urfey's *Wonders in the Sun: or, The Kingdom of the Birds*. This failed to draw the town for more than nine perform-ances, though the first five made a consecutive run—a rarity then: but the jolly ballad tunes, many of which D'Urfey printed in *Wit and Mirth, or Pills to purge Melancholy*, did become popular,

and the comic songs were later inserted most unsuitably in a production of *King Lear*.

But it is not surprising that *Wonders in the Sun* was not a greater
success, for only a week before, on March 30, 1706, Christopher Rich
had presented his new Italian opera, *Camilla*, the music arranged
by Nicolo Haym from the original score of ten years before by
one of the Bononcini brothers—some experts say Giovanni, and
some his younger brother Marcantonio, the libretto Englished by
Mr. Northman, and all sung in English by the following English
singers: Mrs. Tofts, Mrs. Lindsey, Leveridge, Ramondon, Turner,
Hughes and 'the Boy', whose name was Holcombe—with the
addition of the one foreigner, 'Mrs. Joanna Maria', who, strangely
enough, sang at both rival opera theatres.

Camilla was not only a success, it had more revivals and more
performances in the eighteenth century than any other opera.
Mr. X thought it a fine work—'royal', he called it (incidentally, he
said its admirable music was by Giovanni Bononcini), and after
his criticisms of the earlier operas, he approved of the universal
applause it got because it was performed 'in a more regular method
than any of the former (though much of its beauty was lost in the
English language)'. He remarked that

before this every man that had the least smattering in music undertook to compose an opera, but upon the appearance of *Camilla* all their projects vanished into
nothing: they who before bragged of their undertakings were now ashamed to
own 'em, and they who had valued themselves upon having almost finished
their work began now to deny they had so much as set about it, so that at
least six or seven embryos of operas that had no being but in the airy conceptions of their pretended composers became abortive, and everyone joined
in the admiration of *Camilla*.

So for the moment, as Italian opera was a success only when it
was Englished, there was no grave risk of the English stage being
swamped by it. After all, of the three operas performed at the
Queen's in 1706 only one was Italian, while at least fourteen
English plays were given. Still the novelty of Italian opera did
seem to forebode danger to many people, and in 1706 the critic
John Dennis expressed his fears in no uncertain way in an essay
which in its very title was outspoken. He called it

An essay on the operas after the Italian manner which are about to be established
on the English stage, with some reflections on the damage which they may
bring to the public.

In the preface he makes it quite clear that he is only attacking operas that were all sung, not the English dramatic operas, and comments that while stage-plays have recently been criticised as being immoral,

the Italian opera . . . is a diversion of more pernicious consequence than the most licentious play that ever has appeared upon the stage.

His chief point is that the Italian language is not as vigorous as that of the ancient Romans but is made up of 'soft and effeminate measures', which makes sense on the stage give way to sound, and he seems to think that every day conversation has equally deteriorated.

In the essay itself he hopes that

while the English arms are everywhere victorious abroad, the English arts may not be vanquished and oppressed at home by the invasion of foreign luxury,

and goes on to say that

in whatever countries operas have been established after the manner of Italy they have driven out poetry from among the people,

so that now (1706) there has not been a poet in Italy for a hundred years and there is none in France, as Boileau is too old. In England now few plays can do without singing and dancing, for

the generality of our audiences are far more capable of a pleasure of sense than of a delight of reason.[7] Now music that is not subservient to reason, especially if it be soft and effeminate, is a mere delight of sense, and, as somebody has observed that friendship grows insipid to those who have tasted of love, it grows exceeding difficult even for those who are capable of the severe delights of reason to make a pleasing return to them.

Dennis remarks how hard it is to give up sensual pleasures when they have become habitual, and claims that as music that has nothing to do with common sense must be only sensual, even an unintelligent footman may judge it better than his presumably more intelligent master.

He thinks that the vigorous English language with its strong consonants

cannot be pronounced without very frequently shutting the mouth, which is diametrically opposite to the expressing of music:

and as music is essentially not vigorous, the mind easily becomes slack, and

the whole man is dissolved in the wantonness of effeminate airs.

Incidentally, he remarks on the fact that foreigners are applauded for singing and dancing in London, when English performers doing the same would be damned—not quite true in view of the popularity of the English artists, but obviously the undampable clique of would-be artistic connoisseurs aired their ignorant disparagements of native talent, as they always do to the present day.

In the choruses of Greek Tragedy, Dennis said:—

music is only for the sake of the sense, in the opera the sense is most apparently for the sake of the music.

(Where good composers were concerned, Dennis was, of course, wrong, but second-rate composers and second-rate connoisseurs have always claimed that artistic or effective music is all that matters—I once produced an opera in which the composer expected some sixty singers and dancers to be able to leave the stage in two short bars of music and refused to add more, as it would have spoiled the musical shape of the work.) Dennis rather implies that he does not rate the Italian operas in London very high, for he says that

though the opera in Italy is a monster, 'tis a beautiful harmonious monster, but here in England 'tis an ugly howling one,

and he says it is as stupid to transplant such a native sort of music as it would be to expect the Kent or Sussex farmers to grow olives, oranges or muscatels instead of corn, fruit or hops: at the end he gives a warning:—

Let us take heed that as we have taken the opera from the nations which we despise, it renders us not contemptible to those very nations.

[1] In Allardyce Nicoll's invaluable lists at the end of his *Eighteenth Century Drama: 1700–1750* the Italian operas are far fewer than the English musical shows, without including the numerous pantomimes and drolls.

[2] Francesca Margarita de l'Epine also signed herself Françoise Marguerite. Was she Italian–French?

[3] See p. 180 *sqq.*

[4] Called by Cibber *The Triumph of Love*, probably confusing it with either *The Temple of Love* (1706) or *Love's Triumph* (1708).

[5] Allardyce Nicoll and Löwenberg record only two performances fifteen days apart which seems unlikely for a novelty in a new theatre. Was Downes perhaps right in this as in other matters?

[6] The claims and proposals and figures are quoted from the Lord Chamberlain's records printed by Allardyce Nicoll in *Eighteenth Century Drama: 1700–1750*.

[7] It is unfortunate that the word 'sense' may either stand for what is sensible or for one of the senses, and still more unfortunate that Dennis uses it in both meanings. However the context makes it clear which he means.

CHAPTER TWO

Italian Singers Introduced

WHETHER Dennis was right or not about Italian opera being soft and effeminate, it certainly was 'about to be established on the English stage'. One of the first signs was that foreign singers began to take over parts from the English singers in 1707—and not at the Queen's, but at Drury Lane, where Rich must have changed his patriotic mind: Maria Gallia replaced Miss Cross in *Arsinoe* on February 18, and on March 8 the male soprano Valentini, as Valentino Urbani was called, replaced Hughes in *Camilla*. Valentini, Cibber remembered, was the first distinguished Italian singer and a fine actor

but with a throat too weak to sustain those melodious warblings for which the fairer sex have since idolised his successors. However, his defect was so well supplied by his action that his hearers bore with the absurdity of his singing in his first part of Turnus in *Camilla*, all in Italian, while every other character was sung and recited to him in English.

As Cibber later recorded, the managements began to pay 'extraordinary prices to singers, dancers and other exotic performers' —'exotic' meaning, of course, 'foreign' (an invariable guarantee of brilliance to the would-be knowledgeables).

In the meantime, Thomas Clayton, encouraged by the success of his first operatic attempt *Arsinoe*, decided, as the 1709 critic Mr. X said, 'to compose another worse than the first'. This was a full-length all-sung English opera and was given at Drury Lane on March 4 as a counterblast to the invasion of Italian music— *Rosamond*, the libretto by Addison, the music by Clayton in imitation of the Italian style and with Maria Gallia in the title-part, no doubt as a sop to the fashionable audience that swarmed after the foreigners.

Addison sincerely and by no means unsuccessfully aimed at combining dramatic sense with the new Italian style of music— he certainly was praised by Thomas Tickell for his libretto in verses that were printed with the text and which begin:—

> The opera first Italian masters taught,
> Enriched with songs, but innocent of thought.

> Britannia's learned theatre disdains
> Melodious trifles and enervate strains,
> And blushes on her injured stage to see
> Nonsense well-tuned and sweet stupidity.

Tickell says to Addison:—

> Thy style hath matched what Ancient Romans knew,
> Thy flowing numbers far excel the new:
> Their cadence in such easy sound conveyed,
> That height of thought may seem superfluous aid:
> Yet in such charms the noble thoughts abound,
> That needless seem the sweets of easy sound.

Unfortunately, as will be seen, Clayton's music was perhaps too 'easy' and 'needless', though it seems to have taken him a year to write. Mr. X wrote that one of the embryo operas made abortive by *Camilla*

struggled through and mounted the stage on purpose to frighten all England with its abominable music, and this was the celebrated *Rosamond*, with the expectations of which the town had been full for a year together.

When at last it did appear it lasted only three nights, and Mr. X suggested that had it not been for a judicious outlay of money it would have lasted even less. He goes on to say of Clayton's two operatic attempts:—

I observed before, the first was a filthy fardle of old Italian airs, but I can't say the same of this, for indeed I don't know what to make of it.

He sums it up by saying

this opera is no better than a confused chaos of music, where there is everything and nothing, and for my part I think the only thing to be liked in it is that it's short: and I believe if a reward was to be ordained for him that made the worst music in the world, the author of *Rosamond* would have reason to say he had not lost his labour, since he would have an undoubted title to the gratification.

Incidentally when the writer says 'author' he obviously alludes to the composer and this is worth remembering, because the librettist, Addison, was praised highly for his work. At the same time I think the choice of the word author—creator—shows that an opera at this time was thought of as a combination of everything that contributed to the entertainment, and not merely as a musical work that inevitably had words attached to it: all the comments of the time point to this conclusion that though tunes or singing may have drawn an audience, as they always do, that same audience as a whole expected stage excitement, acting, and at least a modicum of sense.

Rosamond was followed on April 1 by a pasticcio, a hotch-potch of music, by Scarlatti, Giovanni Bononcini, Albinoni, Gasparini and Steffani, cooked up by a German, John Christopher Pepusch, who had been in the Drury Lane orchestra for the last seven years, to a libretto by the Frenchman, Motteux, who had worked on *Camilla* and Saggione's *Temple of Love*, all under the supervision of a Swiss refugee, John James Heidegger, the 'Swiss Count', as he was called.

The new work was called *Thomyris, Queen of Scythia*, and was performed by an all-English cast except for Margarita de l'Epine, having been launched by a subscription organised by Heidegger, who, though no musician, made up with his gift of the gab what he lacked in personal looks—he was so hideous that he won an ugliness contest in which he just defeated an old woman by having her bonnet clapped on his head.

Thomyris called forth all Mr. X's scorn. The arranging of this pasticcio he attributes to Heidegger, whom he labels—by stating that his title of Count hails from the Land of the Moon—as another bogus but speciously artistic foreigner who, like Grabu, was able to get on with influential people and cash in on the growing fashion: as he says:—

It's something extraordinary that a person who knows not what composition, playing, or singing, or any other thing belonging to the profession means, should be taught by necessity how to make an opera. I hope I shall oblige the world in imparting so beneficial a secret to mankind, which will turn to a more profitable and certain account than the study of alchemy, or the philosopher's stone. The receipt is as follows:—

(Now comes the most biting description of how to put together a pasticcio opera—of which there were so many in the eighteenth century.)

Pick out about an hundred Italian airs from several authors,—good or bad, it signifies nothing. Among these make use of fifty-five or fifty-six of such as please your fancy best, and marshal 'em in the manner you think most convenient. When this is done, you must employ a poet to write some English words, the airs of which are to be adapted to the Italian music.

In the next place you must agree with some composer to provide the recitative, and promise to give him—in case the opera is performed—as little as possible: by this means you'll run no risk, being at little or no expense.

When this is done, you must make a bargain with some mongrel Italian poet to translate that part of the English that is to be performed in Italian: and then deliver it into the hands of some amanuensis, that understands music better than yourself, to transcribe the score and parts.

In the last place cajole the town into a lusty subscription, and—let this piece of patchwork, which you call your opera, though you know nothing of the matter, take or not—you can't fail of putting four or five thousand guineas into your pocket: for no less did the Count get by his doughty opera of *Thomyris*.

He goes on to say that if, after following this advice, you get blamed, you need only laughingly claim that you are justified on the grounds that the earlier and more skilful operas failed to make a third as much for their authors. He is, however, fair enough to admit that there were some fifteen or sixteen good airs in *Thomyris*, which was why it was not a failure, while there was not even one in all the other operas from *Arsinoe* in 1705 till 1709, with the great exception of *Camilla*, which was so unusually good that a repetition of its standard was not to be expected.

About a fortnight after *Thomyris* Addison's prologue to Edmund Smith's play, *Phaedra and Hippolitus*, further deplores the invasion of the London theatre by foreign nonsense:—

> Long has a race of heroes filled the stage
> That rant by note and through the gamut rage,
> In songs and airs express their martial fire,
> Combat in trills and in a fugue expire,
> While lulled by sound and undisturbed by wit,
> Calm and serene you indolently sit,
> And from the full fatigue of thinking free,
> Hear the facetious fiddles' repartee.
> Our homespun authors must forsake the field,
> And Shakespeare to the soft Scarlatti yield.

In the winter revival of *Camilla* at Drury Lane, Valentini and the Baroness replaced two English singers (though the Baroness tried to sing in English) and Valentini also appeared in the winter performances of *Thomyris*. So the infiltration continued, and the polyglot performances of opera meant that many English straight actors were losing their salaries, as Cibber wrote in his preface to *The Lady's Last Stake*, which was produced in December 1707:—

The use of their labour was to be swallowed up in the pretended merit of singing and dancing. I don't offer this as a reflection upon music (for I allow and feel its charm), but it has been the misfortune of that, as well as poetry, to have been too long in the hands of those whose taste and fancy are utterly insensible of their use and power.

He went on to say that the solution, which 'could never be beat into the impenetrable heads' of those in charge, was that operas and plays should not be run jointly: the present system was disastrous to both:—

Nay, even the opera, though the town has neither grudged it pay nor equipage, from either the wilfulness or ignorance of the same general, we see was not able to take the field till December.

In actual fact *Camilla* opened on November 15, but the criticism of the 'general', Owen McSwiney, the factotum of Drury Lane, was justified, especially as the opera was subscribed to by society— as Cibber wrote in the same play:—

when once a woman's the fashion, everybody follows her: she fills like a music-subscription,—though there's nothing in't, nobody will be out on't.

To judge from his *Apology for His Life* (1740), Cibber had long been advocating a union of the two companies, with actors at one theatre and singers at the other: this had only been prevented by Rich trying to cash in on music and acting at both. At the Queen's a revival of *The British Enchanters* was the only operatic production in 1707 among about fifteen plays including the first performance of *The Beaux' Stratagem*.

In December, however, the order was made to give plays at Drury Lane and operas at the Queen's, and at the beginning of 1708 Owen McSwiney leased the Queen's, Haymarket, in his own name, and got a monopoly of Italian operas in London, which he gave under the management of Heidegger twice a week, on Tuesdays and Saturdays, beginning with *Thomyris* and *Camilla*. Drury Lane at once—in February—ridiculed these operas with an interlude played in Buckingham's stage satire *The Rehearsal* and called *Prunella*. The author, once an actor and mimic, Richard Estcourt, printed on the title page

The sense and music collected from the most famous masters.

This he meant sarcastically, for he followed it with a quotation of Rochester's line

As charms are nonsense, nonsense seems a charm,

and he adds a note saying he will soon publish the complete opera of which *Prunella* is only a part, with a preface in praise of the fineness and delicacy of operas and the difference between an Italian opera and an opera in Italy.

In his preface to *Prunella* he says:—

I must own I attempt not to invade or abuse anyone's diversion, and could wish that my profession, which happens to be speaking, would afford that I should like no speaking better—though I must confess, if I am run away with by an air overnight, the nervous sense and admirable reason it is fraught with brings me back again in the morning.

He also adds, no doubt burlesquing the printed librettos:—

Pray note that all the airs that are marked thus, (") with, double commas are not performed to prevent being tedious, and all that are not inserted are left out.

The satire of the work itself chiefly consists in the use of tunes from *Arsinoe*, *Camilla* and *Thomyris* with words more or less similar to the originals but colloquialised so as to be suitable for characters who, instead of being royal, live round Covent Garden. As an example, which shows how well-known by now *Camilla* was, here are the words of one aria sung by Mrs. Tofts in that opera:—

> Fortune, ever known to vary,
> Now grown weary,
>   Changes to a smile her frown.
> Joys unknown are near attending,
> Never ending,
>   Happy hours move gaily on.

Here is the *Prunella* version which would fit the notes to the repeated lines of the original, though in print it looks unlikely:—

> Father is resolved I shall marry,
> Mammy has made him weary,
>   And has changed to a smile his frown:
> Joys of marriage, undividing,
> Till death abiding,
>   Honeymoon moves pleasing on.

A few days after *Prunella*'s first night the Queen's presented another Italian opera translated by Motteux, called *La Pastorella* in Italy but renamed *Love's Triumph* for London: this, too, was performed by a mixed cast including no less than three foreigners—the Baroness, de l'Epine and Valentini. This was another opera damned by Mr. X:—

If small villages are rendered famous in Italy by the loss of some battles fought near 'em, *The Triumph of Love* [sic] will grow notorious in *gradu musicati* for the desolation it brought upon the Queen's, which was so great that the then undertaker was constrained to abandon operas, foreseeing that a *Triumph of Love,* or two more, would of necessity undo him.

It had, he said, been a puppet opera for Cardinal Ottoboni in Rome—each puppet costing at least a hundred pistoles (about £80)—but Valentini had ignored this by putting it on the stage: he had left out almost all the recitative and had added 'a great number of noisy airs, that seemed to vie with each other which should be loudest': he had introduced choruses and dances 'after the French fashion', and had so changed the pastoral original that

that sort of milk which nourishes the happy shepherds on the fertile Arcadian plains grew hard and sour, and so curdled in the stomachs of those that tasted it, that they were surfeited with the first meal and dared not venture a second time on such disagreeable unwholesome food.

The Swiss Count, according to the writer, did know that he was ignorant, but Valentini had such a great opinion of himself that he thought

no one capable of directing him, but doing everything out of his own head, it's no wonder he has so grossly miscarried, and that his frequent mistakes have made the world entertain a mean opinion of his judgement.

He managed, however, to take a benefit night on the last of the opera's eight performances.

Although that opera might not have been successful, few plays succeeded

> without song or dance,
> Without Italian airs or steps from France,

as the Prologue to *The Maid the Mistress* said at Drury Lane in June 1708. A month later Vanbrugh prophesised much the same thing when he wrote on July 27 to the Earl of Manchester,

I lost so much money by the opera this last winter that I was glad to get quit of it, and yet I do not doubt that operas will thrive and settle in London.

The new 'undertaker' at the Queen's, McSwiney, like Vanbrugh before him, was 'so constrained to abandon operas' in 1708 that he failed to open his autumn season till December. Then, however, the famous male soprano, Nicolini, joined the other three foreigners at the Queen's. Cibber later recorded that this singer, 'by pleasing the eye as well as the ear, filled us with a more various and *rational* delight' (the italics are Cibber's).

His first appearance was in another mixed-language performance—this time of Scarlatti's fourteen-year-old *Pyrrhus and Demetrius* on December 14: the recitative was sung in English, for the sake of the plot no doubt, and the arias half in English and half in Italian to suit the singers—Nicolini, Valentini, the Baroness and de l'Epine, and their English rivals Mrs. Tofts, Cook, Ramondon and Turner.

Mr. X wrote that *Pyrrhus and Demetrius* had other arias added on to Scarlatti's fine music by the same adapter who arranged *Camilla*—Nicolo Haym—quite unnecessarily, but not incompetently: as it was produced soon after the death of Queen Anne's consort, Prince George of Denmark, it seemed too melancholy, but by 1709 it had become really popular and, as the writer shrewdly said, 'I think the public very seldom out in their judgement'. After commenting on the music, which he thought contained fine recitatives, some extremely beautiful airs, occasional longueurs, but a splendid second act—apart from a bad start and finish—he goes on to point out faults in what he clearly considers to be of the first importance in an opera—the logic and sense of the plot. Without retelling the story, his criticisms can be seen to be sound:—

This opera begins great and masterly, it ends low and poorly. No one knows what's become of Marius and Cleartes—

(obviously prominent characters earlier)

—as Deidamia is led out to suffer for her treason, Demetrius, being a true knight errant, on a sudden quits his former mistress, for whose sake he had made such a stir in the preceding acts, and consents to marry Deidamia on purpose to save her from the gallows.

There are some other improprieties in this opera, so that it's to be wished the person who has taken so much pains with it already would add a finishing stroke: a little more will make it a perfect piece, it being already the best we have on the English stage, abounding in extraordinary good airs without one that can be called mean or indifferent.

These inconveniences ought to admonish those who undertake to write words for an opera, to be more careful in the conduct of it.

But what may have been lacking in the opera itself was more than made up by the performances of Mrs. Tofts, Valentini and Nicolini—as Cibber recorded, 'three such excellent performers in the same kind of entertainment at once England till this time had never seen', and in this one winter McSwiney cleared a reasonable profit.

Pyrrhus was kept in the repertoire of the Queen's till May 1709, together with the good old standby *Camilla*, though in that opera more foreigners took the place of the English artists—for now not only did de l'Epine play the part the Boy had played, Prenesto, according to the published songs, but Nicolini, Valentini and the Baroness all appeared in it: this was a sad change from the original all-English production and one that struck many of the audience as ludicrous in spite of the fine singing—as W. R. Chetwood wrote forty years later in his *General History of the Stage*, it was

an odd medley—Mrs. Tofts, a mere Englishwoman in the part of Camilla, courted by Nicolini in Italian, without understanding one single syllable each other said or sung and on the other hand Valentini courting amorously in the same language a Dutchwoman that committed murder on our good old English with as little understanding as a parrot.

The operas this year were eked out with only five English plays at the same theatre.

In March 1709 a new Italian pasticcio, *Clotilda*, was given at the Queen's in Italian–English for some seven performances,[1] and this, Mr. X said, was an even worse medley than *Thomyris*: he blamed Heidegger again:—

He engaged the Venetian painters to make a new scene:[2] he introduced the novelty of Spanish habits on the stage, rarely or never seen in an opera before,— and I'm of opinion they will never be seen again: he drew out a guard of Moors to attend his Spanish monarch . . . but alas! it was all in vain.

There were, he said, some good airs by Bononcini, Scarlatti and Contini, but,

like rich embroideries on an ill-fashioned coat, which serve only to expose the ignorance of the tailor that knew not how to make a right use of such costly trimmings,

they merely showed up the whole: there was no real recitative and no composer's name was given, which was 'very prudent'.

By now the Italian invasion seemed to be gaining ground and

Mrs. Tofts temporarily left the stage and began to suffer mental disorder—whether from not unnatural resentment at the foreign flooding of the opera world or not—which often took the form of imagining herself still to be Camilla, Queen of the Volscians, singing her popular aria 'I was born of royal race'.

But the apparent success of opera started to wilt: as Cibber wrote, it soon

like the fine wife of a roving husband, began to lose its charms, and every day discovered to our satiety imperfections which our former fondness had been blind to.

This may have been partly due to the fact that in 1709 the new actors that went over to McSwiney at the Queen's—Wilks, Doggett, Cibber and Mrs. Oldfield—improved the acoustics of the house by narrowing it and lowering the ceiling, thereby removing 'those hollow undulations of the voice formerly complained of' and no doubt showing up imperfections of singing.

Much had been hoped from the novelty of opera—as Cibber wrote:—

By the short experience we had then had of operas, by the high reputation they seemed to have been arrived at the year before, by their power of drawing the whole body of nobility, as by enchantment, to their solemnities, by that prodigality of expense at which they were so willing to support them, what mountains did we not hope from this mole-hill?

But alas! the fairy vision vanished, this bridal beauty was grown familiar to the general taste, and satiety began to make excuses for its want of appetite: or, what is still stronger, its late admirers now as much valued their judgement in being able to find out the faults of the performers, as they had before in discovering their excellencies.

The truth is that this kind of entertainment being so entirely sensual, it had no possibility of getting the better of our reason but by its novelty, and that novelty could never be supported but by an annual change of the best voices, which, like the finest flowers, bloom but for a season and, when that is over, are only dead nosegays.

Cibber noticed what is still true, that invariably 'the nicest connoisseurs in music fall into such various heresies in taste, every sect pretending to be the true one'—and such a state of affairs invariably springs from and leads to a lack of common sense and general good taste.

It was perhaps symbolic of the partisan enthusiasm for what each sect thought opera should be that the old theatre in Dorset Garden—the stage which launched English dramatic opera of the

Shadwell type for which Purcell had written such finely drawn and yet theatrically exciting music—was pulled down in June 1709.

---

[1] This and all similar figures are taken from Allardyce Nicoll's invaluable dated lists of performances in his *Eighteenth Century Drama : 1700–1750*.

[2] W. J. Lawrence wrote in an article on 'The early years of the first English Opera House' in *The Musical Quarterly*, Vol. VII, 1922, that 'a new set of scenes painted by two famous Italian artists lately arrived from Venice' was added to the Queen's stock in May: there is some discrepancy here.

CHAPTER THREE

A Critical Discourse upon Operas

THE momentary enthusiasm for Italian opera was not truly shared by 'the whole body of the nobility', for, as Cibber recorded, an unfortunately anonymous

Nobleman of the first rank, then in a high post and not out of court favour, said openly behind the scenes, 'It was shameful to take part of the actors' bread from them to support the silly diversion of people of quality.'

There were many music-lovers, too, who were not prepared to accept Italians as necessarily the finest singers, though they were quite ready to welcome musical stage-works from any country provided they were good of their kind, intelligible and dramatic.

So in 1709 somebody thought it high time to try to put matters right by publishing anonymously *A Critical Discourse upon Operas in England, and a Means proposed for their Improvement*, which gives the comments on all operas from *Arsinoe* to *Clotilda* that I have attributed to Mr. X. His *Discourse* was added to *A Comparison between the French and Italian Music and Operas, translated from the French* of the Abbé Raguenet.[1]

Interesting as it is, the *Comparison* itself has no bearing on operas in London, but some of the notes added by the translator are of great value in building up a picture of the first years of Italian opera in London as seen at the time. Here is his view of the difference between the botched-up pasticcio opera and a real opera:—

Old pieced-up operas are not what fall so properly under our consideration in this place. They having been formerly performed on some other theatres are occasionally fitted up for a present convenience or necessity, and several airs are altered or omitted, according to the fancy or ability of the singers, without the approbation or knowledge of the composer. Sometimes whole scenes are changed and are thereby rendered incoherent, when they are revived to answer an emergency in case a new one that's upon the stocks should have the misfortune to be disliked.

But this liberty is by no means allowed in a new opera, where the singers are not suffered to alter anything, but to observe in every particular the composer's directions. The music in these operas has generally speaking as great a connexion as the words, and the poetry is conducted with as much regularity as the music will admit of.

Mr. X, the translator, thinks that Italian operas are the best models and in them

the heroic parts are made to speak with propriety enough: their thoughts are just and the style heightened as much as the nature of the thing will admit, for a studied sublimity or purity in lines designed for music is useless and improper, since the ear will naturally be more employed in listening to the notes than the words.

Commenting on the statement by the Abbé that France has more bass singers than Italy and that they are suitable for such characters as kings, gods and the like, the translator very logically stresses a common-sense fact which still is not acceptable in the theatre—an example of how real life cannot be put on the stage:—

I can't think the bass voice more proper for a king, a hero or any other distin-guished person than the counter-tenor, since the difference of voice in man is merely accidental. . . . I can't see why the part of Caesar or Alexander may not properly enough be performed by a counter-tenor or tenor or any other voice, provided—

(and this is interesting, seeing the number of musicians who think that at this period of opera history, the voice was all that mattered)

[provided] the performer in acting as well as singing is able to maintain the dignity of the character he represents.

It is difficult for us to accept the idea of a soprano king, although many real-life leaders of men have had high-pitched voices which by no means imply effeminacy (one of the most uxorious men I know has a colourless falsetto voice): but I think the writer has hit on the truth, both for the stage and real life, that the voice does not matter so long as the right personality is there, but when the personality is not there the conventional association of a deep voice with power is a safer guide.

The French theatre, says the Abbé, prides itself rightly on its choruses and dances, but the English translator says:—

I can by no means approve the unseasonable interruptions the French operas receive from their choruses and dances which frequently top upon the music.

He quotes as an example Valentini's production of *Love's Triumph* in 1708:—

I can't but observe that the pastoral opera performed some time since in our English stage called *Love's Triumph*, though the composition was Italian, yet, being directed by one who can't compose himself—and is consequently improper for such an undertaking, being fit only to sing when his voice will permit him—

(That's a nasty hit!)

—I say, this pastoral, being stuffed out with dance and chorus after the French fashion, was so disrelished by the audience that the second night of its representation the whole town in a manner forsook it and left the undertaker to sit down with the loss.[2]

He goes on to stress the point:—

This is an instance of the nice taste of the English, who could not endure an Italian piece Frenchified as this was, but considered opera purely as a musical invention, able to subsist without dances, which are adventitious, whereas music is essential to it.

(It must be remembered that to him music included a characterised performance of it.)

The French objected to the Italian habit of introducing comic buffoonery scenes, but the footnote to this points out that comic characters may well be introduced if sensibly, as in *Camilla*, in which they 'mingle very naturally with the serious without any interruption of the story'.

The French claimed to have better violinists, oboists and flautists than Italy: the English writer retorted that in London Paisible and Banister were better flautists and the Flemish Loeillet was a better oboist than any in France: he admitted, however, that operatic costumes in France were naturally richer and better than in any other part of the world, as they were paid for in the first place by the King, 'being all right gold and silver', while the costumes in Italy, though they were 'all false and cost very little' were elegant and new for each opera each season and 'they make a good appearance and are by no means to be despised'.

In Italy ornamental passages for the voice were usually sung on the vowel 'a', in France on an indefinite vowel, and, says the translator in his note to this:—

The English singers are guilty of much the same fault: they make their divisions without any choice upon the vowel 'o', 'i', and 'u' indifferently. This is a vicious habit and they would do well to break themselves of it.

(It must be remembered that at this time it was usually the singers who ornamented the music, not the composer.)

He very strongly approved of the bolder chromatics, cadences and dissonances that were to be found in Italian music, rather than the 'soft, easy, flowing, coherent' little tunes of the French, and as examples refers to an excellent song full of vocal harshness in *Clotilda*, which was quite wrongly omitted in the London production, and two in *Pyrrhus and Demetrius* with such wonderful modulation that 'one can't comprehend the meaning of this artful harshness in music better': in fact, Scarlatti

makes use of all sorts of dissonance to express the force of the words, and afterwards resolves 'em so well that indeed the most beautiful concords are hardly so sweet and harmonious as his discords.

(If only we could hear old music with contemporary ears, instead of taking for granted what to them was new and strange!)

The singer Nicolini—his real name being Nicolino Grimaldi— is greatly praised in the footnotes to passages on singing: there it is said that when in London 'Cavaliero Nicolino de Napoli' (he had been ennobled in Italy for his singing),

with his most charming voice and that great use and skill he hath in music never sings but he captivates his audience, and sometimes launches out with such divisions and swellings as one would think it impossible for him to get clear again: and yet, after having held the audience in some suspense, he changes the concern they had for the music into so great a pleasure that they are forced to vent the oppression they had received from such a contravariety in a universal applause.

It must be remembered that a singer at that time often added such ornamentations and crescendi spontaneously and was largely judged from the suitability, effectiveness and difficulty of these inventions, which often might range far away from the general key and only come home to the final cadence satisfactorily when conceived with artistry. Nicolini added a fine realistically dramatic scene to *Pyrrhus and Demetrius* in London, said a footnote, which

notwithstanding its excellent music would have been esteemed as nothing, had it not been performed by one so perfect in the art of acting as Nicolini is.

Nicolini's skill in acting will be referred to again, and it is worth noting not only that his voice was not his sole attraction, but the standard of acting in music must at that time have been very high, or at least more convincingly full-blooded than the average acting of to-day, for, alluding to the Abbé's statement that often an Italian violinist is seized with an unavoidable agony, he tortures his violin, he racks his body, he is no longer master of himself, but is agitated like one possessed with an irresistible motion,

the anonymous translator records that was certainly true of Corelli, 'whose eyes will sometimes turn as red as fire, his countenance will be distorted, his eyeballs roll in agony'.

Nicolini apparently, though he got extraordinary applause for his performance in *Pyrrhus*, did not get as much in London as he used to do in Italy,

which is not to be wondered at, when we consider the English are not yet thoroughly acquainted with the beauties of the Italian music and the force of their words, and consequently they can't be proper judges of the action that is applied to those words: besides the English stage is not accustomed to such acclamations, which are the effects of madness more than pleasure. It is to be observed that Nicolini is the chief actor in Italy.

(Now unfortunately we are quite used to acclamations that are the effects of madness more than pleasure—the Italian colony applauding the worst Italian opera performances, balletomanes the most slipshod fouettés, devotees of film-stars, crooners or band-leaders their little gods—in fact, as Ella Wheeler Wilcox said in a different context, 'Foolish fan!'.)

The construction of each musical scene in French operas is weak, said the Abbé Raguenet, while the Italians, said the translator, always end each scene with 'some air that is sure to please', followed by an exit, and finish each act with 'some full loud song to leave an impression on the audience and draw 'em into a commendation of the opera'. The principle behind this is of course sound, examples quoted in a footnote being the first two acts of *Camilla*, while examples can easily be seen to-day in musical shows which still aim to drop the curtain on some exciting or cumulative scene so as to send everyone away to the bars exuberant and chattering.

The comments on recitative are illuminating, especially to-day when most conductors, musicians and voice-trainers insist on singers vocalising all recitatives with full voice and lovely smooth tone. Raguenet considered that French recitative was better than Italian,

which can't properly be called singing. Their recitative is little better than downright speaking, without any inflexion or modulation of the voice:

the translator pointed out that in French opera the recitatives and the arias were indistinguishable (an insufferable fault, he said) and though he admitted that Italian recitative was difficult to appreciate for people who were not used to it or could not understand the language,

yet they that understand it reckon it the greatest beauty in music, and I believe they are right, considering how much art and knowledge is necessary for the composing, playing and singing it.

He makes a further excellent point:—

Were it not for the recitative, the great number of airs huddled together would soon cloy the audience, and the beauty of one would be lost in that of the other immediately following.[3]

Nicolini, he said, was a past master of recitative, while Valentini was nearly as good, 'and those that endeavour to imitate 'em are to be commended, though they can't arrive at their perfection'.

The *Comparison between the French and Italian Music and Operas* gives such a careful description of the singing of the *castrati*—as far as it could be described in print—that as the translator makes no comment, I presume he agreed with it. That being so, I give it fairly fully so as to convey to some extent what an artificial male soprano sounded like, or at least how his singing struck his contemporaries at the beginning of the eighteenth century. The French author, who was proud of his country's basses, envies Italy her *castrati*:—

Our women's voices are indeed as soft and agreeable as are those of their castrati, but then they are far from being either so strong or lively. No man or woman in the world can boast of a voice like theirs: they are clear, they are moving, and affect the soul itself.

Sometimes you hear a symphony so charming that you think nothing in music can exceed it, till on a sudden you perceive it was designed only to accompany a more charming air sung by one of these castrati, who, with a voice the most clear, and at the same time equally soft, pierces the symphony, and tops all the instruments with an agreeableness which they that hear it may conceive, but will never be able to describe.

These pipes of theirs resemble that of the nightingale: their longwinded throats draw you in a manner out of your depth and make you lose your breath: they'll execute passages of I know not how many bars together, they'll have echoes on the same passages and swellings of a prodigious length, and then with a chuckle in the throat exactly like that of a nightingale they'll conclude with cadences of an equal length, and all this is in the same breath.

(All cadences regularly included a trill leading to the final note.)

Add to this that these soft, these charming voices acquire new charms by being in the mouth of a lover. What can be more affecting than the expressions of their sufferings in such tender, passionate notes? In this the Italian lovers have a very great advantage over ours,

(that is, of course, the French)

whose hoarse masculine voices ill agree with the fine, soft things they are to say to their mistresses. Besides, the Italian voices being equally strong as they are soft, we hear all they sing very distinctly, whereas half of it is lost upon our theatre unless we sit close to the stage, or have the spirit of divination. Our upper parts are usually performed by girls, that have neither lungs nor wind: whereas the same parts in Italy are always performed by men, whose firm piercing notes are to be heard clearly in the largest theatres without losing a syllable, sit where you will.

Voices of *castrati*, he says, lasted thirty or forty years, as opposed to the ten or twelve years of French women sopranos who were obviously expected to act as well,

so that an actress is hardly found for the stage before she loses her voice and another must be taken to supply her place, who being a stranger to the theatre will at least be out in the action, if she comes off tolerably well in the singing, and won't be fit to perform any considerable parts under five or six years' practice.

(Nowadays, of course, opera sopranos are often expected to take over considerable parts with only a few weeks of musical coaching and, if they are lucky, a couple of runs-through of the stage business.)

When the Abbé talks of the skill of the Italian singers in acting and being able to sing without having a conductor beating time, the translator comments that though London of 1709 puts up with some worse acting in the straight theatre than can be seen in the provinces, in the case of opera,

which has been but lately established among us and which consisting for the most part of strangers hard to be got, the audience are apt to disencourage the middling performers that stand most in need of their indulgence—which makes me believe that if the town doth not grow better natured, it will be impossible for the opera to subsist long among us: for in case Nicolini should miscarry either through sickness or some other accident, I know no one the audience will suffer to perform his part, and then farewell to the opera!

With regard to conducting, the translator Mr. X remarks that it used to be customary in French opera to have the master of the music beating time 'on a table put there for that purpose, so loud that he made a greater noise than the whole band on purpose to be

heard by the performer': the conducting was later moved to the
'music room', that is, the orchestral pit or the equivalent, but it
still remained audible:—

The same was observed in London six or seven years ago: but since the Italian
masters are come among us, and the operas have been introduced, they have
put a stop to that ridiculous custom, which was founded more upon an ill habit
than any necessity there was for it, as doing more harm than good: for the
operas are better performed now without it than any piece of music was
formerly, because the eye was too much distracted, being obliged to mind the
beating of the measure and the score at the same time—besides it kept the singer
and the player in too much subjection and fear of errors, by which means they
were deprived of that liberty so absolutely necessary to music, and which gives
a strength and spirit to the notes.

If only all opera-conductors would learn the implied lesson
in that passage, and if only singers would learn their parts so
thoroughly and perform them so correctly—as the French author
said, 'playing, as it were, with the music and singing exactly true'
—then they could regain the disciplined flexibility of the best
Italians of 1709 of whom the Abbé wrote:—

Without obliging themselves to attend either the person that beats the time or
anything else, they have full leisure to adjust themselves to the action, and
having nothing else to do but to express the passions and compose their
carriage, they must certainly act much better than the French, who being not
such thorough masters of music are wholly busied in the performance.

(I am reminded of a story told me by Dino Borgioli of how
Chaliapin once refused to sing in Italy with a young conductor
who, with his head buried in the score, could not tell when the
singer had finished an important bit of business during a long
pause: Chaliapin pointed out that the public were paying to see
him and not the conductor's back. That young conductor may
have learned his lesson, but only too many think their gyrations
should be exciting to the audience and dictatorial to the orchestra
and singers—and indeed if some singers give careless and colourless performances who can blame the conductors?) [4]
The rest of the *Comparison* and the translator's comments point
out that the Italians had the advantage in opera, as they had more
opera-houses than either England or France, which had only one
each, that *castrati* also appeared as majestic women (Nicolini did)
because no woman was allowed in opera in Rome or Düsseldorf or
Vienna 'in the late Emperor's time', that stringed instruments
were better in Italy than France, as were also opera-houses and

stage-machines, and that Italian operas were longer than French operas—the original author said that while French operas lasted about two and a half hours, Italian operas lasted five or six: the translator however said that was not true and that the longest Italian opera took only four hours.

Nothing else from the *Comparison* needs quoting here, except the description of one stage effect, which I cannot help giving as a challenge to all modern stage designers. How with all modern inventions would they theoretically plan the effect? In practice it would certainly be too expensive nowadays. The translator, describing a Hell scene in an opera called *Nerone Infante*, tells how

a prodigious monster appeared, whose mouth opening to the great horror of the spectators covered the front wings and the remaining part of the stage: within his jaws were discovered a throne composed of fire and a multitude of monstrous serpents on which Pluto sat, with a crown of fire on his head and habited in other royal ornaments of the same nature.

Later the mouth of the monster closed, and after a scene between Cupid and a little devil, who was finally 'transformed into a curling smoke that disappeared by degrees',

the great monster expanding its wings began to move very slowly towards the audience: under his body appeared great multitudes of devils who formed themselves into a ballet and plunged one after another into the opening of the floor . . . out of which a prodigious quantity of fire and smoke was discharged.

So far, though complicated, the device could be worked out, but now comes the major problem:—

After this the great monster being got as far as the music-room, and whilst all the spectators were intent upon what was doing and began to fear he would come into the pit, he was in an instant transformed into an innumerable multitude of broad, white butterflies, which flew all into the pit, and so low that some of them touched the hats of several of the spectators—at which some seemed diverted and others were not a little terrified, till by degrees they lodged themselves on different parts of the theatre and at length disappeared.

He goes on to say that while this 'sufficiently employed the eyes of the spectators'—as well it might—

the stage was refitted and the scene changed into a beautiful garden with which the third act begun.

The translator of the *Comparison* was clearly an opera enthusiast, but that he did not welcome the makeshift examples that were introduced to London up to 1709 can be seen from his addition to the *Comparison* (if the writer is the same). This he called *A Critical Discourse upon Operas in England, and a Means proposed for their Improvement*, which he began by saying:—

Some years ago they gave the name of opera to all those plays here in London as had any musical dialogues intermixed with scenes, for no other reason in my opinion but because there were several choruses and dances added after the manner of the French.

Some time after one Mr. Clayton,[5] newly returned out of Italy,

laboured might and main to compose an English opera, called *Arsinoe* which according to my judgement as little deserved the name of an opera as the pieces before mentioned.

He admits, however, that the earlier dramatic operas often were of value because of Purcell's music, but proceeds to comment adversely on most of the operas from *Arsinoe* onwards: I have already given the operatic criticisms of this prejudiced, but by no means unperceptive, Mr. X.

After his outspoken criticism of operas in England during the last four years the unknown writer describes 'a means proposed for their improvement'. He begins by putting his finger on the chief fault behind pasticcio-arranging:—

Operas patched up out of the composition of several different masters are not likely to succeed unless they are prepared by some person that is capable of making an opera himself.

He goes on to stress that because an opera has been a success in one country it will not necessarily be a success in another—'the very climate may be said to have influence upon it'—and he claims quite reasonably that

an experienced composer that is well acquainted with the taste of the country wherein he lives is the only person proper to prevent such inconveniences.

He cannot understand how the town encouraged such a cheat as the 'Swiss Count', Heidegger:—

Operas will never come into perfection here till these sort of monsters are forbid the stage: but I'm of opinion the English will in time grow more refined in their taste in music, and won't stand in need of my exhortations to quell this pest that annoys the republic of music with as much bravery as their ancestors heretofore destroyed the wolves that had for a long time infested the nation.

(Unfortunately there are always well-meaning enthusiasts who in their ignorance and out of their kindness to poor animals are only too ready to accept such wolves as grandmotherly friends—especially after a war—and fail to see they are only encouraging the frauds to eat them up.)

No operas therefore ought to be received but such as are entire and of one author, or at least prepared by a person that is capable of writing different styles so artfully as to make 'em pass for one.

But what will most contribute to the dignity of operas is that besides the addition of some more decorations to those we have already—

(So the scenery was still important.)

—all the words ought to be sung in Italian, being a language the most proper for music of any other in Europe: music seems to have been born with it, and consequently loses much of its native beauty when it appears in a foreign dress.

(Those who may seize on this to bolster up their argument that Italian is the only language to sing in should notice that, though the writer accepts Italian as being the best language for singing, his chief objection is to having Italian music sung in a translation—which is obviously to be avoided so long as the audience either understands the original or is content to understand nothing.)

He goes on to recommend the practice of all good composers of all centuries by saying that they

ought to consult the capacities of the several performers and dress out their parts accordingly—this being a material point, and indispensably necessary to fix operas upon a lasting foundation.

Now comes an interesting comment on the differences between opera in Italy and opera in England, especially with relation to the audiences—a comment, which on the whole is as true to-day as it was then:—

They ought likewise to avoid a too servile imitation of the Italian composition, since an opera with no more than ten or twelve good airs in it will pass in Italy, whereas here in England five or six bad ones are sufficient to damn the whole composition, the taste of the town in this particular being so exceeding nice and tender, insomuch that of all the operas that are at present in Italy, I don't think one of 'em will go down here without some alterations: Camilla indeed is to be excepted, though probably had not that been the first it would not have passed free from censure.

(In this he is so correct that of all operas produced in Italy up to 1709, apart from those already mentioned, only three were presented in London in the eighteenth century, and those achieved no success—all by Gasparini, *Il più Fedel fra i Vassalli* (1703) as *Antioco* in London, 1711, *La Fede Tradita e Vendicata* (1704) as *Ernelinda* in London, 1713, and *Ambleto* (1705) produced in London 1712. Indeed, no other operas of lasting merit had been produced in Italy up to this time and none were to be seen there for many years.)

He goes on to stress the difference between the Italian and British audiences:—

There are but few masters capable of composing an opera in Italy and much fewer in England. There the people having a settled inclination for music, every little thing pleases and contents 'em whereas our acquaintance with it is but of a fresh date, so that we are not yet grown so partial to it as to excuse any of its defects, but expect everything in the highest perfection.

He also says that the accompaniment in an opera should be as good as the melody and the taste of the whole:—

In short an opera that would be received here ought to be in some measure an extract of the best music in the world, all of a piece, without degenerating into anything low or trifling.

Upon which account a composer that might make an opera in Italy in a month's time can't complete such a one as I think fit for the English stage in less than twelve. So that it is not to be wondered if they who have entertained another opinion of the English taste have found themselves deceived, and have miscarried in their undertakings—and I look on it as an undoubted maxim in music (the business of which is to regale the ear, as it is that of painting to entertain the eye) that whatsoever is good ought to please, and whatever pleases ought to be esteemed good.

(How many people who pretend to good taste fail to see the truth in this and invent a contradictory maxim for their own satisfaction—that whatever pleases must be cheap and what is difficult must be good! The translator of the *Comparison* and the author of the *Discourse* certainly knew what he was talking about—and not only where the early Italian operatic importations were concerned.)

[1] Those who wish to look up the *Discourse* in the British Museum will not find it catalogued under that title, but under the *Comparison between the French, etc.*

[2] This does not mean that there were only two performances. See p. 175.

[3] I wrote this while working on the production of *Katya Kabanova* at Sadler's Wells, and was delighted when the conductor, Rafael Kubelik, told the singers, as I had often done, not to sing so much, so that when they did sing the

effect would be enhanced. Continuous singing—or perhaps one should say, vocalising—is as monotonous as continuous arias would have been to the eighteenth century. I pointed out to one singer that I do not believe anyone can satisfactorily listen to a series of the most beautifully sung gramophone records without a break for a cigarette, drink or occasional word, and he admitted he failed to listen to the long-playing *Tristan* on end, for there was no way of stopping the ears from getting tired, as is done automatically in the theatre by the use of the eyes.

[4] That same conductor, now not unknown, still often has his head in the score.

[5] Printed as 'Cl——n', as are other names in the discourse.

CHAPTER FOUR

Steele and Addison

WHILE *Clotilda* at the Queen's only lasted seven performances in 1709, the old *Camilla* had thirteen up to the summer vacation, and the new *Pyrrhus* achieved no less than twenty-two in spite of the mixture of languages. On Monday, April 18, Steele recorded in *The Tatler* that the performance of *Pyrrhus* on Saturday was received with great applause—this was its twenty-third performance since its première in December—and added this comment:—

> This intelligence is not very acceptable to us, friends of the theatre, for the stage being an entertainment of the reason and all our faculties, this way of being pleased with the suspense of 'em for three hours together and being given up to the shallow satisfaction of the eyes and ears only, seems to arise rather from the degeneracy of our understanding than an improvement of our diversion.

He came to this conclusion because

> a great part of the performance was done in Italian, and a great critic fell into fits in the gallery at seeing not only time and place but languages and nations confused in the most incorrigible manner. His spleen is so extremely moved on this occasion that he is going to publish another treatise against the introduction of operas.

That critic, Dennis, was always prone to lose control of his temper when his tenets were outraged,[1] but though the dramatic principle of the unity of time and place might seem all-important to his reason, a polyglot performance would naturally appear ludicrous to anyone of common sense—though recently such performances have been given in London and tolerated by many.

In spite of the jumble, however, even performances in jumbled languages were worth seeing for one thing at least—Nicolini's performance, which captivated Steele's imagination, however much his reason might boggle at the whole presentation: he saw *Pyrrhus* again on Friday, December 30—its thirty-sixth performance since it was produced on December 14 a year before—and this is what he wrote:—

> I went on Friday last to the opera and was surprised to find a thin house at so noble an entertainment, till I heard that the tumbler was not to make his appearance that night.

This must not be read as invented sarcasm, for dancing, singing and speciality acts of all kinds were performed at this time before, during and after acts of all shows—acrobats even appeared during *Othello* in September of this year, and the contortionist might well draw a public: Steele, however, did not miss him:—

> For my own part I was fully satisfied with the sight of an actor who by the grace and propriety of his action and gesture does honour to a human figure as much as the other vilifies and degrades it.
>
> Everyone will easily imagine I mean Signor Nicolini, who sets off the character he bears in an opera by his action as much as he does the words of it by his voice. Every limb and every finger contributes to the part he acts, inasmuch that a deaf man may go along with him in the sense of it. There is scarce a beautiful posture in an old statue which he does not plant himself in, as the different circumstances of the story give occasion for it. He performs the most ordinary action in a manner suitable to the greatness of his character, and shows the prince even in the giving of a letter, or despatching of a messenger.

He even compares him to the disadvantage of the straight actors of the day—Betterton, Wilks, Doggett and Cibber, Mrs. Barry and Mrs. Oldfield:—

> Our best actors are somewhat at a loss to support themselves with proper gesture, as they move from any considerable distance to the front of the stage: but I have seen the person of whom I am now speaking enter alone at the remotest part of it, and advance from it with such greatness of air and mien as seemed to fill the stage and at the same time commanded the attention of the audience with the majesty of his appearance.

These actors at the Queen's appeared in some nine plays this year.

On January 10, 1710, Nicolini appeared there in a new Italian opera, *Almahide*, based on a play by Dryden: it is not known who wrote either the libretto or the music—though Burney thought the music more like Bononcini's than that of any other composer, but it is known that this was the first opera entirely sung in Italian that achieved success. The singers of the opera were Nicolini, Valentini, de l'Epine, Cassani and Isabella Girardeau but between the scenes there were vocal interludes of English songs and duets sung by the popular Mrs. Lindsey and Mrs. Cross with the comedian Doggett. Italian opera then, although at last sung entirely in Italian, still paid lip-service as it were to the English singers it was ousting, and the difficulty of the language was largely overcome by using a story of an English play which, though first produced thirty-eight years before, had been revived only six years ago.

Two months later, on March 23, at the Queen's, Nicolini was responsible for the first production of another Italian opera, *L'Idaspe Fedele*, with music by Mancini: the cast was the same as for *Almahide*, with the addition of an Englishman, Lawrence, who had to learn his part in Italian. This time there was no singing in English, but possibly the vogue for Italian opera in Italian was now strong enough to draw a fashionable audience, though certainly one of the chief attractions was the fight between the hero and a lion, which became so famous that it should be described.

Artaxerxes, King of Persia, finding that his brother Hydaspes is his rival for the love of the princess Berenice, condemns him to be thrown to a lion in her presence, and in the third act Hydaspes is brought by soldiers into the crowded arena. He has some tender words with Berenice, but a trumpet sounds and the scene goes on as follows in the language of the eighteenth-century translation, which is not only more than free but also of a different scansion from the original Italian—the mood, however, is the same:—

Hydaspes.	For thee, my life, I die.
Berenice.	O my soul! A long farewell!
Hydaspes.	Ah, Berenice! My love!
Berenice.	Hydaspes!
Both.	Oh! Farewell!

> *Berenice places herself on the steps of the amphitheatre with Arbaces and the soldiers: Hydaspes remaining alone in the arena: after which a lion comes out of his den, which, not yet seeing Hydaspes, stalks about looking at the spectators.*

(This of course is to give Nicolini a chance to sing a big aria in as unnatural a situation as the singing of 'Di Quella Pira' by Manrico in *Trovatore* when he should be dashing to his supposed mother's assistance as she is being burnt.)

Hydaspes.	Why dost thou, horrid monster, pause?
	Come on! Now sate thy ravenous jaws,
	This naked bosom tear!
	But thou within shalt find a heart
	Guarded by flames will make thee start
	And turn thy rage to fear! [2]

> *The lion, seeing Hydaspes, flies furiously on him.*

Berenice.	Ah, miserable me! I die!

> *Berenice faints. Hydaspes, grasping the lion's neck with his arms, strangles him: when falling at last on the ground, he sets his foot on his neck in sign of victory.*

After which of course, the crowd shouts 'Viva, Idaspe, viva, viva!'

Hydaspes was a success because of the lion-scene, but the more intelligent members of the audience who were not swayed either by their enthusiasm for melodrama or their pretended knowledge of Italian were very critical of the highfalutin English that was printed as an aid to those who did not understand Italian. Its pompous verbosity and slovenly English led its readers to believe that the original was equally fatuous (and sometimes it nearly was) and that Italian opera was always ludicrous. This was largely the fault of Motteux, who not only sold tea, fans, screens, Japan cabinets, and silks to the Court ladies, but also translated such operas as *Arsinoe*, *Thomyris* and *Love's Triumph*, perpetrating such banalities as

> For thy ferryboat, Charon, I thank thee,
> But thrust me not out, for I come in a hurry.
>
> *Arsinoe.*

> Away, you rover!
> For shame give over!
> So bold a lover
>   Never will pass.
> You press and thunder
> To bring us under,
> Then all you plunder
>   And leave the place.
> Though you are for storming
> And think you are charming,
> Your faint performing
>   We read in your face.
>
> *Thomyris.*

> No more trial,
> Nor denial!
>   Be more kind
>   And tell your mind.
>   So tossed,
>   So crossed,
>   I'm sad,
>   I'm mad.
> No more then hide your good nature,
> Thou dear creature.
>
> *Love's Triumph.*

No wonder, then, that the readers of these English librettos thought them poor stuff compared, for instance, with Dryden's lyrics for Purcell's music, and they were hardly to be blamed for putting the responsibility for the rubbishy style on to the Italian librettists.

As an example of what could be done by a writer who knew more about his craft and the English language than the Huguenot refugee—yet another of them—who combined opera translation with tea-selling and a job in the Post Office, Congreve published in 1710 his libretto for an opera on *Semele*. It was not set at this time, but the text—although not poetry of the first water—showed that it could still be possible to write decent English for singing, and in his introductory argument Congreve made it plain that he well understood the fundamental principles of that great characteristic of Italian opera, recitative:—

It was not thought requisite to have any regard either to rhyme or equality of measure in the lines of that part of the dialogue which was designed for the recitative style in music. For as that style in music is not confined to the strict observation of time and measure which is required in the composition of airs and sonatas, so neither is it necessary that the same exactness in numbers, rhymes, or measure, should be observed in words designed to be set in that manner which must ever be observed in the formation of odes and sonnets.

—and now comes a passage that should be studied by all singers.—

For what they call recitative in music is only a more tuneable speaking: it is a kind of prose in music: its beauty consists in coming near nature, and in improving the natural accents of words by more pathetic or emphatical tones.

To think that most musical people imagine that recitative was a musical formality and that musicalised naturalism of speech was only recently invented under the name of 'sprechstimme'!

In this year of 1710, though now five different operas were performed at the Queen's, three of them being novelties, not less than eighteeen English plays were also given there, including Cibber's famous version of *Richard III*—a spate of drama, like a last effort against the new craze. There were further performances of *Hydaspes* during the last six weeks of the year, but in the meantime Handel had arrived on a visit to London, and he was invited to set a libretto to music for the Queen's Theatre in the Haymarket. At the same time the young manager, Aaron Hill, who was always eager to improve stage works by making scenery more solid than flat, historical costumes more correct and dialogue more natural, planned great improvements in the settings at the Queen's, which he duly showed off in Handel's opera.

Handel made this new work ready in a fortnight by using up several operatic arias he had already had successfully performed, and the result—*Rinaldo*—was produced on February 24, 1711 (Old Style), or, as Löwenberg puts it, March 7 (New Style).[3] In his dedication of the libretto to Queen Anne, Hill, who had prepared the story for Rossi to make into a libretto, expressed his hope 'to see the English Opera more splendid than her mother, the Italian': this he explained in his preface as follows:—

> The deficiencies I found, or thought I found, in such Italian operas as have hitherto been introduced among us were first, that they had been composed for tastes and voices different from those who were to sing and hear them on the English stage, and secondly, that, wanting the machines and decorations which bestow so great a beauty on their appearance, they have been heard and seen to very considerable disadvantage.

The opera *Rinaldo*—or rather the one-man pasticcio such as the author of the *Critical Discourse* recommended—was a great success, partly because of the selected tunes, including 'Cara Sposa' and 'Laschia ch'io pianga', partly because Handel himself played the harpsichord brilliantly at the performances and partly no doubt because of a daring piece of stage naturalism by Hill that Addison not unjustly criticised in the *Spectator* ten days after the first performance.

He began his now famous criticism, which contains fundamental truths of stage direction that are well worth studying, as follows:—

> An opera may be allowed to be extravagantly lavish in its decorations, as its only design is to gratify the senses and keep up an indolent attitude in the audience. Common sense, however, requires that there should be nothing in the scenes and machines which may appear childish and absurd.
>
> How would the wits of King Charles's time have laughed to have seen Nicolini exposed to a tempest in robes of ermine, and sailing in an open boat upon a sea of pasteboard! What a field of raillery would they have been let into, had they been entertained with painted dragons spitting wildfire, enchanted chariots drawn by Flanders mares, and real cascades in artificial landscapes!
>
> A little skill in criticism would inform us that shadows and realities ought not to be mixed together in the same piece, and that the scenes which are designed as the representations of nature should be filled with resemblances, and not with the things themselves. If one would represent a wide champaign country filled with herds and flocks, it would be ridiculous to draw the country only upon the scenes, and to crowd several parts of the stage with sheep and oxen. This is joining together inconsistencies, and making the decoration partly real and partly imaginary. I would recommend what I have said here, to the directors as well as to the admirers of our modern opera.

The most ludicrous example of this inconsistency that actually occurred in *Rinaldo*—which may well have attracted an ignorant audience—is pilloried by Addison like this:—

As I was walking in the streets about a fortnight ago, I saw an ordinary fellow carrying a cage full of little birds upon his shoulders; and as I was wondering with myself what use he would put them to, he was met very luckily by an acquaintance who had the same curiosity. Upon his asking him what he had upon his shoulders, he told him that he had been buying sparrows for the opera.

'Sparrows for the opera!' says his friend, licking his lips, 'What, are they to be roasted?'

'No, no,' says the other, 'they are to enter towards the end of the first act, and to fly about the stage.'

This strange dialogue awakened my curiosity so far, that I immediately bought the opera, by which means I perceived that the sparrows were to act the part of singing birds in a delightful grove: though, upon a nearer inquiry, I found . . . though they flew in sight, the music proceeded from a consort of flageolets and bird-calls, which were planted behind the scenes.

Addison went on to criticise the librettist Rossi for being fulsomely ornate and says that

the first writers among the modern Italians express themselves in such a florid form of words and such tedious circumlocutions as are used by none but pedants in our own country, and at the same time fill their writings with such poor imaginations and conceits as our youths are ashamed of before they have been two years at the university.

This has often been quoted to show Addison's ignorance (especially as he goes on to disparage the 'tinsel of Tasso', from whom the story of *Rinaldo* was taken, by comparison with Virgil, and all contemporary Italian writers by comparison with the Latin classics, which English writers tried to imitate). But Addison was primarily talking of stage literature, and so was quite right to prefer for an English audience a less flamboyant style. He also has been disparaged for sneering at the author because he dared

to call Mynheer Handel the Orpheus of our age, and to acquaint us in the same sublimity of style that he composed this opera in a fortnight. Such are the wits to whose tastes we so ambitiously conform ourselves.

But it should be remembered that English authors, musicians and artists generally had suffered so much and so consistently at the hands of foreign composers from Grabu on (if not before) that they could hardly have been expected to recognise a genius when they heard one, especially as *Rinaldo* must have sounded, and certainly looked quite different from the usual London opera: nor was it any more logical than the others, however carefully Hill had tried, though the magic of the enchantress Armida might excuse a lot.

Why then should Addison or anyone else be expected to drop their prejudice of many years, especially when the boast was made of the short time the composer had spent on the new work—in itself not a compliment, but rather yet another example of the usual patronising sneer of the foreign musician for the stupid London audience? Besides, all the opera-critics of the day were concerned with opera as a whole and not as a concert in costume: to them the stage-action and characterisation was an essential part of the whole, and however good Handel's music might be, his arias could not—for them—make up for the lack of logical dramatic construction, a lack which, it must be admitted, is typical of almost all his operas.

Nor did Hill's stage innovations help, however well intended—as Steele wrote in the *Spectator* ten days later:—

. . . the undertakers of the Haymarket, having raised too great an expectation in their printed opera, very much disappoint their audience on the stage.

The King of Jerusalem is obliged to come from the city on foot, instead of being drawn in a triumphant chariot by white horses, as my opera-book had promised me, and thus while I expected Armida's dragons should rush forward towards Argantes, I found the hero was obliged to go to Armida and hand her out of her coach. We had also but a very short allowance of thunder and lightning—though I cannot in this place omit doing justice to the boy who had the direction of the two painted dragons and made them spit fire and smoke: he flashed out his resin in such just proportions and in such due time that I could not forebear conceiving hopes of his being one day a most excellent player. I saw indeed but two things wanting to render his whole action complete—I mean the keeping his head a little lower and hiding his candle.

Steele also criticised the sparrows and chaffinches for getting into the galleries or putting out the candles instead of perching in the trees as they should, and blamed Hill for only changing the backcloths, and not the side-wings as well, so that 'we were presented with a prospect of the ocean in the midst of a delightful grove'. He also pointed out the ludicrous incongruity of allowing the audience to overflow on to the stage, handsome though they were, for he was 'not a little astonished to see a well-dressed young fellow in a full-bottomed wig appear in the midst of the sea and without any visible concern taking snuff'.

Nine days after his attack on *Rinaldo*, Addison weighed in again on the subject of stage sense with an article on the *Hydaspes* lion-fight, which was still to be seen in 1711—and indeed after that. He begins by saying:—

> There is nothing that of late years has afforded matter of greater amusement to the town than Signor Nicolini's combat with a lion in the Haymarket, which has been very often exhibited to the general satisfaction of most of the nobility and gentry in the Kingdom of Great Britain.

It is worth noting that while the society opera-goers swallowed the lion, so to speak, the town as a whole laughed at it—and, it seems, them. He goes on to mention the rumour that may really have circulated in the cheaper parts of the house, perhaps at the instigation of the management, that a tame lion would be sent each night to be killed by Hydaspes and 'that the stage would be supplied with lions at the public expense during the whole season'. He also facetiously said that according to another rumour Nicolini was expected to subdue the lion in recitative, which was not far from the truth in view of the ludicrous hold-up of the action for music—a far greater hold-up than can be seen from the words alone, for the first two lines of Hydaspes' aria to the lion are greatly extended in true bravura fashion, full of roulades and flourishes, while the lines about the faithful heart are set to a largo movement.

But Addison was not the fool many writers think him: he knew merit when he saw it, and ended the same article with the following eulogy:—

> I would not be thought in any part of this relation to reflect upon Signor Nicolini, who in acting this part only complies with the wretched taste of his audience. He knows very well that the lion has many more admirers than himself—as they say of the famous equestrian statue on the Pont Neuf at Paris, that more people go to see the horse than the king who sits on it.

(Animals and children always steal scenes from the best actors.)

> On the contrary, it gives me a just indignation to see a person whose action gives new dignity to kings, resolution to heroes, and softness to lovers, thus sinking from the greatness of his behaviour, and degraded into the character of *The London Prentice*.
>
> I have often wished that our tragedians would copy after this great master in action. Could they make the same use of their arms and legs, and inform their

faces with as significant looks and passions, how glorious would an English tragedy appear with that action which is capable of giving a dignity to the forced thoughts, cold conceits, and unnatural expressions of an Italian opera.

In the meantime I have related this combat of the lion, to show what are at present the reigning entertainments of the politer part of Great Britain. Audiences have often been reproached by writers for the coarseness of their taste, but our present grievance does not seem to be the want of a good taste, but of common sense.

It is clear that he thought this lack of common sense which encouraged such childish exhibitions was an attribute of 'the politer part of Great Britain'—the society fashionables, in fact.

Incidentally, Nicolini certainly set himself standards, for in 1710, six days before the first performance of *Hydaspes*, he had refused to sing between the acts of a comedy, not only because it would be breaking his contract, but because it 'would prove a real means to vilify and prejudice the opera'.

A few days after his attack on the lion-fight and his praise of Nicolini, Addison wrote a brilliant article on the problem which then was new, but which since has almost become stale—should operas be performed in the original language or in translations? Not being able to foresee the way future opera audiences in this country and America would follow the example of the society poseurs of the early eighteenth century—themselves the successors of the fops who Dryden pilloried for pretending to appreciate French operas by shouting 'Bien!' and pronouncing 'cadence' with a French accent, Addison in his innocence wrote satirically:

there is no question but our great-grandchildren will be very curious to know the reason why their forefathers used to sit together like an audience of foreigners in their own country, and to hear whole plays acted before them in a tongue which they did not understand.

He little knew they would continue to do so for over two hundred years and would sneer at performances they could understand. He pointed out that when, after *Arsinoe*, attempts were made to imitate and also to improve on Italian models, the incompetent authors and composers of London became alarmed and by their own slovenly work

laid down an established rule, which is received as such to this day. *That nothing is capable of being well set to music, that is not nonsense.*

This maxim was no sooner received but we immediately fell to translating the Italian operas, and as there was no great danger of hurting the sense of those extraordinary pieces, our authors would often make words of their own which

were entirely foreign to the meaning of the passages they pretended to translate
—their chief care being to make the numbers of the English verse answer to
those of the Italian, that both of them might go to the same tune.

Thus the famous song in *Camilla*,

'Barbara, si, t'intendo, etc.'
'Barbarous woman, yes, I know your meaning,'

which expresses the resentments of an angry lover, was translated into that
English lamentation,

'Frail are a lover's hopes, etc.'

And it was pleasant enough to see the most refined persons of the British
nation dying away and languishing to notes that were filled with a spirit of
rage and indignation.

It happened also very frequently, where the sense was rightly translated, the
necessary transposition of words, which were drawn out of the phrase of one
tongue into that of another, made the music appear very absurd in one tongue
that was very natural in the other. I remember an Italian verse that ran thus,
word for word,

'And turn'd my rage into pity',

which the English for rhyme's sake translated,

'And into pity turn'd my rage'.

By this means the soft notes that were adapted to 'pity' in the Italian, fell upon
the word 'rage' in the English, and the angry sounds that were turned to 'rage'
in the original were made to express 'pity' in the translation.

It oftentimes happened likewise that the finest notes in the air fell upon the
most insignificant words in the sentence. I have known the word 'and' pursued
through the whole gamut, have been entertained with many a melodious 'the',
and have heard the most beautiful graces, quavers, and divisions bestowed upon
'then', 'for', and 'from' to the eternal honour of our English particles.

All translators should study this passage carefully, and so should
all musical critics who so glibly repeat that Addison had no feeling
for music.

Addison went on to explain that the introduction of Italian
singers led to polyglot performances in which they were answered
by English singers—each in their own language.

One would have thought it very difficult to have carried on dialogues after this
manner without an interpreter between the persons that conversed together,
but this was the state of the English stage for about three years.

At length the audience got tired of understanding half the opera, and therefore, to ease themselves entirely of the fatigue of thinking, have so ordered it at
present that the whole opera is performed in an unknown tongue. We no
longer understand the language of our own stage, insomuch that I have often
been afraid, when I have seen our Italian performers chattering in the vehem-
ence of action, that they have been calling us names and abusing us among
themselves: but I hope, since we do put such entire confidence in them,

they will not talk against us before our faces, though they may do it with the same safety as if it were behind our backs.

In the meantime I cannot forbear thinking how naturally a historian who writes two or three hundred years hence, and does not know the taste of his wise forefathers, will make the following reflection—'In the beginning of the eighteenth century the Italian tongue was so well understood in England, that operas were acted on the public stage in that language'.

It is, indeed, often maintained and pretended that an opera-audience then did in fact understand Italian, while now they understand German and French as well—though nobody has so far claimed that the real English opera-lover also understands Czech and Finnish. For my part, I thoroughly agree with Addison's next paragraph:—

One scarce knows how to be serious in the confutation of an absurdity that shows itself at the first sight. It does not want any great measure of sense to see the ridicule of this monstrous practice: but what makes it the more astonishing, it is not the taste of the rabble, but of persons of the greatest politeness, which has established it.

It should be noted that Addison never maintained that a translation was better than the original, merely that it was more sensible when performed to an audience that did not understand the original. After that last comment he adds one judicious observation on operatic music and one pathetic admission:—

Music is certainly a very agreeable entertainment, but if it would take entire possession of our ears, if it would make us incapable of hearing sense, if it would exclude arts that have a much greater tendency to the refinement of human nature, I must confess I would allow it no better quarter than Plato has done, who banishes it out of his commonwealth.

At present our notions of music are so very uncertain, that we do not know what it is we like: only in general we are transported with anything that is not English—so it be of foreign growth, let it be Italian, French, or High Dutch, it is the same thing. In short, our English music is quite rooted out, and nothing yet planted in its stead.

Soon after this Addison discussed another problem that all translators of sung music should try to solve, but which few attempt—the question whether it is possible to sing the words of one language to the natural tune and lilt of another: Pepys had already hit on the difference between the sound or tune of one language and that of another, but Addison makes it quite clear that, as George Hogarth wrote over a hundred years later in his excellent *Memoirs of the Musical Drama*, in 1838, 'the vocal music of every country must be founded upon the peculiar accent, or modulation, of its spoken language': this of course applies chiefly to recitative, and it is in that connection that Addison discusses it:—

The only fault I can find in our present practice is the making use of the Italian *recitativo* with English words.

To go to the bottom of this matter, I must observe that the tone, or—as the French call it—the accent of every nation in their ordinary speech, is altogether different from that of every other people—as we may see even in the Welsh and Scotch who border so near upon us. By the tone or accent I do not mean the pronunciation of each particular word, but the sound of the whole sentence. Thus it is very common for an English gentleman, when he hears a French tragedy, to complain that the actors all of them speak in a tone: and therefore he very wisely prefers his own countrymen, not considering that a foreigner complains of the same tone in an English actor.

For this reason the recitative music in every language should be as different as the tone or accent of each language—for otherwise what may properly express a passion in one language will not do it in another. Everyone who has been long in Italy knows very well that the cadences in the recitative bear a remote affinity to the tone of their voices in ordinary conversation—or, to speak more properly, are only the accents of their language made more musical and tuneful.

Thus the notes of interrogation, or admiration, in the Italian music (if one may so call them) which resemble their accents in discourse on such occasions, are not unlike the ordinary tones of an English voice when we are angry—insomuch that I have often seen our audiences extremely mistaken as to what has been doing upon the stage, and expecting to see the hero knock down a messenger when he has been asking him a question, or fancying that he quarrels with his friend, when he only bids him good-morrow.

(If anyone who has not been to Italy doubts this, he has only to go into any Italian shop in London to hear enthusiasm or query expressed in tones that our ears associate with threats of violence.)

For this reason the Italian artists cannot agree with our English musicians in admiring Purcell's compositions, and thinking his tunes so wonderfully adapted to his words, because both nations do not always express the same passions by the same sounds.

Purcell's music, and all English music, for that matter—especially when it is full of feeling—always strikes a Frenchman as being lugubrious, as Dent has pointed out. To us, however, almost all the words that Purcell set, if spoken to the rise and fall of the tune to which he set them—and not only in recitative—sound perfectly natural; and the same holds, I believe, with all good composers if judged by the lilt of their own language—it is, in fact, automatic with composers who have really sensitive ears, but it merely sounds forced if cultivated by those who labour to achieve the same result. Stanford taught me that a composer should test the ease and flow of his settings of words by speaking the lines over in the lilt and rhythm of the music *after* they had been set, but to try to compose a tune by copying natural speech is like trying to write poetry by mathematically balancing vowels and consonants.

Addison's wise conclusion then is diffidently put as follows:—

I am therefore humbly of opinion that an English composer should not follow the Italian recitative too servilely, but make use of many gentle deviations from it in compliance with his own native language. He may copy out of it all the lulling softness and 'dying' falls—as Shakespeare calls them—but should still remember that he ought to accommodate himself to an English audience, and, by humouring the tone of our voices in ordinary conversation, have the same regard to the accent of his own language as those persons had to theirs whom he professes to imitate.

It is observed that several of the singing-birds of our own country learn to sweeten their voices and mellow the harshness of their natural notes by practising under those that come from warmer climates. In the same manner I would allow the Italian opera to lend our English music as much as may grace and soften it, but never entirely to annihilate and destroy it. Let the infusion be as strong as you please, but still let the subject-matter of it be English.

A composer should fit his music to the genius of the people, and consider that the delicacy of hearing and taste of harmony have been formed upon those sounds which every country abounds with—in short, that music is of a relative nature, and what is harmony to one ear may be dissonance to another.

The same observations which I have made upon the recitative part of music may be applied to all our songs and airs in general.

Addison did not comment on the only other new opera of 1711, *Antioco*, probably by Gasparini, nor on the fact that while seven different operas were played that year at the Queen's, only three straight plays were given there: *The Sequel of Henry IV: with the Humours of Sir John Falstaff and Justice Shallow* by Betterton–Shakespeare, *The Schoolboy* and *The Careless Husband* both by Colley Cibber—a sure sign that opera was ousting straight plays at the Queen's, but not, it must be remembered, from Drury Lane.

Nor did Addison unfortunately leave us his comments on the first new opera of 1712—the first *Hamlet* opera, *Ambleto* by Gasparini, which had been produced in Venice in 1705—his views on the Italian musicalisation of Shakespeare would have been interesting. Nicolini seems to have been responsible for introducing that opera and was still performing *Hydaspes*, while Rossi, who had written the *Rinaldo* libretto, was responsible for another Italian opera, *Hercules*.

By now it had become fashionable to admire Italian opera (which was now partly financed by the straight theatre) and to ape the habits of an Italian audience, so, just as Dryden had ridiculed the fops of his day, Addison pilloried those who had picked up a little Italian opera-talk. He printed a letter from 'Toby Rent-Free' complaining that

Nicolini refused to gratify me in that part of the opera for which I have most taste.

I observe it is become a custom that, whenever any gentlemen are particularly pleased with a song, at their crying out 'Encore' or 'Altro volto' the performer is so obliging as to sing it over again. I was at the opera the last time *Hydaspes* was performed. At that part of it where the hero engages with the lion, the graceful manner in which he put that terrible monster to death gave me so great a pleasure, and at the same time so just a sense of that gentleman's intrepidity and conduct, that I could not forbear desiring a repetition of it by crying out 'Altro volto' in a very audible voice—and my friends flatter me that I pronounced those words with a tolerably good accent, considering that this was but the third opera I had ever seen in my life.

Yet, notwithstanding this, there was so little regard had to me, that the lion was carried off and went to bed without being killed any more that night.

Now, Sir, pray consider that I did not understand a word of what Mr. Nicolini said to this cruel creature—besides I have no ear for music, so that during the long dispute between them the whole entertainment I had was from my eyes. Why then have I not as much right to have a graceful action repeated as another has a pleasing sound, since he only hears as I see, and we neither of us know that there is any reasonable thing a-doing?

Pray, Sir, settle the business of this claim in the audience, and let us know when we may cry 'Altro volto' (*anglice*, 'Again, again!') for the future. I am an Englishman and expect some reason or other to be given me, and perhaps an ordinary one will serve: but I expect an answer.

On the subject of not understanding what was sung, he later satirised the fashion by inventing an opera-promoter who suggested giving an opera called *The Expedition of Alexander the Great* and said that

Alexander being a Greek, it was his intention that the whole opera should be acted in that language, which was a tongue he was sure would wonderfully please the ladies, especially when it was a little raised and rounded by the Ionic dialect, and could not but be acceptable to the whole audience, *because there are fewer of them who understand Greek then Italian.*

The only difficulty that remained was how to get performers, unless we could persuade some gentlemen of the universities to learn to sing, in order to qualify themselves for the stage;

(This of course has been often achieved during the last fifty years.)

but this objection soon vanished, when the projector informed us that . . . if we want any single voice for any lower part in the opera, Lawrence can learn to speak Greek, *as well as he does Italian*, in a fortnight's time.

Towards the end of April 1712 a brave attempt was made to prove the practicability of an English opera by a young German oboist, John Ernest Galliard, who had come over from Hanover to play for Prince George of Denmark: he set to music a libretto called *Calypso and Telemachus* by John Hughes. Galliard may well have been Mr. X, the translator of the Abbé Raguenet's *Comparison*, as Hawkins thought, in spite of Burney's contrary opinion, but there is no doubt that he did his best to make his music palatable to a London audience, and he certainly must have approved of the preface Hughes wrote to the published libretto, which was 'an essay for the improvement of theatrical music in the English language after the model of the Italians'.

Hughes began by pointing out that theatre-music in London had for some years been provided by Italians with the introduction of their most famous operas, and that their singing had been greatly applauded. As his opera was performed under the same management that encouraged the Italians, he was tactful enough— and perhaps honest enough—to say:—

I am not of the opinion of those who impute this encouragement given to Italian music to an affectation of everything that is foreign. I would rather ascribe it to the ingenuous temper of the British nation that they are willing to be instructed in so elegant an art by the best examples.

But after this justice done to others, there is likewise a justice done to ourselves. It could never have been the intention of those who first promoted the Italian opera that it should take the entire possession of our stage to the exclusion of everything of the like kind, which might be produced here. This would be to suppress that genius which foreigners so commonly applaud in the English, who if they are not always the inventors of arts, are yet allowed to be no ill learners, and are often observed to improve that knowledge which they first received from others.

Although he admits that Italian is a softer language than English, he fails to see why some think English unsuitable for singing:—

Let it be considered whether too great a delicacy in this particular may not run into effeminacy. A due mixture of consonants is certainly necessary to bind the words which may be otherwise too much dissolved and lose their force—and as theatrical music expresses a variety of passions, it is not requisite, even for the advantage of the sound, that the syllables should everywhere languish with the same loose and vowelly softness.

But his chief reason for advocating operas in English is that they must be understood—'and though the airs of an opera may be heard with delight as instrumental pieces without words, yet it is impossible that the recitative should give pleasure when the words are either taken away or are unintelligible' . . .

The great pleasure in hearing vocal music arises from the association of ideas raised at the same time by the expressions and the sounds . . . It is probable too that the pleasure we receive from the most pathetical strains of instrumental music is in part assisted by some ideas which we affix to them of passions which seem to be expressed by those strains. If the airs in operas may be heard with delight for the same reason, even when the words are not understood, yet it is impossible that recitative should give pleasure, which can raise no such ideas, this being not so properly singing as speaking in musical cadences.

He also touches on the question of national intonation noticed by Pepys and Addison when he says 'Recitative music takes its rise from the natural tunes and changes of the voice in speaking and is indeed no more than a sort of modulated elocution.'

Calypso had only five performances in its first season and three five years later: after its fourth performance, however, there was talk that Nicolini was leaving England, which Addison greatly regretted in a notice he wrote the day of the singer's last appearance in *Antioco*, which had been produced in the winter of 1711:—

I am sorry to find by the opera bills for this day that we are likely to lose the greatest performer in dramatic music that is now living, or that perhaps ever appeared upon a stage. I need not acquaint my readers that I am speaking of Signor Nicolini. The town is highly obliged to that excellent artist for having shown us the Italian music in its perfection, as well as for that generous approbation he lately gave to an opera of our own country, in which the composer endeavoured to do justice to the beauty of the words by following that noble example, which has been set him by the greatest foreign masters in that art.

Some others, however, perhaps saw in Nicolini's departure the hope that Italian opera might vanish with him. It was probably at this time that a ribald ballad comparing him to Caligula's horse was written: it was printed by D'Urfey in *Wit and Mirth*:—

THE CRITIC AT THE OPERA

Caponides

Or lyrical remarks made on the famous Signor Cavaliero Nico—— Grimaldi, knighted by the Doge of Venice, and Signor Gallapo Frisco, Caprioli Frontini the Horse, made a Consul by the Roman Emperor Caligula. Set to a tune in the opera of Antiochus.

Some blooming honour get
By valour, some by wit,
And some have titles met
  By the way of Guinea:
But two, most famed I show,
One long since and one now,
Who if you don't allow,
  The Devil's in ye:
Of creatures I discourse,
Who must your liking force—
They must your liking force,
As well as my discourse—
Caligula's fine horse,
  And Nicolini,
  Ni-hi-hi-hi-hi-hi-hi-colini.

A Senator some say
He made his dapple grey
For his Italian neigh—
  A crack-brained ninny:
A Doge too, as appears,
With squeaking caught by th' ears,
Amongst the Chevaliers
  Placed Nicolini:
And, as the Horse did bear
That honour many a year
For squalling notes so clear,
As you shall seldom hear,
So does our Capon dear,
  Dear Nicolini,
  De-he-he-he-he-he-he-ear Nicolini.

The next verse says that some critics think the Horse looks better and is on the whole happier because he has not had Nicolini's rejuvenating operation: that may be so,

But yet by vocal strain
And subtle dint of brain,
'Mongst English gentry vain
  He gets the penny:
He trills, and gapes, and struts,
And fricassees the notes:
Our crew may crack their guts,
  They ne'er will win ye.

For quavering like a lark,
This rare disabled spark
Gets ladies too i' the' dark
Who, though 'tis bungling work,
Will hug this Knight of Mark,
    Smooth Nicolini,
    Ni-hi-hi-hi-hi-hi-hi-colini.

But now to cause our woe,
Why, chanter, will you go?
Fop-bounty still may flow
    And many a guinea:
You leave us, some do guess,
To build a sumptuous place
To seat your noble race
    Like Valentini.
But, though we to our shames
Have paid ye in extremes,
Whene'er you leave the Thames
To roll on ocean-streams,
Pray don't you call us names,
    Sweet Nicolini,
    Swee-he-he-he-he-he-he-heet Nicolini!

Whether the last line of each verse was meant to burlesque the way Nicolini sang with the intrusive 'h', or whether it was merely intended to indicate a typical Nicolini roulade, such as Burney quoted in his *History*, there is no doubt but that the author thought him highly overpaid and highly overpraised by 'the English gentry vain' with their 'fop-bounty'.

Nicolini did leave England for a time, but a few months later Handel returned, and at once prepared a new and extra short opera to a libretto by Rossi, *Il Pastor Fido (The Faithful Shepherd)*. This opened at the Queen's on November 22, 1712, but failed with only seven performances that season—partly no doubt because nobody could replace Nicolini in the favour of society—though it was revived years later when Handel was a name to conjure with among opera enthusiasts. In 1712, however, it was overshadowed by the anonymous opera *Dorinda*, which had eleven performances that season, when ten different operas were given and only the same three plays as in the year before.

This year an enthusiast started to keep a record of all the operas produced in London, which is now among the manuscripts in the British Museum.[4] A note at the beginning entitles it: 'Opera register from 1712 to 1734 by the father of Geo. Colman, Brit.

Consul at Leghorn'. The writer says of *The Faithful Shepherd* and *Dorinda*, 'Neither of these two operas produced full houses'.

But Handel's next opera, *Teseo*, had considerably more momentary success, for it did achieve fourteen performances—one less than *Rinaldo*: Colman recorded after the second night: 'The house was very full these two nights'; but it was never revived, and some five days after its first performance on January 10, 1713, the manager McSwiney decamped, leaving all salaries unpaid.

The Queen's company, who carried on by themselves, were therefore allowed by the Lord Chamberlain about four weeks later to share £162 10*s*., 'being the clear receipt of the opera since Mr. Swiney left the house', and the ugly 'Swiss Count', Heidegger, took over the management of the theatre. He was responsible for another pasticcio, called *Ernelinda*, on February 26, which had six performances in just over two weeks ('The house was very full all these nights', said Colman) and scored ten performances, against *Rinaldo*'s three this year. There was now a growing feeling among all except society theatre-goers that the fashionable Italian opera was killing the theatre, and when Addison's play *Cato*, was produced on April 14 at Drury Lane, Pope—who could hardly be smeared with the accusation that he was disappointedly jealous, as Addison and other serious writers for the theatre not unreasonably were—wrote in his prologue to the play:—

> Our scene precariously subsists too long
> On French translation and Italian song.
> Dare to have sense yourselves! Assert the stage!
> Be justly warmed with your own native rage!

The precarious Queen's gave only four operas and the same three die-hard plays in 1713—no doubt because of the financial situation.

The next six years made it look as if the average audiences, whether swayed or not by the patriotic, jealous or honest critics, had had nearly enough Italian opera, for though new operas were produced each year, none of the new works stayed the course. In 1714 (the year Vanbrugh was knighted), of the five operas performed with two of the die-hard plays, the new *Creseo*, *Re di Lidia* and *Arminio*—both anonymous—did better than Handel's operas except *Rinaldo*, but were never revived. In that year, by the way, opera days were altered from Tuesdays to Thursdays—

the usual days of Wednesday and Friday being banned during Lent—because the Queen after her illness had a 'withdrawing room' on Tuesdays when she played basset, as Colman recorded.

In 1715 (six operas against three plays) the anonymous *Lucio Vero, Imperatore di Roma* (attributed to Nicolini by Colman) did slightly better than Handel's *Amadigi di Gaula*, but not as well as the old favourite *Idaspe*—'the house extraordinary full', as Colman wrote, who also recorded on October 31 that there had been no opera since July 23,

the rebellion of the Tories and Papists being the cause—the King and Court not liking to go into such crowds these troublesome times, but it is hoped in a short time the rebels will be confounded. I shall keep no further account of operas in that exactness as before—perhaps a remark on a new opera now and then as the humour takes.
Vanity of Vanity all is Vanity.

For *Amadigi* incidentally, owing to the many scenes and machines employed, none of the audience was admitted on to the actual stage. The same ruling was made in December 1715, when Purcell's *Prophetess* (*Dioclesian*) was revived for seven days running.

Not that there were no opera enthusiasts of the kind that like to show off: they still attended in a rapt frenzy (as they always do) and applauded so indiscriminately and to such an extent that in the same year the managers of the Haymarket Theatre had to issue the following notice:—

Whereas by the frequent calling for the songs again the operas have been too tedious, therefore the singers are forbidden to sing any song above once: and it is hoped that nobody will call for 'em or take it ill when not obeyed.

In 1716 only one play was given—*The Schoolboy*—and five operas, of which an anonymous *Clearte*, which seemed more successful than the revived and often rewritten *Amadigi*, was just beaten by the once-popular *Pyrrhus and Demetrius*. The year 1717 was the last year in which a straight play was given at the Queen's —the faithful *Schoolboy*—on January 4, and two more anonymous operas, *Venceslao* and *Tito Manlio*, the last new Italian operas to be heard in London for some time, scored only nine performances between them. *Rinaldo*, having been rested for a year, certainly did score ten performances in 1717, but it was outclassed by the old warhorse *Camilla*, with eight performances in January alone and six more that season at the new Lincoln's Inn Fields Theatre, built three years before, and run by John Rich, the son of the late patentee of Drury Lane.

This revival of the Anglo-Italian *Camilla* showed that, although the real Italian opera was just kept going by the support of a few loyalists, it was at least losing its novelty. The Lincoln's Inn Fields Theatre therefore followed the usual theatre custom of looking for what Cibber called 'some new-fangled foppery to draw the multitude', and so after *Camilla* the Anglo-Italian operas *Thomyris* and *Calypso* were both revived with English singers in accordance with the theatre's policy as a counterblast to the Queen's. This was not enough, however—as Cibber said, 'our English music had been so discountenanced since the taste of Italian operas prevailed, that it was to no purpose to pretend to it'. So in 1718 the Lincoln's Inn Fields Theatre tried out a real novelty—for the first time presenting a narrative ballet, the story of Mars and Venus told in pantomime.[5] They made a feature of ballet sequences in a new English opera, Galliard's *Pan and Syrinx* on a libretto by Lewis Theobald, which had twelve performances in 1718, and Settle's comi-dramatic opera *The Lady's Triumph* was given eight times by the all-English cast—the one foreign-born artist being Margarita de l'Epine, who, however, married Dr. Pepusch this year, and so practically achieved honorary naturalisation.

Italian opera at the Queen's, with uninteresting new works and dull revivals, criticised left and right and challenged by the new dancing experiments at Lincoln's Inn Fields, was now only just keeping going, thanks to the leaders of fashion who had just managed to keep it alive for ten years—a sobering thought for all who have been brought up to believe that at the beginning of the eighteenth century Italian opera came, sang and permanently conquered the London stage, winning over all artistic connoisseurs.

---

[1] One one occasion Purcell got rid of him by making him lose his temper: they were in a drinking party and when no one came to answer their call to draw some more wine, Purcell, examining the table, said 'What, no drawer?' Dennis at once left, not wishing to sit with such dishonest company that could make such a bad pun!

[2] A closer—but equally banal—translation which is not too flowerily unfair to the more direct Italian, but which still could not justify the aria, would be :—

O cruel beast, what now?
    You come so fierce and savage
      To tear my breast in two?
    My heart you cannot ravage,
That heart, that still I vow
      Unto my love is true!

[3] All dates in this book up to September 1752, when the calendar was changed, are given in the Old Style.

[4] Add. MS. 11258.

[5] Was this suggested by someone's memory of *The Slighted Maid*? See p. 81 *sqq.*

CHAPTER FIVE

The Royal Academy

By 1718, owing to lack of support and lack of finance, the Queen's closed down for two years—apart from a few months when some French comedians played there, though at the same time Drury Lane went triumphantly ahead with English plays and Lincoln's Inn Fields still played the Englished *Thomyris*—a double refutation of the wishful belief of some opera-lovers that Italian opera was dominating the London stage at this time. Some of the leaders of fashion, however, piqued perhaps because their operatic enthusiasm was not shared by the ordinary theatre-going public, decided that the time had come to prove their superior knowledge of musical style and the Italian language by financing Italian opera.

In doing this not only did they hope to gain themselves credit by supporting a worthy artistic venture, but—convinced that they only had to show the way to be followed by anybody who was anybody—they thought they might also make a fortune out of the speculation, as many of them anticipated they would do out of the no less romantic South Sea Company.

The scheme for sharing in the riches of the South Sea traders and for abolishing at the same time the National Debt had originally been launched by Harley, Earl of Oxford, some fourteen years before. By 1718, however, Spain, which had been said to have been willing to grant trading licences, was at war with England: still speculators were eager to get shares, and speculation, as Dent pointed out in his *Handel*, 'had become the universal fashion'.

£50,000 therefore was raised to establish the Royal Academy of Music in imitation of the French Royal Academy, which was responsible for the Paris opera: shares were £100 each, and the King himself subscribed £1,000. So on May 9, 1719, the Lord Chamberlain approved the new society, and on May 14 he empowered Handel to go abroad to engage the famous *castrato* Senesino and any other artists he thought good enough

The Academy had a governor, a deputy-governor and twenty directors—the first attempt by a board of distinguished amateurs to organise an artistic venture of professionals, and as this was such a momentous precedent, I give the cast-list of one of the first operatic governing bodies,[1] complete with a description of each individual as far as I have been able to find it out. I have tried to be fair, but it may be that others may find in these individuals—apart from the obvious three—more suitable qualities than those that led, I think, to the inevitable failure that resulted from their appointment. The descriptions I have found in the *Dictionary of National Biography, Burke's Extinct Peerages*, etc.

The Governor was Thomas Pelham-Holles, Duke of Newcastle, aged 26: he was 'nervous, pompous, always in a hurry, and always behindhand: ignorant of common things, and not learned in any sense'; he was afterwards nicknamed 'Permis' for his sheepish way of addressing George II's Queen and Princesses: he was a turncoat. The Deputy-governor was Robert Benson, Lord Bingley, of Yorkshire, aged 43: he was the son of a dishonest father, of mean extraction and of little worth: a Privy Councillor and a turncoat, he 'disobliged both sides so much that neither will ever own him': he was an enthusiast for architecture.

Among the Directors there was a Yorkshire contingent and an Irish contingent: in the former there was William Pulteney, Esq., aged 35, M.P. for Holderness in Yorkshire and Privy Councillor, later Earl of Bath, a highly intellectual, eloquent and witty classicist, extravagant and with a great love of money—another turncoat: there was Conyers d'Arcy, Esq., second son of the Earl of Holderness, M.P. for York and Master of Horse for Anne and George I, a brother-in-law of another Director, the Duke of Portland, aged 37, the son of William III's Dutch favourite: there was Bryan Fairfax, Esq., aged 43, the son of a Yorkshire politican, a collector of books and pictures.

The Irish contingent was headed by Richard Boyle, Earl of Burlington and Earl of Cork, aged 24, the patron of Handel: he was all for outside show, but lavish and without envy: an enthusiast for architecture, he rebuilt Inigo Jones's church in Covent Garden and Burlington House, Piccadilly, which was satirised by Hogarth, for masquerades and operas. There was John, Viscount Chetwynd of Bearhaven, County Cork, and Baron of Rathdowne, County Dublin, aged about 34, the Receiver-General of the Duchy of Lancaster and Envoy Extraordinary to Madrid in 1717: there was Colonel James O'Hara, aged 29, son of

Baron Tyrawley, and later Baron Kilmaine of Ireland, a popular wit, who was said by Walpole to be 'imperiously blunt, haughty and contemptuous, with an undaunted portion of spirit, a great deal of humour and occasional good breeding', but was considered 'singularly licentious, even for the courts of Russia and Portugal': there was Francis Whitworth, Esq., the younger brother of Charles, afterwards Baron Whitworth in the Irish Peerage, though of a Staffordshire family, and Major-General Wade, aged 46, also an Irishman, more solid than brilliant, who, though he lacked initiative and was perplexed by responsibility, was an M.P., a Privy Councillor, the subduer of the Old Pretender's supporters, had been at Saragossa, and in 1708 was second in command to General James Stanhope, afterwards the first Earl of Stanhope.

Philip Dormer, Lord Stanhope, aged 25, was also a Director: he was a pedantic classicist and, after a tour of Flanders, a gallant gamester and orator: he was Gentleman of the Bedchamber to the Prince of Wales in 1715, but stayed friendly with the King; he had been an M.P. before he was 21, and was a friend of Pope, Arbuthnot and Swift; he was known then for his tact, and is now famous for his letter-writing when he succeeded his father as Earl of Chesterfield.

The two Directors best fitted to deal with opera were Sir John Vanbrugh, aged 55, the architect-dramatist, who had built the Queen's Theatre and later built Claremont House, Esher, for the Duke of Newcastle—he was accepted by society for his wit and his handsome looks—and Colonel Blathwayte, who had been a pupil of Alessandro Scarlatti and an amazing harpsichordist at the age of 12, when Kneller painted his portrait, which is in the Music School at Oxford.

Other military Directors were John Dalrymple, Earl of Stair, aged 46, a general under Marlborough, who had won his wife by appearing at her bedroom window and so endangering her reputation—he had intrigued for the Hanoverian succession, had been Minister Plenipotentiary in Paris, where he lived *en prince* from May to December each year from 1715 to 1734, and later, when his fortune was impaired, cultivated turnips and cabbages, and Brigadier-General James Dormer (related to Lord Stanhope?), aged 40, the grandson of the Master of Ceremonies to Charles I, Charles II and James II, a member of the Kitcat Club, who had been at Blenheim and Saragossa.

Other Directors were Charles Douglas, Duke of Queensberry, aged 21, who later supported Gay over the licence for *Polly* with his wife, who loved balls and masquerades; James, Earl of Waldegrave, a Jacobite turncoat and a diplomatist; James Bruce, Esq., who later succeeded his brother as Earl of Cardigan, possibly of the same family as the Barons Bruce of Whorlton, Yorkshire, and Thomas Coke, of Norfolk, Esq., about whom I can find nothing.

The interrelation of many of the governing body through family, county, country or military service is remarkable, but though they may have been genuinely enthusiastic about opera, which of them on the face of it had any qualifications that are necessary for running an opera-house, apart from perhaps three of them? Lord Burlington and his mother had had Handel staying with them for three years—he had written *Amadigi* under their roof: Vanbrugh was a theatre-man and Blathwayte was musical, but the architectural knowledge of the one or the military experience of the other hardly added to their operatic knowledge.

Apart from these three, was there one whose inclusion on that board is not a solemn warning to all who have the appointing of artistic boards of governors and trustees? Unfortunately we are so bound by tradition that, just as we accept the untrue fact that Italian opera successfully dominated the London stage from the start of the eighteenth century, largely through Handel and the Royal Academy of Music, so we set up the same sort of constitution for propagating art and music—influential and titled amateurs in not necessarily the best sense of the word—ignoring the true fact that the originals—for all their good intentions and enthusiasms—quickly brought their project to disaster.

The Academy's first season opened on Saturday April 2, 1720, with Porta's *Numitore*, the libretto by the Academy's contracted poet, Rolli. Apart from Holy Week, the Queen's—now a real opera-house—set out to give two performances a week, *Numitore* being played five times running. Then Handel's new *Radamisto* was produced on April 27 and more arrived for the first performance than the theatre could hold—after all, Handel was intended to be the great attraction: there were ten performances of it that season. *Numitore* had two more performances, and *Narciso*, with music by Scarlatti and Roseingrave, which followed the eighth

Radamisto, had only five performances and, like *Numitore*, was never revived. Strangely enough, though perhaps wisely, in view of the apathetic feeling of the London audience to Italian opera, the singers that season were half English, half Italian—Anastasia Robinson, Mr. Turner Robinson, Mr. Gordon, Baldassari, Durastanti and Galerati, with Mrs. Dennis in *Numitore* and Mr. La Garde in *Radamisto*: the part of Radamisto was sung by Signora Durastanti, who had been engaged by Handel in his talent-search the year before.

Though he had not been able to get Senesino, as requested, he had found several excellent singers at Dresden: they, however, were not available for London until, after being disgruntled by Handel's tempting offers, as Dent thinks, they had been dismissed from Dresden. They then came to London in the autumn of 1720—Senesino (i.e. 'the man from Siena', whose real name was Francesco Bernardi), Boschi, Berenstadt, Berselli and Salvai.

Before they could open, however, the Directors had to ask on November 7 for £5 per cent from each subscriber to cope with expenses—a proof that they had not even run their first season properly—besides, the South Sea Bubble burst that year. At last they opened the winter season at the King's (as it now was) in November 1720, giving two performances a week—usually Wednesday and Saturday—until June, the closing month for social events.

The first opera was one that may have been seen in Rome by Lord Burlington five years before and written by Predieri, Löwenberg thinks, but now reset by Bononcini with the libretto suitably altered by Rolli—*Astarto*. It was a great success with twenty performances that season.

Radamisto was revived in January 1721, Durastanti now playing a woman's part and leaving the hero to Senesino, but even so it had only seven scattered performances—a shock to Handel's supporters both then and now. A pasticcio, *Arsace*—a version of Orlandini's *Amore e Maesta* of 1715—was given eight times running, and at the end of February Sir John Edgar, in a journal called *The Theatre*, satirically rejoiced that at last 'the delight of sound has prevailed over the pain of sense'. As a proof he goes on to say:—

The following song is written by a person who has offended very much by mixing a little understanding in his composures, but has expressed his penitence and reformation by a contrary practice, as will appear by the following song, which is admirably well set to music by a famous Italian Master. . . .

i.

So notwithstanding heretofore
Straightforward by and by
Now everlastingly therefore
Too low and eke too high.

ii.

Then for almost and also why
Not thus when less so near
Oh! for hereafter quite so nigh
But greatly ever here.

It is not to be doubted but this piece will meet with applause, for it gives no manner of disturbance to the head, but merely serves to be added to sounds proper to the syllables. . . . The particular words were indeed translated for the master and he gave them dying notes accordingly, for upon the supposition that lovers are to be constant and unhappy, as they are equally so in all nations, the force, the pathos, is most admirably laid upon the word 'everlastingly' with a due impatience in the notes on 'by and by'.

Now he comes out with the accusation that there is only one form of sense left—that is a sense of profit, and he says that the opera merchants have

a stock laid in to impose upon the stupidity of their admirers, and it is expected that there will be a nightly succession of bubbles in numbers large enough who will part with their cash, as well as their understanding, to support a mechanic and mean profit raised by gentlemen of honour and quality upon ingenuous arts.

Could anything be clearer than this accusation of speculative chicanery? Or can it be pretended that this is merely a malicious, unfounded libel, and that all the noble directors of the Royal Academy were really honest and knowledgeable patrons of the arts? Even if they were honest, they were not knowledgeable, as the sequel will show.

The Theatre goes on to stress the parallel between the South Sea subscribers and the Academy subscribers by quoting the former stock at 174, which may well have been the figure at the time (though it did reach 890), and Opera Company stock at $83\frac{1}{2}$. The next issue, March 5–8, becomes more satirical:—

At the rehearsal on Friday last Signor Nihilini Beneditti rose $\frac{1}{2}$ a note above his pitch formerly known. Opera stock from $83\frac{1}{2}$ when he began: at 90 when he ended.

Alluding to that information, there is a letter in the next issue from one Musicorus pointing out that Beneditti—what a good name!—was injured by the Board of Directors insisting he should play an unsuitable part: he made this clear to them:—

he set forth in the recitative tone the nearest approaching ordinary speech that he had never acted anything in any other opera below the character of a sovereign or at least a prince of the blood, and that now he was appointed to be a Captain of the Guard and a Pimp, etc.

Satirical as this was, and aimed more at the singers than the Directors, it surely implied that the Directors did in fact interfere in the running of the opera-house, which they might better have left in the hands of Handel, Rolli or even Heidegger, who was officially in charge.

Handel was concerned with only one new operatic work in the 1720–21 season, *Il Muzio Scevola*, for which he and the new King's composers, Ariosti and Bononcini, each wrote an act—not, as is often said, as a competition which was won by Handel, but, as Dent thinks, following Burney, so as to save time. It had eleven performances (far fewer than Bononcini's own *Astarto*), while the last new work of the season, Ariosti's *Ciro*, or *L'Odio e l'Amore*, had only eight. In this year incidentally the King was godfather by proxy to Durastanti's daughter.

D'Urfey now weighed in with some more sarcasm against opera in general. He published three *New Operas* in 1721, one of which was *The Two Queens of Brentford*, which he describes as a musical farce or comical opera, being the sequel to the *Rehearsal*. In this comes the following scene:—

Bayes.   I have contrived another opera rarity. It has always been a great beauty in 'em to get a lion or a bear in to put one of the chief actors in distress, who, being very outrageous upon the poor fellow that was covered in the monster's shape and to show his extreme valour, has often beat and bruised him unmercifully. . . .

Smith.   Oh, nothing more natural in an opera than a lion, Mr. Bayes.

Johnson.   Ay, or the creature that goes about with long ears would do very well.

The idea is that the hero, one of King George's officers, should meet a 'seeming lion', in reality a Scotch conjuror, who,

hearing his melodious and delicate trillo, is so alarmed that after two or three flourishes and light buffets received, he sings the bass part in a dialogue with him and afterwards a Scotch song, where giving him the victory he saves the breath of one and the bones of the other.

In a poem he published this year D'Urfey again alludes to the opera

> When Caponides trills and squeaks
> And nonsense with the audience takes.

By July of 1721, only sixteen months after the first production by the Royal Academy, the Directors had made their sixth call on the subscribers for money, and Burney's calculations on the extravagant methods of the distinguished Board are worth quoting here:—

Now as £50,000 was the original sum subscribed, the first call of £5 per cent amounted to £2,500. And as all the several calls which I have seen advertised in the papers of the times are for £5 each, except the last (which was £4) we may fairly suppose that a sum nearly amounting to £15,000 had been sunk in a little more than a year from the establishment of the academy.

Not all the subscribers paid up, and by November another call was made, closely followed by a 'general court of the corporation of the Royal Academy of Music' to choose new directors—as they did each year—and the following day the Duke of Manchester was elected as a new deputy-governor, while on November 25 it was announced that each subscriber would have to pay up ten guineas 'on the delivery of his ticket', five more on February 1 and five more on May 1, in the hope that fifty operas might be presented that season.

As far as I can see, only some six operas were in fact performed in the 1722 season, the first being Handel's fair success, *Il Floridante*: but Bononcini had two, *Crispo* and *Griselda*—eighteen and sixteen performances respectively—with the result, as Dent points out, that the Academy could declare a dividend of seven per cent —another blow for Handel's admirers, as Dent's explanation in his book on Handel must also be:—

Bononcini's music was pleasing and, after a far longer experience than Handel's, he naturally wrote what singers enjoyed singing . . . . Besides, Bononcini was a stranger and a novelty; Handel was becoming a national institution—indeed, he was well on the way to becoming an English composer.

One reason perhaps why these two Bononcini operas were popular is that they hit the growing sentimental taste of the day: kings and emperors ruled the operatic world for several years to come, but they only pleased the public when they showed that royalty, too, had its feelings. Sir Richard Steele, who is always said to have been jealously prejudiced in his criticism of Italian opera, showed in his play *The Conscious Lovers*, which was produced in the same year as *Crispo* and *Griselda*, that many of the audience could appreciate charm, though they might still regret a lack of depth:—

Indiana. First give me leave to thank you for my tickets.
Beverley junior. Oh your servant, madam! But pray tell me,—you now, who are over partial to the fashion, I fancy, must be the best judge of a mighty dispute among the ladies, that is, whether *Crispo* or *Griselda* is the more agreeable entertainment.
Indiana. With submission now I cannot be a proper judge of this question.
Beverley. How so, Madam?
Indiana. Because I find I have a partiality for one of them.
Beverley. Pray which is that?
Indiana. I do not know—there's something in that rural cottage of Griselda, her forlorn condition, her poverty, her solitude, her resignation, her innocent slumbers, and that lulling 'Dolce Sogno' that's sung over her: it had an effect upon me that—in short I never was so well deceived at any of them.
Beverley. Oh now then! I can account for the dispute:—*Griselda*, it seems, is the distress of an injured, innocent woman, *Crispo* that only of a man in the same condition: therefore the men are mostly concerned for Crispo, and by a natural indulgence both sexes for Griselda.
Indiana. So that judgement, you think, ought to be for one, tho' fancy and complaisance have got ground for the other. Well, I believe you will never give me leave to dispute with you on any subject: for I own *Crispo* has its charms for me too—though in the main all the pleasure the best opera gives us is but mere sensation. Methinks it's pity the mind can't have a little more share in the entertainment. The music's certainly fine: but in my thoughts there's none of your composers come up to old Shakespeare and Otway.

From now on, relying on the promised support of the noble Directors of the Academy and their unpaid-up shareholders, Italian operas were churned out for the King's Theatre, and, encouraged by his backers, Handel did most of the churning. For the 1722–3 season he produced the successful *Ottone, Re di Germania* and the unsuccessful *Flavio* against Ariosti's successful *Caio Marzio Coriolano* which, Colman said, 'pleased much', and Bononcini's short-runned *Erminia*. It was in 1723 that Durastanti left England, and the short, ugly, brilliant singer, Cuzzoni, first appeared with a great reputation and a higher salary than other singers—£2,000 and a benefit for the season. She made her debut in Handel's *Ottone*, after he had threatened to throw her out of the window for objecting to one aria, and was an instant success, as the *London Journal* said on January 19, with

a numerous audience, who are ever too fond of foreign performers. She is already jumped into a handsome chariot and an equipage accordingly. The gentry seem to have so high a taste of her fine parts that she is likely to be a great gainer by them.

Music now became fashionable, as John Gay pointed out to Dean Swift in February 1723 :—'There is nobody allowed to say "I sing" but an eunuch or an Italian woman. . . . Folks that could not distinguish one tune from another now daily dispute about the different styles of Handel, Bononcini, and Attilio' (Ariosti). '. . . In London and Westminster in all polite conversations Senesino is daily voted to be the greatest man that ever lived.' Despite this Handel's new *Flavio* was not a success, perhaps because it was so short—it began at eight instead of the more usual six or six-thirty. In the same year, however, *Le Mercure* announced that some Italian actors from the London opera would perform in Paris, though the visit does not seem to have materialised.

Bononcini's *Farnace* was the first new work in the 1723–4 season, but failed, while Handel's *Giulio Cesare in Egitto* was a real success in competition with Bononcini's successful *Calfurnia*, Ariosti's *Vespasiano*, which 'did not please', and a pasticcio *Aquilio*, which failed and in which Durastanti sang for the last time before returning to Italy.

In November Handel's successful *Tamerlano* opened the 1724–5 season, and after Ariosti's failure *Artaserse* Handel's triumphant *Rodelinda* started a new fashion for the ladies with the brown-and-silver dress Cuzzoni wore, and Vinci's *Elpidia* was by no means a failure, though Ariosti's *Il Dario* only had five performances.

Although Bononcini had no opera performed that year, he was evidently still thought of as Handel's chief rival by musical London, headed by the King and Queen for Handel against the Prince of Wales and Dr. Maurice Greene for Bononcini, for John Byrom recorded that in May 1725 he had met

Bob Ord, who was come home from Cambridge, where he said he made the whole Hall laugh at Trinity College and got himself honour by my epigram upon Handel and Bononcini, and in June he published that epigram, which afterwards was attributed to Swift or Pope:—

> Some say, compared to Bononcini,
> That Mynheer Handel's but a ninny:
> Others aver that he to Handel
> Is scarcely fit to hold a candle.
> Strange all this difference should be
> 'Twixt Tweedledum and Tweedledee!

But then Byrom had hated *Giulio Cesare* and hoped he would never see another opera.

By 1725 it was the fashion to be opera-minded, for in that year an anonymous writer published

A Letter to my Lord . . . on the present Diversions of the Town with the true Reason of the decay of our dramatic entertainments.

He thought that all theatrical performances were bad except the operas:—

Our operas indeed are in perfection: we have a composer or two, and two singers that cannot be excelled, if rivalled, by any in the universe. But yet I have a complaint against them—'them', I cannot say, but against our immoderate love for them. . . .

I own, my lord, the charms of music and dote on them: I can dwell on the delightful tone of Senesino's voice or attend to the pleasing extravagances of our little warbler Cuzzoni with as much rapture as anyone, and more, I believe, than most people: but, however, it is with grief I see music banish everything else from our discourse, it is with regret, I see our fiddlers looked on as the first geniuses of our nation, and that a man must make harmony his study to be fashionable in company.

He goes on to say that at White's Club men of wit and letters, instead of discussing Shakespeare or Virgil, now talk only of fugues, counterfugues and divisions:—

we are as great pedants in music as any the University can produce in the classics.

Yet even this might be tolerable in those who are judges of it, in those who have a delicate ear and taste: but the infection reaches further, even to them who are entirely ignorant of the science, who have no relish for it, no satisfaction in it, who are weary of an opera before it is half finished, and these generally, if not always, make a great part of the audience.

Opera-making in England seems by now to have become formalised, to judge from a letter written in September 1725 by the Modenese Representative in London, the Abbate Giuseppe

Riva, to the historian Ludovico Antonio Muratori and quoted (in English) by Streatfeild in the *Musical Quarterly* for July 1917. In this he gives the following advice to a would-be librettist. In England, he says:—

they want few recitatives, but thirty arias and one duet at least, distributed over the three acts. The subject-matter must be straightforward, tender, heroic, Roman, Greek, or even Persian, and never Gothic or Longobard.

For this year and for the two following there must be two equal parts in the operas for Cuzzoni and Faustina: Senesino is the chief male character and his part must be heroic: the other three male parts must proceed by degrees with three arias each, one in each act. The duet should be at the end of the second act, and between the two ladies. If the subject has in it three ladies, it can serve, because there is a third singer here.

In actual fact Cuzzoni's brilliant and beautiful rival, Faustina, had at that time only been announced, and did not arrive in England till 1726.

The 1725–6 season was practically Handel's with *Scipione*, produced on March 12, 1726, just after his naturalisation, and *Alessandro* on May 5 in which Faustina Bordoni, Cuzzoni and Senesino appeared together for the first time in London with the result that there were no less than twelve performances within a month. The noble patrons of opera, however, failed to encourage the publication of the latter, only two or three of the Academy directors subscribing to it.

But the great success of 1726 was another revival of the perennial Anglo-Italian *Camilla* at Lincoln's Inn Fields in November— twenty-three performances in the 1726–7 season, ten more than either of the last Handel operas, no doubt because many people 'liked it for old acquaintance sake', as one music-lover did, though she was not enthusiastic, seeing that 'there is not many of the songs better than ballads'. This critic was Mary Granville, now the second wife of Alexander Pendarves, whose first wife had been the Lady Dorothy Burke, who had spoken the prologue to *Dido and Aeneas* at its first performance at the Chelsea school in 1690.

By this time the great Senesino had gone back to Italy for a holiday, and as Faustina and Cuzzoni—the only other two attractions—were at daggers drawn, the Italian opera at the King's was not too healthy, as the prologue to the *Camilla* revival shows:—

Ye British fair, vouchsafe us your applause,
And smile, propitious, on our English cause!
While Senesino you expect in vain
And see your favours treated with disdain,
While 'twixt his rival queens such mutual hate
Threats hourly ruin to your tuneful state,
Permit your country's voices to repair
In some degree your disappointment there.

The disappointment with the King's was that that foreign-occupied theatre did not open as usual in November 1726, in spite of rumours—Mrs. Pendarves went to see *Camilla* that month, after having heard Cuzzoni sing that morning, so that her senses 'were ravished with harmony' and then commented, 'They say we shall have operas in a fortnight, but I think Madame Sandoni and Faustina are not agreed about their parts'. She was wrong, however, as the season did not start at the King's till January 7, 1727, with Ariosti's *Lucio Vero, Imperatore di Roma*, which had only ten performances in this and the following seasons. Nearly three weeks later Mrs. Pendarves was glad that Faustina, 'the most agreeable creature in the world', was going to sing with Cuzzoni and Senesino and that 'we are to have our senses ravished by her melodious voice'. Did she prefer her to Mme. Cuzzoni-Sandoni?

By now the music of an opera was becoming of more importance by itself than the combination of music with words, story, scenery and the other ingredients—or so it appears from James Moore Smythe's play of January 27, *The Rival Modes*, in which it is said that 'the composers of our operas scorn to call in the assistance of good poetry, that they may show how the science of music can shine by itself'.

Four days after that play, Handel's version of the Alcestis story, *Admeto Re di Tessaglia*, was produced, and successfully had nineteen performances between January 31 and April 18. To judge from Burney's comments on it, this opera certainly appealed to the pure musicians—in the printed libretto, for example, at the start of the second act, Burney says:—

a horrid symphony to express the cries and shrieks of tortured souls is announced, but instead of wild jargon and hellish dissonance, Handel has given us a regular overture with one of the most artificial chromatic fugues that was ever produced, in which the subject . . . is reversed in the answer, and then interwoven and carried on as a counter subject throughout the movement.

The musicians were also intrigued by the use of French horns in a hunting aria. Colman said of the *Admeto* performances 'during all this time the house filled every night fuller than ever was known at any opera for so long together'.

Lewis Theobald's pantomime opera, *The Rape of Proserpine*, produced about a fortnight later at Lincoln's Inn Fields, also implies that music and singing was becoming more important, for the author complains that foreign singers are so highly paid that good scenery cannot be afforded. In one of the songs in the play was sung

> Here be de Haymarket, vere de Italian Opera
> Do sweetly sound
> Dat costa de brave Gentry no more as
> Two hundred thousand pound.

But it must not be thought that only the jealous English playwrights and musicians were critical of operas in which bad-quality words and sentiments were excused because the music was of good quality: one anonymous Italian writer inveighed heavily against them in an essay that was translated and published this year, called *Advice to the Composers and Performers of Vocal Music.* It should be studied by all such artists of to-day.

In this the author said:—

> The greatest perfection of vocal music is that it be made subservient to the words, or—to speak more plainly—that the composer takes particular care to express the sense of them, rejecting the most pleasing movement which is improper for that purpose, and contenting himself with a more indifferent one, which answers that end—by which means he takes the surest way not to please those alone who have skill in music, but others also, who only give attention to the words.

He points out that a composer who sets a 'fine, brisk air' to words of a different character is like Horace's painter,

> who, when he was required to paint one who had escaped from shipwreck with the loss of everything, could paint nothing else but a cypress-tree.

On the other hand, some composers, he said, even when they do hit on the right music are inclined to

> spin out the thread of their fancy through all the possible variations of counterpoint and modulation.

After all,

It is not the great number of notes that moves the passions, but a few disposed in due time and place, and modulated with art and judgment.

The growing tendency was for the symphonies or introductions before the arias to be extended, and

if a stop be not put to it, the singer will be made to give place to the instruments and the orchestra will be more regarded than the voices.

It was all-important to see that the accompaniment fits the mood and that the new trick of writing in unison with the voice should not be over-used: at times an indifferent song heightens what follows. A singer needs an excellent voice, fine taste, perfect intonation, ability to learn how to keep exact time, sing the words with expression and keep the voice steady,

embellishing the composition with proper graces.

The great aim of a real artist should be to know when to use vocal effects such as legato or staccato, and he should know his own abilities,

but selflove, which often blinds persons of good sense, and the applause the singer meets with from the multitude often corrupts his judgment, so that he comes to fancy himself a much more excellent performer than he really is, and to flatter himself that he merits the applause that is given him, although it has no better foundation than mere caprice or the want of judgment and good taste in those who extol him.

The vanity of self-satisfied singers, than which there is probably nothing more colossal in the world, was well exemplified in May 1727, when Faustina and Cuzzoni appeared together in Bononcini's *Astianatte*. Each was excellent, though in different ways. Quantz, the flute-player and composer who taught Frederick the Great the flute, heard Cuzzoni in London this year, and told Burney that she

had a very agreeable and clear soprano voice, a pure intonation, and a fine shake: her compass extended two octaves, from C to c in alt. Her style of singing was innocent and affecting: her graces did not seem artificial, from the easy and neat manner in which she executed them: however, they took possession of the soul of every auditor by her tender and touching expression.

She had no great rapidity of execution in allegros, but there was a roundness and smoothness which were neat and pleasing. Yet with all these advantages it must be owned that she was rather cold in her action, and her figure was not advantageous for the stage.

She was, in fact, squat, dumpy and very plain.

Faustina, on the other hand, though tiny, had a perfect figure and a lovely face, and of her Quantz said that her mezzo-soprano voice

was less clear than penetrating. Her compass now was only from B flat to G in alt, but after this time she extended its limits downwards. She possessed what the Italians call 'un cantar granito': her execution was articulate and brilliant.

She had a fluent tongue for pronouncing words rapidly and distinctly, and a flexible throat for divisions, with so beautiful and quick a shake that she could put it in motion upon short notice, just when she would. The passages might be smooth, or by leaps, or consisting of iterations of the same tone, their execution was equally easy to her as to any instrument whatever. She was doubtless the first who introduced with success a swift repetition of the same tone.

She sung adagios with great passion and expression, but was not equally successful if such deep sorrow were to be impressed on the hearer as might require dragging, sliding, or notes of syncopation and tempo rubato.

She had a very happy memory in arbitrary changes and embellishments, and a clear and quick judgment in giving to words their full power and expression. In her action she was very happy: and, as she perfectly possessed that flexibility of muscles and features which constitutes face-playing, she succeeded equally well in furious, amorous, and tender parts: in short, she was born for singing and for acting.

Burney recorded that Cuzzoni on the other hand used embellishments sparingly, but excelled in rubato singing, while 'her intonations were so just and fixed that it seemed as if it were not in her power to sing out of tune'.

Tosi, who had set up in London as a singing-teacher for some time, considered their merit to be above praise,

for with equal strength, though in different styles, they help to keep up the tottering profession from immediately falling into ruin.

He remarked that

the pathos of the one and the rapidity of the other are distinctly characteristic. What a beautiful mixture it would be, if the excellencies of these two angelic beings could be united in a single individual!

Unfortunately these angels had begun to quarrel, partly no doubt through Cuzzoni's temper, but largely through the fatuous idolatry of their respective admirers—the Countess of Burlington, Lady Delaware and most of the men, headed by Sir Robert Walpole, for the lovely Faustina, Lady Pembroke and Lady

Walpole leading the rival camp—though Lady Walpole had scored in society by getting them each to sing at the same soirée, while the other was taken to examine some curious china. Quantz recorded that

the violence of party for the two singers, Cuzzoni and Faustina, was so great that when the admirers of one began to applaud, those of the other were sure of hiss—on which account operas ceased for some time in London.

The singers themselves came to blows on occasion, but the climax was reached at the ninth performance of *Astianatte* by Bononcini on June 6, 1727, and the *London Journal* reported the event four days later:—

A great disturbance happened at the opera, occasioned by the partisans of the two celebrated rival ladies, Cuzzoni and Faustina. The contention at first was only carried on by hissing on one side and clapping on the other, but proceeded at length to the melodious use of cat-calls and other accompaniments, which manifested the zeal and politeness of that illustrious assembly.

The Princess Caroline was there, but neither her Royal Highness's presence nor the laws of decorum could restrain the glorious ardour of the combatants.

The fracas, it must be noted, was caused, not by the riff-raff in the gallery, but by the society leaders who—we are always taught —did so much for opera: it was commemorated by this often-quoted epigram which stresses that fact:—

> Old poets sing that beasts did dance
> Whenever Orpheus play'd:
> So to Faustina's charming voice
> Wise Pembroke's asses bray'd.

The whole situation was satirised in an anonymous one-act play called *The Contretemps, or, Rival Queans*, which was later attributed—wrongly, Nicoll thinks—to Cibber. The scene of this 'small farce', as it was called, was 'the Temple of Discord near the Haymarket': with a chorus of Dukes, Lords and 'Tupees' [2] with cat-calls in their hands and bells round their necks, Heidegger (though, like all the names, his is indicated by dashes) begs F - - - - and C - - - - to make friends:—

Heidegger. With bright Faustina we lose all our beams.
    And Dukes must die when sweet Cuzzoni goes.
Handel.   Nor shall the Saxon ever more compose.

Heidegger, the High Priest to the Academy of Discord, and Handel, the Professor of Harmony to the Academy, fail to stop

Faustina, Queen of Bologna, and Cuzzoni, Princess of Modena, insulting each other. Senesino, the Chief of the Choir, begs them to desist:—

.Senesino. If no respect you have for Senesino,
Think of what sums you leave of ready rhino!

In an aside he admits that he takes bribes from each of the ladies, who blacken each other's characters, Cuzzoni attacking Faustina's morals, while Faustina enlarges on Cuzzoni's ugliness: they soon begin to box at each other, but Handel says

Let them fight it out.
Oil to the flames you add to stop their rage:
When tired, of course their fury will assuage.

For the moment they stop to take breath, but soon, to an accompaniment of cat-calls, serpents and cuckoos, they start up again:—

Faustina lays flat Cuzzoni's nose with a sceptre, Cuzzoni breaks her head with a gilt leather crown: Handel, desirous to see the end of the battle, animates them with a kettledrum: a globe thrown at random hits the High Priest on the temples: he staggers off the stage.

'M - - n - - o', the 'Violino Primo to the Queen of Bologna to keep Her Majesty's Body in tune', and Sandoni, the 'Basso Continuo, and Treasurer to the Princess of Modena' (and in real life Cuzzoni's husband) take shelter behind the scenes:—

the Queen loses her head of hair and the Princess her nose in the skirmish: at last the Goddess of Discord inspires Cuzzoni with more than mortal bravery, she plies her antagonist so warmly the Queen is obliged to fly—the Princess follows: Senesino creeps from under the altar where he lay hid, and moralises in the following simile—,

which is about a fight of two bull-dogs just over a dry bone: he then brings the play to an end by pointing the comparison:—

The pageant glory of a title thus
To rage provokes each caterwauling puss:
So much to show of greatness is their care,
They'll lose the substance for a puff of air.

It is just possible that the rivalry that the two prima donnas inspired in their followers was stronger than the rivalry between themselves, for after the coronation of George II they appeared together again on November 27, 1727, at the start of the new season, with Senesino back from his holiday, in Handel's fairly successful *Riccardo Primo, Re d'Inghilterra*. In spite of this reunion of the three popular stars, however, Mrs. Pendarves wrote only a fortnight later:—

I doubt operas will not survive longer than this winter: they are now at their last gasp: the subscription is expired, and nobody will renew it. The directors are always squabbling, and they have so many divisions among themselves that I wonder they have not broke up before. Senesino goes away next winter, and, I believe, Faustina, so you see harmony is almost out of fashion.

But the greatest setback to Italian opera—far greater than the Faustina–Cuzzoni affair, the directors' quarrels, or the constant drain on the subscribers (the recent call on them was the nineteenth in seven years)—was the production at the Lincoln's Inn Fields Theatre on January 29, 1728, of *The Beggar's Opera*.

It has always been said that this was a satire on Italian opera, but it seems to me that the truth of this has been misunderstood, for musically it is utterly unlike the Italian opera of that period—or, for that matter, opera of any country or style except its own, the ballad opera style which it inaugurated. Brought up as we are, to think of opera as music first and foremost, I wonder that nobody has queried the often-repeated statement, for *The Beggar's Opera* has no recitatives, no *da capo* arias, and no arias of the accepted kind so much admired by the Italian opera enthusiasts—*aria d'agilita, aria fugata, aria di bravura*, and the rest. Nor is there any allusion to Italian opera or singers, except the Beggar's statement that 'I have not made my opera throughout unnatural, like those in vogue; for I have no recitative'—though no doubt the quarrel between Lucy and Polly echoed the Faustina–Cuzzoni dispute.

Surely the truth of the statement must lie in the fact that *The Beggar's Opera* lyrics are brilliant satires of the sort of verses that were printed as English versions of the librettos of the Italian operas. The lofty figurative lines such as

> Virgins are like the fair flower in its lustre,
> Which in the garden enamels the ground:
> Near it the bees in play flutter and cluster,
> And gaudy butterflies frolic around.

were well in the style of the highfalutin English 'improvements' of Italian opera lyrics—and indeed far better than most of them—

but the extravagant simile was shown to be ludicrous by being brought down to earth—or rather the gutter—with a bang in the next lines:—

> But, when once pluck'd, 'tis no longer alluring:
> To Covent Garden 'tis sent—as yet sweet:
> There fades and shrinks, and grows past all enduring,
> Rots, stinks, and dies, and is trod under feet.

To the average London theatre-goer at the time a stage entertainment was primarily one of words and thoughts and actions: music might be used, as was scenery, to enhance the drama, and sometimes perhaps to colour it beyond its merit, but the drama was of prime importance. It was natural, therefore, that every critic of Italian opera looked first at the dramatic content as exhibited in the words, and as the majority knew little, if any, Italian, the words they looked at were the hack translations. It was these that were ridiculed in *The Beggar's Opera*, not the musical conventions of Italian opera, which, as Dent says,[3] 'could at that time have been ridiculous only to quite unmusical people': the music of the operas might be tolerated, or even admired, when there was a good tune, though the fops affected musical jargon, and the singers might excite enthusiasm by the amazing things they could do with their voices, though they were being paid far too high salaries compared with the London actors, but if the words—or what purported to be the words—were stupid, they well deserved to be pilloried.

So the satirising of the words in *The Beggar's Opera* drew a large part of the audience to Lincoln's Inn Fields, the well-known tunes drew those who liked something they could hum or whistle (which is why they preferred *Camilla* to Handel), the political hits drew others (even Sir Robert Walpole himself, the head of the Government), the down-to earth criminal setting drew all who were sick of the kings, queens and emperors of the Italian opera with their trains and their huge plumed head-dresses, the wit drew everyone who liked a laugh, and Lavinia Fenton drew all the men. Even Mrs. Pendarves admitted its success, though she artistically deplored the fact that

the taste of the town is so depraved that nothing will be approved but the burlesque. The *Beggar's Opera* entirely triumphs over the Italian one.

So no wonder that the whole town flocked to see it. In the one year there were over a hundred performances—a huge number at a time when the biggest and rarest successes at the Italian opera only managed just over twenty a season: those hundred odd performances were at Lincoln's Inn Fields and the new little theatre in the Haymarket, and they do not include the performances at Bartholomew Fair in August and Southwark Fair in September.

The morning after its second performance on Wednesday, January 31, *The Beggar's Opera* was mentioned in the *Journal* as follows:—

On Monday was represented for the first time at the Theatre Royal in Lincoln's Inn Fields Mr. Gay's new English opera, written in a manner wholly new and very entertaining, there being introduced instead of Italian airs about 60 of the most celebrated old English and Scotch tunes. There was present there, as well as last night, a prodigious concourse of Nobility and Gentry, and no theatrical performance for these many years has met with so much applause.

Among the nobility and gentry was the Duke of Argyle, who was heard by Pope in the next box before the first act was over saying, 'It'll do—it must do! I see it in the eyes of 'em!' which gave Gay's friends great comfort, as the Duke had a reputation for having a finger on the taste of the public as well as having good taste himself. As Pope said:—

He was quite right in this, as usual: the good nature of the audience appeared stronger and stronger every act, and ended in a clamour of applause.

Henry Carey celebrated the success of *The Beggar's Opera* with a ballad called 'Polly Peachum' to the tune of his own 'Sally in our Alley'. the first two verses of which, with their allusions to Rolli, the Italian librettist at the King's, and the three chief singers there, run as follows:—

> Of all the toasts that Britain boasts,
>   The gin, the gent, the jolly,
> The brown, the fair, the debonaire,
>   There's none cried up like Polly.
> She's fired the town, has quite cut down
>   The Opera of Rolli:
> Go where you will, the subject still
>   Is pretty, pretty Polly.
>
> There's Madam Faustina Catso!
>   And the Madame Catsoni,
> Likewise Signor Senesino,
>   Are tutti abbandonni!

Ha, ha, ha, ha! Do, re, mi, fa
Are now but farce and folly.
We're ravished all with Toll, loll, loll,
And pretty, pretty Polly!

From February 2 to March 5 it ran continuously—a rare happening, when the normal procedure in a theatre was to have not more than three or four performances of the same show in a week. The *Journal* recorded that it continued to attract, 'to the great mortification of the performers and the admirers of outlandish opera in Haymarket'. On February 15, in a letter to Swift, Gay satirically wrote:—

Lord Cobham says that I should have printed it in Italian over against the English, that the ladies might have understood what they read. The outlandish (as they now call it) hath been so thin of late that some have called that *The Beggar's Opera*: and if the run continues, I fear I shall have remonstrance thrown up against me by the Royal Academy of Music.

On March 20 Gay wrote to tell Swift that the show was still drawing crowds,

and as yet there is not the least probability of a thin audience, though there is a discourse about the town that the members of the Royal Academy of Music design to solicit against its being played on the outlandish opera days, as it is now called.

Soon after *The Beggar's Opera* opened, Mrs. Pendarves wrote:—

Yesterday I was at the rehearsal of the new opera composed by Mr. Handel. I liked it extremely, but the taste of the town is so depraved that nothing will be approved of but burlesque. The *Beggar's Opera* entirely triumphs over the Italian one. I have not yet seen it, but everybody says it is very comical and full of humour: the songs will soon be published.

So great was the English triumph that she went on to say that the Italian opera

will not survive after this winter: I wish I was a poet worthy the honour of writing its elegy. I am certain, except for some few, the English have *no real taste for music* [*sic*], for if they had, they could not neglect an entertainment so perfect in its kind for a parcel of ballad singers. I am so peevish about it that I have no patience.

Handel's new opera *Siroe* opened three weeks after *The Beggar's Opera*, on February 17, most auspiciously, with George II, Queen Caroline and the three Princesses in the audience, and scored eighteen performances. But the success of *The Beggar's Opera*, which the same Royal party had already seen, was undoubtedly outshining the King's opera, as a letter in the *London Journal* of March 23 pointed out.

The author, supposed to have been honest Dr. John Arbuthnot, the late Queen Anne's physician, a keen musician and a friend of Swift, Pope and Gay, commented on the 'neglect into which the Italian operas are at present fallen', remarking that to 'some true Britons' (obviously including himself), who refused to yield to foreigners on any point,

they were a ridiculous, senseless and unnatural diversion: yet, as their interest was espoused by people of the most polite taste, they continued to gain ground to such a degree that the whole nation seemed in a short time almost unanimous in the encouragement of them.

Our English language was by degrees discarded with our English music: we appeared to be so entirely converted to an Italian taste that we were not able to bear with any voice which was produced under our own climate. In short, we were grown so nice as to see even the Italians themselves glad of our leavings.

He went on to say that at the moment there were in London three voices

as have never been equalled in any age, and a composer who is able to set each of them off to the best advantage, with such a band of musicians to accompany them as is not to be matched [4] in Europe—to say nothing of the decorations of the stage.

Unfortunately the chief result had been rival parties over the merits of Faustina and Cuzzoni, and argument had become more important than the opera which they both enhanced: in fact— and here the author blows sky high the belief that the intelligent aristocracy benevolently encouraged the introduction of Italian opera to London:—

it will not be hard to judge whether that excellent fondness for Italian operas, which has of late years overrun the nation had proceeded really from a true taste of good music, or only from a violent affectation of it.

Much as the author liked *The Beggar's Opera*, he wished it hadn't been produced at that moment, as it was doing a disservice to a better sort of entertainment (was this sarcastically meant?), largely because it was performed four nights a week,[5] while the Italian opera could be seen only twice a week. That season at the King's Theatre the author thought the Academy had given of their best, 'for we have never had three such operas performed in any one season as have been in this,[6] and yet the house has seldom been filled, which was a demonstration that our relish for Italian music was decaying'.

Rich had been clever, he said, to cash in on the true English taste for ballad-tunes, but that had increased cat-calls at the opera: the author wished the galleryites might cultivate the good behaviour they used to have (what is it that starts those excellent critics indulging from time to time in a spate of self-advertising booing irrespective of the merits of the entertainment?), but the fundamental fault was more deep-seated, the author believed:—

For my own part I cannot think it would be any loss to real lovers of music if all those false friends, who have made pretensions to it only in compliance with the fashion, would separate themselves from them—provided our Italian opera could be brought under such regulations as to go on without them. We might then be able to sit and enjoy an entertainment of this sort, free from those disturbances which are frequent in English theatres, without any regard, not only to performers, but even to the presence of Majesty itself.

In short my conclusion is that, though so great a desertion may force us to contract the expenses of our operas as would put an end to our having them in as great perfection as at present, yet we shall be able at least to hear them without interruption.

Another shrewd critic, Roger North, about this time wrote in his *Musical Grammarian*:—

As all things from low beginnings grow up to their full magnitude, so our operas were performed by English voices—nay, the Italian of foreign operas were translated and fitted to the music; nay, more—some scenes were sung in English and others in Italian or Dutch rather than fail, which made such a crowd of absurdities as was not to be borne. But now the subscriptions with a Royal encouragement hath brought the operas to be performed in their native idiom and up to such a sufficiency that many have said Rome and Venice, where they heard them, have not exceeded.

Now having brought our English opera music to this pass it will scarce be manners to throw any censures at them: but, be they very great and good, there is no such perfection upon earth to or from which somewhat may not a *buon cento* be added, or subtracted, and perhaps altered for the better.

He now makes a good point:—

One thing I dislike is the laying too much stress upon some one voice, which is purchased at a dear rate. Were it not as well if somewhat of that was abated and added to the rest to bring the orchestra to nearer equality? Many persons come to hear that single voice who care not for all the rest, especially if it be a fair lady: and observing the discourse of the quality critics, I found it runs most upon the point who sings best, and not whether the music be good and wherein.

He goes on to object that a series of solos without any concerted numbers is a fault in operatic composition, though he admits that the musical standard of recent operas composed in England seems higher than that of operas imported from Italy.

1728 then seems to have seen the birth of serious musical criticism as opposed to satirical comment, though the satirists were by no means finished—as will be seen.

[1] This list as given by Burney and Hawkins really belongs to 1721 (see Deutsch's *Handel*) but as it is the earliest complete list of directors I give it here.

[2] This word refers to the fops who wore the newly fashionable wigs or toupées.

[3] *Handel.*

[4] 'Marched' in the original.

[5] This is only roughly true: after its opening run from January 29 to March 5, which seems to have been continuous apart from January 30, the weeks of March 4 and 11 had only three performances, while the week of March 18 had only two—while after that the number of performances seems to have varied between four and one per week, to judge from Allardyce Nicoll's invaluable handlist of plays in his *Eighteenth Century Drama: 1700–1750*.

[6] *Riccardo* and *Siroe* were two, but which is meant by the third is uncertain, as Ariosti's *Teuzzone* had only three performances, and Handel's revived *Alessandro* (which was probably the third) only two.

CHAPTER SIX

The Touchstone

In this same year of 1728 Pope dismissed the Italian opera as a 'harlot form' in his *Dunciad*, saying that

> Rolli the feather to his ear conveys
> And his nice taste directs our operas,

and in the passage that foretells the rising of imperial Dullness from booths via theatres to Court:—

> Already Opera prepares the way,
> The sure fore-runner of her gentle sway.

He thought the arias affected, the singing effeminate, and a pasticcio a hotch-potch.

In this year, too, James Ralph, an American by birth who lived at Hammersmith, published a half-serious half-satirical book which had a far-reaching effect on opera in England, entitled

The Touchstone, or historical, critical, political, philosophical, and theological essays upon the reigning diversions of the Town. In which everything antique or modern, relating to music, poetry, dancing, pantomines, choruses, catcalls, audiences, judges, critics, balls, ridottos, assemblies, new orators, circus, bear-garden, gladiators, prize-fighters, Italian strollers, mountebanks, stages, cockpits, puppet-shows, fairs, and public auctions, is occasionally handled. By a person of some truth and some quality.

He called himself 'A. Primcock', of an ancient family with innumerable branches of ribald names of careful and, nowadays, unprintable significance, claiming he had sung in opera in Paris and never missed good or new operas or plays.

In his preface he says he will start with operas, which for him meant the Royal Academy productions: 'The operas therefore being looked upon as the centre of the beau monde, I begin with them', dealing with their history, merits, failings and how to 'adapt them to the taste of this nation in general'—one of their failings being the omission of choruses, though choruses of catcalls could be heard. Claiming that he is writing to appeal to English common sense, he satirically sneers at Swift's *Gulliver's Travels*, which had been published two years before:—

I suppose no flying islands, enchanted castles, or fancied regions to amuse them. I bring home no pygmies of six inches, or giants of sixty foot to moralise and talk politics to them, nor speaking brute to preach to them.

After all, he says, 'every fool' can invent: he is dealing with facts.

He starts his comments on operas by briefly sketching operatic history from the priests of Cybele and Greece through *The Siege of Rhodes* to the dramatic operas of the Shadwell type, which were 'regular stage-plays, larded with pieces of occasional music, etc.—embellished with scenes, machines, French dancing-masters, long trains and plumes of feathers', only *Albion and Albanius* being a real opera. As for the others, he said:—

I absolutely deny them that title, that term implying a regular, complete musical entertainment, which they never could arrive at till they entirely came into a finished Italian plan: nor do we bestow the name of opera on any drama but those where every word is sung.

Dramatic operas might have equalled their prototypes, Greek tragedies, 'could they have supplied the necessary expenses essential to the grandeur of such a design'. They held the stage with two rival houses ruining wit by sound and show, till Clayton produced *Arsinoe*, which, being

true homespun British manufacture, cut out in the Transalpine fashion, and some others of that stamp, pleased as long as they were a novelty: but they only instructed us to have a relish for better music.

Next came translated Italian operas, and then

an Italian singer or two crept in by degrees to charm us with something new and unintelligible: and this pretty motley performance pleased for some time: but, some good sense still remaining among us, the absurdity of that conversation *à la Babel* was so notorious that it was looked upon as more inexcusable than having the whole performance in one proper, though foreign, language.

He praises the King's Theatre for the general standard of production: 'we may boldly say we excel anything Italy ever knew (as to one particular stage) both in composition and performance'. It had held its ground in spite of attempts to dislodge the Italian operas and recesses for breathing-time, 'and as an Italian opera can never touch the comprehension of above one part in four of a British audience, it is very probable their theatre will be crowded as long as we are a nation'.

At the same time 'the bare name of an Italian opera as established at present among us is to the last degree shocking to the ears of many honest inhabitants of this metropolis'. In the first place it is unintelligible:—

'What, be attentive to what is gibberish to us?'
'Chattering monkeys!'
'Ridiculous apes! We spend our money and lose our time, and perhaps only be cursed or laughed at!'

Secondly, some hate the recitative, others object that there is no dialogue:—

They die with laughing to hear a tyrant rage and storm in a vast regularity of sounds, a general sing at the head of an army, or a lover, swanlike, expire at his mistress's feet, and that there is not an imperial mandate, a word of command, or billet-doux delivered but in expressive flats and sharps.

Thirdly, all singers are paid too highly, especially the foreigners:—

'Intolerable!'
'So many hundreds!'
'For a thing of nothing!'
'A voice!'
'A mere "ha-ha".'
'Nasty pussies! Odious filthy things!'
'Let them stay at home and starve, or sing at reasonable rates!'

Fourthly, he deals with critics whose standard is Aristotle or Rapin (the meticulous French historian for England about 1700):—

An opera throws them into convulsions, one part is ridiculous, another improbable, a third unnatural, a fourth improper, a fifth irregular, and so they run themselves out of breath—

He then answers all these points. First Italian is the best language for singing and foreign voices are better:—

Some women we boast of and boys, but the first generally lose their voices before they begin to learn and are then ill taught, as the latter are obliged by nature to part with theirs, by the time they know anything of the matter.
A tolerable bass voice we may meet with by chance in an age, but as we are denied the liberty of artificially tuning the pipes of those performers who are neither men nor women, and who are the foundation of the Italian operas, I do aver that I think it impossible to form a perfect and complete musical entertainment of our own people or in our own language.

As proof he quotes the revival of *Camilla* at Lincoln's Inn Fields in 1726:—

Their endeavours, though headed by a great master and supported by some people of the best fashion and interest, in a few weeks did but expose to the ridicule of everybody that had any notion of music their wretched performance: and even then those that made the best figure on their stage were foreigners.

'Tis true that representation had a run—as they term it—and brought several full houses, but I speak of its merit and not its success: the first was obvious to every ear, the last was forced by a party during the vacation of the Italian opera.

At that time the Haymarket standard was probably higher than in Italy, while English singing had never been so bad:—

I was so unfortunate as to be obliged once to sit *Camilla* [1] out, to the great disquiet of my ears: nor have I perfectly got rid of the headache it gave me yet.

Apart from Mrs. Barbier and his old friend Leveridge, he says

I could have sworn the stage had returned the favour the audience sometimes does them and played a full chorus of cat-calls upon us.

'This season' the Lincoln's Inn theatre put on a revival of *Thomyris*:—

but that being rather a better opera, and more justly performed than the other, the town would not go near it. So finding their finances run very low by striving to do well, they thought it absolutely necessary to do something very bad in order to retrieve their undone affairs.

This indeed they have happily effected in conjunction with a great poet: and by giving us something more execrable in relation to music than the world ever dreamed of seeing on any stage, they are made: and we run mad with joy in being so agreeably disappointed.

That 'execrable' work was, of course, *The Beggar's Opera*, sung, he says, by voices with a cockney raucousness which, though usually it 'shocked most ears and set most teeth on edge at turning the corner of a street for half a moment, when thrown into a regular entertainment, charms for hours'. In fact its title was most suitable, considering the 'rags of poetry and scraps of music joining so naturally'.

Did the author really hold these views, or was he being as sarcastic as his ribald preface and his allusion to Gay as a great poet seems to imply? Whether he did or not, his answer to those who wanted either all aria or interpolated dialogue was sensible:—

It is impossible to have a perfect musical drama without recitative: no ear can support the whole being all air. . . . The recitative is but a tunable method of speaking, and in the article of music but refines upon speech as far as polite comedy excels common conversation or tragedy in heroics the ordinary style of the great.

If recitative is wrong, then 'greater absurdities and inconsistencies' should be banished from stage plays: it is not so bad as the sparkling nonsense, gilded fustian, and pompous bombast in most, if not all, our tragedies, nor so improper as the quaint double entendres and forced similes squeezed out in the midst of misfortunes or at the point of death. . . . In short, nothing is ridiculous that executes a regular design.

If all is sung, all should be sung: 'nor can I observe anything in singing a conversation-piece more absurd or ridiculous than a familiar dialogue in heroic rhyme'.

As for the high salaries, which are regrettable, the excuse is that 'we are arrived now to so piquant a *gout* in music that nothing but what is super-excellent will pass. What pleases at Venice or Rome may chance to be hissed at the Haymarket.' Besides, a north-easter in July may rob the singers of their voices, so they deserve high salaries, and 'such an entertainment cannot be supported but by the tip-top performers of the world'. At the same time 'it would be unreasonable to expect that the directors of the Hay-market Theatre should amuse us at their own private expense', so there must be crowded houses every night to make it pay.

Next for the Aristotelian critics: they always 'damn all amusements where spirit and life prevail over their unanimated works of clay'. Opera is not like drama and is not bound by rules: Dryden's definition of an opera is good enough: at the same time many opera-lovers regret that there is 'too great simplicity or sameness in those amusements'. Why, for instance, are there now no choruses, no dancing, no machines?

The author says he likes operas, but sympathises with patriotic and Protestant music-lovers who dislike 'singing as well as praying in an unknown dialect'. He therefore offers a suggestion to the directors of the opera who

can never hope for a set of singers, natives of this island, equal to what we are supplied with from abroad (as long as our laws in relation to emasculation confine that small ceremony to the bodies of our brutes).

The suggestion is that English history or fable should be ransacked for stories to be translated into Italian for the operatic stage, and then our honour would be safe. *Dick Whittington*, for instance, had been suggested by someone who

went so far in the design as to procure a puss or two, who would purr tolerably in time and tune, but the inconveniences arising from the number of vermin requisite to be destroyed in order to keep up to the truth of the story blasted that project.

245

Now Ralph's satire is given full rein. *Valentine and Orson*, though well known, was really a foreign story, and anyway where could one find two finer bears than at the Haymarket? (Handel and Heidegger, I presume.) *The Seven Champions of Christendom* would not do, the Academy 'not being able to furnish so many heroes at a time'. *St. George* might do, with the Garter and a troop of Knights of the Bath and their esquires—another hit at the Academy Directors—but where was the dragon, unless a baby one from the 'Af - - - - n Company' would do: then Boschi could sing St. George's horse with Senesino on his back and Palmerini inside the dragon and there would be the 'newest and finest duet that ever was heard, viz. between the horse and the dragon'. (Tactfully no name is spelt out in full.)

The Dragon of Wantley with choruses would be good, and so would *Robin Hood*, although, as 'no singer in Europe can top the part of Little John but Berenstadt, we must suspend that performance till his return to bless our eyes'. *The London Prentice* has the advantage of the 'valuable incident of a lion-scene', and Cuzzoni in breeches would make a delightful *Tom Thumb*, while *Chevy Chase* 'will admit of a good number of French horns, which have been lately received at the Haymarket with tolerable success'—notably in *Admeto*.

If any critic objects that these stories are not about royalty, as opera-stories usually are, he should remember *Griselda*, the story of Patient Grisel, which was performed 'to the entire satisfaction of several audiences as pure as crowded'. (Apart from royal characters such as Theseus or Tamburlain, Handel had specifically included among his opera titles up to this time Kings of Germany, the Lombards, Thessaly, England, Persia and Egypt— the last four in the last two years.)

The Children in the Wood would be admirable, allowing for 'a vast deal of the pathetic, the wonderful, and the terrible, the distinguishing characteristics of music as well as poetry': besides, there was always the ugly Mr. Heidegger,

who has always graciously condescended to act any part in life, which could amuse this nation in a polite way: his countenance (though far different from his nature) will best become the Uncle's cruel part, and some of our present composers have a few savage songs ready composed adapted to his face and character in this opera. As Faustina's shake and graces qualify her to appear as the first old woman in Europe, she can play the old nurse. Senesino and Baldi

will make a couple of chopping infants: and as they can equally act the parts of
boys and girls, the Academy shall determine which shall be male, which
female . . . Boschi and Palmerini may be very happily introduced as two
hobgoblins to frighten the Uncle out of his wits. . . .

Anastasia Robinson, as the old maiden aunt, 'in conjunction
with the lamentable Dotti would move most feelingly in a funeral
chorus', and the Academy could dress the show cheaply in accordance with our old English custom, while as for 'our little warbler
Cuzzoni', seeing that

her size and voice will furnish out a mighty pretty bird, she shall sing the
part of the Robin Redbreast which covers the dead Children with leaves: she
shall be ushered in by a Cocksparrow and allowed two Tomtits to hold up
her tail. N.B. the composers of *Elpidia* and some other later operas will be
the proper masters to set this drama to music.

So Ralph did not think much of Vinci, who wrote *Elpidia*, or,
apparently, of the Italian opera in general, and his tongue must
have been in his cheek when he sneered at *The Beggar's Opera*.

He claimed that these stories of low life would not encourage
fights between prima donnas as grand stories did: there would be
'no room for conceit, no dispute who shall be Empress, Queen or
Princess, no rivalship but in love, when contending nymphs and
shepherdesses strive and scold and sing to gain Senesino's heart'.

They would also allow for greater latitude in composition and
'destroy that schism which at present divides our lovers of music':
each composer could excel in his own way. Handel could express
'the rage of tyrants, the passions of heroes and the distresses of
lovers in the heroic style', Bononcini 'sighing shepherds, bleating
flocks, chirping birds and purling streams in the pastoral', Ariosti
'good dungeon scenes, marches for a battle, or minuets for a ball
in the Miserere'(?).

Handel would warm us in frost or snow by rousing every passion with notes
proper to the subject, whilst Bononcini would fan us in the dogdays with an
Italian breeze and lull us asleep with gentle whispers.

As for recitative, 'the generality of our audiences have a secret
distaste to it, and many, even of our patrons of music, are shocked
with it'. It has been suggested that one singer should sing the
recitative in English, 'and then at an air his Italian counterpart slip
from behind his robe or jump out of his pocket and sing the air'—

but perhaps it might not work! Why not, then, dance the recitative, like the old pantomimes 'and our modern grotesque dances?' Everyone understands, of course, what a dance is about and there is a tune, so why should the hero not make love to a Princess in a 'minuet step or a sprightly caper or a strong bound'? Certainly a King in a rage can cuff and kick far better than he can speak or sing.

The real answer to the expense of opera is a larger house that can accommodate all classes, not merely the leaders of society: then the best singers and instrumentalists could be afforded and 'not a tinker or cobbler should miss an opera'—after all, in Venice 'every gondolier can whistle his opera-air and judge of harmony!' Why not take money and land from one of the London hospitals to build an opera-house? It still would be put to the same use, housing the old and infirm and educating young and helpless orphans 'in a genteeler manner'—or, better still, why not put some of our aged and sickly into an opera?

Nowadays, Ralph says, tunes from the operas are 'stole or borrowed from the Haymarket', and put into ordinary plays or played between the acts

improved by the additional excellencies of a hoarse oboe [2] or a screaming little flute, which by the strength of imagination we are to believe Senesino and Cuzzoni.

At the same time,

I flatter myself that by this time every thinking Briton is convinced that an Italian opera is an innocent and perfect entertainment and may be rendered as improving as agreeable: it may indeed be disordered in some parts of its constitution, but labours under no disease that is incurable.

Why are there no choruses in Italian operas? In *Rinaldo*

a chorus of wild sparrows was let fly behind the scenes, but they were never heard—the Undertakers being out in their choice of a singing-bird—nor seen but in their effects upon the ladies' heads.

It would have been better to have flutes and artificial nightingales for such a scene, but operas ought to finish with a grand chorus in harmony, as they always used to in the good old days when 'elbow-chairs danced' (as in *Dioclesian*) 'flower-pots sung, ghosts walked, and devils flew to divert us'. Besides, it would give employment to the poor!

As for the audience, cat-callers cleverly can

distinguish with the greatest ease whether the poor hare of a poet or composer is only to be merrily run down by way of pure diversion, or killed outright for the benefit of the critical kennel.

The opera audience is different from the theatre audience:—

The inhabitants of the boxes at the playhouse make up pit and box at the opera. The pit at the playhouse is the first gallery in the opera. The first gallery and middle part of the upper gallery in the playhouse have no representatives in the opera—there are few of that country who care to part with a crown for a song.

As for the gentry at each end of the upper gallery in the playhouse, they enjoy that entire region to themselves at the opera with space to range and liberty to make as much noise as they please.

Ralph wished such cat-callers could be cat-o'-nine-tailed, and noted that all the audience spent most of the time at an opera in talk and boredom, aping critics who quoted others and ran with the pack.

He gives a sample of the dialogue to be heard at the Haymarket at that time (which can still be heard today):—

Beau Modish. I suppose your ladyship honoured the new opera with your presence?
Lady Plyant. Certainly, Mr. Modish. I never miss the first night.
Beau Modish. Was your ladyship mightily pleased?
Lady Plyant. I cannot say. But so-so—tolerable enough—what I minded of the thing: but I shall not declare myself till its character is established by the town.
Beau Modish. Was it approved of by that audience?
Lady Plyant. Some strange creatures seemed in raptures. The claps came from the gallery, but few admirers below stairs—and those mightily ill-dressed.
Beau Modish. Then it must be damned stuff.

And so on. Ralph ends his remarks on the operas of London by saying that *The Beggar's Opera* had an 'incredible run, while *Radamisto* and *Siroe* are performed to almost empty benches'.

---

[1] He prints the names with dashes, thus '*Ca - - - - la*.'
[2] 'hoatboy'.

CHAPTER SEVEN

Handel and his Rivals

THE Italian opera was certainly dying again at the start of 1728. Handel's *Tolomeo* was produced in May, but had only seven performances and in the dedication Haym commented on the decline in popularity of opera, in spite of the fact that in this opera were Faustina, Cuzzoni, Senesino and the novel French horns. After that three performances were given of *Admeto*, the last—on June 1 —being the last performance of opera under the auspices of the Royal Academy, an institution, as Burney says,

in the support of which the whole sum of £50,000 [1] originally subscribed seems to have been sunk in less than seven years, besides the money produced by the sale of tickets and that which was taken at the door for the admission of non-subscribers.

So Mrs. Pendarves was right—for the moment Italian opera was dead, and as a final feeble gesture *Camilla* and *Thomyris* were given again in the winter of 1728 at Lincoln's Inn Fields as well as *The Beggar's Opera*.

The chief singers left England, Senesino—according to one correspondent of 1729,[2] 'playing an ungrateful part to his friends in England by abusing 'em behind their backs and saying he'll come no more among 'em', though he was said to have 'built a fine house with an inscription over the door to let the world know 'twas the folly of the English had laid the foundation of it'.

Handel, however, tried again in the winter of 1729 (in which year no spectator was allowed on the stage during an opera) with a new lot of singers. Apart from reviving some of his older works, he produced seventeen new operas in the next thirteen years, but of these only three achieved any sort of success—*Poro, Re dell' Indie* (twenty-four performances), *Ariadne in Crete* (twenty-two) and *Alcina* (twenty-four). Of the rest most had less than twelve performances, while his last, *Deidamia*, had only three.

The Beggar's Opera, however, had started off a series of English ballad operas, some of them on the stories Ralph had jokingly suggested, and most of these were revived again and again

throughout the century. Of the host of Italian operas which were
tried out, many of which attempted to imitate the British comedy
works or were chosen because they were comedy works, few
made their mark—of about a hundred produced between 1729
and 1750 only ten were ever revived, and only one—Lampugnani's *Rossane* of 1743—totalled in its revivals as many as thirty-
two performances.

From 1729 the Italian operas were more than well matched by
the English musical stage-works, which admirably supported the
criticisms or ridicule of the foreign works which were still being
written. In 1729 the Prologue to the popular burlesque by
Samuel Johnson of Cheshire, called *Hurlothrumbo, or, the Supernatural* commented

> Diamonds to swine are despicable things,
> Lost to the mole the vernal verdure springs,
> And adders hiss, though Senesino sings:

while the Epilogue, by John Byrom, stressed the fact that only
nonsense was then tolerated on the stage and prophesied

> Handel himself shall yield to Hurlothrumbo,
> And Bononcini too shall cry 'Succumbo'.

In the same year Cibber recommended writing in English so as to
be understood in his Prologue to *Love in a Riddle*:—

> let your sounds have sense,
> Old England will with English throats dispense,
> And take what's well designed for excellence.

In 1730, soon after Handel's *Partenope*, Fielding's play, *The
Author's Farce*, was produced, in which the scene is the other side
of the Styx and all the characters are dead, including Signor Opera,
Don Tragedio, Sir Farcical Comic, Dr. Orator and Monsieur
Pantomime. Signor Opera announces his arrival in the under-
world as follows:—

> Claps universal,
>   Applauses resounding,
>   Hisses confounding,
>   Attending my song:
>   My senses drowned,
>   And I fell down dead,
>   Whilst I was singing, ding, dang, dong.

The Goddess of Nonsense hopes to marry Opera, but he already has married her daughter, Mrs. Novel: Nonsense is angry, but gives him a chaplet as her Archpoet, Count Ugly (Heidegger, of course) points out to her that Opera, when alive,

> Long in the world your noble cause he fought,
> Your laureate there, your precepts still be taught.

He goes on to urge his own merits:—

> But if from dullness any may succeed,
> To that and nonsense I good title plead:
> Nought else was ever in my masquerade.

Nonsense herself now replies:—

> No more! By Styx I swear
> That Opera the crown shall wear.

and promptly bursts into an aria:—

> Away each meek pretender flies:
> Opera, thou hast gained the prize:
> Nonsense grateful still must own
> Thou best support'st her throne.
> For her subscriptions thou didst gain
> By thy soft alluring strain,
>   When Shakespeare's thought
>   And Congreve's brought
> Their aids to sense in vain.

Later one Sir John Bindover and a Constable come to arrest Luckless, an author and the master of a puppet-show:—

Luckless.   For what?
Sir John.   For abusing Nonsense, sirrah.
Constable.   People of quality are not to have their diversions libelled at this rate.
Luckless.   Of what do you accuse me, gentlemen?
Sir John.   Shall you abuse Nonsense, when the whole town supports it?

A month after *The Author's Farce*, Ralph took up the cudgels again, this time under his own name in a burlesque called *The Fashionable Lady, or Harlequin's Opera*, in the manner of a rehearsal. In this one Ballad is going to have an opera performed for his son's wedding, but Meanwell is surprised he should so dishonour the occasion:—

Meanwell.   A modern opera, in my opinion, would be but a poor entertainment at any marriage.

Modely.   Your English opera, I grant you, but your Italian would do honour
             to a prince's marriage.
Meanwell.   Yes, sir, I believe as much as any other part of the ceremony.
Modely.   Some people, sir, who have not been happy in an ear for so refined
             an entertainment have affected to condemn it only to conceal
             their weakness.
Meanwell.   And some people, sir, from a very fashionable absurdity have
             affected to be in raptures at a beauty they did not understand.

They start quarrelling, as Ballad says, 'about squeaking recitatives,
paltry eunuchs, and a thrill of insignificant outlandish vowels':
after all, Ballad reminds them, even a parish clerk

             knows more of true music than you and all your Senesinos put
             together. Parish clerks, quotha! they are angels to such effeminate
             warblers.
Modely.   Abominable comparison! A parish-clerk and Senesino! An Eng-
             lish opera and *Radamisto*!
Ballad.   An English opera and *Rad-dad-da*—Confound this Italian! It ties
             up a man's voice like the appearance of a ghost at midnight!

He sings the praises of *The Beggar's Opera* in the following
terms:—

a certain English opera that shall be nameless . . . a masterpiece of art, the glory
of its author, the delight of a whole nation. It ravished the nobility, men,
women, and children, enchanted the city, and strolled all over the country.

Ballad is even prepared to fight for English opera and plans one
with Mr. Drama. The fashionable Modely, however, says, 'I
feel a sort of an antipathy to an old English tune, that shocks
me worse than the setting of a saw or a concert of midnight cats
in a gutter', and later asks Meanwell.

             Is not music the politest entertainment in the world?
Meanwell.   Yes, for your men of mode, who have not sense enough to
             relish anything beside—creatures that, like a certain wise animal,
             are all ear.

The following year, 1731, Handel's *Poro*—with Senesino, who
had returned, after all—had sixteen performances at the King's,
and scenes from his *Acis and Galatea*, with Gay as librettist
(originally performed 1719), were performed at Lincoln's Inn
Fields: but both were surpassed in popularity by the ballad opera
(called an opera) *The Devil to Pay* at Drury Lane, which held the
stages of London for fifteen years.

No opera had any real success in 1732. At the King's Handel's

Ezio 'did not draw much company' with five performances in January, and his February opera, *Sosarme, Re di Media* had only eleven—though Colman said it took with the town, while an anonymous *Lucio Papirio, Dittatore* 'did not take'. At Lincoln's Inn Fields Scarlatti's *Telemachus* was given only once, while at the little Haymarket Theatre, Carey's opera after the Italian manner but in English, with music by Lampe, *Amelia*, managed to last twelve performances.

At the end of that year Aaron Hill made another attempt to improve the standard of opera in England by writing on December 5 to Handel—who, after all, he had introduced to England twenty-one years before—with suggestions that were even more sensible than his earlier attempts to improve stage decor. In this letter he wrote as follows:—

Having this occasion of troubling you with a letter, I cannot forbear to tell you the earnestness of my wishes that, as you have made such considerable steps towards it already, you would let us owe to your inimitable genius the establishment of *music* upon a foundation of good poetry, where the excellence of the *sound* should be no longer dishonoured by the poorness of the *sense* it is chained to.

My meaning is that you would be resolute enough to deliver us from our *Italian bondage* and demonstrate that English is soft enough for Opera, when composed by poets who know how to distinguish the *sweetness* of our tongue from the *strength* of it where the last is less necessary.

I am of opinion that male and female voices may be found in this kingdom capable of everything that is requisite, and I am sure a species of dramatic opera might be invented that by reconciling reason and dignity with music and fine machinery would charm the *ear* and hold fast the *heart* together.

Such an improvement must at once be lasting and profitable to a very great degree and would infallibly attract a universal regard and encouragement.

I am so much a stranger to the nature of your present engagements that, if what I have said should not happen to be so practicable as I conceive it, you will have the goodness to impute it only to the zeal with which I wish you at the head of a design as solid and unperishable as your music and memory.

This most sensible suggestion of Hill's, though it did not have the result he hoped, may quite likely have borne fruit, for it is remarkable that it was after this that Handel found his most lasting greatness in oratorios in the words of which there is greater strength and beauty than in most of his operas and in which his music—though it may at times have been borrowed from his earlier more secular works—seems to be so joined to the sense of the words that the two can hardly be remembered separately. Handel also soon discovered many excellent English singers.

For the time being, however, Handel stuck to his operas and his usual and perhaps perfunctory method of writing them. In any event, neither his operas nor anyone else's had much success in the 1732-3 season, at the beginning of which John Rich opened the new theatre in Covent Garden—on December 7. At the King's Theatre, Handel's *Orlando* was given twelve times, but an anonymous *Catone* only five: at Lincoln's Inn Fields Carey's *Teraminta*, with music by Handel's amanuensis J. C. Smith, lasted three performances only, and Arne's re-setting of Addison's old *Rosamond* only seven—but that was often revived. So, too, was the Tom Thumb *Opera of Operas*, but that burlesque had only six performances in its first season at the little Haymarket Theatre, where Thomas Lediard's English opera, set by Lampe, *Britannia*, lasted only four in spite of the fact that it was given

with the representation of a transparent theatre, illuminated, and adorned with a great number of emblems, mottoes, devices and inscriptions, and embellished with machines in a manner entirely new.

Handel was therefore not sweeping to success at the King's, though he occasionally had fair successes himself, at least with his followers. Then in 1733 his opponents began to take a hand, and Mr. Johnson of Cheshire wrote in *The Blazing Comet* 'to the poets of future ages', implying that in his opinion Handel was not the greatest composer of all time:—

In these days lives in London without encouragement the famous Mr. Bononcini, whose music for celestialness of style I am apt to think will demand remembrance in the soul after fire has destroyed all things in this world: and I, that have translated his sounds into our own English language, cannot say enough of this great man, who is rivalled by Mr. Handel, a very big man, who writes his music in the High-Dutch taste with very great success: so when you peruse these two masters, you'll guess at the men and blush for the taste of England.

So there were some people who thought the sixty-year-old Giovanni Bononcini greater than the 'very big' Handel, thirteen years his junior, in spite of rumours that he had submitted another composer's work as his own in a competition for the Academy of Ancient Music—rumours which he haughtily refused to refute. Some years before, indeed, the Duchess of Marlborough had offered him a yearly income of £500 not to compose any more for the Haymarket Theatre—though her artistic taste may have been swayed by her dislike at having to pay Vanbrugh for building Blenheim Palace.

In 1733, then, society was divided for and against Handel—he charged increased prices for his oratorios: the King and Queen were for him and against him was the Prince of Wales and his set, who combined together to start what was called the Opera of the Nobility at Lincoln's Inn Fields Theatre. The first work to be produced by the anti-Handelians was the twenty-year-old *Arianna e Teseo* by Porpora, renamed *Ariadne in Naxos*: that was on December 29 and it had twenty-four performances that season, but was never revived. Handel at once retaliated with *Ariadne in Crete* at the King's on January 26, 1734: this only had seventeen performances in the season, but it did have five more at the beginning of the next.

In February 1734 Mr. Johnson of Cheshire wrote a vituperatively sarcastic and lengthy letter-pamphlet attacking Handel: it was entitled

Harmony in an Uproar: A letter to F – – d – – k H – – d – l, Esq., M – – r of the O – – a H – – e in the Haymarket, from Hurlothrumbo Johnson, Esq.: Composer Extraordinary to all the theatres in G – – t B – – t – – n, excepting that of the Haymarket. In which the rights and merits of both O – – s are properly considered.

This was printed in 1751 in the *Miscellaneous Works of the late Dr. Arbuthnot*, but A. W. Ward considered it was not by Arbuthnot, and in view of Johnson's championing of Bononcini there seems no reason why the title page should be wrong in attributing it to him.

He begins by saying that he had long wanted a talk with Handel, but

being sensible of the almost insuperable difficulty of getting at you, I bethought me a paper kite might best reach you, and soar to your apartment, though seated in the highest clouds, for all the world knows I can top you, fly as high as you will. . . .

(Handel's unapproachability has since been equalled by that of a more recent brilliant composer, equally protected by his distinguished patrons and friends.)

I have been told and made to understand by your betters, Sir, that of late you have been damned insolent, audacious, impudent, and saucy. . . . Why this discord? Why these stupendous alarms in the affairs of harmony? Why has music made so confounded a noise that the great guns upon the Rhine and in Italy affect not our ears deafened with an eternal squall or chatter about operas?

Now Johnson launches the attack, which shows not only the violent feelings of the anti-Handel party roused by his self-satisfied superiority, but this partisanship of his supporters, which had tried to prove his ascendancy in the opera-world by packing the Haymarket in the past. I should stress the fact that neither I nor, I think, Hurlothrumbo Johnson are attacking Handel as a musician—indeed, Johnson makes it quite clear that Handel's music was attractive, at the least: it seems that the music in his operas was considered better than his operas by some judges, but the attack—whether it is an attack by Johnson or by Handel's enemies satirically quoted by Johnson is not really clear—is more an attack against the idea that Handel is the one and only composer.

Johnson begins vigorously:—

First for thee, thou delightful musical machine! Why hast thou dared to rouse the roaring lions and wily foxes of the British nation who, but for pity, could tear thy very being to atoms in the hundredth part of an *allegro* minim, make crotchets of thy body and semiquavers of thy soul, and with the powerful breath of their nostrils blow thy existence beneath the lowest Hell?

Handel may claim, says Johnson—and here we can catch a glimpse of the facts behind the satire—that when Senesino left England other and better singers were provided, that it was impossible for Handel to abide by the 'unreasonable and savage proposals' made to him, that though he may have been misled or have judged wrong in raising the price of tickets (which he did for oratorios on opera nights), he has already been sufficiently punished—and anyway the productions warranted 'so extravagant a price'. To this the answer is that

all you assert is false, utterly false, damnably false: and that you're an impudent liar and a scoundrel and a rascal, and so God confound you and rot you and yours to all eternity and ten times worse than all that.

Handel's partisans in the chocolate and coffee-houses sneer at the Lincoln's Inn Fields singers, including Senesino, who had had a row with Handel, but Handel deserves punishment, and so is arraigned in an imaginary trial.

Handel is sworn in ('So help you, Music!') on 'the two operas of Ariadne, alias the Cuckoo and the Nightingale'—that is, of course, the Porpora *Ariadne in Naxos* and the Handel *Ariadne in Crete*.

I   257

The charge is then read:—

1. You are charged with having bewitched us for the space of twenty years past, nor do we know where your enchantments will end if a timely stop is not put to them—they threatening us with an entire destruction of liberty and an absolute tyranny in your person over the whole territories of the Haymarket.

2. You have most insolently dared to give us good music and sound harmony, when we wanted and desired bad, to the great encouragement of your operas and the ruin of our good allies and confederates, the profession of bad music.

3. You have most feloniously and arrogantly assumed to yourself an uncontrolled property of pleasing us, whether we would or no, and have often been so bold as to charm us when we were positively resolved to be out of humour.

Handel pleads guilty, but in defence asks, 'Wherein have I offended?' The court replies that he is no composer for five reasons: he has not got an academic degree, he refuses to be tied by rules and have his genius cramped:—

Thou Goth and Vandal to just sounds: we may as well place nightingales and canary-birds behind the scenes and take the wild operas of nature from them as allow you to be a composer: an ingenious carpenter with a rule and compass will succeed better in composition, thou finished irregularity!

He made a mess of singing the psalms one Sunday in a country church, and everyone could criticise him as follows, 'You can no more dance a Cheshire hornpipe than you can fly down a rope from Paul's Church. A composer and not dance a Cheshire-round! Incredible!' And for a final accusation, 'By God, you have made such music as never man did before you, nor, I believe, never will be thought of again, when you're gone.' He had practised sorcery for twenty years:—

If at any time a squeak of one of your fiddles or the tooting of a pipe was heard, Hey bounce! we pricked up our ears like so many wild colts—away danced the whole town, helter skelter, like a rabble-rout after a mad bull, squeezing and pressing and shoving, and happy were they that could be squeezed to death.

He got the dead to fight his battles for him—Theseus, Orlando, Alexander or Caesar against the pastoral princess of any other composer—and if he did have a Christian hero—Rinaldo or Amadis—he introduced a wizard. By his witchcraft, too, though other composers were praised their operas were never well attended, but everybody was hurried away by some of your infernal agents to crowd your houses: and when we would have locked up our wives and daughters from your power,—Presto pass! they whipped through keyholes or chimney-tops to you.

There is now a hope that the Lincoln's Inn Fields Theatre may 'put an end to your charms and knock off the fetters we have so long wore'.

Handel may ask, Why set up another opera-house to ruin the Haymarket. The answer is that if we don't, the nation will be ruined. If he then asks how opera can ruin the nation, the reply is:—

How, you dog? How could it be sooner effected than by an opera—that source of expense, luxury, idleness, sloth and effeminacy, and all that—a damned set of Italian squeakers and fiddlers?

Besides, two such institutions will let our own people share a little in the receipts, and anyway the mistake can then be more clearly seen.

Johnson now quotes, through his imaginary court, what is thought of Handel by other composers, who were mostly connected with the rival theatre of Lincoln's Inn Fields:—

The whole musical world is united against you: the King of Aragon (*the arrogant Carlo Arrigoni* [3]) swears you want softness; Signor Porpoise (*obviously Porpora*) finds you deficient in roughness: Mr. Honeycomb protests that he cannot adapt one air of your composition either to his eyes or nose (*Geminiani,* [4] *who loved dealing in pictures and was said to nose out other people's compositions to rewrite*) and they are such stuff as is only fit for the throat of a Carestini or a Strada (*two of Handel's new lot of singers*): Mr. Gaynote vows you produce no pretty thing—that is to say, pleasingly pretty to tickle the ladies (*Galliard, who wrote light and charming pieces for Rich on pantomime lines*); Dr. Pushpin (*obviously Pepusch*) affirms you are no mathematician, and Dr. Blue (*otherwise Greene*) roundly asserts in all companies that you are quite void of spirit and invention. Nay, I can produce an Italian nobleman, whose musical judgement is universally allowed of—especially if his spectacles are on—who has assured me that you know no more of harmony than he does of the tricks of a faro-table or a bowling-green.

(Was this last character meant for the twenty-three-year-old Count Francesco Algarotti?)

Johnson went on:—

As for that indefatigable Society, the Gropers into Antique Music and Hummers of Madrigals (*the Academy of Ancient Music*), they swoon at the sight of any piece modern, particularly of your composition, excepting the performances of their venerable President—

(This must, I think, have been John Eccles, whose first compositions date from about 1680, and who annually composed odes for special occasions, though in retirement till his death the year after this satire.)

—whose works bear such vast resemblance to the regular gravity of the ancients, that when dressed up in cobwebs, and powdered with dust, the Philharmonic spiders could dwell on them and in them to eternity.

Finally, Johnson attacks Handel with one of his own weapons— a cantata, the words translated 'in the modern taste from the original Italian of that incomparable dramatic poet, Signor Rowley-Powley' (that is, of course, Paolo Antonio Rolli, the Haymarket librettist, the Anthony Rowley of 'A frog he would a-wooing go'). The cantata is entitled 'L--- J--- T--- Triumphant', which I take it to mean 'Lincoln's Inn Theatre Triumphant'.[5] It is to be sung to the tune of 'Welcome, Joan Sanderson', and begins:—

Chorus.   Welcome sweet Porpora to Britain's shore,
          Ariadne now adds to our musical store.
Air.   O my sweet Porpora,
          Tis a fine opera:
       We will play it then o'er and o'er,
       And over again nights full three score,
       Till the whole world comes near us no more. *Da Capo.*
Duet.   This opera will no further go.
       Hark ye, Sir Treasurer, why say you so?
       It will not do, it ne'er can do,
       Without you get in *Don Ferdinando.*

(The second Nobility opera, but by Arrigoni,[6] produced February 8, 1734.)

Chorus.   He must come to, and he shall come to,
          And he must come to, whether he will or no.
Recit.   Welcome, sweet Aragon, over the main!
       Is *Don Ferdinando* safe landed from Spain?

(Arrigoni had come from Brussels to London some time between 1728 and 1732.)

Air.   O my dear Aragon,
          This is a paragon:
       We will play it over again,
       And over again, to free us from pain,
       All in the tweedledum, deedledum strain. *Da Capo.*

Duet.   Alas, the poor Don no longer can go,
           Then there is an end of all our fine show:
           If this won't do, how shall we get money?
           Why, await the arrival of Madam Cuzzoni.
Chorus. She must come to, and she shall come to:
           If she'll not come to, this never will do.

(Cuzzoni returned to London for the Lincoln's Inn Fields Theatre about a month after *Ferdinando*, which only lasted four performances, and repeated her previous success in *Ariadne*.)

Johnson finishes by giving a long account of how he came to the World of the Moon and set up an opera, but when the moon-calves set up their own popular opera (and the 'majority of its inhabitants have their ears placed so near their backsides that they frequently sit upon them') he came home for love of his country: why doesn't Handel do the same? In any event the time has come

for the better entertainment of the Court, nobility and gentry to contrive some method of gently blowing into the air one opera-house and all concerned in it.

Johnson's sarcastic satire may miss its mark—or rather makes it uncertain which opera he is attacking, unless indeed he is attacking both; but it at least is an enlarged reflection of what was said at the time about both houses.

[1] But see Theobald's probably satirical estimate, p. 229. The difference of money value between then and now must also be remembered.

[2] See Streatfeild *Handel*.

[3] In the winter of 1733, according to this pamphlet, when Arrigoni had given concerts in London, that 'Trolly Lolly Composer . . . , a stupid cantata-thrummer' (alluding to his playing on the lute and his *Cantate da Camera* published London 1732) 'would not allow that Handel could compose or Senesino sing'.

[4] By comparison with the other names Otto Deutsch (*Handel* 1955) seems right to identify Honeycomb as the alliterative Holcombe, but his first published work is dated 1745 and the 'eyes and nose' allusion cannot now be made as applicable to him as to Geminiani.

[5] Other names are similarly suggested:—*A - - - ne* and *F - - - di - - do*.

[6] From the title-page of the libretto 'Londra 1734' as quoted by Sesto Fassini in *Il Melodrama Italiano a Londra nella prima metà del settecento* (1914). This confirms that this 'Cantata' refers to the first two Nobility operas and their composers. Deutsch, by repeating Burney's wrong attribution of *Ferdinando* (really *Fernando*) to Porpora, complicates the simple interpretation of the 'Cantata' and confuses it further by thinking *Ferdinando* may also refer to the eagerly expected Farinelli. There is nothing to show that that singer might come from Spain, though his patron, Emperor Charles VI of Germany, had been closely concerned with the earlier 'Spanish Succession' quarrels and he himself later had close ties with Philip V of Spain and his son.

CHAPTER EIGHT

Comedy Operas Triumph

In the season of 1734-5 the fight between the rival opera-managements came to a head. Handel moved to the two-year-old Covent Garden Theatre supported by the King and Queen and but few others, leaving the King's, Haymarket, for the Nobility company—supported by the Prince of Wales and most of society—which started brilliantly with twenty-eight performances of Hasse's *Artaserse*. Handel began more leisurely: his first new work was an entertainment for one performance only, *Terpsichore*, and then merely provided an overture for the three performances of an opera called *Oreste*, but in January he presented his *Ariodante*, which reached twelve performances. This was, however, surpassed by sixteen performances at the Haymarket of Porpora's *Polifemo*, though the next Nobility opera, *Issiphile*, by Sandoni, was given only four times. In April Handel went ahead with twenty-two performances of *Alcina*, which Mrs. Pendarves heard at a private rehearsal—she commented on 'a whole scene of charming recitative', said there were 'a thousand beauties' and considered Handel a necromancer. The last new opera of the season, Porpora's *Ifigenia in Aulide*, rated only three performances, but on balance Hasse and Porpora between them outclassed Handel in new works.

But Mrs. Pendarves implies that this rivalry was doing damage, for she wrote to Dr. Swift on May 16, 1735, to tell him:—

Our operas have given much cause of dissension: men and women have been deeply engaged, and no debate in the House of Commons has been urged with more warmth. The dispute of the merits of the composers and singers is carried to so great a height that it is much feared by all true lovers of music that operas will be quite overturned. I own I think we make a very silly figure about it.

The chief singers over whom their followers quarrelled were Carestini and Strada at Covent Garden and at the King's the brilliant new *castrato*, Farinelli, and Senesino, who had deserted Handel to sing for the Nobility and who drew a far larger audience.

The Nobility again scored at the start of the 1735-6 season with

Veracini's *Adriano in Siria*, which had seventeen performances in all. In December 1735 the theatre in Goodman's Fields revived Purcell's *King Arthur* as *Merlin, the British Enchanter*, and on March 2 a pasticcio called *Orfeo* started fifteen performances at the Opera House in the Haymarket. Handel in the meantime had produced nothing new, though he had revived some of his oratorios at Covent Garden.

Three days after the first performance of *Orfeo*, however, the town was captivated by Fielding's 'dramatic satire on the times', *Pasquin*, in the form of the rehearsal of two plays, the second of which, a tragedy called *The Life and Death of Common Sense*, is an attack on foreign entertainers. In this the 'honey-drops' of Farinelli's voice are mentioned and Queen Common Sense learns that

> Queen Ignorance is landed in your realm
> With a vast power from Italy and France
> Of singers, fiddlers, tumblers and rope-dancers.

(The last two categories incidentally were then performing at Sadler's Wells, which explains the allusion when Common Sense is encouraged with the words

> Shakespeare, Jonson, Dryden, Lee and Rowe
> Thou wilt not bear to yield to Sadler's Wells.)

Soon the news comes that

> the warlike Queen
> Of Ignorance, attended with a train
> Of foreigners, all foes to Common Sense,
> Arrives at Covent Garden.

(Only the malicious would consider this applicable to-day.)

At the end Queen Common Sense is killed and music is heard, whereupon the onlookers comment—

Fustian.   What hideous music, or what yell is this?
            Sure 'tis the ghost of some poor opera-tune.
Sneerwell. The ghost of a tune, Mr. Fustian?
Fustian.   Ay, sir. Did you never hear one before? I had once in mind to
            have brought the apparition of Music in person upon the stage in
            the shape of an English opera.

The Epilogue makes a heartfelt appeal to the audience:—

> Banish all childish entertainments hence!
> Let all that boast your favour have pretence,
> If not to sparking wit, at least to sense!

263

With soft Italian notes indulge your ear,
But let those singers, who are bought so dear,
Learn to be civil for their cheer at least,
Nor use like beggars those who give the feast:
And though, while Music for herself may carve,
Poor Poetry, her sister-art, must starve,
Starve her at least with show of approbation,
Nor slight her, while you search the whole creation
For all the tumbling scum of every nation!

On March 30 the opera audience was asked not to encore the singers, for operas had been elongated beyond endurance by partisans, who indulged their fancies. Mrs. Pendarves wrote to Swift again on April 22, 1736, and told him:—

When I went out of town last autumn, the reigning madness was Farinelli: I find it now turned on *Pasquin*, a dramatic satire on the times. It has had almost as long a run as the *Beggar's Opera*, but in my opinion not with equal merit, though it has humour.

No doubt she preferred Handel's new opera, *Atalanta*, which opened on May 12, but it had only ten performances, though it had been produced for the marriage of the Prince of Wales and was presented with allegorical scenes of congratulation and with fire-works.

Handel's next new operas, *Arminio*, *Giustino* and *Berenice*, all produced in the spring of 1737, scored only nineteen performances in all, while at the rival opera-house Hasse's *Siroe* and Pescetti's *Demetrio* had twenty-four between them in the same season when, as Burney said, opera was on the decline: indeed the Nobility opera ended in June. But these and other less successful and now-forgotten new operas were surpassed by an English musical work that was produced at Covent Garden in November 1737: this was a brilliant and true musical satire on Italian opera called *The Dragon of Wantley*—one of Ralph's suggested subjects—the libretto by Carey, the music by Lampe. It had no less than sixty-seven performances in its first season and was constantly revived. Even Handel himself admired it.

When it was published, Carey wrote in his dedication to Lampe:—

Many joyous hours have we shared during the composition of this opera, chopping and changing, lopping, eking out, and coining of words, syllables, and jingles, to display in English the beauties of nonsense so prevailing in the Italian operas. This pleasure has been since transmitted to the gay, the good-natured, and jocular part of mankind, who have tasted the joke and enjoyed the laugh.

In 1738 Handel returned to the King's with the new opera star Caffarelli in *Faramondo*, *Alessandro Severo* (a pasticcio) and *Xerxes* (*Serse*), in which comes the famous Largo aria 'Ombra mai fu', but these only averaged under seven performances each, as against ten for Pescetti's *La Conquista del Vello d'Oro*, also at the King's, which by now was again virtually the only opera-house. The Nobility had given up the fight—as Cibber said, opera singers were then getting as much as £1,400 a year and therefore

those gentlemen of quality who last undertook the direction of them found it ridiculous any longer to entertain the public at so extravagant an expense, while no one particular person thought himself obliged by it.

Cibber put the blame entirely on the singers and their conceit:—

There is too in the very species of an Italian singer such an innate, fantastical pride and caprice that the government of them (here at least) is almost impracticable. This distemper, as we were not sufficiently warned or apprised of, threw our musical affairs into perplexities we knew not easily how to get out of.

There is scarce a sensible auditor in the kingdom that has not since that time had occasion to laugh at the several instances of it: but what is still more ridiculous, these costly canary-birds have sometimes infested the whole body of our dignified lovers of music with the same childish animosities—ladies have been known to decline their visits upon account of their being of a different musical party.

Caesar and Pompey made not a warmer division in the Roman republic than those heroines, their countrywomen, the Faustina and Cuzzoni blew up in our commonwealth of academical music by their implacable pretensions to superiority!

He thought it impossible to afford two first-rate singers of the same sex in one opera even if the public paid double prices. If only they could be dealt with drastically!

What a pity it was these forward misses and masters of music had not been engaged to entertain the Court of some King of Morocco that could have known a good opera from a bad one! With how much ease would such a director have brought them to better order!

The city of Parma had tried to combine star singers, but failed:—

Imperial Rome fell by the too great strength of its own citizens! So fell this mighty opera, ruined by the too great excellency of its singers! For upon the whole it proved to be as barbarously bad as if malice itself had composed it.

(Those who cannot imagine how fine stars can combine disastrously should listen to the delicate 'Goodnight' quartet from

Martha as sung competitively by the superb singers Caruso, Alda, Jacoby and Journet.)

So by the end of 1738 London opera was again in a bad way (Burney said it had been 'a very calamitous season')—even Handel could not open at the King's in the autumn as usual, Heidegger having failed to get subscriptions, and starting on January 16, 1739, could only last four months. In 1740, as Burney wrote:—

The opera, a tawdry, expensive and meretricious lady, who had been accustomed to high keeping, was now reduced to a very humble state and unable to support her former extravagance.

In fact opera was only played at the little theatre in the Haymarket, and the singers were put on half-pay, Burney said. Two now-forgotten operas of that year, *Meridi e Selinunta* (a pasticcio) and *Olimpia in Ebuda*, by Hasse, did, however, have thirty-two performances between them—worth mentioning to show that Handel was not always in the lead and that tastes were changing, as can be gathered from Mrs. Pendarves's description of the fine lady who admired and hated to excess, detested Handel's oratorios and only liked a dancer who kicked a tambourine while naked to the waist. In 1741 Handel's last opera was given—*Deidamia*—which lasted only three performances, and that at Lincoln's Inn Fields Theatre.

In the winter of 1741 the Italian opera started up again under Heidegger, this time without Handel, but with a noble committee headed by Lord Middlesex—another example of leaders of society encouraging the arts: but the aims of the thirty-year-old peer may not have been entirely musical, for he paid extra salary to Signora Panichi, known as the Muscovita, for 'secret services', as Walpole said, though singing was not one of her talents. Rolli was still there, but gradually Middlesex allowed his assistant manager, the conceited Abbé Vaneschi, not only to run the opera-house, but also to line his pockets well.

Instead of Handel, who had now decided that oratorio was a better proposition than opera, they imported Galuppi, whose music was lighter than Handel's. According to the great librettist Metastasio, Galuppi never bothered much about the words he was setting, but his tunes became fairly popular, though none of his operas had more than seventeen performances in a season and he left London after two years, and Lampugnani took his place.

From 1742 to 1748 none of the thirty-odd Italian operas produced in London had any success with the public, though books
on the history of opera in England might mention Galuppi's
Scipione in Carthagine (1742) when an imported elephant broke
through the stage at a rehearsal and Veracini's *Rosalinda*, based by
Rolli on *As You Like It*, which was produced in 1744. In the latter
year Mrs. Pendarves—or rather Mrs. Delany, as she had become
the year before—perhaps following Dryden, prepared a libretto
from *Paradise Lost* for Handel to set, which, alas! he never did,
maybe because of his oncoming paralysis.

There was no autumn season of opera in 1745 due to the threat
to England by the Young Pretender, but on January 7, 1746, the
King's reopened, newly rebuilt in honour of the popular Duke
of Cumberland, with Gluck's specially written *La Caduta de'
Giganti* to celebrate his defeat of Bonny Prince Charlie—in this
opera, by the way, one of the male giants was sung by Signora
Frasi.

After this time, swayed by the English taste for comedy ballad
opera, more and more Italian comedy operas were given,[1] but
apart from Pergolesi's *La Serva Padrona* in 1750, none had more
than an ephemeral success for some time. After the 1747–8 season,
when Middlesex and his subscribers were heavy losers, Croza
made the experiment of giving only comic intermezzi without
any serious operas, but the following season the buffo singers,
fresh from Italy, and the composer Ciampi, performed at the
little Haymarket, having quarrelled with Croza, the manager at
the King's who decamped in the spring of 1750.

Serious composers of opera were now tending to exploit the
singers' technique at the expense of the emotion and drama that
grew out of the words. The poet Thomas Gray, who in 1739,
when he was twenty-three, had hated the Paris opera with its
cracked voices, bad orchestration and ballets that intruded on dis-
connected stories, but had loved the fine opera-singing at Reggio
in Italy two years later: now however in 1751, when his friend
Mason had written his *Elfrida* in imitation of Greek tragedy and
had commented on the inability of modern music to express
poetry, Gray, after giving his opinion that the Greeks

might sing better than the French, but I'll be burnt if they *danced* with more
grace, expression, or even pathos. Yet who ever thought of shedding tears at a
French opera?,

went on to say:—

If modern music cannot, as you say, express poetry, it is not a perfection, but a deterioration. You might as well say that the *perfectionnement* of poetry would be the rendering it incapable of expressing the passions.

In 1753 operas—even serious operas—began again under Vaneschi but the year's greatest success was Cocchi's comic *Jealous Lovers (Gli Amanti Gelosi)*, played by the Giordani family, of whom the elder sister, Burney says, was so admired both as a singer and an actress that

she was frequently encored two or three times in the same air, which she was able to vary so much by her singing and acting that it appeared, at every repetition, a new song and she another performer. The music of the burletta, by Cocchi, was not of the first class: however the part of Spiletta was so admirably performed that it became the general name of the company.

In the autumn of 1754 the great singer Regina Mingotti arrived, and was so popular that she at least kept the manager, Vaneschi, out of debt, if not out of jail, for the time being: but in 1756 he followed the example of his predecessors and decamped, whereupon Mingotti took over the management for a year with the help of the violinist Giardini, who, Burney said, used to get more applause than any other individual artist, apart from Garrick.

In 1757, Mingotti having given up, another popular singer, Colomba Mattei, and her husband, 'made interest for the chance of speedy ruin and obtained the management', as Burney says, 'the nobility having paid too dear for their experience to wish again to resume the government of so expensive and froward a family', as opera singers. It is, however, worth noting that if the earlier noble committees had known more about theatre management there would have been no precedent for the extravagant demands of the singers.

Mattei tried to achieve some policy of standard by engaging the popular Cocchi as resident composer, but without much result, though Thomas Gray told Mason at the beginning of 1759—the year in which Handel died: 'Here is a very agreeable opera of Cocchi's, the *Cyrus (Ciro Riconosciuto)*, which gave me some pleasure', and later in the same year he said it was 'very pretty'.

In 1760 Mattei engaged a comic-opera troupe headed by the Paganini family, with a fine singer, Elisi, for the serious opera:

of them Gray wrote in December 1760, 'Here is a delightful new woman in the burlettas: the rest is all Bartholomew and his fair: Elisi has been ill ever since he came, and has not sung yet.' The Paganina was certainly a success: Walpole said that she 'has more applause than I almost ever remember: every song she sings is encored', and Burney, recording her success in Galuppi's *Il Filosofo di Campagna* in January 1761, wrote:—

This performer, though not young when she came hither from Berlin, increased in reputation so much during the run of this opera that, when it was her turn to have a benefit, such a crowd assembled as I never remember to have seen on the like occasion before or since: indeed not one third of the company that presented themselves at the Opera-house doors were able to obtain admission.

Caps were lost and gowns torn to pieces without number or mercy in the struggle to get in. Ladies in full dress, who had sent away their servants and carriages, were obliged to appear in the streets and walk home in great numbers without caps or attendants. Luckily the weather was fine and did not add to their distress by rain or wind, though their confusion was greatly augmented by its being broad daylight and the streets full of spectators, who could neither refrain from looking or laughing at such splendid and uncommon *streetwalkers*.

This enthusiasm is worth noting to show that comic opera not only proved at least as popular as the more serious works when sung with spirit, but also gave a new lease of life to the opera-house. Gray's letter to Mason on January 22, 1761, not only makes this clear, but epitomises the whole situation:—

The Opera House is crowded this year like any ordinary theatre.

(So opera was not ousting drama even now!)

Elisi is finer than anything that has been here in your memory, yet, as I suspect, has been finer than he is. He appears to be near forty, a little pot-bellied and thick-shouldered, otherwise no bad figure: his action proper and not ungraceful. We have heard nothing, since I remember operas, but eternal passages, divisions, and flights of execution: of these he has absolutely none, whether merely from judgement or a little from age, I will not affirm. His point is expression, and to that all the graces and ornaments he inserts (which are few and short) are evidently directed. He goes higher (they say) than Farinelli, but then this celestial note you do not hear above once in a whole opera, and he falls from this attitude at once to the mellowest, softest, strongest tones (about the middle of his compass) that can be heard.

The Mattei (I assure you) is much improved by his example, and by her great success this winter. But then the Burlettas and the Paganina! I have not been so pleased with anything those many years: she too is fat and about forty, yet handsome withal, and has a face that speaks the language of all nations. She has not the invention, the fire, and the variety of action that the Spiletta had, yet she is light, agile, ever in motion, and above all graceful: but then her voice, her ear, her taste in singing—Good God!—as Mr. Richardson the painter says!

(That her personality was at least as strong as her voice indicates that vocal technique is not always the chief requisite for an opera-singer.)

English opera was becoming more and more successful— Arne's light comedy opera *Thomas and Sally* at Covent Garden in 1760 and his fine serious opera *Artaxerxes* (1762) at Covent Garden, in which, however, he had two Italian male sopranos, Tenducci and Peretti, as Arbaces (which was later played by tenors) and Artaxerxes (later played by female sopranos). This infuriated Charles Churchill, the author of the *Rosciad*, in which he wrote:—

> never shall a truly British age
> Bear a vile race of eunuchs on the stage:
> The boasted work's called national in vain,
> If one Italian voice pollute the strain.

In the same year Count Algarotti's book on opera technique, *Saggio sopra l'Opera in Musica*, was translated into English: in it he is very scornful of the slovenly methods of opera composers of the day, who did little to co-ordinate scenery, arias, recitatives, ballets into the one whole that operas well might be if only the librettist could once again be the prime architect—or if the composer himself was competent enough to be his own librettist, just as Arne had made his own translation of Metastasio's *Artaserse* for himself. In 1762 Arne also had a great success with his lighter, *Love in a Village* at Covent Garden, and the following year Purcell's *King Arthur* was again revived, first in January and then again the following December: 1763 was the year Mattei engaged J. C. Bach as opera composer.

Things were in a bad way at the King's Theatre, which still was the prime opera-house for Italian opera, and in 1763 [2] some anonymous author published a pamphlet entitled

A fair enquiry into the state of operas in England.

Although it is not in the plan of this book to deal with the various managements of opera in London, their struggles, their aims and their chicaneries, this pamphlet, which incidentally is well worth reading for its sensible constructive criticisms, does give a picture of how the opera-houses were then run, and so shows a very good reason why the Italian opera just jogged along from now on without making any great mark and why the English works, which depended more on the box office than on the subscriptions of patrons, were usually far more successful.

The author begins straight and to the point:—

It has been thought a taste for Italian music was not general enough in our country to support the expense of an opera, and this entertainment, after many struggles, seems now sinking into absolute decay from the prevalence of that opinion.

Whether that is so or not:—

This entertainment stands now upon the verge of a precipice, and it must be a tender, as well as a resolute hand that is stretched out to save it.

Tis certain the opera deserves some regard, as it is the entertainment of the highest ranks and as it gives a variety among other polite amusements. If it be true, as has been pretended, that the produce of the best seasons does not defray the charge, it will be in vain to think of restoring it in England: but if it shall appear on the contrary that the receipts of moderate houses are more than equal to the expense of the very best operas, there will be need only to explain and ascertain this to the Nobility, who have always been their support, to the fixing them upon a secure and lasting foundation.

The author believes that the expense could have been covered by the revenue, but that

a great part of it has fallen into the hands of persons who contributed nothing to the entertainment, and that a number of unnecessary officers of the house have been enriched, while the performers starved. This has always been the case: it has been long a complaint, and 'tis fit that at length it should be known.

He now comes down to brass tacks:—

Whosoever undertakes operas enriches the *proprietors* [3] of the house, clothes and scenes, but the restraints and hard conditions under which they are let render it nearly impossible anybody else should be gainers.

While the Nobility were pleased to honour the operas with their direction, the representations were elegant in the highest degree, and but for this unseen and unnecessary charge, they would have found at that time a lasting establishment.

The performers were proud to receive the commands of their *patrons*, and those honourable persons had no views but for the *improvement* of the entertainment: they had *spirit* to procure whatever was excellent, and taste to distinguish where excellencies lay.

So far it is praise for the noble committees of the past, but now comes a qualification which is serious, though it is expressed—naturally—in terms that excuse the governing body:—

While the opera was under this regulation, everything was elegant; everything answered and exceeded the expectation, except the balance of the account, Those who managed became *losers*—but all the while the receipts of the house were much more than equal to the *necessary expense*.

Yet to this we are to attribute the decline of operas in *Britain*:—The Noblemen were perfect judges of what was worthy of their audience, but they were kept in the dark as to the real profits.

(How easily and how often this can happen!)

They did not condescend to look into the innumerable lesser articles of the account, and these were in the hands of persons whose custom was to delude those that dealt with them. The Noblemen lost because they were imposed upon, and they gave up the management because they *lost*. This is the short history.

(This seems to imply they were in it for speculation and certainly shows they did not know enough to take a practical and inquiring interest in it.)

Now, the author says, those in charge *only* think of what they can get out of it and therefore underpay the singers so badly that

good singers will not come over, unless to serve a different sort of masters: worse and worse will therefore be employed, and the entertainment itself must in the end certainly cease.

Operas are now frequented by few except the subscribers and their friends— and on half the nights not even by those. It cannot be supposed those great personages who slight them now will contribute to them again under the same management: we see, perhaps, this winter the last that will be performed in *England*, unless the conduct be entirely altered.

The author now says that there is an easy remedy: he may not have all the facts—though he thinks he has—but at least he is

a person wholly unconcerned, one who has no motive but his regard for the *entertainment* and his apprehensions of its absolute destruction.

(Poor honest man! Did nobody ever tell him that if he had no personal axe to grind he would be told he had his facts wrong, and that if his facts were right he would be accused of grinding his own axe?)

He is convinced that opera can and must be self-supporting: recently the artists themselves had tried to run it, but, being foreigners, they were easily tricked out of their profits, for profits there were:—

Estates were got by the opera, while the noblemen were fleeced and the performers starved.

This depends on calculation and may be proved from facts which cannot be contested.

If we set the expense of operas at the highest, twenty good houses with a moderate subscription will pay the charge of a season. There remain thirty therefore, reasonably computing, for advantage. Perhaps there never was a year in which the opera did not produce enough to pay for itself, though the money fell into wrong hands. Four thousand pounds has been frequently the profit of a season, and it is easy to see much more than this may be got every winter under a fair and rational management.

The best performers will bring good houses, otherwise expenses must be retrenched and watched professionally:—

A banker will be the proper *treasurer* of the cash: nor can it be needful to keep an army of *carpenters* in pay—it will be enough to employ them when they are wanted. It is ridiculous even to absurdity that a man should have a large salary for an office to which he appoints himself at the letting of the house.

(Even nowadays one has heard stories of theatre-managers leasing theatres and then acting as managers for the incoming lessee, who is then charged for use of the manager's office, which he would have, anyway! In the past there have been cases of managers leasing their theatres to outside companies of which they themselves are directors. Times never change much.) Now he comes to economies:—

Three pounds a week for a carpenter to be ready for fear he should be *wanted* and who, if he is wanted, is paid for his work beside, is an extravagance and folly so barefaced that one could scarce believe it real: nor is there any reason the managers—

(i.e. the incoming opera impresarios)

should be obliged to pay an exorbitant sum nightly for lighting the house, when reputable tradesmen offer to do it twice as well for a fifth less expense.

Who is authorising the expenses?

If one man shall make such demands, and another order their payment, independent of those who are at the expense of the entertainment, 'tis certain who must gain and who be ruined.

The opera-house should be leased together with scenes and wardrobe and the performers engaged for three years, which will give the artists encouraging security, and will allow backers more incentive to improve the scenery and more time to get back their expenses. Now things are very different:—

It has been usual to take the house under sad limitations, with dirty scenes and without a sight of the wardrobe, and with a certain profit to those who give no pleasure to the audience.

A board of six or eight subscribers with a knowledgeable accountant need only meet two hours a week: they should be given a complete inventory and should account for all in it at the end of their three years' tenancy, but should be allowed to engage who they like and have entire control of the opera-house—except for 'Assemblies or Masquerades'.

The Nobility of *England* will not conceive the direction of these performances beneath their notice, since they are sensible that in other nations this care is usually taken by persons of the highest rank purposely to keep it out of mercenary hands in which it could not prosper. . . . The qualifications for the conducting of such an entertainment are the natural qualities and accomplishments of persons of great rank—taste, spirit, and a dignity accompanied with politeness to give weight to the commands and at the same time make them pleasing.

The treasurer, who could also be deputy to the directors should have

some skill in the *Italian* language and a perfect knowledge of our own, with a little taste in poetry. He should be qualified to judge of the sense and to *translate* the opera without rendering it ridiculous.

These are talents which might be easily found, but if those who have managed operas have been of a rank too mean for such moderate accomplishments, much less could we expect in them the higher requisites.

Perhaps that is the real trouble—those in charge are incapable as well as money-grubbing:—

The ignorance of such a person may lead him to prefer the meanest writers when *Metastasio* is as readily before him, and in that opinionated obstinacy which always accompanies ignorance he may cut out so much of those which are better as to reduce all to one level. If the singer adds what he likes, when such a Manager has cut out what displeases him, the performance must become one great absurdity.

I am grieved to say the *English* have been content to admit such Managers, and to receive such operas: but 'tis hoped it will be so no more.

A Manager thus destitute of knowledge and influenced by mercenary views, would select the most indifferent performers because they would come cheaper, and we should be sure to see the best unemployed, because they were too good for his service.

Indeed we see it now. Persons are suffered at the opera who would be rejected at the meanest theatres abroad: no capital performer of any kind appears, and yet the Nobility pay the same price as when they had the best representations.

Of late two incidents have occurred at the operahouse which seem to threaten the finishing stroke to that entertainment—the introduction of *Italian* shades, a larger kind of magic lantern, an expedient so low that it would disgrace a puppet-show, and proposals for a smaller subscription for a less number of operas in the season.

(We still occasionally have a magic lantern instead of scenery or practical stage properties—projection scenery it is called.)

Fewer performances will not be cheaper over the whole season, nor will that mean a lower rate of hire for scenes and wardrobe or smaller salaries:—

Having a smaller number of representations cannot lessen the expense of the principal performers, for they must live the winter, whether they sing two and thirty times or fifty—and sufficient care is always taken to prevent their singing anywhere else. 'Tis evident therefore we can have no capital performer upon such terms, and there requires little knowledge to find out that an opera without capital performers is ridiculous.

If benefits are given them instead of more pay, it is a second tax on the subscribers: but perhaps this may be a new method in the place of those *imaginary* agreements which were shown to the Nobility to procure a large subscription, though the money was never intended to be paid to the performers.

If the Nobility will please to take the opera out of this kind of management, it will be easy to make it flourish.

It cannot subsist upon these terms: nor is there any reason those who subscribe so largely to the support of that entertainment should submit to them. There are performers to be had, and they would come joyfully, for to all foreigners *England* is Elyzium.

There was a temporary improvement in the state of Italian opera in London in 1764, thanks to 'the most powerful and voluminous soprano that had been heard on our stage since the time of Farinelli', Burney says: this was the singer Manzoli, and Burney wrote,

We are now arrived at a splendid period in the annals of the musical drama, when, by the arrival of Giovanni Manzoli, the serious opera acquired a degree of favour to which it had seldom mounted since its first establishment in this country.

The expectations which the great reputation of this performer had excited were so great that at the opening of the theatre in November with the pasticcio of *Ezio* there was such a crowd assembled at all the avenues, that it was with very great difficulty I obtained a place, after waiting two hours at the door.

In spite of his eulogy of this period, it would seem that Burney cannot, however, find more to say of it than that Manzoli was brilliant in some otherwise unsuccessful operas: indeed, for sheer popularity the brilliant two-year-old Irish burletta *Midas* by Kane O'Hara at Covent Garden was more successful.

One of the results of the sad state of affairs at the Italian opera was that English works attracted a larger public, and new English stage-composers emerged. Arnold came to the front in 1766 with his *Maid of the Mill*, which rivalled the success of Piccini's *Gli Stravaganti*, and the charming *Buona Figliuola*, produced in October and November of that year. According to the new policy the popular comic operas were given on the less-frequented Tuesday evenings, while the less popular serious works were left to the other opera day, the crowded Saturday. These last two operas, by the way, were constantly revived, the latter—in which Lovattini was the great draw, at whose retirement comic opera lapsed, according to Burney—each year for nineteen years, popular no doubt in part because it was based on Richardson's twenty-six-year-old famous novel, *Pamela*.

In the 1768–9 season, when no serious operas were given, Dibdin started his successful career as a comic-opera composer with *Lionel and Clarissa* and *The Padlock*. Gluck's *Orfeo* was given in 1770 with additional music by J. C. Bach and Guglielmi, but the following season there were again no serious operas. Dibdin scored heavily in 1773 with *The Deserter*—his arrangement of Monsigny's original—after having produced fifteen other stage works in five years, and he followed it up with *The Waterman* in 1774.

In 1775, when the famous soprano Agujari, whom Mozart so much admired, was paid as much as £100 a night for singing two songs, Linley collaborated with Sheridan in *The Duenna*, Paesiello's *La Frascatana* was the success of 1776, and in 1777 Arnold's *Spanish Barber* appeared, which is notable as being the earliest existing musical version of *The Barber of Seville*, and which includes a calumny aria and songs from Beaumarchais's own operatic original as I believe—but this is not the place for such an exposition.

In 1780 William Jackson, who well understood the proper balance between words and music (to judge from his preface to his published songs) collaborated, in *The Lord of the Manor*, with Lieutenant-General Burgoyne (if he was the author), who deprecated in his preface the use of recitative in English works, preferring the dialogue to be spoken, while the music should be kept subordinate.

The following year, in his *Lives of the Poets*, Dr. Johnson printed his opinion of Italian opera as 'an exotic and irrational entertainment', which has often been quoted as a damning definition of all opera, and anyway should carry a negligible amount of weight in view of the fact that the Doctor was far more eager to air his views to listeners who had no courage to contradict him than he was to be humble enough to enjoy any work of art: on the other hand, 'exotic' merely meant 'foreign' or 'outlandish', and 'irrational' was universally applied to the Italian opera with its lack of sense. In the passage concerned he was writing of John Hughes, whose *Calypso and Telemachus* was produced in 1712, and said that his aim was to 'oppose or exclude the Italian opera, an exotic and irrational entertainment, which has been always combated and always has prevailed'.

Dr. Johnson was even wrong in stating that Italian opera always prevailed: it was always being resuscitated and kept alive by its irrational patrons, but through the latter half of the eighteenth century it seldom lived long enough to draw the town, as the English works did. These may have been of an inferior type, but they were largely first-rate of their kind, whereas the average Italian opera seen in London after 1750 was a pale second-rate shadow of the supposedly higher type.

In 1782 the Italian opera in London was in a bad way again: Garrick and Arne had revived and adapted Purcell's *King Arthur*, Shield produced his successful *Rosina* (1782) and *The Shamrock* (1783), and about this time comparatively recent French operas by composers such as Grétry or Monsigny, translated and adapted by composers such as Dibdin, Linley, Shield, or Arnold, were given frequently, while *The Dragon of Wantley* was revived for the last time at Covent Garden, which looks as if the public had forgotten or failed to recognise the object of its satire. The comic Italian operas still held their public—*La Serva Padrona*, revived again in 1783, and *Gli Stravaganti* in 1784, while *Orfeo* was specially revived for Tenducci in 1785, with Gluck's music made more palatable by the addition of music by Handel and Anfossi as well as J. C. Bach, who had assisted before. In 1785 there seems to have been no Italian operas.

In 1786 one John Williams published the first part of his *Children of Thespis*, a poem which gives accounts of all the stage performers of the day: in this he sings the praises of an English singer, the twenty-three-year-old Mrs. Crouch, who had sung the part of Venus in the *King Arthur* revival—

> When Dryden's gay Venus comes forth with a smile
> To chant the bless'd boons of her favourite isle,
> The soul of great Purcell it bursts from the tomb,
> And listening flutters with joy round the dome.

He blamed Dibdin, however, for writing scraps of trash and catchpenny stuff.

In the next year, when Cimarosa's *Giannina e Bernardone* and Dalayrac's *Nina, ou la Folle par Amour* were given in London with success—the latter in English, as were all the French works at this time—the second part of *Children of Thespis* contained praise for another even younger singer, the German-born Elizabeth Weichsell, already well-known by her married name of Mrs. Billington:—

> Behold a blithe siren, high priz'd and high finished!
> Fall back, ye meek songsters, abashed and diminished!

At the same time she could be criticised for her cultivation of technique at the expense of emotion:—

> She oft wants the gentle assistance of ease,
> And seems more intent to surprise than to please.

In 1787 also the London-born Anna Storace, who had created the part of Susanna in *Figaro* the year before in Vienna, made her London debut at the age of twenty-one in Paesiello's popular *Le Gare Generose*.

In 1788 the third part of *Children of Thespis* contained a scathing allusion to opera, which

> at best
> Is an error-made monster and national jest:
> Manufactured the reason of man to affright,
> Insulting our wit, while it flatters the sight.

There was also a violent criticism of the great German singer, Madame Mara, who had come to London as a child violinist in the fifties but had returned in 1784, and sung in the Handel Commemorations of that year and the next, in *Didone Abbandonata*, a pasticcio, in 1786, and Handel's *Giulio Cesare* in 1787. Of her the poem said she was 'baseborn and invidious' and went on:—

> As the bounties of Britain with speed overtake her,
> Hear the vocalised idiot blaspheming her Maker:
> When the pit echoes round with 'Charmante' and 'Cara',
> She roars with *fierté* 'One God and one Mara!'

(so echoing what had been said fifty years before by an adoring female admirer of singing and included by Hogarth in one of his pictures of 'The Rake's Progress'—'One God, one Farinelli!').

Paesiello's *Barbiere di Siviglia* was a success of the year 1789, but it was surpassed by the fifty performances of *The Haunted Tower*, by Anna Storace's brother, Stephen. He followed this up with *No Song, No Supper* in 1790 and *The Siege of Belgrade* in 1791.

In the same year William Jackson published his *Observations on the Present State of Music in London*, in which he claimed that at that time most grand-opera arias were defective in melody, while few opera-buffa arias were anything but nonsensical: English operas, on the other hand, wisely used tunes 'which were composed when melody really existed' and which can be appreciated by an audience

after they have been gaping to take in some meaning from the wretched imitations of Italian bravura and pathetic songs, which alas! are but 'the shadows of a shade'.

Nowadays he fears that 'what is least felt is most applauded', but while the overture to an Italian opera now 'never pretends to much', an English overture does at least try to 'have an air somewhere'. He then reflects that the craze for Lully in the seventeenth century stopped the development of French music, and says with some justification:—

The harm which Lully did in France Handel has done and will continue to do in England.

In 1792 Gluck's *Orfeo* was given in English for the first time—but now with additional music, not only by Handel and J. C. Bach as before, but by Sacchini, Weichsell and Reeve as well. It is so easy for writers on opera to praise Italian opera in general, and to blame the English operas, comic operas, burlettas, musical dramas, interludes and the rest for adding and adapting, but this is exactly what the average Italian opera did: the only difference was that the Italian works were usually mere tedious hotchpotches, while the English works—adapted and arranged by experienced theatre-musicians—were amusing or exciting hotchpotches. Storace's *Pirates*, which was produced in the winter of 1792, was a successful example of what could be done by borrowing when the borrowing was done by a brilliant man—even from

himself, thereby bearing out what was said as long ago as 1709 [4]
—that

Operas patched up out of the compositions of several different masters are not
likely to succeed unless they are prepared by some person that is capable of
making an opera himself.

Storace's operas certainly succeeded, though he borrowed and
imitated, and in the opinion both of his contemporaries and of
those who know his works it was a great loss to opera when he
died as early as the two geniuses to whom he was compared,
Purcell and Mozart.

There were few new successes or productions of special interest
over the turn of the century, except for Arnold's *Children in the
Wood* of 1793 (yet another hint taken from Ralph [5]), Cimarosa's
Matrimonio Segreto (based on the 1766 play by Colman and
Garrick, *The Clandestine Marriage*), Bianchi's *La Vendetta di Nino*,
Storace's *Cherokee* (all of 1794 and all later revived), Martiny Solar's
La Scuola dei Maritati and *L'Isola del Piacere* (both later revived and
both produced in 1795, in which year Gluck's *Alceste* was given its
first real stage performance in London for the benefit of the fine
singer Banti, who had made her début in *La Vendetta di Nino*),
Gluck's *Iphigénie en Tauride* (1796) and Paesiello's *Nina, o sia La
Pazza per Amore* (1797). The chief revivals during this time were
La Buona Figliuola, *Il Barbiere di Siviglia*, *Il Matrimonio Segreto*, *The
Maid of the Mill*, *Midas*, and other English works of similar type—
all, be it noted, comedies.

Mozart had died in 1791, but though a great deal of his music
was known here and some included in other people's stage works
(Leporello's Catalogue aria was probably included in Gazzaniga's
Don Giovanni Tenorio, o sia il Convitato di Pietro in 1794), no opera
of his had been performed as such in London during his lifetime.
That had to wait till the nineteenth century had started, and with
it criticism became rather more a professional matter than it had
been up to 1800.

[1] Between 1700 and 1750 only some seven were given: between 1750 and 1800
there were 129 Italian comedy operas as against 157 Italian serious works.

[2] The pamphlet is undated, but 1763 is the dating according to the British
Museum.   [3] The italics all through are as in the original.

[4] See p. 189. Incidentally one of his loveliest melodies from this opera
'Softly slumb'ring on the ocean' was later adapted for a Catholic Easter hymn.

[5] See p. 246.

PART THREE

Up to 1914

SENSE

Interior of the 1809 Covent Garden Theatre when
reconstructed as the Royal Italian Opera, as it
appeared on the opening in 1847 to a contemporary
artist

CHAPTER ONE

Mozart Operas Introduced

ON Saturday, March 15, 1806, readers of *The Times* who patronised the operas at the King's Theatre in the Haymarket were interested to notice that

Mrs. Billington respectfully informs the Nobility, Gentry, and the Public that her benefit night is fixed for Thursday, March 27, when will be performed a grand serious opera with choruses, entitled *La Clemenza di Tito*, entirely composed by Mozart—the most celebrated ouvrage of that great composer, and the only one of his composition ever produced in this country. To which will be added favourite ballets.

Elizabeth Billington—at that time about forty years old—had long been popular as a singer both in England and Italy: her mother had been a successful singer, her father, Carl Weichsell, was principal wood-wind player at the King's Theatre, and she herself had appeared as a child prodigy under ten years of age as a pianist with her brother Charles—who afterwards led the orchestra at the King's and occasionally conducted at Covent Garden when his sister sang there—as a violinist. When she went to Italy, Sir William Hamilton persuaded the King of Naples to hear her, with the result that she was engaged to sing at the San Carlo opera-house in an opera, *Inez di Castro,* especially composed for her by Bianchi. Unfortunately an immediate eruption of Vesuvius was, according to the more superstitious Neapolitans, the result of the appearance on the stage of a heretic Protestant from England, and things might easily have gone sadly wrong for her if her operatic performances—often in works specially composed for her by Paesiello, Paer and Hummel—had not been so enthusiastically received.

On her return to England her services were eagerly sought after, for her voice, though not powerful, was not only extensive in range, but sweet and flexible, and her singing was pure and musicianly (she had composed two sets of piano sonatas before she was twelve). Her appearance on the stage always ensured a large audience, and for her benefit nights—that is, the nights on which a leading artist was entitled by contract to the proceeds of the theatre, except for certain qualified expenses—there was always a great rush for tickets, which were advertised as being obtainable from Mrs. Billington herself at 42 Leicester Square.

To musicians there was the further interest of the first presentation of a Mozart opera on the London stage. The implication in the announcement is, of course, misleading, as many of his compositions had been heard before in London, even some of the music from his operas, but either at concerts or inserted into other stage-works. But perhaps it is not surprising on reflection that the first Mozart opera to be seen in London was one of his last two, for although it was already fifteen years old in 1806, it would probably seem less old-fashioned than one of his earlier stage-works. Perhaps with the object of making it even more up-to-date, the original Italian libretto by Metastasio, first set to music by Caldara in 1734, and already altered for Mozart by C. Mazzola in 1791, was even further changed for the London of 1806 by S. Buonaiuti.

For those who were not enthusiastic about opera and who were not especially excited by either a Mozart novelty or by Mrs. Billington, there was also the probability of enjoying a little variety in the 'favourite ballets' which, as was the custom of the day, were to be performed between the acts of the opera: so those who were only anxious to see and be seen among the nobility, gentry and the public were probably intrigued when, on the morning of the performance, the title of the ballet was announced as

La Surprise de Diane; ou, le Triomphe de l'Amour: composed by Mons. Rossi.

The next morning the *Morning Post* contained the following appreciation of the event:—

Last night this elegant theatre was crowded to an overflow, a just tribute to the great talents of Mrs. Billington. It must have been highly pleasing to this lady, on her benefit night, to see the whole of the boxes and the pit occupied by persons of the first distinction.

On her entrée she was greeted with repeated plaudits. She sung with uncommon effect, and seemed anxious to repay with every exertion the approbation and attention of so splendid and numerous an audience.

The music of *La Clemenza di Tito*, the production of that great composer Mozart, was heard with delight. The Overture was much admired, and the Leader, Mr. Weichsell, exerted himself with the whole orchestra to render every justice to one of the greatest composers the world ever produced.

Mr. Braham sung admirably, and the duets between him and Mrs. Billington were indeed a delectable treat. Signora Griglietti made her first appearance: she has a pretty voice, a pleasing person, and we have no doubt will prove an acquisition. Righi and Rovedino also filled their respective parts with great credit.

The scenery, dresses, decorations, etc. were at once elegant and appropriate, and we have no doubt that *La Clemenza di Tito* will be often repeated to crowded audiences.

It is not surprising that this first account of a Mozart opera in England was a report rather than a criticism: after all, the occasion was a benefit night and a society event: the Prince Regent himself was present and, as reported in the same paper in a column headed 'Fashionable World', a large number of the 'persons of distinction' among the audience went on to Mrs. Fitzherbert's Grand Assembly at her house in Tylney Street, Park Lane, 'one of the most magnificent houses in town':—

The whole world of fashion (with a very few exceptions) were present: among whom we noticed the following distinguished personages:—

His Royal Highness the Prince of Wales, Dukes of Kent and Clarence, Prince and Princes Castelcicala, Their Excellencies the Imperial, Sardinian, and Swedish Ambassadors.

—to say nothing of innumerable dukes, duchesses, marquesses and marchionesses.

Of the other singers only Braham was in the same class as Mrs. Billington—indeed, six years before they had been vehement rivals for popularity in Milan. He was a fine, if rather flashy singer, lacking in refinement—the exact opposite of Mrs. Billington—but he was full of dramatic vigour, especially when singing his own popular ballad type of songs, which he liked to introduce at every opportunity. Poor Signora Griglietti apparently was too overcome at appearing with two such popular singers, for two days after the performance *The Times* critic wrote that

Mrs. Billington gave the charming airs allotted to her with the most powerful effect. Signora Griglietti made her *début* on the occasion, and though under the most evident alarms gave the promise of future excellence.

The same critic considered that this opera by Mozart

would have established his reputation as a great composer, if it had not been already acknowledged in every part of Europe.

It was performed a second time the day that notice appeared—Saturday, March 29—this time with divertissements and a 'Heroic

Ballet' entitled *Tamerlan and Bajazet*, and the *Morning Post* of Monday wrote:—

The Grand Serious Opera of *La Clemenza di Tito* drew a crowded house on Saturday night: nor will it fail to be of lasting attraction. The music is exquisitely fine, and in all its parts the most fastidious critic must acknowledge it to be a 'chef d'œuvre' of the art. Mrs. Billington was heard throughout with rapture, and Mr. Braham sung admirably. Two duets by him and Mrs. Billington were 'encored' with renewed applause.

It was not, however, kept in the repertoire, though after the first performance the *Morning Post* had had no doubt it would be 'often repeated to crowded audiences'.

On the day of the second performance of *La Clemenza di Tito*— Saturday, March 29, 1806—there was advertised in *The Times* a performance for that night at the German Theatre, Leicester Place, Leicester Square, called the Sanssouci, of a mixed programme including the popular comic opera *Adolf and Clara*, a Pantomime Dance, and

for the first time,[1] a new Musical Piece by Mozart, called *The Enchanted Flute*: and to conclude with the Optical Ballet.

The *Morning Post* did not name Mozart but added 'under the immediate patronage of her Majesty'. Dalayrac's *Adolphe et Clara ou Les Deux Prisonniers*, which had been first produced in Paris in 1799, had been seen in English at Drury Lane in 1804 and in German at the Sanssouci in 1805, and so was presumably popular enough to warrant the risk of presenting with it a strange Mozart novelty. Obviously *The Magic Flute* must have been cut drastically to fit into a quadruple bill, but unfortunately I have so far been unable to find out what the critics then thought of this fantastic twin of *La Clemenza di Tito* or what the intriguing phrase 'the Optical Ballet' meant. Perhaps both the ballet and the Mozart opera were performed with some development of the 1763 (?) magic-lantern[2]—the eighteenth century equivalent of the modern ultra-violet stage transformation.

In the five years after Mrs. Billington introduced Mozart opera to London some dozen Italian operas which are now only names were produced for the first time in London, as well as an English opera, *The Circassian Bride*, by the twenty-three-year-old Henry Bishop: this was enthusiastically received on February 23, 1809, but the night after its first performance the theatre—Drury Lane—

was burnt to the ground and the score was destroyed. In 1810 he was appointed composer and musical director at the year-old new theatre at Covent Garden.

1809 had been the year of the Covent Garden riots against the increase price of seats and against the engagement for her fourth season in London of the expensive foreign singer, Catalani, in whose place the rioters patriotically preferred Mrs. Billington, Mrs. Mountain and Mrs. Dickons, according to the print of the riot.

In 1811 a benefit night for the singer, Mme. Bertinotti Radicati, was announced for Thursday, May 9,

on which evening Madame Bertinotti, anxious to comply with the wishes of the British musical world, for the performance on the stage of an Opera Buffa of Mozart's, will have the honour to present the Opera *Cosi fan tutte*, which will be performed on that night only.

It was to be given, of course, 'with a Divertissement and Ballet', and tickets were to be obtained from Mme. Bertinotti at 29 Princes Street, Hanover Square. The other singers were announced to be Tramezzani, Cauvini and Naldi as Guglielmo, Fernando and Alfonso, with Collini as Dorabella and Cauvini's wife as Despina. The thirty-five-year-old Teresa Bertinotti, not having the voice or execution for Fiordiligi's arias, cheerfully sang in their place other arias, as was her practice—usually seizing the opportunity to choose some written by her violinist-composer husband, Felice Radicati. She made a great personal success with the audience, whose spirits were not damped by the pouring rain in which many of them had watched the laying of the foundation stone of Vauxhall Bridge by the Prince Regent's deputy that morning, and on May 30 *Cosi fan tutte* was put on again—this time for the benefit of the Ballet-Master of the King's, Vestris, with the addition of the new ballet *Ildamor and Zulema*.

After its next performance on the following day it became part of the repertoire and was played six times between then and June 18, its second regular performance on June 4 being the occasion of a great scandal, when the Princess of Wales[3] was said to have remained seated during the playing of 'God Save the King' at the performance, though it was George III's seventy-third birthday. Unfortunately I have not found any criticisms of the actual production, and after June *Cosi fan tutte* went out of the opera repertoire for many years.

Two days after the national anthem incident the excellent character-bass Giuseppe Naldi announced in *The Times* for his benefit night

for the first time in this country the celebrated comic opera composed by Mozart and entitled *Die Zauber Flöte; or, Il Flauto Magico*, and which has ever experienced the most enthusiastic reception in Vienna, Berlin, Amsterdam and Paris.

Other famous cities—apart from about fifty German towns— might have been added to the list, for since its first performance in 1791 it had also been produced at Prague, Warsaw, Cracow, St. Petersburg, Moscow and Berne. The phrase 'for the first time in this country' may have been substantially correct, as the 1806 performance must have been cut to ribbons: on the other hand, it either might have been used as a catch-penny boost or deliberately used to claim that this 1811 production was the first in London that to any extent truly resembled Mozart's original composition.[4]

It was certainly shortened—though probably not to the extent of the advertised 1806 version—for with it were given the usual divertissement and ballet: but to fall into line with the supposed taste of the fashionable opera-goers, who had come to believe that Italian operas were the acme of classically cultured art, the original German libretto by Schikaneder was translated for the English audience into Italian by G. de Gamerra, and in that language it was sung. Again the papers throw no light on this performance, though one called it 'delightful'. *The Times* disregarding the opera in favour of Astley's popular show in which

the wonders achieved by the horses at the Royal Amphitheatre in the brilliant spectacle of *The Tyrant Saracen and the Noble Moor* become every hour more interesting by the glorious deeds effected by the British cavalry in the late victories.[5] Such a lively representation of a real battle was never before exemplified.

The following year, however, the papers did notice Mozart, when *La Clemenza di Tito* was revived on Tuesday, March 3, with Griglietti, who had been in the first London production five years before, Tramezzani, who had recently appeared in *Così fan tutte*, and the great Catalani herself. On this occasion the preliminary announcement stressed that the opera was being given 'for the first time' in London, which was probably justified by the succeeding statement:—

The music by Mozart, as originally composed; the poetry by Metastasio.

implying, no doubt, that the Billington version had been strongly adapted.

The 1812 critics, however, whether because they were hearing the real Mozart score in all its modernity, unsoftened by 'arrangement', or whether because they were no longer influenced by the kindly atmosphere of a popular benefit night, not only criticised the performance in considerable detail, but pulled no punches. Here is what *The Times* wrote after due consideration two days after the first performance of this revival:—

The opera on Tuesday was admirably performed in its principal parts; and if the highest powers of voice and acting could do justice to the music of the great opera composer of Germany, the audience had a right to be gratified with the leading characters of this opera: yet our taste is still so far native as to make us regret that this music and those powers were employed upon a subject so bare that nothing like the interest of a plot could be felt through it.

The first thing, then, that this critic asked for from an opera was a logical and interesting story: at the first performance for the coronation of the Emperor Leopold as King of Bavaria in 1791 Titus may well have stood for the ideal of a kindly despot, but to a London audience of 1812 he must have seemed a weak turncoat, giving up the idea of marrying Servilia on finding she loves Annius, agreeing to marry Vitellia, who had complained of his lack of interest in her, tearing up the death-warrant he had already signed on finding his friend Sextus had planned to murder him and had fired the Capitol, and on Vitellia's confession that she had planned the conspiracy pardoning everyone. London of 1812— except perhaps the artistic set of society—would far rather have seen Sextus and his fellow-conspirators thrown to the wild beasts in the arena, or at least escape in a wild pursuit on some of Astley's horses. As *The Times* most shrewdly remarked, though the critic did not know that Metastasio had died in 1782 aged eighty-four nine years before Mozart wrote the opera,

Nothing can be more destitute than this plot; and yet it was this—such was the taste of the stage in countries where the decay of political freedom spread through all the departments of intellectual effort the same spirit of tameness, weakness, and monotony—that Metastasio selected for the subject of a drama to be set by Mozart.

As for the twenty-year-old music:—

The fame of the composer is now almost beyond criticism, and want of delight at his works will probably be attributed in the critic to want of taste: but his composition, if it has all that can be given by science, probably bears the exclusive impression of science too strongly and too unremittingly for the general ear; and the pleasure with which the few scattered airs that occasionally relieved the ponderous and laboured character of the composition were received, might have persuaded the admirers of the unmitigated German School that taste, nature, and simplicity might in some instances at least be advantageously substituted for chromatics and cadences, the crashing of disjointed harmonies, and the array of scientific discordance.

Not that all the music sounded 'too modern':—

Yet if the strength of science has in this opera been sometimes employed like the unwieldy vigour of the giant of old, to produce only more irreparable confusion, it has sometimes wrought its miracles of labour: and perhaps in the whole range of music prowess nothing could be a finer instance of difficulty attempted and admirably overcome than the chorus at the end of the first act, in which the people mourn for the supposed death of Titus.

Two of the airs, 'Deh prendi un dolce amplesso', in which Vitellia and Annius express their mutual gratitude, and 'Deh perdona', in which Sextus gives up his claim to the hand of Vitellia, were highly applauded: but they were of a character totally distinct from the general opera.

The overture—a composition peculiarly adapted to the powers of the German School, and in which nothing is expected but instrumental display and 'regular confusion'—was ably performed and encored.

In his notice of the performers *The Times* critic makes it quite clear that he is not interested in voice alone, but that he regards singing, acting, costume and everything as mutually contributing to a finally welded-together character, on whose emotion the effect on the audience depends.

Catalani had recovered from her cold, and her acting and voice were both in their usual excellence. Her dress on her first appearance was magnificently arranged, and the glittering diadem, the head wreathed like an antique bust, the scarlet tunic and the looped and tasselled drapery gave the full impression of regal grandeur to a face and form fitted, beyond all that we have ever seen, to the expression of dignity and grace—the softness of a woman mingled with the solemn and tragic majesty of a fallen queen.

Tramezzani's acting was such as left little to be desired, and the audience expressed their approbation by the loudest applause. The inferior characters admit of considerable improvement, and if Signora Griglietti is in future to support the character of Annius, it might be expedient to make her costume a little less of the doubtful gender.

There are several interesting points worth noting in these last few lines: Tramezzani's acting is praised, while his singing is not specifically mentioned, being apparently included in the general term 'acting', which, after all, includes speaking when applied to plays: the inferiority of the smaller parts was well in keeping with Catalani's invariable wish to be the great star—at an enormous salary—with 'four or five puppets', as her husband said, supporting her: and finally poor Griglietti, who seems fated to make a mess of her performances, was obviously forced to follow the eighteenth-century practice of having a *castrato* part played by a woman on occasion—a practice that by 1812 was becoming more essential with the decline of popularity for the male soprano.

La Clemenza di Tito was given several times between March and June—by which time it was announced as a 'favourite' opera —and its last performance this season was on June 20, when its Roman dignity, its academic modern music and its lack of plot were to some extent enlivened by the interpolation after the first act of 'the favourite Scotch Divertissement of *Peggy's Love*'. But before we laugh too heartily and patronisingly at the ingenuous bad taste of the period shown by such a mixture, let us remember that nowadays, when an opera is broadcast in this country, we have interpolations between the acts—on one occasion a talk on Lewis Carroll, who certainly would have appreciated the ironic joke.

---

[1] This has, I think, not been noticed before. 1811 is always given as the date of the first London performance.

[2] See p. 275.

[3] Presumably the Prince Regent's wife, though their daughter was called Princess Charlotte of Wales.

[4] Compare the 'first acted' of *Psyche*, pp. 126–8 n.

[5] In the Peninsular War.

CHAPTER TWO

Figaro, Don Giovanni, The Barber

IN 1812—the year, as all musicians know, of Napoleon's retreat from Moscow—Figaro introduced himself once more to the London stage—but in two forms. The first was on the farewell benefit night of the dancer Des Hayes, when, under the patronage of the Prince Regent, Spontini's *La Vestale* with Catalani and Tramezzani was followed by the usual divertissements and 'a new Grand Ballet in three Acts, called *Figaro, ou les Noces du Comte Almaviva*'. This danced version of the *Barber of Seville* story by Duport on May 16 was followed on June 18 by a charity performance at the King's in aid of the Scottish Hospital, under the usual committee of titled patrons: the advertisement read: 'For the first time in this country the celebrated Opera of *Le Mariage de Figaro*: the music by Mozart.'

The cast, which included Catalani and Naldi, was entirely foreign with the exception of Mrs. Dickons, who was remembered from the nineties as a lovely Polly in *The Beggar's Opera*, and who was announced as 'from the English stage, being her first appearance at this theatre'. She played the Countess with Catalani as Susanna, and it says much for the English singer that she was able to hold her own against the popular foreign star, while in the letter-scene their duet was received with overwhelming applause. The following morning the *Sun* commented:—

> Mozart's standard opera of *Figaro* was performed last night with a strength of musical talent which has seldom been displayed at one time at this or any other theatre. Mrs. Dickons, who commenced her engagement as 'second Donna', seemed to be animated with a spirit of rivalship, which produced exertions far beyond what we have ever witnessed, even from this charming singer. The surprise which this new display of her powers excited drew down thunders of applause at the close of almost every cadence.

In view of the modern German-founded interpretation of the Countess as a tragic matron, who would be far better employed looking into the Feld-Marschallin's mirror in *Rosenkavalier* rather than skittishly changing clothes with her maid and hiding the page-boy in girl's clothes in her closet, it is interesting to see that in 1812, when the original Mozart interpretation cannot have been forgotten, the Countess was played by a Polly Peachum. Such a type is much nearer to the eighteen-year-old girl of Beaumarchais's story, who after three years of marriage might well be expected to show the little smiles and frowns that Mozart indicated and that are so regularly disregarded by all middle-aged vocalists who seem to suggest they ought to be singing something fruitier. That Mrs. Dickons was in fact at this time about forty will not surprise theatre-goers who can call to mind many actresses both past and present who at that age have convincingly acted young girls in plays.

It is more surprising—and indeed, as a later quotation will show, it surprised even the contemporaries—that Catalani was a good Susanna, for she was always ready to exhibit her powers as a singer even to the extent of appropriating to herself Cherubino's 'Voi che sapete', and especially exulting in showing she could sing louder than anyone else—she once sang Figaro's 'Non piu andrai' at a concert to show how she could top the brass. Queen Charlotte always felt she wanted cotton wool in her ears when Catalani sang, and once when a wit was asked if he was going to York to hear her, he said he'd hear her better where he was.

There was not much space in the papers for detailed criticism in view of the disturbed political situation arising chiefly out of the pathetic decline of George III: at the end of the performance

M. Tramezzani came forward and sang 'God Save the King'. He was joined in the chorus by the whole of the audience, most of whom testified their loyalty by shedding tears. The Duke of Cambridge who was present was particularly affected at this display of the public affection for his venerable Sire, and was himself strongly agitated by the same emotions.

No doubt, though, many of the audience must have been in a sentimental mood, as they probably came to the performance not only to aid the Hospital but also because the preliminary announcement had said that at the end of the first act of *Figaro* 'will be revived (expressly for the occasion) the favourite popular Scottish ballet of *Peggy's Love*: composed by M. Didelot'.

Figaro was repeated for Naldi's benefit on June 25th, and on Saturday, two days later, it went into the regular bill: the *Courier* of June 29, however, made it clear that there were more important matters to notice than the opera:—

Political occurrences have prevented us from paying that attention which this superb establishment deserves. Whether we view the Opera or the Ballet, it is established on a scale astonishingly high, when we consider the general situation of Europe. Catalani! Anything we can say in praise of her is but the repetition of a tale a hundred times told. But her air in *Figaro* on Saturday night was sung in a manner that did honour even to her.

The *Courier* then proceeded to give a much longer notice of the ballet—which *The Times* tore to pieces: but apart from the European situation, space was needed for such important things as strong argument against Jenner's new-fangled vaccination and the state of the British prisons, while that very evening Mrs. Siddons retired from the stage as Lady Macbeth.

Tito was revived in 1816, and the following year on Saturday, April 12, at the King's Theatre, *Don Giovanni* was performed in London for the first time. For the first time, too, Mozart was overwhelmingly established as an opera-composer, and the critics vied with each other in their appreciations, which were, however, tempered with good common sense that took into account all the facets that went to make an opera, even suggesting improvements where weaknesses showed. On the morning of Monday, April 14, the critic of the *Sun* wrote:—

On Saturday was represented at this theatre for the first time in this country Mozart's Grand Opera of *Don Giovanni*, and in a style highly creditable to the managers of that establishment. Although unknown here as a public spectacle, this work in private has long been a favourite study with all true musicians and amateurs of music. It is this circumstance which could alone enable us to give any distinct account of the performance: the beauties it comprises are so numerous, so various, and of so high an order, as to exceed, if presented for the first time to the contemplation, the grasp of the most powerful mind.

The *Sun* was full of praise for everything up to the last scene:—

but still above all this, excellent and inimitable as it is, our astonishment is excited by the supernatural effects which accompany the first speaking and the introduction of the Statue in the supper scene—all here is terrible, obscure, and undefined—our blood absolutely runs cold. Never do we recollect any such impression produced from a combination of musical sounds.

In the evening the *Courier* came out with the following:—

That highly celebrated opera, the *Don Juan* of Mozart, was, after being announced for many weeks, at length brought forward on Saturday evening. So much has already appeared in the papers on the music, the history and merits of this grand composition, that little of the critic's duty remains to be performed. We can but place on record what had been so generally anticipated: and on the present occasion we have pleasure in stating that the success of *Don Juan* was eminent and complete. The acting throughout was just and spirited, the music was delightfully executed, and the new scenic decorations were picturesque and splendid.

The critic then goes on to talk of the cast and begins with Giovanni himself:—

Ambrogetti acquitted himself with extraordinary energy: and with respect either to vocal or dramatic action we have rarely seen any performance more powerful than his, from the opening of the second act to the conclusion of the supper scene, where the statue and a host of devils beset Don Pedro's murderer.

Naldi's Leporello was a piece of comic and assured extravagance, which relieved the sombre complexion of the crimes upon which it was employed. Crivelli [Ottavio] was correct enough, but overpowered by superior organs.

Some of the airs by the female performers displayed much taste and feeling, and the noble, and often terrible and thrilling harmonies were poured forth by the assembled corps of singers with masterly precision.

Among the decorations of the opera must be noticed the striking view of the cemetery and equestrian statue in the second act, where the shades are managed with unusual depth and softness, and the moonbeam is thrown with prodigious effect upon the ghastly figure of the horseman. . . .

The music is altogether of the highest cast, the melodies are original and enchanting, the harmonies profound and full of genius. . . .

The house overflowed in every part, all the private boxes were filled, and in the pit there was scarce room to stand. From the beginning to the end the pleasure derived from the performance was manifested by continual plaudits. So many of the airs were encored that it was not until near eleven the opera finished.

The opera was given a second time the next day, Tuesday, April 15, and of that performance the *Courier* wrote:—

It is not easy for persons not present at the performance of the opera of *Don Juan* to conceive the impression which it makes on the auditors. Those whose taste has been cultivated to a critical knowledge of the art find in it such delicious harmonies that they express their enjoyment with enthusiasm, while the untutored ear feels equal delight from the influence of the varied melodies with which it abounds, and which by turns are pathetic, exhilarating, sublime, terrific, and playful. It went off last night with increased effect. The house presented the crowd of a Saturday night. The pit was full before the opening of the curtain that the overture might not be lost.

What an achievement: that the pit—the stalls of today—was full before the curtain went up!

The critic next dealt with the actual music, though it is remarkable that he cannot think of the music without the dramatic situation:—

Mozart's music appears to us not only of a higher rank, but of a different order from that of almost every other composer. It appears to us a more perfect eloquence, a medium for sentiment and passion of the most exalted kind: he seems always to take the tone suited to the action, and to transfer the emotion to the mind of the hearer. We quote, as an example, the first movement that occurs to us.

Don Juan in the 10th scene of the first act learns from Leporello that he has dexterously contrived to remove Elvira, who was the impediment to his designs on Zerlina, out of the way. His joy of this, his exultation, know no bounds: he cannot express his delight—he begins impetuously the air 'Fin ch'han del vino' full of riotous transport and abandonment to the feeling of the moment. It seems a pure effusion of the mind. This was sung with great effect by Ambrogetti: his volubility and his articulation are surprising. The impulse seemed to seize on the audience: he was encored with unanimous plaudits.

(How often does the singer nowadays think only of how fast he can sing this aria, without giving any thought as to why he is excited in anticipation and ignoring the fact that Mozart's *presto* in $\frac{2}{4}$ applies to the quavers.)

Another charming instance occurs in the scene following that last mentioned. Zerlina, the peasant girl, is endeavouring to pacify her jealous lover, Masetto, but without effect—her caresses, her wiles, her fears, the whole artillery of female blandishments is exhausted—without the least preparation from the orchestra, without any of the symphony to intimate that an air is about to be sung, she begins that charming movement, 'Batte, batte, O bel Masetto!'—it proves an irresistible appeal to the tenderness of her lover—he relents, and our perfect sympathy accompanies him: we are not surprised that he could resist no longer. The peasant himself just after seems to wonder at this effect, for he says 'See now, how this little syren contrives to bewitch me'. This is the true magic.

An elegant specimen of Mozart's taste is the canzonet in the second act, 'Deh viene alla finestra', which Don Juan sings to attract the notice of his mistress to bring her to the window. A soothing tenderness pervades this air, which is at the same time simple, manly and unaffected. The accompaniment was written originally, we understand, for the mandoline: but as that instrument is too weak to produce any effect in so large a theatre, it was played by Weichsel on the violin, and produced a very masterly effect . . .

Another of our favourites is the song of 'Vedrai carino', sung by Zerlina to console her lover, Masetto, who had just before received a severe beating from Don Juan in the disguise of Leporello. The music assigned to the part of Zerlina is of a more simple and popular cast than that of any other in the opera: it is in fact beautifully in harmony with her character, as drawn in the drama.

The same critic wrote in *The Times* of the same date, but added some well considered criticisms:—

Some trifling errors occurred in the conduct of the drama, which we notice solely from a desire we entertain that it should be in all parts perfect.

In the masquerade scene Don Juan in his attempt on Zerlina should carry her into the adjoining apartment, at which moment her cries (which produce so marked an effect in the music) alarm the company, and bring them to her assistance. Instead of this, she invokes help by her shrieks at a time when she is surrounded by the peasants and consequently in no sort of danger.

And on the first night in the supper scene the musicians and servants remained on the stage all the time the spectre is addressing Don Juan: whereas it is evident that they should fly in alarm—unless they can be supposed to be accustomed to such visitors. Leporello too, who should hide himself under the table, prefers continuing his supper to being placed in so inglorious a situation. These errors, however, were last night corrected.

He went on to give some more details of the performance:—

Madame Camporese gave us great pleasure in Donna Anna: her acting was very good, and her singing chaste, unaffected, and full of feeling.

Ambrogetti's Don Juan is his celebrated character: it is that on which his reputation on the Continent is more particularly founded: he is indisputably one of the best actors we have seen on the boards of this theatre.

Naldi acted and sung with great spirit, but we have heard him more accurate in his execution.

He then goes on to make a criticism of the habits of the audiences of the day:—

There is one custom which in all our public performances of music, but particularly in the present instance, where a work of such peculiar merit is in question, we should be very glad to see reformed: we mean that of yielding (in a way very honourable, no doubt, to the taste and feeling) to the impulse of admiration excited by a fine passage, and interrupting it by an applause which, however judicious in itself, is perfectly ruinous to the effect. The end of the movement or piece is the proper time to testify approbation.

He finally praises both the libretto and the taste of the London public:—

The poetry of this opera possesses considerable merit. Our classical readers, who are fond of parallel passages, will perhaps be amused by tracing the idea of Leporello's song of 'Madamina' to one of Anacreon's odes, and also to one of Ovid's amatory elegies.

We take leave of this opera with regret. The enthusiasm its representation has excited is an unerring testimony to the true musical taste that prevails in this country.

The house—quite unexampled on Tuesday evenings—was as much crowded as a Saturday.

The *Sun* of the same day was no less enthusiastic:—

Don Juan again drew a bumper last night, and bids fair to enrich this theatre, being unquestionably the finest opera ever produced on these boards.

By now young Henry Bishop began to see that Mozart's music might appeal to a wider audience if it was carefully selected with a few additions of his own—and sung to English words. Already Mozart's music had been used in English entertainments—the latest being a performance at Drury Lane on April 17, 1817, of what the *News* called a

gigantic mass of Oriental show and insipidity *Elphi Bey or the Arab's Faith*, with music by Mozart, Attwood and Horn.

Bishop now started to adapt for English ears *Don Giovanni*, which was given a month after its first London production on May 30, 1817, in its altered state. Whether or not Bishop's version was merely cashing in on the growing popularity of Mozart, or whether it did anything to increase it, *Figaro* and *Giovanni* were frequently performed at the King's right into the spring of 1818.

On March 7 it was announced that a new composer would be introduced that evening to London by a performance of an opera he had written in daring rivalry of the proved composer Paesiello, who had already achieved fame by his version of the same opera, *The Barber of Seville*. Later the public were told that it was postponed to Tuesday, March 10, and that in it

Signor Garcia will make his first appearance in this country.

A further notice said:—

The subscribers to the opera and the public are respectfully informed that the chair doors at the west side of this theatre, communication from Pall-Mall, are thrown open as heretofore.

These doors are still to be seen leading from the Opera Arcade to the back of Her Majesty's Theatre in the Haymarket.[1]

Garcia was the Almaviva, Naldi the Figaro, Ambrogetti Bartolo—who now plays both Giovanni and Bartolo?—Madame Fodor Rosina, and Angrisani Basilio. *The Times* and the *Observer* of March 11 were enthusiastic: this is what *The Times* said:—

The music is by Rossini, a young composer of extraordinary merit, now living, who enjoys great celebrity in all parts of the Continent. This opera is the first specimen of his composition which has been submitted to the judgment of an English audience.

Taken as a whole perhaps, it bears marks of haste, and still more of extravagance: but we are persuaded that all persons who have carried the study of music to the last degree of refinement must have been delighted and astonished by the occasional touches of genius, the variety and originality of his style.

The general character of Rossini's music is extreme ornament, the perfect reverse of what is called the simple style: but his resources in that line and the fertility of his invention seem almost unlimited. It is probable that its effect may lessen by frequent repetition: the first impression, however, is delightful.

The particular pieces with which we were most struck were a song by Rosina 'Una voce poco fa', another by Basilio descriptive of the effects of calumny . . . a quintet near the end of the first act, and the latter part of a trio in the second beginning with the words 'Zitto, zitto, piano, piano'.

Garcia was much praised, though his voice was thought to be somewhat on the decline, still

The character of Count Almaviva . . . requires a good actor as well as an accomplished singer, in both respects he did it complete justice.

The *Observer* went further:—

A more perfect representation *in all its parts* we have never witnessed: the music combining enchanting melodies, scientific harmonies, and at the same time truly dramatic: the variety and novelty of the modulations, the fire and sprightliness infused into all the accompaniments, are truly rapturous to the ear, and stamp him, as a musician, a perfect master of nature and of his art. The Finale to the first act and the quintets in the second are beyond all praise.

There was praise for Garcia:—

His figure is good, his voice clear and sonorous, his execution most rapid and articulate, his intonation just, his science great, and his acting excellent.

There was praise for Naldi, Ambrogetti and especially for Fodor as Rosina:—

The slight fioramentes with which she just touched particular passages were the triumph of delicacy and sentiment: it was the southern breeze that tremulously swept through an orange grove, waking the sweetness of its blossoms, but forbearing to scatter the slightest of its leaves.

There was praise for the scenery, praise for the orchestra:—

Weichsel, their accomplished conductor, led them with his accustomed intelligence and animation: his incessant attention to the singers and to the business of the stage is truly laudable.

The *Courier* of the same date, writing of the most varied music in the opera, said of it:—

We have heard none, not even of Mozart, in which darkness seemed to have so little crept.

But four days later the *News* did its best to counteract all this eulogy: Rossini, according to that paper, was a composer

who is considerably more admired on the Continent (where the ankle of the Prima Donna is more critically examined than the music of her part) than he is ever likely to be in this country.

His style is less remarkable for its variety than for the prodigality of ornament which rather characterises than adorns it. There is no originality about
it, either in passion or fancy. . . . We do not know whether impudence or
genius is most remarkable in a composer who sits down to repeat a story which
has already been so delightfully told by one of the great masters of his art: but
we may in some degree settle the point by fancying how we should estimate
the modesty of any worthy gentleman who should announce a *new* comedy to
be called *The Midsummer Night's Dream*, or a *new* tragedy of *Macbeth* or *Othello*.

In the *new Barber of Seville* we therefore looked with some eagerness for some
touches of genius or nature—some wildness of fancy at once graceful and
original, which should justify the boldness of an attempt for which no other
excuse could be invented—but we were disappointed.

Indeed, with three or four exceptions, the music of the opera is considerably
more flat and commonplace than anything we recollect lately to have heard:
and its whole surface is laboured into an artificial richness by an accumulation
of a thousand small graces, which would scarcely have been used by any
musician of moderate taste—even if he possessed no splendour of imagination.

'Una Voce' was one of the exceptions: the next was

the concluding part of an intolerably tedious trio beginning with the verse
'Zitto, zitto, piano, piano', which is very delicious in its expression, though
common enough in its melody. 'La Calunnia' is a song when the effects of
calumny are described under the figure of the wind: the accompaniment begins
with a soft murmur, which goes on and on till it swells into the roar of a tempest
through a thousand ingenious gradations, without ever degenerating into a
vulgar imitative harmony.

When we have named these pieces we believe our readers are acquainted with
everything good in the opera. We cannot speak very indulgently of the new
performer. His voice is artificial . . . and he has but one attitude and one action
in singing, which he uses most unmercifully on all occasions.

(Who is right when critics are poles apart?)

Bishop soon followed with his English version of *The Barber*
on October 12 to show that he could improve Rossini as well as
Mozart, which he did by adding airs by himself and Paesiello, and
by getting Mrs. Dickons—still the great favourite with those of
the London audience who understood English better than Italian
—to sing Rosina. In March of 1819 *Figaro* was performed
at Covent Garden Theatre for the first time—suitably altered by
Bishop, with Mrs. Dickons repeating her enchanting performance
as the Countess. The papers were all enthusiastic: *The Times*, in
commenting on the translation of Mozart's opera, remarked that

it shows that the beauty of his music is perfectly independent of language, and
that in any form it cannot but charm and captivate.

As for the additions to Mozart's numbers:—

Some compositions have been joined with these, that suffer not a little by a comparison with Mozart: but on the whole the lovers of music will find in the opera a source of great enjoyment.

The Times thought the scenery lovely and welcomed the appearance of Mrs. Dickons and Catherine Stephens (another popular Polly Peachum twenty-five years old) together in the same show while

Liston played Figaro, and though the part is a little too serious for him, gave it in a very effective manner.

The *Morning Post* was most appreciative and the *Sun* said:—

The piece itself is very amusing, and was rendered still more so by the manner in which it has been brought forward.

Do these appreciations of Bishop's alterations stultify the same critics' opinions on the real Mozart? Can one be quoted as showing how some critics have sometimes seen the light and another showing how stupid the critics were? Or was criticism in those days more objective than it is now—might it not be fact that Mozart pleased the Mozart audience and that Bishop-Mozart pleased the rest, and perhaps did a lot to introduce the real Mozart to those who would never have bothered otherwise? Besides, is badly performed Mozart really better than excellently performed Bishop? There has for many years been a grave danger that enthusiasts may think that anything labelled Mozart is necessarily good, and their reverence tends to make them over-value inferior performances and scorn any that attempt to infuse such enthusiastic life into the operas as was the natural aim of the first performers of them in England with the knowledge or report of Mozart's own interpretation still in their heads.

Of the other operas that were produced in London up to 1819 only a few won temporary popularity, and though I have quoted opinions on many eighteenth-century works which are now little more than names in operatic history to show the changing taste, it would seem superfluous to quote criticisms of nineteenth-century productions which are now forgotten by the side of many works which are still included in the London operatic repertoire of to-day.

In their own time Cimarosa's *Gli Orazi ed I Curiazi* and Mayr's

Che Originali (later called *Il Fanatico per la Musica*) excited the London of 1805 and 1806 and were constantly revived, but no other opera, apart from those already mentioned, caused any sensation till Paer's *Agnese di Fitz-Henry* (1817), in which Camporese sang the part of the daughter (her first season on any stage) and Ambrogetti terrified the audience with distressing realism as the mad father, having spent days studying lunatics in an asylum —women fainted, other members of the audience left the theatre and the run was cut short as a result.

The chief revivals during this time were Paesiello's *Barber* and *La Frascatana*, Shield's *The Poor Soldier* (formerly called *The Shamrock*), Storace's *No Song, no Supper* and Piccini's *La Buona Figliuola*. Cimarosa's *Matrimonio Segreto*, Arnold's *Maid of the Mill* (with additional music by Bishop) and Storace's *Haunted Tower* were among other revivals, while Arne's *Artaxerxes* (also improved by Bishop) had its last revival at Covent Garden.

Rossini made such a success with his *Barber of Seville*, or, as it was then called, *Almaviva, o sia l'Inutile Precauzione*, that for the next six years his operas practically ousted all other Italian operas from the London stage. *Almaviva* was followed a month later by *Elisabetta, Regina d'Inghilterra*; in 1819 came *L'Italiana in Algeri* and *L'Inganno Felice*; in 1820 *Cenerentola* and *Tancredi* (which was constantly revived in the next forty years); in 1821 *La Gazza Ladra* and *Il Turco in Italia* (*La Clemenza di Tito* was revived again this year); in 1822 Rossini's *Mosè in Egitto* was given under the less religious title of *Pietro l'Eremita*, and was a great success, though on the first night the basket-work soldiers, who should have been precipitated from a breaking bridge into the waves, got stuck and nearly caught fire instead. In these last two years, by the way, more was spent at the King's on ballet than on opera.

In 1823 four Rossini works were given:—a concert version of *Ciro in Babilonia o sia la Caduta di Baldassarre*, and on the stage *Ricciardo e Zoraide* and *Matilde di Shabran* (that was the year of Bishop's *Clari, or the Maid of Milan* with 'Home, sweet home' in it), and in 1824 Rossini's *Zelmira* and *Semiramide* were produced, Rossini playing the piano in the orchestra for the former.

[1] See frontispiece.

CHAPTER THREE

Lord Mount-Edgcumbe's Reminiscences

THE year of 1824 is important in the history of opera in England, for two events took place of which one was to be of great value to all future operatic historians and the other was not only sensational to the audiences of the day but had a considerable effect on later operatic presentations. The former was the publication of the *Musical reminiscences of an old amateur for fifty years from 1773 to 1823*, the author being Richard Edgcumbe, the second Earl of Mount-Edgcumbe. He had seen his first opera, Hasse's *Artaserse* arranged by Giordani, when he was nine years old, and fifty years later his reminiscences dealt chiefly with Italian opera, he having been, as he says, 'passionately fond of music when music was really good, and having lived in what I consider as one of its most flourishing periods, now, I lament to say, at an end'.

The great value in the book is twofold—the descriptions of famous singers of the day by a real lover of music (he actually had his own opera *Zenobia* performed in 1800 with Banti in the lead), and his comparisons of taste and style between 1773 and 1823— and what greater change could there be than from soprano heroes, male or female, to baritone leading men in opera?

This is not the place to quote all Mount-Edgcumbe's comments on all the singers he heard, but a brief survey of the abilities of some will contribute something to an impression of operatic taste in his time. He was not content to admire the voice or technique, however fine, and evidently valued skill in acting, which the majority of the better artists had as well. At fifteen he heard the dignified but low-born Gabrielli, 'the best prima donna of her time', as Dido in Sacchini's *Didone Abbandonata* (1775), but the one thing he remembered later was 'the care with which she tucked up her great hoop as she sidled into the flames of Carthage'. The flames, of course, in those days would have been real, so it says a deal for the skill of the singer, dressed as she was in the grandiose fashion of the day magnified for the stage, that she could negotiate her way.

Pacchierotti, the male soprano who came to London three times

303

between 1778 and 1790, and whom Mount-Edgcumbe heard in 1778, was, he says, 'the most perfect singer it ever fell to my lot to hear': he had perfect taste and feeling as well as technique— he never sang the same aria twice in the same way—and though ungainly, was impressive, and such a good actor it never mattered whether the audience understood Italian or not. In 1780 came the powerful tenor Ansani, 'a spirited actor'. Mount-Edgcumbe records that the most admired serious operas of those days were the *Rinaldo* of Sacchini, the pasticcios *L'Olimpiade* and *Ezio*, Bertoni's *Quinto Fabio* and Rauzzini's *L'Eroe Cinese*—where are they now?

In comedy opera—and of course he is speaking of Italian comedy opera—the handsome Sestini was a good actress, but her voice was 'gritty and sharp (something like singing through a comb)'; she was best in lively airs and was very popular, though not with connoisseurs. Piccini's *La Buona Figliuola* was very popular in the late seventies, though not so well sung as it had been by Guadagni and Lovattini ten years before, though of course Mount-Edgcumbe had not heard them personally—Guadagni, incidentally, was a male contralto, and in the early fifties had sung for Handel, in the *Messiah* and *Samson*, the parts originally written for Mrs. Cibber. When Catalani had revived *La Buona Figliuola* in 1810, taste had changed and the music sounded odd to the audiences of that day: *La Frascatana* was more successful.

Mount-Edgcumbe went abroad when he was twenty, and on his return admired Mara in a pasticcio *Didone* in 1786 for her bravura singing, but says that she was no actress and showed little feeling. He must have seen her, too, in Mortellari's *Armida* the same year with the male contralto Rubinelli, who also had *Giulio Cesare* revived and altered to please the King and all who liked old music: he had a voice of limited compass and agility, but fine and round, and sang with excellent taste.

Comic opera, the author said, began to improve about 1787, especially with the return to her mother country of Anna Selina Storace, the daughter of the Italian contrabassist Stefano Storace (originally Sorace), who had settled in England about 1750. It is worth quoting much of what Mount-Edgcumbe says of her, Mozart's first Susanna in *Figaro*—if only to give a well-deserved jolt to those who persist in thinking of the character as a delicate Dresden-china figure of exquisite gentility:—

She had a harshness in her countenance, a clumsiness of figure, a coarseness in her voice and vulgarity of manner, that totally unfitted her for the serious opera, which she never attempted. But her knowledge of music was equal to anything and she could sing well in every style.

She even sang in Westminster Abbey.

In her own particular line on the stage she was unrivalled, being an excellent actress, as well as a masterly singer.

After she left the stage, she often came back to it to perform at Drury Lane,

where the English opera was raised to an excellence not known before by her singing and that of Mrs. Crouch, Mrs. Bland, Kelly and Bannister and under the direction of her brother Stephen Storace, who composed, or rather compiled, several very pretty operas, of which *The Haunted Tower* and *The Siege of Belgrade* still remain favourites and are frequently played.

Anna Storace's voice, says Mount-Edgcumbe, was of the sort that soon cracks and grows husky.

From 1788 to 1790 the male soprano Luigi Marchesi was popular: he was good-looking, acted spiritedly, had a huge range and great technique, was incomparable in recitative and passionate scenes, and if only he had not been so eager to show off, would have been faultless, said Mount-Edgcumbe, who thought Rubinelli the most simple singer, Marchesi the most brilliant and Pacchierotti the most touching. Michael Kelly, who had created the parts of Basilio and Curzio in *Figaro* and was great friends with Mozart, was a good musician and not a bad singer—having studied in Italy—but was rather vulgar, like all English singers, Mount-Edgcumbe says (though Kelly was Irish). After 1790 Mara often sang in London again and 'could not sing ill, but was not exactly suited for the *pretty Polly* of the *Beggar's Opera*, one of the characters she there assumed'.

The Venetian gondolier's daughter, Brigitta Banti, whom Mount-Edgcumbe heard in Italy in 1785 and then for many years in London, where she studied as a girl up to 1780 and where she returned in 1794, was, he says, 'far the most delightful singer I ever heard'. She was a bad musician and could not read a note of music, but once she had learned her music she sang it with more pathos than any: she had an amazing compass and sang with even tone and great agility. She was particularly successful in Gluck's *Alceste* (1795), in which three arias were always encored, and in his *Iphigenia in Tauris* (1796), but was equally successful in Paesiello's *Serva Padrona* (1794). Mount-Edgcumbe says he never wished for another singer.

In 1802 Mrs. Billington returned from her triumphs in Italy to take the place of Banti, and when they both sang together for Banti's benefit in Nasolini's *Merope*—Banti singing the tenor part!—the audience, which overflowed on to the stage, gave them each an equal ovation. Mrs. Billington, according to Mount-Edgcumbe, looked young and pretty, with a very high and flexible head-voice, sounding like a flute, but, like Mara, she showed no feeling, never changed her facial expression, and was no actress: neither she nor Mara could sing recitative well.

Grassini, who sang in London between 1804 and 1806, on the other hand, was an excellent actress and very handsome, but her deep contralto voice was rather monotonous without 'one octave of good natural notes' and in the higher register 'she produced only a shriek, quite unnatural and almost painful to the ear'. (It is only fair to say that others thought her voice more delightful than any (De Quincey) and that she excelled in combining the music with the action, dying like Mrs. Siddons and reaching to the soul of the hearer (Sir Charles Bell).[1]) Grassini was taken up by society, but, says Mount-Edgcumbe, 'of her *private* claims to that distinction it is best to be silent'. The difference between Grassini and Mrs. Billington he sums up as follows:—

the deaf would have been charmed with Grassini, while the blind must have been delighted with Mrs. Billington.

John Braham, born Abraham, who had sung at the Scala, Milan, with Mrs. Billington, had a voice, Mount-Edgcumbe says, of the finest quality, force and occasional sweetness, had a great knowledge of music and '*can* sing extremely well': unfortunately he often sings in an unpleasant falsetto, forces and adopts an 'over-florid and frittered Italian manner', while at times he is coarse and vulgar in the English manner—in fact, anything to gain applause.

Angelica Catalani had sung in London and the provinces from 1806 to 1813 (she later returned in 1824 and again in 1828). Perhaps Mount-Edgcumbe gives a clearer picture of her than of any other singer, and in doing so shows the very contradictory things that drew the audience of the day to the opera-house. Her voice, he says, was of an uncommon quality and capable of exertions almost supernatural. Her throat seems endued (as has been remarked by medical men) with a power of expression and muscular motion by no means usual, and when she throws out all her voice to the utmost, it has a volume and strength that are quite surprising, while its agility in divisions running up and down the scale in semitones, and its compass in jumping over two octaves at once, are equally astonishing.

(So much is praise: now comes the criticism.)

It were to be wished she was less lavish in the display of these wonderful powers, and sought to please more than to surprise: but her taste is vicious, her excessive love of ornament spoiling every simple air, and her greatest delight (indeed her chief merit) being in songs of a bold and spirited character, where much is left to her discretion (or indiscretion) without being confined by the accompaniment, but in which she can indulge ad libitum passages with a luxuriance and redundancy no other singer ever possessed, or if possessing ever practised, and which she carries to a fantastical excellence.

She is fond of singing variations on some known simple air, and latterly has pushed this taste to the very height of absurdity by singing, even without words, variations composed for the fiddle.

All this, Mount-Edgcumbe says, amounts to a misuse of voice, and he was reminded of the 'late noble statesman' who, being unmusical, when he was told a performance was difficult, remarked he wished it had been impossible. Catalani 'detested Mozart's music, which keeps the singer too much under the control of the orchestra and too strictly confined to time, which she is apt to violate', and yet she was the first London Susanna, and excellent. (Incidentally Mount-Edgcumbe returns later to his regret that Mozart and others allowed singers no headway by making them subservient to the orchestra.) As for Catalani's acting, in serious opera she was majestic, forcible and expressively varied, but though she could be as tragic as Mrs. Siddons, she had a charming smile and could even seem simple.

With all her faults therefore (and no great singer ever had so many) she must be reckoned a very fine performer, and if the natural powers with which she is so highly gifted were guided by sound taste and judgment, she might have been a perfect one.

He later says, 'I consider Catalani to be the last great singer heard in this country whose name is likely to be recollected in musical annals' and after her departure in 1813 because she could not buy the opera-house and so reign supreme, 'a new era began in our opera'.

Of the lesser singers in about 1811 the handsome actor Tramezzani was 'one of the most agreeable tenors I ever remember to have heard': with him in *Cosi fan tutte*—'which was admirably acted in every part'—were Madame Bertinotti and Naldi, 'an excellent buffo' (who incidentally was killed in 1820 by the bursting of a newly invented pressure-cooker in the Paris rooms of his friend, the tenor Garcia). Mrs. Bland was one of the few English singers who could sing Italian so purely: but, then, her maiden name had been Romanzini: Mrs. Dickons had been excellent as the Countess in *Figaro*, but otherwise made little mark on the Italian opera stage. Of all the women singers he had heard, Grassini was all grace, Catalani all fire and Banti all feeling:

They were all likewise but indifferently skilled in music, supplying by genius what they wanted in science, and thereby producing the greatest and most striking effects on the stage.

It seems, therefore, that the greatest change in the style of singing in the fifty years up to 1824 was from the skilled technique of the earlier period allied to dramatic power to natural instinct combined with effective technique.

As for the operas themselves, Mount-Edgcumbe regretted that by 1824 there was no longer the distinction between serious and comedy operas—all now were *semiseria*, half and half, and all singers now sang all types of opera. Recitative, as the eighteenth century understood it, was on the way out and the dialogue

is now cut up (and rendered unintelligible if it were worth listening to) into *pezzi concertati*, or long singing conversations, which present a tedious succession of unconnected, ever-changing *motivos*, having nothing to do with each other: and if a satisfactory air is for a moment introduced, which the ear would like to dwell upon or hear modulated, varied, and again returned to, it is broken off before it is well understood, or sufficiently heard, by a sudden transition into a totally different melody, time and key, and recurs no more—so that no impression can be made or recollection of it preserved.

(It must be remembered that it was the Mozart-type of concerted finales and accompanied dialogue that Mount-Edgcumbe found so disconcertingly 'modern' in comparison with the easily intelligible and shapely *da capo* arias and simple *sprechstimme* recitative of the past.) He also complains:—

Single songs are almost exploded, for which one good reason may be given, that there are few singers capable of singing them. Even a prima donna, who would formerly have complained at having less than three or four airs allotted to her, is now satisfied with one trifling cavatina for a whole opera.

Even the types of voices have changed: tenors had taken the place of the old male sopranos, and even these 'have become so scarce that Italy can produce no more than two or three very good ones'. There seem to be more basses, with the result that they are

thrust up into the first characters, even in serious operas where they used only to occupy the last place, to the manifest injury of melody and total subversion of harmony, in which the lowest part is their peculiar province.

A bass singer is now called '*basso cantante* (which by the bye is a kind of apology, and an acknowledgement that they ought not to sing)'; to give them melody is like getting the double-bass to play the first violin part: their voices are 'too unbending', not sweet enough for solos—though they will serve in comic operas, and too separated from female voices to be used in duets—'Yet three or four basses now frequently overpower one weak tenor, who generally plays but a subordinate part'.

To this Mount-Edgcumbe puts a footnote, which is illuminating:—

It has always surprised me that the principal characters in two of Mozart's operas should have been written for basses, namely, Count Almaviva and Don Giovanni, both of whom seem particularly to want the more lively tones of a tenor.

After all, he points out that in *La Clemenza di Tito* the first and second male parts were written for sopranos, and the part of Sesto 'was never so well sung here as by Madame Camporese'.

In the old days, he says, the two first acts of a serious opera always ended with a duet for the first man (i.e. soprano) and first woman, and the third with a terzetto in which the tenor joined, while 'the inferior singers never joined in any concerted piece': now, however, there were, instead of songs, numberless quartets, quintets and sextets—in effect, so many finales, 'such as were never used but at the end of the acts of comic operas, to which alone they are appropriate'.

These new concerted pieces, longer than six of the old arias put together, are usually ended

by a noisy crash of voices and instruments in which the harmony is frequently distracted, each personality engaged in the scene having perhaps to express a different passion, and the whole vocal part almost overpowered by so loud and busy an accompaniment that the voices themselves are nearly lost.

It is really distressing to hear the leading voice strained almost to cracking in order to be audible over a full chorus and full orchestra, strengthened often by trumpets, trombones, kettle-drums and all the noisiest instruments.

To his ears this was mere noise: he liked some choruses, but not if they were long, in view of the inadequacy of the chorus-singers:—

No opera choruses are very good and they should not be long, because being to be sung by memory and by bad singers, it is next to an impossibility that an intricate or elaborate composition should be sung well anywhere, and at our opera they are generally most miserably performed.

Nowadays, he adds, lungs are more important than voices:—

In these levelling days equalisation has extended itself to the stage and musical profession: and a kind of mediocrity of talent prevails, which, if it did not occasion the invention of these melodramatic pieces, is at least very favourable to their execution.

(The musical dramas of the end of the eighteenth century—such as *The Haunted Tower*—had led the audience to expect big acting and exciting situations in opera, even though Ambrogetti's mad father might have gone too far: but the insistence on drama had naturally led to a neglect of the poetry that used to be associated with music—anyway, of contemplative or philosophical poetry on which the old composers used to spread themselves.) As Mount-Edgcumbe says:—

All the new dramas written for Rossini's music are most execrably bad and contain scarcely one line that can be called poetry, or even one of common sense.

As for the Rossinian opera in general :—

we have for the last two or three seasons been satiated in this. That he is possessed of genius and invention cannot be denied, but they are not guided by good taste and may be deemed too fanciful: neither are they inexhaustible, for he is so rapid and so copious a writer that his imagination seems already to be nearly drained, as no one is so great a plagiarist of himself.

All Rossini sounded the same to Mount-Edgcumbe, which is not surprising, as now each piece must have 'as many different subjects as would make three or four' in the old days.

La Gazza Ladra was full of loud concerted pieces and noisy instruments that were quite out of keeping with the touching subject: *Tancredi* was liked, and there *were* two or three pleasant bits of music in it,

but when the principal, or at least the favourite, song of a first man in a *heroic* opera is not only capable of being converted into a quadrille, but appears better adapted to that purpose than any other, all idea of its propriety and fitness for its situation must be put totally out of the question.

The aria in question, 'Di Tanti Palpiti', he thought was merely a French *contredanse*: half Rossini's operas, even the 'sacred oratorio', *Mosè in Egitto*, had been quadrilled:—

Were it possible so to convert Handel's, we should deem it a *profanation*.

Mount-Edgcumbe had heard that Rossini's operas sounded better without voices, as they were less important than his arch and laboured accompaniments. In the old days songs were written with the minimum of accompaniment,

which, if sung as written, would be cold, bald and insipid. It was left to the singer to fill up the outline, to give it the light and shade, and all its grace and expression, which required not only a thorough knowledge of music, but the greatest taste and judgment. No one ever worked on such a canvas like Pacchierotti.

(So much for those academic purist singers and conductors of to-day who think Handel is all crotchets and quavers as printed!)

Mount-Edgcumbe recorded that *Mosè*, *Otello* and *Turco in Italia* were Rossini's best: *Barber* had a moderate success, while *Cenerentola*, *Italiana in Algeri* and *Elisabetta* had none. *Donna del Lago* and *Ricciardo e Zoraide* were liked, but Mount-Edgcumbe could hardly find one song in either of them. Rossini so 'engrossed the stage' that no other operas except *Don Giovanni* and *Figaro* (and the unsuccessful *Tito*) were performed.[2] Mozart he admitted was really great, though sometimes too German in style, but the

frippery and meretricious style of modern music is to the ear like tinsel to the eye. I think I may venture to predict that Rossini will not long have ceased to write before he will cease to be remembered.

Mozart, on the other hand, like Handel and Haydn, was 'sterling gold' and would last.

After Catalani left London in 1813, opera stopped being fashionable and was nearly deserted, Mount-Edgcumbe says, and in 1816 the singers comprised a medley of Russian, Spanish, French and English performers, with but few Italians. He never liked Fodor for singing through her teeth, though her Zerlina in *Don Giovanni* made her popular, Ambrogetti was not a good singer, but a fine actor, and with Camporese—'genteel, ladylike' both on the stage and off—filled the theatre with *Don Giovanni* and *Figaro*: Belloc, plain and coarse-voiced like Storace, but not so good, was all right in comedy but shocking as Tancredi, though she sang well: de Begnis was a good buffa and very popular, but Colbran Rossini, Rossini's wife, was 'entirely passée'. Catalani returned in 1824, still expensive, but her attraction was not great and her performances were few: 'her powers are said to be undiminished, her taste unimproved'. The best in 1824 was Pasta, who had been little noticed in Camporese's first year, but now was a finished singer and an excellent actress. At the end of the 1824 season, Mount-Edgcumbe records,

all the contents of the Opera-house have been advertised for sale: interminable disputes and litigation, mismanagement, and repeated losses seem again to threaten ruin to the unfortunate King's Theatre.

And so he ends.

[1] v. Grove.
[2] Nearly but not literally true.

CHAPTER FOUR

Freischütz to The Bohemian Girl

THE other outstanding operatic event of 1824 which must have convinced Mount-Edgcumbe that now at last the end of the opera world he knew had come with even a more hideous racket than even Rossini could produce, was the first production in London of Weber's *Der Freischütz*, only three years after its première in Berlin. This took place on July 22 at the Lyceum, which had been built under the direction of the composer Dr. Arnold in 1798 for the presentation of English operas and other musical pieces: he, however, had failed to get a licence, but his son, Samuel James Arnold, had been more successful, and opened it in 1809 as the English Opera House with operas, melodramas and musical farces: he had rebuilt it in 1815.

The *Freischütz* was performed—in accordance with the title of the theatre—in English with a sub-title *The Seventh Bullet* and the music adapted by W. Hawes. The more reputable papers were rather at a loss, as it was so unlike the operas they, and Mount-Edgcumbe, were used to, but as it was definitely like the melo-dramatic plays with music that they had seen at that theatre be-fore, they judged it accordingly.

The Times, which had announced it as 'a new musical per-formance of an extraordinary character', said that in anticipation it had 'excited a great sensation in its favour which its representa-tion is doomed, we fear, in some measure to disappoint'. The critic, after pointing out that it at once became popular when it was first produced in Germany,[1] naturally stresses the supernatural scenes, especially the Wolf's Glen in which 'a phantasmagoric hunt is seen (or rather ought to be seen, for this part of the scene failed) in the clouds'.

He goes on to comment on the difficulty of the music, which, he says, with

the complicated nature of some parts of the drama entitle it to the most favour-able consideration, while the exertions which have been made in its production are highly praiseworthy. . . .

When the witches and devils, and toads, and skeletons get well into their several parts, we have no doubt they will make very respectable beasts: and as soon as the fireworks are made sensible of the manner in which they ought to go off, the scene of the incantation will be a very powerful one of its kind.

In the meantime the directors of this theatre must have the praise of having made a very bold effort to introduce at the English Opera a piece of first rate excellence, and which is no less creditable to their good taste than to their spirit.

The *News* called it 'a regular opera of the "German horrific" character', and lists the effects of the Wolf's Glen scene:—

the melting of the lead, amidst the warring of the elements, the frantic demeanour of divers evil spirits, ghosts, goblins, toads, and other reptiles, who shower down fire and change the colour of the moon and the cataract in the glen to that of blood—all these were represented with the entire of the appalling horrors of the *rampant* melodrama, of veritable German extraction. Mr. Bennett (Caspar) who 'mouthes' terribly and 'saws the air', was here in his element.

The critic sums up:—

Our opinion of the composition as a dramatic work may be inferred from what has already been stated: in truth it is humble enough—inferior to 'Frankenstein' in appalling interest, and a body unworthy of the soul of harmony by which it is animated.[2]

The Overture awed all into breathless silence and attention: it was performed with much power, aided by an enlarged orchestra consisting of about forty instruments. It was loudly encored.

But its worst fault 'is its wearisome length. Every part of it tires'.

The *Observer* was frankly disturbed:—

To the nature of this story as a groundwork for opera there can be no just objection. . . . Of the music we speak not without hesitation. Fame had raised an expectation that the *Don Juan* of Mozart would find a rival in the *Freischütz* of Weber. This expectation has not been realised.

That the music has merit, extraordinary merit, is true: but it is not the merit of vocal music. Its chief excellence is instrumental. . . . Much of the music is addressed to the professor rather than to the general auditor, and seems better fitted to instruct than to please. It is too full of discords, and they are sometimes introduced most unfortunately so as to break the chain of melody as soon as a few of its links have been developed. . . . The owl-like chorus did not seem to please the audience. . . .

The whole thing must have been very expensive.

No wonder the critics were puzzled: whatever Mount-Edgcumbe thought about Mozart's German type of music, this was the first really German music to be heard in London, for the only German composers whose work was known in London were the Italianised Mayr and Winter. But though the critics were at a loss, the public—always the final judges—lapped up the excitement of it all, and before the year was out four more versions of it had been given in London—at the Royal Amphitheatre a melodrama version in August, at the Surrey Theatre in September the opera again as *The Demon of the Wolf's Glen, and the Seven Charmed Bullets*, at Covent Garden in October as *The Black Huntsman of Bohemia*, and at Drury Lane in November as *Der Freischütz* with additional music, of course, by Bishop.

In June 1825 the *Morning Post* printed the following:—

A correspondent in the *Harmonicon* states that *Der Freischütz* is considered on the Continent the first of modern German compositions, and *Il Crociato* the first of the modern Italians. Meyerbeer combines the easy, flowing and expressive melodies of Italy with the severer beauties, the grander accompaniments of the German school. . . . Let us hope then that the Twin Sisters, when they appear before a British audience, may be duly appreciated, and rewarded according to their merit.

Meyerbeer's *Il Crociato in Egitto* (*The Crusader in Egypt*), which had been in rehearsal for some time, was the cause of much excitement in London—and not only with the opera audience who might be presumed to be interested in the first opera they had a chance of seeing by the new thirty-three-year-old composer. The chief part was to be sung by the last of the *castrati*, Giovanni-Battista Velluti: no male soprano had been heard in London for twenty-five years, so curiosity alone was sure to guarantee a full house—apart from the fact that as Velluti had been Pasta's teacher, he must be well worth hearing for his singing.

The newspapers, of course, exploited this old-fashioned novelty, some enthusiastically, some vituperatively, and when, after many postponements owing to the unusually excessive rehearsals under Velluti himself that the production entailed—Meyerbeer began as he meant to go on, on the grand scale—the final rehearsal took place at the King's Theatre on June 29, the excitement was immense. There was a large paying audience for this dress rehearsal—the proceeds, bought up beforehand by the manager, Ebers, for £700, going to Velluti for his benefit as producer, and the performance was complete with the full band of the theatre 'and the extra military ones'.

The *Morning Post* remarked:

Never was there a greater enthusiasm excited: and the house, which had to boast of a numerous and fashionable audience, echoed again with the applause bestowed on the exertions of the whole establishment. . . . The public has in expectation one of the greatest musical treats enjoyed for many seasons.

The Times, however, came out on the other side—the side of British respectability:—

Our opinion was that the manly British public and the pure British fair would have been spared the disgust of such an appearance as that of Velluti upon any theatre of this metropolis. . . .

Humanity itself should rise against such a violation of decency—such an outrage upon feeling. But women! Can women too attend the scene? Can British matrons take their daughters to hear the portentous yells of this disfranchise of nature, and will they explain the cause to the youthful and untutored mind?

The question was answered the next day, June 30,[3] when the real first night took place—as a counterblast to the scandalously exciting attraction at the King's, Drury Lane put on *Macbeth* with Kean followed by *Der Freischütz*! The next day the *Morning Post* printed a long and detailed criticism and report, most of which is well worth reading: it began by objecting to the 'revolting beastliness' of a certain morning paper 'which has so effectually excited *public horror and disgust*', and went on to describe the performance:—

The opera having commenced, it proceeded without the slightest interruption until the change for the scene in which Velluti was to appear. Here some delay took place, and it excited partial disapprobation; but after a short pause the audience seemed to understand that the apprehensions of the singer might be the cause, and a loud burst of applause broke forth from all parts of the house.

The scene was immediately shifted, and Signor Velluti made his entrée amidst the most astounding and universal plaudits. As these subsided we heard a solitary hisser; but he did not venture to disturb the silent attention of the audience when it became fixed, and the business of the opera proceeded in the ordinary way.

(Mount-Edgcumbe thought the applause was planted: Ebers denied this.)

The work itself, the *Morning Post* thought, had been somewhat over-rated,

when the work has been without qualification placed at the head of all modern compositions. It is delightfully rich in melody, and its vocal as well as its instrumental harmonisation command high admiration.

But it certainly cannot be said that Meyerbeer compares with Rossini in his production of orchestral effects, or that he attains in any way to the genius displayed in the finest conceptions of that master. *Il Crociato* is a work far more polished, and perhaps more varied than any single opera which Rossini has produced. . . . But great as are its particular as well as its combined beauties, it would be impossible to select any given specimen that would for a moment bear comparison with the splendid gems of the *Tancredi*, the *Barbiere*, the *Gazza Ladra*, the *Mosé*, the *Ricciardo*, or indeed any one of Rossini's works.

Meyerbeer, the critic said, had less genius, but more industry than Rossini, and some of the music was charming:—

The Canzonetta is perhaps the most generally pleasing thing in the opera. The first part of it, sung by Mlle. Garcia, was the only thing *encored*. The Canone is exceedingly beautiful and written with masterly science. The Quartetto, 'O Nome Clemente,' and the duos in the last scene were the other favourites with the audience.

The chorus sang badly, but Velluti was mostly excellent:—

His school, or manner, is one of the best that has ever been heard in this country. It is not generally florid, but when he uses ornament, it is luxuriant and highly expressive. The great charm of his singing is its peculiar finish and delicacy.

(It would seem then that, like all the best singers of bel canto, Velluti used cadenzas and all decorative figuration to express emotion, not as a technical display: this he also handed on to Pasta.)

Of the voice itself, it cannot be disguised that there are defects about it which ruin many of the fine intentions prompted by the singer's feeling and judgment. The tone, when forced, is not always true, and the sweetest tones which perhaps were ever heard are occasionally mingled with others which music can scarcely own.
    When these occurred, some disapprobation was now and then expressed, and - every attempt to call for a repetition of Velluti's songs was effectually opposed. The greater part of his exertion, nevertheless, was rewarded with most rapturous applause.

As for Mlle. Garcia, who had made her debut as Rosina the year before in the *Barber* with her father, she was now only seventeen, and this was her first serious part, 'in which', the *Morning Post* said,

she not only gave some exquisite singing, but proved that her dramatic talents are not limited to comedy. Both her singing and acting frequently reminded us of the genius of Pasta. This young lady will certainly gain an eminence in her profession which few have passed.

Mount-Edgcumbe, who had thought her only very promising as Rosina, believed that she

317

in time, by study and practice, would in all probability under the tuition of her father—a good musician, but (to my ears, at least) a most disagreeable singer —rise to eminence in her profession.

Both critics were right and she did indeed rise to 'eminence in her profession', as they both said, becoming known during her tragically short career and to future generations as Malibran.

The Times, as might be expected from its preliminary campaign against the production, had other views on the performance. The critic began by sneering because the distinguished audience,

many of whom have passed a considerable portion of their lives in Italy, far from their own sturdy rough-toned peasantry, may delight in such forced fruits, such costly exotics: but, nurture them as they may, they never will suit the unsophisticated palate of that people who for years fought the battles of Europe, and came from the contest victorious.

There was some loose thinking here, as in the audience was at least one who had certainly been victorious in Europe as can be seen from this gossip paragraph from the same article:—

Amongst those who were most prominent in supporting Velluti we observed the Duke of Wellington and a party, Lord Maryborough, and a lady for whom we feel too much compassion to mention her name.

(Wellington was a keen lover of music and himself encouraged Malibran with an enthusiastic prophecy.)

The Times persisted that the house was chiefly packed by professors of music and Italians, who were

determined, we suppose, that Italian customs, however humiliating or degrading, ought to be supported by the sons of Italy when in a foreign land.

(In this the critic may have been right, for so often enthusiasts fail to remember that patriotism is not enough where art is concerned, and only this year, while I am writing this, an Italian opera company which is less than adequate in almost every particular has been duly applauded by compatriots and extolled by the descendants of Dryden's would-be artistic fops.)

As for Velluti's voice, *The Times* critic said it had

the shrillness of a woman's voice, but not the sweetness. At times it burst upon us with all the discordance of a peacock's scream, or that of a superannuated lady scolding her servants —they are convertible terms: at other times his notes were sweet and soft and flexible. . . . His cadences are delicate and expressive.

He was best in two duets, but there was a ribald section of riff-raff in the house, for, as the critic said, 'gallery imitators stopped encores'.

For this opera there was no divertissement or ballet between the acts, but even so it was an outsize opera, for the *Courier and Post* mentions that it was not over until just twelve o'clock. The Sunday paper, the *Telescope*, of July 3 said that it was

a feast of music and a splendid spectacle: and the drama itself, though the incidents are sufficiently incredible, not absolutely impeachable of nonsense.

That critic remarked of the audience who supported Velluti:—

Among the most enthusiastic of the applauders we observed a good many *young* ladies of fashion in the boxes: and indeed we do not know when we have seen so many delicate hands beating their snow-white gloves to pieces on behalf of a new favourite upon the boards.

(Was *The Times* wrong in its opinion of the British fair? Or was their enthusiasm actuated by artistic appreciation or by an inherited memory of the days when society ladies swooned over each male soprano with the confident approval of their menfolk?)

The *Sunday Times* enlarged on what *The Times* had said, but most other papers disagreed with such unreasoning abuse, though the *Common Sense and Weekly Order* did not think Velluti's voice very good, 'nor is its compass very great: we do not recollect that it ever ascended above G or that it descended below C sharp'.

Whatever were the true merits of Velluti's singing, he certainly was a great artist, to judge from his pupil Pasta, and he certainly was a draw, even after *Il Crociato*, for while he received £600 salary for the few weeks left in that season plus the £700 Ebers paid him for his benefit, for the following season he had £2,300. In July of 1825 he sang with success in the *Barber* and again in *Il Crociato*, when the faithful *Morning Post* of Monday, August 1, remarked:—

Meyerbeer's beautiful opera was repeated on Saturday night, and its attractions seem to defy even the heat of the weather and a closing season. . . . The opera went off with its usual success.

From now on for about twenty years most operas newly produced in London were given in English, although Italian works were given in Italian. Some of the operas given between 1825 and 1845 are still well known, at least by name, especially through gramophone records, but few of them are given more than an occasional performance in this country: so as the contemporary opinions quoted in this section of the book deal only with the more usual English repertoire of operas—apart from such a historic landmark as *Il Crociato*—there is no room for critiques on Weber's *Oberon* or Spontini's *La Vestale* (1826), Mozart's *Seraglio* (first performed in English at Covent Garden in 1827), Auber's *Masaniello* or Marschner's *Vampyr* of 1829.

The operatic event of 1830 that seems of special interest nowadays was the first introduction to London of a Bellini opera. To the London audiences of the day, however, it did not make a great effect, because they were so Rossini-minded—there had been over twenty Rossini productions in London in the eleven years since the first was given, the last three being *Le Comte Ory* and a pastiche *Ivanhoé* (as *The Maid of Judah, or The Knight Templars*) of 1829, and a three-act ballet version of *Guillaume Tell*, given after the *Barber* on March 6, 1830 (evidently as what might now be called an operatic trailer).

When Bellini's three-year old *Il Pirata* then was given on April 17, 1830, *The Times* was not enthusiastic about the composer:—

Signor Bellini is a very young composer, whose labours are supposed to have received the secret help of more experienced hands in the construction of this opera. . . . As a musical composition the opera is not destitute of merit, with the exception of the overture, which was very weak and puerile. It is deficient in concerted pieces, because the incidents of the drama hardly afford situations which call for any: but a pleasing vein of melody prevails throughout the whole.

The *Morning Post*, though apparently kinder, was really more damning:—

The music is extremely pretty, and comprises several melodies which we have no doubt will become favourites: its lively and sucré quality is such that we occasionally almost imagined it to be the medium of comic rather than of serious action.

Finally this critic remarks that 'the general character of the opera decidedly assimilates to the Rossinian school', which is not surprising as all young composers were imitating Rossini.

The performance of *Il Pirata* was followed by a ballet-version of *La Sonnambula*, though Bellini's operatic version was first performed in Milan a year later, and a month after *Il Pirata* Rossini's operatic *Guillaume Tell* was given at Drury Lane in a Bishop adaptation as *Hofer, the Tell of the Tyrol*—it was not given in its proper form in London for another eight or nine years.

In 1831, after Auber's *Fra Diavolo* was introduced to London in an adapted English version, a Donizetti opera was given for the first time on July 8—*Anna Bolena*. As so often at this time, to ensure a large and friendly audience it was produced at the King's on a benefit night—for the great Pasta. It was finely performed, with Rubini as Lord Percy, Lablache as Henry VIII and Pasta as Anne Boleyn, who had more acting to do than singing, the critic of both the *Sun* and *The Times* said:—

The energy of Medea, the dignity of Semiramide, the tender pathos of Desdemona, the profound affliction of Mary Stuart, and that fascinating littleness which forms the charm of her mad scene in *Nina* were all displayed in turns.

The composer did not get such praise:—

There is a great deal of good music in the opera, and the hand of a master is visible throughout, but imperfections are also abundant. In some parts Rossinian recollections have strongly prevailed, and in others Bellini's *Pirata* has supplied the model.

There was also an imitation of the Tyrolese air, that Henrietta Sontag had made famous, while in the last scene 'Home, sweet home' was introduced.

The *Morning Post* said it was so well performed that it was impossible to judge the music at first hearing (interesting that acting could in those days be so good in opera that the music took second place):—

There are no airs that particularly strike the attention or impress the memory, yet is this work always above mediocrity. We have long come to the conclusion that all writers after Rossini must more or less be followers of his style, and last night we were impressed with the conviction that Donizetti composed his opera with not only the music of Rossini in his mind, but also strains of more recent birth—the strains of the universally-known and admired Auber.

Twenty days after *Anna Bolena*, on July 28, 1831, Bellini's *Sonnambula* was performed for Rubini's benefit night, but *The Times* seems to have completely ignored the performance, while the *Morning Post* printed only nine lines after the second performance on Saturday, July 30, in which, while admitting that Pasta's aria at the end was 'one of the most effective' ever heard from her, the critic said of the music that 'its prevailing character is sprightliness rather than depth'. More attention was paid when, on August 1, the new London Bridge was opened.

Two ineffective Donizetti operas were given in 1832. *L'Esule di Roma, ossia Il Proscritto* and *Olivo e Pasquale*, but the latter caused *The Times* to make a trenchant comment that has not always been inapposite even since April 2, 1832, when it was printed:—

It is impossible not to be struck with the slovenly and disgracefully incorrect manner in which the English translations of the libretti are executed. Can no one be found to do them who knows anything of the Italian and English languages? There is hardly a sentence the text of which has not been grossly perverted. These books have, in fact, no translations at all. The English writer affects to give an adaption of his own in blank verse, and he only succeeds in making it the most absurd and stupid trash that ever was seen in print.

Meyerbeer's *Robert the Devil* was also given in London in the same year, twice in English versions within two days at Drury Lane and Covent Garden and in French at the King's, but the great success of the year 1832, surprising as it may seem to-day, was the production at the King's of Beethoven's twenty-seven-year-old *Fidelio* on May 18 in German.

Although the wind was flat at the start of the overture, the whole performance was superb, largely, the *Morning Post* implied, owing to Schroeder-Devrient as Leonora, who

possesses a pleasing face and fine person: the voice is a fine soprano, which she exerts to the best advantage, being a first-rate musician, and possessing taste and judgement in the highest degree. As an actress she is not surpassed by Pasta, whom she more than equals in feminine grace.

(The acting, in fact, made no less impression than the music and the singing, and at times was 'electrifying', this critic said.)

Her exclamations on the discovery of her husband, her throwing herself before him as a shield against the dagger of his foe, her shrieks of wild joy at the happy termination of their distresses, and her final exultations, were all master strokes of that art which seems to leave all art behind and become nature itself, and elicited applause even equal to that bestowed upon her singing.

(How many Leonoras of to-day would be capable of exclaiming or shrieking with wild joy or exulting, even if they were allowed to by experts who believe that vocalisation is admirable and emotion cheap bad taste?) The chorus-singers were far better than were usually heard in England—it was a foreign company—and the whole production was 'a treat that has never been surpassed, even if equalled, in a London theatre'.

That *Fidelio* was such a triumph surprised even the opera-going public of the day, to judge from the notice in *The Times* which said that 'contrary to our expectation it proved completely successful'. In the first place, the plot was simple, as all good opera plots should be, in the second place

the music, like all Beethoven's compositions, abounds in novel and powerful effects of harmony, and the scoring in some parts of the orchestral accompaniments must have astonished those whose notions of operative composition are derived solely from the productions of the Rossini school.

Schroeder-Devrient was, this critic also said, 'electrifying' in the dungeon scene, and Haitzinger, though tremulous in slow passages (which might have been thought intentionally effective in his great aria), was excellent: 'the choruses merit no less praise than those of the *Freischütz*. One of them, a chorus of prisoners, was rapturously encored'.

The overture also, had to be played twice, and

indeed, owing to the multitude of encores, the audience might almost as well have waited to the end, and insisted on a repetition of the whole opera.

In fact even after the final solo calls were taken the whole of the finale had to be done again.

In June 1832 Bellini again failed to impress the London critics with *La Straniera*, which *The Times* thought was definitely not good, being too noisy and melodramatic, although there were some sweet airs in it, and in 1833, after Malibran had sung in Bishop's English version of *La Sonnambula* at Drury Lane, *Norma* was given at the King's for Pasta's benefit night on June 20—only to be completely ignored by *The Times* and to be dismissed by the *Morning Post* four days later as follows:—

We cannot however award any high praise to this opera of Bellini's. It is lamentably deficient in original ideas (Rossini, as usual, being the source principally drawn upon) and but for a certain dramatic character discernible in its music would, unusually short as it is, put the patience of the audience to a somewhat severe test.

The admirers however of the singing and acting of Pasta will do well to see her in this opera. The Ballet of *La Sylphide* with Taglioni followed. The house was crowded.

1833 was a year in which great objection was taken to the constant presenting of foreign operas and foreign singers at the two great national theatres, though as the writer of one of the many letters to the *Courier* said, anticipating more recent opinions:—

Nobody supposes that the lessees of Covent Garden and Drury Lane are actuated by any desire to uphold the English Drama: that is not their affair: their business is to make money, and to that end they must present the public with that which the public will go to see.

(To-day, of course, the prime business of Covent Garden with its Arts Council grant is to present opera and ballet, while Drury Lane is one of the few theatres large enough to be likely to produce the necessarily high guaranteed royalties required by the popularly desirable and microphonically publicised American musicals which were often designed for smaller theatres, but whose merits are not automatically enhanced by enlargement.)

One of the results of the protests of 1833 was the opening of the newly built English Opera House—the Lyceum—on nearly the same site as Arnold's earlier English Opera House which was burnt down in 1830, and four British operas were given there in 1834: Loder's *Nourjahad*, Barnett's often-revived *Mountain Sylph* and *Hermann, or The Broken Spear* and *The House of Aspen*, both by the twenty-nine-year-old Scotsman John Thomson, whose *Shadow on the Wall* was given at the English Opera House in 1835 and who became the first Professor of Music at Edinburgh, only to die when he was thirty-six. Bellini's *I Puritani di Scozia* was also given in 1835 at the King's as well as his *Beatrice di Tenda* in 1836, but by the end of that year, though Balfe had begun to restore opera in English at Drury Lane with his first two, *The Siege of Rochelle* and *The Maid of Artois*, the latter of which he wrote for Malibran, the English Opera House reopened with a season of Italian comic opera, beginning with Donizetti's *L'Elisir d'Amore* on Saturday, December 10.

None of the performers in *L'Elisir* are remembered to-day, but as *The Times* said,

on the whole, there was sufficient to constitute a delightful evening's entertainment: the plot was good, the music pleasing, the singing everything that could be desired, and the band excellent.

The *Morning Post* remarked that though the house was tolerably filled, the audience was not brilliant and fashionable as at the King's, which in the opinion of many is as attractive as the opera itself. We greatly question whether the love of Italian music is sufficiently advanced in this country to make this experiment successful.

Between the acts, this critic said, the overture to *La Gazza Ladra* was played, which was 'not creditable to the taste of the director'. Benedict should have been conducting, but the opportunist Balfe took his place and the *Morning Post* critic wished he had been singing instead. On March 10, 1838, in the first English *Magic Flute* (apart from Bishop's altered version of 1819) Balfe did sing— Papageno.

Several other minor Donizetti works had been given in 1837, and then on April 5, 1838, at Her Majesty's—as the King's was renamed—in the presence of Queen Victoria with an excellent cast including Persiani, Rubini and Tamburini, *Lucia di Lammermoor* was given its first London performance—only for *The Times* to say that it was better performed than written, for, 'like other Italian operas, it is rather a succession of scenes than any attempt at a plot or regular drama', and after all Donizetti 'is but of a mediocre school'. The *Morning Post*, however, did say there was cheering at the end. Still more Donizetti operas were given in the next three years—*Lucrezia Borgia* in 1839, *Torquato Tasso* in 1840 (as well as Spohr's *Faust* and *Jessonda*), *Fausta* and *Roberto d'Evereux, Conte d'Essex* in 1841 and *Gemma di Vergy* in 1842.

1842 was the year of the London production of Meyerbeer's *Huguenots*, which lasted four hours and a quarter on the first night and which *The Times* did not like, though the critic had to

commend the judgement of the manager in not rendering the massacre too shocking, but in alleviating the feelings of the audience by spicing it with a touch of broad humour. When one gun only was fired, the three victims fell dead, which created a pleasant spirit of mirth—a spirit much heightened upon the discharge of the other two guns which followed their decease.

The contrivance also of allowing the green curtain to descend before the artillery was discharged was exceedingly comic, the audience, who were leaving, being perpetually refreshed with right merry shouts of laughter.

Donizetti had three more London first nights in 1843: the first two were the unremembered *Adelia, ossia La Figlia dell' Arciere* and the opera with the one famous gramophone-recorded aria, *Linda di Chamounix*, but with the third he really came into his own at last with the one opera of his that has taken the fancy of present day English audiences—*Don Pasquale*.

It was produced at Her Majesty's on Thursday, June 29, 1843, on Lablache's benefit night with Grisi as Norina and Mario as Ernesto. There seems to have been no notice in *The Times*, which may have disregarded benefit-night premières, although it was repeated on July 1, 4 and 6—the last date being the night for Grisi's benefit. The *Morning Post*, however, recorded that the first performance, including the ballet that followed the opera, was not over till one in the morning, but that even at the time of writing 'our sides are still aching with what we took in—even the listless Adonises in the stalls were for once convulsed out of all propriety': not did the opera only convulse these curled youths, whose ancestors drooped in Dorset Garden Theatre and whose descendants, by type if not by birth, still clutter up the crush bar at Covent Garden; the ladies, too, laughed till their whale-bones cracked, the critic said, adding as a final comment on the would be society audience—'And only think of this taking place in a country where to laugh in public is a grievous sin'.

Lablache was excellent as Don Pasquale with his white camelia —the next morning white camelias were sent to his house by the dozen—and so was Grisi, while all the music, which was well worthy of the author of *L'Elisir*, certainly warranted encores: in fact this opera 'most triumphantly shows that Donizetti's genius has not been frittered away by the wonderful rapidity of composition in which he indulges'. Most unusual for opera buffa, the scenery was excellent, and there could be no question but that every performance would be packed by genuinely enthusiastic audiences and not by 'Drawing-room' people:—

Thanks to the caprice of fashion, ladies no longer dare to come and display those feathered headdresses with which the boxes were filled formerly, and which, with a shake of the head of the proud wearers, told the less favoured mortals, 'You see, *we* go to Court.'

Don Pasquale was the twentieth Donizetti opera to be given in London within thirteen years and it was not the last, but in the same year Balfe seized the chance offered him by Bunn of Drury Lane and hurriedly wrote a new score to go with Bunn's libretto of *The Bohemian Girl*, his earlier setting for which Balfe had largely used up for his French opera *Les Puits d'Amour*.[4] The result certainly pleased the public, even if the critics were not wholeheartedly enthusiastic. The *Morning Post* said the evening was a triumph and justified the expensive production—'A greater reck-lessness of outlay has never been witnessed.' The story was based on the ballet *La Gipsy* written by de St. Georges for Fanny Elssler in 1839 in Paris (not to be confused, *The Times* said, with Tag-lioni's *Gitana*), and set in Austria with a Pole as hero instead of in Scotland with a Jacobite, as in the ballet. The music, said the *Morning Post*,

will certainly add to the reputation of Mr. Balfe, for, although it abounds with many reminiscences, it contains more sterling originality than any of his former works.

At the same time one could constantly sense the 'Irishman struggling with the Italian', and there were some blemishes, notably the absurd scene at the end of Act I when the whole com-pany is praying in the foreground while the child is being kid-napped in the background. It was also regrettable that there was no recitative :—

As it is, the words had about the average quantity of 'Ahs! and Ohs!—What do I see?—What do I hear?—It is, it must be, my child!—Oh, never!' and the accompanying melodramatic etceteras.

Still, there was no doubt that the publishers would make a very good thing out of it, having paid Balfe £450 for his copyright and Bunn £100 for his. *The Times* pointed out the weaknesses and also the good points, such as the Gipsy Chorus, the Prayer, 'I dreamed I dwelt' (twice encored), Arline's fine duet with Thad-deus, 'The heart bowed down', 'When other lips' and 'When the fair land of Poland', and finally said 'It was a complete thing, and the success seemed complete also'.

But though *The Bohemian Girl* gave a much-needed spurt to British opera at the time, it failed to hold the field against all comers and in 1845, when London suddenly had a spate of operas sung in French (including *La Favorita* and *Lucia di Lammermoor*), the one new Italian opera introduced a new composer, Giuseppe Verdi.

[1] He says in Munich, which Löwenberg quotes as the eleventh German town to perform it after the Berlin première on June 18, 1821.
[2] Mary Shelley's *Frankenstein* with its monster was published in 1818.
[3] Löwenburg in the 1st edition wrongly gave June 3 : it had been announced for such an early date, but was in fact postponed several times. This is corrected in the second edition.

⁴ So much is known, but it now seems that, when in Paris, Balfe started *La Bohémienne* with his friend de St. Georges, then used music from that to fit adequately Bunn's libretto, which was partly old and partly new translated from de St. Georges, who later completed the French version for which Balfe wrote recitatives and from which Sir Thomas Beecham and I reconstructed the version that was performed during the Festival of Britain at Liverpool and Covent Garden in 1951. This is not the place to go into the fascinating detective-story of *The Bohemian Girl*, the clues to which I discovered from Balfe's note-books when working on the production, but briefly:—the Cavatine at the end of Act II of *Les Puits d'Amour* 'Que de graces, que de charmes' is identical with one of Balfe's many rough settings of 'When other lips' in Add. MS. 32669 in the British Museum, while the false accentuations all through *The Bohemian Girl* (so unnatural to a singer of Balfe's repute and so untypical of him as a composer) vanish when the English score is joined to the words of the (apparently later) French version—typical being 'I dre-*eamed* I dwe-*elt* in ma-*ar*-ble halls' compared with 'A mes *pieds* dans un *doux* servage'.

CHAPTER FIVE

Ernani to Faust

ERNANI, the *Pictorial Times* said on Saturday, March 8, 1843, the morning of its first performance, was

the production of a young but prolific composer, Giuseppe Verdi, of whose talents Italy is just now making great boast, and whose fame she is doing her best to spread and secure.

His greatest admirers claim for him the merit of entire originality: but in this they are rather outstripping justice and discretion, since his real position and character as a composer may be fairly summed up in one sentence, the soundness of which time will most certainly demonstrate—Verdi is another Donizetti.

Is that not praise enough for any young Italian, who neither seems to understand the scientific depths of German harmony, or the rapid expressions of the school of France?

The same critic said the music was

characterised by its easy, melodious flow, and light, graceful, pointed instrumentation. Its sentiment is simple and familiar, its originality slight, its inspiration rather that of champagne than of port or burgundy.

He also thought that the gem of the opera, 'Ah, morir', was 'certainly destined by its beauty to the cruel, mangled immortality of the pavement through the instrumentalists of the peripatetic organ-grinders.'

The *Observer* of March 9 says that the music 'is of a highly dramatic quality, which after all is a capital substitute for sterling excellence'.

The *Morning Post* the next day pointed out that *Ernani* had in the one year since its première in Venice been played on upwards of fifty Italian stages, and after writing six operas Verdi

has been elevated by the voice of his countrymen to the throne formerly filled by Donizetti and that child of passionate melody, poor Bellini—

(who had died ten years before at the age of thirty-four)

Donizetti seems to be now devoted more to the search of the *auri sacra fames* than to the evocation of that fine imagination which marked his bygone efforts. Verdi is the only worthy successor to the intensity of Bellini—he has sought his lyrical promptings in the scores of the German writers: we do not by this mean to assert that his operas possess the same deep contrapuntal knowledge, but by his orchestration, which to the unobservant may press unheeded, the entire construction and feeling of the music changes as the scene shifts. . . .

This power of admirable adaptation is one of Verdi's leading excellencies, and one which must ultimately place him on a level with contemporary composers.

The Times, careful as ever, says the house was 'brilliantly attended' in spite of the cold weather, but denies that there is any sign of Verdi founding a new school of composing: his work is that of the ordinary modern Italian school, and though his instrumentation is superior, his pleasing melodies are neither original nor striking, and in that respect his operas are 'not yet equal to the better works of Donizetti'.

London tried to take Verdi to their hearts as they had taken Rossini, but none of his operas that were produced here during the next three years made much mark—*I Lombardi alla prima Crociata* and *Nabucodonosor* (as *Nino*) (1846), *I due Foscari* or *I Masnadieri* (1847) [1] or *Attila* (1848), though he wrote *I Masnadieri* expressly for London and the great Jenny Lind created the part of Amalia in it. Donizetti's *Daughter of the Regiment* was given in 1847, and 1849 was another year for operas in French—Auber, Boiëldieu, etc., as well as Flotow's *Martha* in German. In 1850 there were more French operas—Halévy and Thomas, as well as *Freischütz* in Italian, and in 1851 another well heralded young composer had a work performed in London for the first time—Gounod, then thirty-three.

The opera was his first, *Sapho*, which had been given for the first time on any stage only four months before in Paris. In London it was performed on August 9, 1851, in Italian, and was by no means a success. The *Observer* the next day praises the scientific writing, which the musicians may admire, but the general opera-goer,

who requires his ear to be tickled by nothing but melody, will not at first be satisfied: but the opera will obtain a hold upon the musical world, and, mounted in the admirable style it is, and sung by such exquisite musicians—[Tamburini, Tamberlik, and Viardot–Garcia]—it cannot fail to be numbered as a stock piece.

The Times pulls no punches at all:—

The characteristics of his music are want of melody, indecision of style, ineffective treatment of voices, inexperience in the use of instruments, accompanied by an affectation of originality disclosed in strange and unsuccessful experiments, excess of modulation, monotonous in itself and proceeding from inability to develop phrases, contempt of established forms, and general absence of continuity, vexing the ear with beginnings that rarely arrive at consummation.

The *Sun* reports the curtain descended to but faint applause, and says that the opera is

not calculated to produce an effect upon the stage, but that its composer is a young musician from whom great things may reasonably be expected. . . . In the music there are many and great beauties—beauties too, which would grow upon the ear by repetition of the piece.

Surprisingly, that critic thought, Gounod failed to write melody in the vocal music through striving after originality, though the instrumental music was full of it.

The *Morning Post* blamed the libretto which was

so clumsy, so deficient in interest, that an overwhelming sense of tedium is produced which could scarcely be relieved even by the genius of a Mozart or a Beethoven. Out of such materials, therefore, it will be necessarily inferred that much could not be made by M. Gounod, who is neither Mozart nor Beethoven.

The writer goes on to say that there are traces of a dramatic instinct, and that Gounod 'is rarely open to the reproach of using hackneyed slang of the day, and if he does not reach the beautiful, he not infrequently lights upon the novel'. The same conclusion, however, is come to that his vocal melody is not as good as his instrumental melody, probably because 'we should imagine that the composer had never studied the human heart very deeply, or that he was deficient in the means of expressing his thoughts with perfect freedom'.

Besides, this was a classical subject and, as the *Observer* had said, Gounod had 'in his original capacity of Catholic priest, devoted himself *toto coelo* to the study of Catholic ecclesiastical music'.

Two years later Verdi was given another chance to shine in London and failed abysmally—at least with the critics—when *Rigoletto* was produced on May 14, 1853, at Covent Garden— Her Majesty's closing this year for three years. The *Morning Post* of May 16 is eloquent on the subject:—

After an unusual delay, which occasioned many impatient demonstrations from the audience, Signor Costa gave his directorial tap at about half-past eight o'clock, when the band commenced a lugubrious strain, in which pompous successions of minor common chords and sudden explosions of diminished sevenths by turns saluted our ears.

The trombones said nothing with brazen solemnity, and the kettle-drums, with sullen dub, murmured prophetically of coming storms, but neither melody, nor harmony, form, nor substance, was there to fix our attention, or take root in our memory.

In the first glittering scene there were countless chandeliers and a vulgar dance tune, while Mario's first aria as the Duke, 'Questa o quella per me', was remarkably commonplace and insipid, and also too low for him.

After this some dances were prettily executed to music which presented a very curious mixture of the *rococo* minuet style and that of the modern Casino. Then the amorous duke made love to one Countess Ceprano, personated by a Miss Smythson (who seemed frightened out of her senses), her jealous husband looking daggers in the background.

As for the scene of Monterone's curse:—

The situation is highly dramatic, but with Verdi's inexpressive and frightfully ugly music (though this was admirably sung) it fell flatly upon the audience, who showed no signs of real excitement.

Rigoletto's speech, beginning 'Ch' io gli parli', is absolutely hideous: the constant straining after strange harmonic effects which characterises the reply of Monterone is scarcely less offensive, and the following chorus . . . sung by the now infuriated courtiers, to the tune of the above-mentioned galop, played *prestissimo* and *fortissimo*, forms a worthy conclusion to this first scene, which contains some of the very worst music we ever had the misfortune to listen to.

The duet between Rigoletto and Gilda was beautifully sung,

delightfully accompanied, and containing some of the best passages we have yet heard, though still very poor as a whole. . . . The jolly *dansante* music which Verdi has set to that portion of the duet which, according to the situation and the words, . . . should express tender solicitude and pure love, will doubtless delight the admirers of the 'genial' Italian. We think it detestable, grossly wrong in conception, vulgar and ugly.

The quick movement at the end, however, led to an encore. The critic also remarks on the duet that 'Signor Verdi ought to know that the oboe is about the worst instrument which could be selected to sing with the voice'. 'Stringera O vergine' was sung by Mario divinely to thunders of applause: but as for 'Caro nome', which should illustrate the 'delightful sensations' with which the duke's assumed name 'fills the young maiden's bosom':—

its intrinsic merits are very slender. The quaint and odd instrumentation may however please certain admirers of musical eccentricities, but we do not wish to be reckoned among these.

Gilda, of course 'made a swan-like end, according to the approved fashion which the public had been taught to admire in the operas of *Lucia, Lucrezia Borgia, Ernani*, etc.' and the concluding scene was beautifully done by all and

nothing could possibly be better than the scenery, costumes, decoration, groupings, etc., etc., but still we cannot set down this opera as a great success, even with the public.

Our opinion of Signor Verdi's powers is well known: and as his present work is rather worse than better than previous productions by him, which we have already condemned, it will be unnecessary to enter into painful details.

This opera is certainly not so noisy as the *Ernani, Attila, Masnadieri* or *Anato*, but it contains other grievous faults, for which the mere absence of 'row' cannot compensate.

(*Anato* was the name given to *Nabucodonosor* when revived in 1850.)

The only concerted piece in the score having the slightest pretension to merit is a quartet in the third act (encored), but amongst the solos we cannot find one melody possessing true beauty or originality. . . . The harmonies . . . are frequently very far-fetched, and at times completely inadmissible: the choral voicings are generally deficient in clearness and resonance, and the instrumentation confused and unimaginative.

Of the rich resources of the stringed band, Signor Verdi scarcely avails himself at all. He assigns to it throughout most humdrum passages, except in one instance, where in an accompanied recitative for the baritone he essays some novel effects with the violoncellos and double basses, *divisi*, only: but the whole being low in pitch, the result is so rumbling and indistinct that we cannot congratulate him on the success of his enterprising efforts. A few passages assigned to wood wind instruments only come out pretty well, but these constitute those fatal exceptions which are said to prove a rule.

(Before that criticism is laughed at as being unperceptive, it must be remembered that all opinions are relative, not only considering the person who holds those opinions, but also the time in which he holds them. Is it surprising that an ear which had only recently managed to assimilate Rossini, Bellini and Donizetti, should boggle at the comparative crudities of early Verdi? Judged purely analytically, the introduction to *Rigoletto* is in fact as described by that critic—especially as everyone of that day expected melody in some form and a regular overture: that the present day can see beauties to which the past was blind does not mean that the past was wrong.

It is all a question of relativity: because we know that Handel

333

wrote some wonderful music (and are ignorant of the fact that a lot of it was adapted by him from some other work), it does not mean that the operas that contained it were good operas. Besides, it must be noticed that the critics of the mid-nineteenth century did attempt to do what the eighteenth century had been pleading for—judge according to common sense: almost all their criticism of the music of an opera is joined up to either the dramatic situation or characterisation or to the effect on the public—both of which are essentially theatrical matters. Nowadays the average opera-lover is prepared to admire a good singer's good performance of a good aria, without ever considering that it might be the wrong colour of voice, the wrong style of singing or the wrong aria for the situation.)

The *Morning Post* was not alone in its condemnations. The *Sun* said that the opera

partakes greatly of the usual character of Signor Verdi's productions: and, we think, judged by this standard alone, *Rigoletto* would have but a poor chance of becoming a permanent favourite in this country. As a dramatic performance, however, its success we are assured will be as great as that of any opera which has hitherto been produced on the Italian stage.

(So it was to be the drama of the piece that would save it—and, come to that, how many serious operas have lasted that have not been excitingly dramatic?) This critic thought that it would always be a success with great artists such as Ronconi, the original Rigoletto here, whose acting was the success of the evening: his singing, too, 'was all that could be desired', while Mario had little to do but sing sweetly and powerfully, which he did 'in a style right worthy of the *primo tenore* of the world'. The scenery by Beverley 'was a worthy example of the great advances which the art of scene-painting has made of late years'.

The *Observer* said the performance was better than the score: Rigoletto's voice was weighty enough to 'overcome the confusion' of the accompaniment of his recitative before meeting Sparafucile, the scoring of his duet with Gilda was too noisy but nearly triumphant as performed, 'Farmi veder le lagrime' was 'unmelodious', but sung by Mario with feeling: only 'La Donna e mobile' would probably become popular: the quartet was good, but from then on the score flagged while the dramatic interest increased, and except for Rigoletto's recitative at finding the body there is nothing remarkable in the music. Nor would this be remarkable more than the rest, but for the force and feeling which Ronconi threw into its execution, and by which he almost electrified the house.

The Times agreed that *Rigoletto* was put on well, apart from the feeble ballet, but that it would have no more success than did *Masnadieri*: 'the reason is that there is very little interest in the music. . . .' The story is a 'monstrous rhodomontade', and as for words to describe the music, 'a very few will suffice to record its beauties. Its faults we have not space to describe'. In *Nabucco* and *Ernani* there were tunes, here there are none, only imitations and even plagiarisms from other composers, and in aiming at simplicity Verdi has hit frivolity. *Rigoletto* in fact is 'the most feeble opera of Signor Verdi (except *Luisa Miller*)'—which was not seen in London till 1858—'. . . the most uninspired, the barest, and the most destitute of ingenious contrivance'. As for the plagiarisms, the critic finds music from Benedict, de Beriot, *L'Elisir, I Martyri* (by Donizetti) and—in Rigoletto's meeting with Gilda in the palace—a travestied phrase from the famous duet in the *Huguenots*.

After the third performance the *Era* wrote:—

The opinions we at first entertained have undergone no mutation: subsequent representations have only served to strengthen our assertions that the character of the libretto is a bar to its ever becoming popular, and that the music has not in it the element of success.

Ronconi, unquestionably a great man among great artists, Mario, and Mlle. Bosio, who had to sustain the principal parts, inimitable and energetic as their acting was, failed—as they ever must—in making an opera effective which has in it principles antagonistic to refined taste.

That critic also says that *Norma* on Thursday was 'a pleasing relief to *Rigoletto*'. Were all those critics wrong all the time?

Two years later, on May 10, 1855, the critics relaxed a little when they attended the first performance in London of Verdi's *Trovatore*—all except the *Morning Post*, which was as violent as before:—

If Signor Verdi be really the 'Speranza di Italia', we cannot congratulate that once favoured land of song upon its expectations, for a more uninspired or uncultivated composer never yet succeeded in attracting public notice. . . .

If the unanimous opinion of the best musicians of every country be of any value, then must he be driven from the heights of Parnassus as one who has been puffed up to them by the 'vile breath' of the mob, but who possesses not the magic pass-word which alone can procure admittance amongst the elect.

The Italians are very national, and, like the Chinese, have erected a huge and interminable wall around their flowing land, with this difference that theirs is made of prejudice, whilst that of the Celestial Empire is of stone. Both, however, are equally hard, and stupidly exclusive.

Verdi, in that critic's opinion, was not as good as Bellini, Donizetti, Rossini, Cherubini, Spontini or Cimarosa, as he could only write vulgar tunes, with commonplace scoring, maudlin pathos and fustian passion. As an example of the fustian passion he goes on to quote the printed description of the Count di Luna's appearances: first 'in a violent passion', secondly 'in an excess of fury', thirdly with 'the gestures and voice of a maniac', then he 'looks fiercely about him', 'and his subsequent conduct betrays such unrestrained fury, as makes us suspect very strongly that he is not quite right in the head'.

There were some fine dramatic scenes finely acted, especially by Viardot-Garcia as Azucena, but why, he asks, must heroines of modern opera have to fall about so instead of acting, as Rachel could, with their faces? 'A trained tumbler will presently be required as the heroine of modern Italian opera.'

The *Observer* recognised that Verdi was the representative of 'young Italy', 'as Wagner has been identified with a movement similar in spirit, though very unsimilar in practice, in Germany', but thought that his music was limited, certainly in construction, though

to say that it is uneffective would be absurd. . . . Constructive ingenuity is one of the last things in the world that Verdi has, or apparently cares to have: but there is a certain speciousness of treatment which is telling—a decision and boldness of detail which oftentimes produces a striking *ensemble*.

The melodies are gay and voluble, and of genuine Italian physiognomy, the native triviality of the themes being compensated for by a prettiness of vein which, we can easily understand, the public will not dislike. . . .

On the whole, there is more harmony of general effect and less of mere patchwork or haphazard composition than in any other work of Verdi's, except *Ernani*, with which the English public are familiar. . . .

It is probable that, like the *Rigoletto*, it will increase in favour with those who relish the light and rhythmical modes of the modern Italian school and become a permanence.

(So already *Rigoletto* was appealing to the public.)

The Times was even more enthusiastic in a notice that must be read with the knowledge that in 1855 the Crimean War was on, and the very day the notice appeared news came that the new electric telegraph wire was actually at work between Sebastopol and London:—

Seldom indeed has an opera enjoyed such undisturbed good fortune. From all which, nevertheless, it must not be deduced that a new *chef-d'œuvre* has appeared: by no means: *Il Trovatore*, though it exhibits Signor Verdi in his best holiday attire, is hardly destined to raise him in the estimation of real judges. . . .

Signor Verdi is accepted as one of the popular European composers . . . even the military bands of our august ally, the Sultan Abdul Medjid, have learned to play some of his most sonorous melodies. He is neither a Rossini, nor an Auber, nor a Meyerbeer: far from it: but he is not, as some would insist, a nonentity—almost as far, indeed, from that as from the others.

(It is interesting that at that time Auber was included as a worth-while opera-composer.) The absence of an overture was not regretted, as Verdi 'is no great adept at "absolute" instrumental music': the soprano had to strain in her first aria, 'but it is useless to remonstrate with Signor Verdi on this head': the opening chorus of gipsies was trite, but 'Il balen' was 'pretty certain of popularity, although the opening melody is ill-defined'. 'Di quella pira', on the other hand, was noisy and square-cut, and was redeemed only by the singing of Tamberlik: Viardot-Garcia sang Azucena with feeling, though her voice was 'not what the composer might have desired'.

A year later Verdi had another opportunity, with *Traviata* on May 24, 1856, at Her Majesty's, which was now open again after Covent Garden had been burnt down two months before. This time he had a success—or rather the fascinating Piccolomini as Violetta had a great success. The *Observer*, it is true, thought that this opera was 'unquestionably among the principal works of its composer. It is light, cheerful, full of melody, and abounding in skilfully constructed harmonies'.

The Introduction to it 'embodies in brief the leading themes of the score', and a long run was predicted, for Piccolomini's success had not been paralleled in the musical world, the critic said, since the debut of Jenny Lind:—

Those who had the opportunity of listening to her execution of the plaintive and expressive aria 'Addio del Passato' and of witnessing the extraordinary histrionic talent she manifested at the same time, will not readily let its memory perish from their minds.

As for the death-scene—'It was truth to nature carried to the last point to which it could go in acting: while in singing it was unsurpassable for expression and for sentiment'.

The Times, which had thundered against the 'foul and hideous horrors' of the subject in advance, thought that the work was really a play set to music—'the book is of far more consequence than the music, which, except so far as it affords a vehicle for the utterance of the dialogue, is of no value whatsoever'. But the great expectations—not for Verdi, but for Piccolomini—were fully realised (the *Morning Post* was no less enthusiastic about her great acting and singing, which was æsthetic rather than technical). Her real forte was charm, for it was said she sang well without being a singer, and acted well, though no actress. Here is some of *The Times's* description of her acting in the scene where Violetta is insulted by Alfredo:—

> Except in the Camille of Mademoiselle Rachel, we scarcely remember to have seen such an instance of the bodily frame breaking up, as it were, through the aggression of mental anguish. Mademoiselle Piccolomini trembled from head to foot under the influence of the insulting language—the hands clutched convulsively and wandered about uncertain—it was evident that the mind was so absorbed in its own suffering as to have lost its control over the limbs.
>
> In this situation she *did not* utter a note, but nevertheless she monopolised to herself all the attention of the public, who contemplating that mute figure forgot the insipid air by which her movements were accompanied.

'Di Provenza,' by tradition, the critic said, 'the great song of the piece, produced scarcely any effect whatsoever', and no art could have rendered Alfredo's songs fascinating.

Three more Verdi operas were produced in London in the next four years: *Luisa Miller* in 1858—the year Covent Garden was rebuilt in the form we know it today—first in English at Sadler's Wells and then less than a week later in Italian at Her Majesty's, when it failed in spite of being sung by Piccolomini; *Les Vêpres Siciliennes* in 1859 at Drury Lane, and *Ballo in Maschera* in 1861 at the Lyceum: none of these, however, converted the anti-Verdi-ites.

In 1863, however, Gounod took London—both the audience and the critics—by storm with *Faust*. It was produced in Italian at Her Majesty's on Thursday, June 11, with Titiens as Marguerite, Giuglini as Faust, Gassier as Mephistopheles and Santley as Valentine. The critics undoubtedly recognised it as a success, though they naturally pointed out some weaknesses. The *Morning Post* on June 12 first dealt with the prelude:—

> There are three kinds of instrumental preludes to an opera—the overture, which prepares the mind for what is to come by its general character and sug-

gestiveness, without anticipating any of the themes of the opera itself . . . then the overture which does borrow the melodies of the coming opera, and lastly the simple 'introduction' which, chiefly through Meyerbeer's influence, has grown much into fashion of late years, and the latter form of prelude is that adopted by M. Gounod in his *Faust*, and it is not the only point of resemblance between him and the famous composer of *Les Huguenots*, whose dramatic forms he has followed in the opera under notice with singular persistency and success.

The critic could not point to any piece of music in the work that was 'absolutely beautiful'—after all, Gounod was not as good as Spohr, whose *Faust* of 1816 had been produced in London in 1840, but the quartet and the end of the garden scene were good:

The 'Canzone del Re di Thule' is perhaps a little too sorrowful and meaninglessly odd in harmony . . . but still it is striking in itself, and likely to linger upon the memory of the most blasé musician.

All the second act was good, while the first act waltz and the Jewel song were likely to be popular. The serenade, soldiers' chorus, duel trio, death of Valentine and the end of the opera were also good. The whole production was excellent, apart from 'the make-up of some of the principal performers'—imagine a music critic of to-day having both the space and perhaps the inclination to bother about the make-up.

Firstly Faust should not be an old man, as Signor Giuglini represents him in the first act—

Goethe said that Faust was 'a man of middle age, not an image of tottering senility'.

We also object to the beard Signor Giuglini wears when he is transformed into a youthful cavalier. He would look much better without it, and it is unnecessary.

We also object to the coiffure of Madlle. Titiens: that long flaxen hair does not suit her face, and there is no necessity for her to wear it.

We would also remind M. Gassier that Mephistopheles ought to be habited like a travelling German student of the olden time, and not appear in the conventional costume of a stage devil. His red feather too should stand up straight upon his hat, which M. Gassier's did not, and Mephistopheles ought to be lame, which M. Gassier was not.

The *Sun* of the same date said that *Faust* was 'one of the most brilliant and decided triumphs which had ever been witnessed' in this country.

It grasps with the hand of a master all the outward life of the story—all the emotion and all the character that float upon the surface—but it scarcely reaches to the grandeur which is inseparable from such a theme.

Mephistopheles is its weakest conception—'He is drawn with all the lithe and supple traits of the *familiar* of a wizard, rather than the august and terrible complacency of the Prince of Evil himself.'

This critic also praised the same music that the *Morning Post* did, but also liked the Thule ballad, 'that in its plaintiveness and melody we have rarely heard surpassed'. The chorus of old men in the Kermesse scene was encored, and Gounod—under whose direction the production was wrongly rumoured to have been rehearsed—took a call after the Garden scene. The critic then had a word for Marguerite—'If the queenly dignity of Madlle. Titiens was scarcely adapted to the traits of the simple and confiding maiden, she rose to every other requisition of the character', and after the Church scene 'she reached a height of tragic excellence which belongs to her alone'. As for Mephistopheles, 'M. Gassier was a very able and expressive Mephistopheles—looked at from the composer's point of view': and finally, 'The house, we need not add, was crowded in every portion, and the one impression at the fall of the curtain was that an admirable work had been most perfectly presented.'

The *Observer* on June 14 was as enthusiastic:—

It is seldom that public opinion has so surely expressed itself, and in terms which leave so little room for suspicion or mistrust. The audience 'went' for the music from the first note to the last, and the future popularity of this opera can hardly be a matter of question.

After first considering Gounod's brilliant treatment of all the facets of the story the critic then dealt with the music:—

Gounod's forms of melody are various, and not at all times pleasing, but in his warm and felicitatious instrumentation, in which there is sufficient fullness without actual depth, or even any feature of remarkable originality, there is an obvious and abiding charm. . . . Nor is the art of strongly and emphatically individualising the personages of the drama absent.

He adds 'Salve, dimora!' to the musical excellencies: this, he says, 'may be pronounced, without wrong or dispute, the gem of the opera. There are few things in the realms of lyrical art which excel this in graceful feeling'. The Soldiers' Chorus,

though slightly vulgar, is too broadly cast, too decisive and exhilarating, too frank and jubilant, not to please mightily. . . . The serenade sung by Mephistopheles is dry in outline and unfriendly to sing.

340

Unlike the *Morning Post* this critic thought Titiens was ideal
and sang the part of Marguerite 'in a way that it will not be
M. Gounod's good fortune to have it sung at any other English
theatre'. (He was soon proved a bad prophet.)

It may be mentioned that she . . . looked—if distance did not lend a false enchantment to the view—as innocent and guileless in her long golden hair, as
poet or painter could imagine in their best dreams of the original.

(The parenthesis must have been back-handed politeness, for
Titiens was not the slightest of prima donnas.) As Valentine, Mr.
Santley 'gave a masterly exposition of whatever music fell to his
share'. In all the opera was a triumph: 'Its success was unmis-
takable—a success the more remarkable, as the miserable fate of
Sapho, by the same composer, is not yet forgotten by the habitués
of the Royal Italian Opera.'

In *The Times* on June 15 there appeared one of the more
pompous essays:—

A more striking example of the influence of music over the mind and intelligence of modern Europe could hardly be cited. Had the original piece
concocted by MM. Jules Barbier and Michel Carré been translated and brought
out in Germany as a mere drama, it would not have been tolerated. The spirit
of intellectual nationality would have cried out against it as a desecration.

But the muse now most courted in the land of beer and pipes and meta-
physics—the gentle Euterpe—was enlisted to excuse and sancify the sacrilege
by the aid of her melodiously persuasive tongue. A lyre was suspended to the
neck of the maimed Goethe, and, lo! he was metamorphosed into a wandering
minstrel, hobbling while he sang, but singing with such eloquence that his
compatriots were induced to overlook the defect in his gait for the flow and
smoothness of his numbers.

After making the Greek Sappho more or less an infliction, the *Médecin malgré
lui* of Molière a sombre lyric comedy ('un opéra malgré le médecin'), *Philémon
et Baucis* prolix shepherds, and Monk Lewis's too famous romance a dull
pasticcio,[2] M. Gounod conceived the happy idea of taking the French *Faust* as
the subject of an opera, and thus at a bound, from the most respectably un-
popular, to become the most respectably popular of actual French composers.

The writer admits that

it is unquestionably the opera of the last ten years which has found the greatest
number of admirers, not excepting even Signor Verdi's *Il Trovatore*, with
which however we feel no inclination to compare it. . . .

The conductor Arditi, *The Times* said, had supervised the rehearsals,
as Gounod had only arrived at the eleventh hour.

The introduction was 'too vague, and in its harmony too much after the manner of Wagner to please the lovers of unadulterated music'. The first scene and the Kermesse with the waltz were good, but the Jewel song was 'rather common, however catching, in itself, and quite out of keeping with the simple, uncoquettish character of Margaret'. The end of the Garden scene, when the fatal embrace is given and exchanged, was 'a piece of unmitigated Wagnerism', while the Serenade 'reduces the arch-fiend into a very melodramatic sort of imp—a "bottle imp" at the best. It is plain that M. Gounod has more sympathy with lovers than with devils'. Still, when all is said and done:—

On the whole *Faust* is a work which, if not remarkable for wealth of melodic invention, or for musical conception and contrivance of a very high order, is full of merit, never—or very rarely—dull, and carried through triumphantly.

Three weeks after *Faust's* première at Her Majesty's all the critics, professional and amateur, had to have second thoughts, because on July 2, 1863, *Faust* was produced at Covent Garden, also in Italian, but with Gounod's original Marguerite, Marie Miolan-Carvalho. The performance was not over till nearly one in the morning, but on July 4 the *Morning Post* wrote:—'Anything better "put upon the stage", to use the accepted form of speech, it were difficult to imagine.' The writer said that Covent Garden stuck closer to the composer's design 'than the director of the rival house thought proper to do', and Valentine's death now took its right place before the scene in the cathedral instead of after it, as was done at Her Majesty's—where the temptation scene took place outside the cathedral.

The *Observer* especially praised the scenery:—

Upon Marguerite's garden Mr. W. Beverley has expended extraordinary pains, and a more extensive and elaborate 'set' has seldom been seen. The stage is studded with beds, and the gravel walks that lead to the private gate, or lose themselves in the remote distance through vistas of overhanging trees, are little short of perfect, absolute reality.

Here too we have some charming incidental effects, depicting the approach of evening, and the soft blue light of the summer moon, in whose pale rays the guilty figures of Faust and Marguerite shine with silvery distinctness.

The change from the outside of the cathedral, when Valentine was killed, to the inside for the temptation scene was done by 'an intricate mechanical contrivance'.

This critic preferred the rival order of scenes and indeed the whole rival production:—

In other respects the performance shrinks in value when contrasted with that of Her Majesty's Theatre. Madame Miolan-Carvalho, notwithstanding the stress that is laid upon the fact that the composer had her especially in his eye when he wrote the opera, and that she embodied the part of the heroine for some three hundred nights at the Théâtre Lyrique, is not equivalent for Mlle. Titiens.

She looks the part, it is true . . . but her delivery of the music is thin and tremulous, and, though generally neat and dexterous, is but little animated by the passion and feeling which characterise her distinguished contemporary.

Tamberlik, he thought, was not such a good Faust as Giuglini, while M. Faure, as Mephistopheles,

sings with his accustomed elegance, but without the essential point and definition, or picturesque significance. As a dramatic portraiture it is inferior to that of Signor Gassier. Neither one nor the other, however, do much with the original idea, which, it would seem, must be left to the imagination rather than to the actor.

The Times was patriotic:—

The first performance may not have been altogether irreproachable, but if M. Gounod was unsatisfied with the second, he must either be difficult to please, or—like so many foreigners, not precisely 'Mendelssohns' or 'Spohrs'—unwilling to admit, what is nevertheless unquestionable fact, that the best English orchestras are also the best in Europe . . .

(far better, the writer said, than the scratchy strings and imperfectly tuned wind 'of that overlauded establishment, the Théâtre Lyrique'.)

The bright and penetrating tone of our fiddles, the rich sonority of our tenors and violoncellos, the weight and importance of our basses, to say nothing of the instruments of wood and brass and percussion, all in the hands of first-rate professors, must have proved a rare feast of sound for one whose heart and soul—as his dramatic music plainly shows—are rather in the orchestra than on the stage.

The Marguerite *The Times* found reticent and cold, while 'M. Faure's first costume—a suit of glaring crimson—is as diabolically unwarranted as can well be conceived'—an interesting comment for those of us who have come to believe the Devil is always in red, especially in *Faust*.[3]

The *Morning Post* had more to say two days after its first notice:—

343

Mme. Miolan, from the first moment that she comes upon the stage, seems to be oppressed with a painful foreboding of the dreadful fate that awaits her. Anything more sedate or solemn than her bearing it were difficult to imagine. She walks about more like a somnambulist than a consciously living being . . .

Her singing throughout (though her last act is most entitled to praise), excepting a tendency to rise above the pitch—unpleasantly evident on the first night—and a certain French thinness of tone, is exceedingly clever and artistic, and she looks the character to the life.

The *Sun* evidently preferred the Covent Garden production, to judge by its critic's opinion of Marguerite and Mephistopheles:—

The Margaret of Mdlle. Miolan, if somewhat wanting in the intensity proper to the remorse and grief of the last act, displays a most poetic sense of the opening of her passion in the second, where throughout the garden scene the singular delicacy with which Mdlle. Miolan makes the growth of an emotion that, in its entire faith in its object, never for a moment loses its purity, is a *chef d'œuvre* that cannot possibly be eulogised too highly.

M. Faure, also, in Mephistopheles has added another to the substantial list of his many admirable impersonations. The satanic irony with which he infuses it—especially in the serenade—is of itself a distinctive feature that is as faithful as it is effective.

This critic liked the music, 'which the public are already beginning to appreciate as among the most spirited, tender, and at times original, that has been heard in this country for many years'.

All the critics agreed that *Faust* was a success, but varied in their appreciation and differentiation of the two almost simultaneous productions. Luckily there exists a comparison of both made by Henry Morley at the time, and published by him in *The Journal of a London Playgoer from 1851 to 1866*. He was an LL.D., and Emeritus Professor of English Literature in University College, London, but these qualifications can add no authority to his opinions on plays and operas, which in themselves are authoritative and observant enough. His views on the two *Fausts* are so illuminating and so instructive that they are worth quoting here in their entirety for Gounod experts, musical historians and singers to study and enjoy. He is, I believe, only wrong on one point, that is when he states that Gounod approved of both versions: Gounod had no hand in the version played at Her Majesty's and was displeased that his name had been used in connection with that presentation. Here, then, is what Henry Morley wrote under the date July 11, 1863:—

The difference between the representations of M. Gounod's *Faust* at Her Majesty's Theatre and at Covent Garden is so great and so distinctly marked that I believe it to have been designed by the author (who assisted at the production in each case), with no small advantage to his own work, and no prejudice at all to either house.

There are two ways of reading Goethe's *Faust*: it may be read literally as the story of a village girl whose plain substantial love is stolen from her by unholy arts, who is betrayed and forsaken, yet in her hour of uttermost distress finds pity in heaven: or it may be read mystically as a soul's tragedy of the devil's war against the innocent.

At Her Majesty's Theatre we have the real, at Covent Garden the ideal side of the conception. But the ideal to a great extent includes the real, and is clearly the point of view from which especially the music was composed. Goethe's own sketches of Margaret present distinctly in ideal outline the image of a real and artless village girl. That is the Margaret of Mdlle. Titiens, who plunges substantially into an abyss of love, and with the help of Signor Giuglini brings out in the garden scene the whole material and sensuous charm of the music.

Madame Miolan-Carvalho, who has been taught by M. Gounod himself how he intends her part of Margaret to be played, and for whom its music was written, represents not so much the girl as the girl's soul. Even in the dressing of the part this is remembered. Until her fall she walks in virgin white, the idealisation of the character marked strongly by contrast of her dress with the gay peasant costumes of the other girls. Betrayed and forsaken, the white has been changed for grey. After the death of her brother, his last words laying his death at her door, she enters the cathedral with dress black as ink—no white, but in great sleeves like wings about the arms she lifts in prayer. In prison she wears grey again, with a white lining, and she ascends at last in pure white to the skies.

In her acting Madame Miolan-Carvalho represents first the still pure maiden spirit on the way to church when Faust first meets her. Afterwards, re-entering her garden, prayer-book in hand, and through a strain of sacred melody wondering who was the stranger that accosted her, she does not fling away Siebel's flowers, but drops them unconsciously as she submits with an innocent grace to the fascination of the devil's jewels.

When Faust and Mephistopheles arrive, at the first near approach of Mephistopheles to Margaret there is a sudden jar in the music, Margaret is fluttered and half faints, and there is an exclamation of defiant hatred from the disguised fiend: but that first shock of the contending principles underlies natural dialogue that accounts otherwise for the fiend's cry and for Margaret's faintness.

In the Haymarket reading of the piece the thought here intended is conveyed: but it seems rather a small detached effect than, as at Covent Garden, necessary to the harmony of the entire performance. In the more spiritual version Margaret under fascination does not seek Faust, hardly dares to look at him, delivers her love up wonderingly: and so throughout until the closing plaint of Margaret at her window, which she begins sitting, and during which she rises pressed with the magical longing to her full height in the window, Madame Miolan-Carvalho maintains to the last the sense that it is Mephistopheles, not Faust, who has achieved the cruel victory.

In Mephistopheles as represented by M. Faure, instead of M. Gassier's hunted Figaro, we have a malignant fiend, striken with deadly terror, quaking, shrinking, gnashing his teeth, when Mephistopheles is banned with the crosses on the sword-hilts of the students.

His mocking serenade at the door of forsaken Margaret is no longer the almost incomprehensible excrescence it appeared as given by M. Gassier in connection with the other reading of the opera. Here we have seen in the drama, and felt in the music, a conflict between a pure soul and a mocking fiend: and the serenade, as given by M. Faure, has mockery for its natural tone, but is the devil's cruel song of triumph in its motive.

A transposition of scenes in this act, as performed at the Haymarket Opera, seems to confirm the impression that M. Gounod meant to show separately at the London houses the two sides, spiritual and human, of his work.

In the Haymarket version the fiend's interference with the prayers of Margaret takes place with diminished emphasis outside the cathedral, and is followed by the killing of Valentine and his curse on his sister, which forms the climax of the act. This is transposed from the original arrangement and the effect of the change is to bring out with more emphasis the material incidents of the story, and to throw its allegorical sense more into the background.

At Covent Garden the original order is restored. The curse has fallen upon Margaret before the struggle in the church of the despairing soul with the demon who lurks to betray it, and that conflict forms in a great cathedral scene the climax of the act. Mephistopheles speaks to his victim from within a side-chapel, where, by a skilful arrangement of the lights and shadows, he stands like a spectre.

Again—to hurry at once to the end—the redemption of Margaret's soul is not represented slightly by a transparency, but dwelt upon in a substantial group that fitly crowns an opera remarkable even at this house for the luxurious completeness of its stage-appointments, and so brings the allegory to its right, emphatic end. But Faust is held to his bargain.

At the Haymarket, where he is chiefly shown as one of a pair of human lovers, he is, I believe, with M. Gounod's consent, saved.

And let me not forget to mention how finely in the rendering of Madame Miolan-Carvalho the soul of Margaret, strong in prayer and victorious over the tempter, at last strides forward and stands fearless breast to breast with its great enemy.

I hope that this comparison may show as clearly to others as it did to me what Gounod was really aiming at in *Faust* and prevent them dismissing so lightly, as I used to, the composer who, through his early ecclesiastical training and his realistic literary contemporaries, was, I believe, much more akin to Goethe than is apparent from a casually romantic glance at the score.

Six months after the Covent Garden production *Faust* was given again in London at Her Majesty's, but in English, and for this performance on Saturday, January 23, 1864, a new cavatina was, as the *Morning Post* said,

added by M. Gounod expressly for Mr. Santley, whose rare abilities—whether musical or histrionic—scarcely found full play in the character of Valentine as it originally stood. The chivalrous brother of Margarita had, indeed, but a single important scene, and that an ungrateful one, acted even with the masterly skill displayed by Mr. Santley in dealing with its gloomy, vindictive horrors, and the physical inconveniences inseparable from singing while stretched full-length upon the ground.

The new cavatina, 'E'en the bravest heart' was 'rapturously en-cored'. In this new production Sims Reeves was, in the opinion of *The Times*, a better Faust than either Giuglini or Tamberlik, while the long shake in the Jewel song

is for the first time as intended. Madame Carvalho could never execute it in tune, while the imposing voice of Mlle. Tietjens could never accommodate itself to its light and glib delivery but Mme. Sherrington does it to perfection.

In 1864 also Gounod's *Mireille* was given in London for the first time, and in 1865 Meyerbeer's *L'Africaine*. Two more operas by Verdi—*Forza del Destino* and *Don Carlos*—and Gounod's *Romeo and Juliet* were produced in London in 1867, and two more French operas—*Hamlet* and *Mignon*, both by Ambroise Thomas—appeared in 1870. But three weeks all but a day after *Mignon* the critics and the audience anticipated having their preconceived operatic prejudices excitingly jolted when the first performance in London of a Wagner opera was given.

[1] The year Covent Garden opened solely as an opera-house with Rossini's *Semiramide* with the all-star cast of Mario, Grisi, Persiani, Tamburini, Ronconi and Alboni with Costa conducting, having deserted Her Majesty's with the orchestra and the last four singers. See illustration, p. 282.

[2] *La Nonne Sanglante* (The Bleeding Nun), founded on the novel *The Monk*, never produced in England: *Médecin malgré lui* and *Philémon* had not been seen in England when the above was written.

[3] When I produced *Faust* at Sadler's Wells I had a vituperative unsigned letter saying that the writer was ashamed to have brought her young daughter to see a Mephistopheles who was not in scarlet with green spangles on his eyelids, which was "the traditional costume".

CHAPTER SIX

The Flying Dutchman to Carmen

THE FLYING DUTCHMAN was produced on Saturday, July 23, 1870. Incidentally it is interesting how many operas in the nineteenth century were produced for the first time in London on a Saturday, evidently to ensure as full a house as possible, just as in the old days up to about 1812 new opera productions had been tried out on the benefit night of a popular singer when again a good house might he expected. *The Flying Dutchman* was given in an Italian version by Salvatore Marchesi, both a singer and a teacher, whose wife later became so well known through her brilliant pupils of whom Melba was the last. In the cast were two English-speaking singers, Santley as the Dutchman and Signor Foli (the Irish Foley) as Daland, while three little-known Italians, Perotti, Rinaldini and Corsi played Erik, the Helmsman and Maria, and the Croatian pupil of Mme. Marchesi, Ilma di Murska, played Senta.

Monday's *Morning Post* liked most of the music, especially noticing that the

glorious duet for two basses, 'Patria, famiglia', in which two distinct melodies are supported by the accompaniment of a third, and the fine chorus with which the act concludes, created an amount of enthusiasm absolutely astonishing.

The critic also picked out the chorus

for female voices, with a sweet and characteristic melody and pleasing harmony in three parts, at the end of which there is a laugh in which all the women indulge, which is treated in a very novel fashion, a chromatic descending passage in chords of the sixth and third: it was wonderfully startling and expressive.

The 'perfectly novel duet between Senta and the Dutchman' was also remarked on, as was the surprising and regrettable omission of the ghost chorus.

The Times was glad that the *Holländer* of 1843 was the first Wagner opera to be heard in London instead of the *Tannhäuser* of 1845 because the later work was so much more difficult to assimilate:—

If we are to welcome such music and ultimately to adopt the Wagnerian doctrine of the 'Art-work of the Future', it is as well to begin from the beginning—with an opera, in short, composed when the Prophet was more like other men. We have always thought, moreover, that Herr Wagner's very best, because least extravagant, dramatic work was the *Holländer*, which, amid much that is incoherent and formless, contains some genuine music, and the promise of more to come. Every step since taken in advance of it seems to us a step in the wrong direction. . . .

Strange to say, considering the attraction one might suppose would attach to an opera by a composer who, in one way and another, has been the incessant talk of the musical world for more than thirty years, and scarcely any of whose dramatic music, occasional selections at concerts allowed for, is known in England, the house was not very full. In revenge, however, the audience was uproarious from first to last.

The overture which provides material for all the most important dramatic situations of the opera, was loudly encored, and no wonder, the execution being beyond reproach. Happily Herr Wagner allows few opportunities for encoring in the course of his work, and had Signor Arditi been satisfied with acknowledging the applause, instead of repeating the overture—perhaps the least coherent, certainly the noisiest piece of the whole—he would have acted more discreetly.

There was great applause all through, probably, *The Times* thought, because the audience 'found themselves in the presence of something quite new and strange, something for the greater part unlike anything whatever they had previously witnessed'.

After the second performance, which was also applauded, *The Times* reported that there was again a very poor attendance, 'which does not say much for the sincerity of those who have so long been crying out for an opera by Herr Wagner, and who keep away now that it is offered to them'. The critic said that it was obvious Wagner had been influenced all through by Weber:—

True he had not the gift of melody to anything like the extent possessed by Weber, but he had a much larger faculty of development; and perhaps a more remarkable instance could scarcely be cited than the *Holländer* of the power of making something—a great deal indeed—out of little or nothing.

Seeing how unsatisfactory the chorus-writing was, it was just as well the ghost chorus was cut, but Santley was superb, though the part was low for him:—

The difficulty of keeping the intonation true when at times the voice part and the accompaniment seem to be hardly in the same key can only be appreciated by musicians: and the way in which Mr. Santley manages this is worthy all praise.

He had also studied the part well from a dramatic point of view.

The Senta of Mdlle. di Murska is a veritable 'creation'. Highly as we have thought, from the beginning, of the histrionic genius of this lady, she has never before so triumphantly vindicated her right to stand foremost among the lyric artists of the day. . . .

A finer piece of acting than that of Mdlle. di Murska in the scene where the Dutchman is unexpectedly introduced to Senta by Daland, her father, and she beholds the vision of her dreams bodily realised before her, we cannot recall. . . .

Mdlle. di Murska has had many successes in London, but not one more legitimate or more unanimously recognised than this. Henceforward the romantic personage of Senta will be inseparably identified with her name.

The article ends by saying that

the production of the *Olandese Dannato*, late as it came in the season, has, in the opinion of all who care for serious art, done honour to an enterprise already distinguished by the introduction of Weber's *Abu Hassan* and Mozart's *Oca del Cairo*, by the revival of Rossini's *Otello*, and by the production in an Italian dress of the *Mignon* of M. Ambroise Thomas, next to M. Gounod's *Faust* the most generally popular of modern French operas.

The *Morning Post* was more enthusiastic:—

The music with which Wagner has described this story in his opera is of the most remarkable character: utterly unlike any operatic music familiar to the British public, and possessing none of the characteristics of an evanescent popularity, there are few melodies the average London publisher would care to disseminate, because the difficulty of the treatment places them far above the usual style of stuff which the ladies of the present generation have been led by the publishers to believe is taste-improving.

But as music, it is music for the thoughtful and educated musician, and for effect it would be only powerful upon a less favoured audience when presented in the style written by its author, and not through the medium of arrangements, which can after all only reflect weakly the power of thought in the composer. The instrumentation is wonderful, and so contrived that the interest of the performer in his respective part is almost as great as the pleasure derived by the hearer from the combination of the several instruments.

It was not so good on the stage as it ought to have been, but the production was

attended with as great a success as if it had been an inferior and music-seller's opera. Each artist engaged accomplished his and her several portions in the admirable manner—admirable for the reason that knowing, as every artist must know, the blind prejudice against any music not of the 'lum-ti-tum' school— the characteristic of which is the solo arpeggio accompaniment with two bars' start to impress the time, and a watery melody harmonised in thirds with a portion in sixths—knowing this prejudice, it is hard to find words sufficiently forcible to express the gratitude which every true artist must feel towards the singers for the very fine manner in which the difficulties of the music were mastered.

He then has a nice hit against the morals of the average opera or play:—

Not only is novelty in music a bar against its sudden reception, but purity of plot weighs against it. There is positively nothing in the words which sets before the public in an outwardly respectable form any of the sad and (except on the stage) nameless vices which undermine virtue and social happiness. It cannot be interesting, the fatigued novel-reader will say, but the audience gathered to hear it were of such a stamp as to undoubtedly pronounce it not only interesting, but elevating and edifying both morally and musically.

A warm reception by such an audience ought to have the greatest weight with the directors, for they were representatives of many shades of opinion: and that, however varied the feelings with which each member of the audience came prepared to listen, the result proved that the success of Wagner's *Flying Dutchman* was another blow to the unreasoning prejudice entertained against music which has hitherto denied a hearing, and which will in no distant day fill opera houses to the brim.

It is not surprising that the first Wagner opera in London was so calmly received: talk of the new music was by now rather stale, except for the initiates, and the fears of the more orthodox were not realised in the testing-time, just as the long-dreaded operation is less terrifying when it happens—besides Wagner's music had often been heard outside the opera-house. Not that everyone accepted it: *Punch* printed the following on August 6, 1870,

Gee Woe, Wagner!

(A Solo by Mr. Crusty, after hearing a Selection from the opera *Tannhäuser*)

> The music of the future, eh?
>> Well, some may think it pleasant!
> But when such trash again they play,
> I'll for the future hope I may
> Not be among the present!

Five years later, when *Lohengrin* was given for the first time in London at Covent Garden on May 8, 1875—also in Italian, and when at the Royalty Theatre Offenbach's *La Périchole* was being played with a last-minute stop-gap opera, *Trial by Jury*, the *Observer* harked back to the *Dutchman*, saying:—

There was nothing in it to shock the most rigid stickler for the 'ancient ways', nor did it in any way indicate a tendency towards those bold innovations which distinguish the later works of Wagner from his own earlier writings, as well as from the writings of Mozart, Beethoven, Weber, Rossini, Meyerbeer and other popular composers who have during the past century furnished music to the civilised world.

As for *Lohengrin*, the critic of the *Morning Post* especially praised the 'new and beautiful scenery, gorgeous costumes, glittering suits of armour, and a small army of supernumeraries'.

The music was roughly considered the same as before—the orchestra was predominant, while the voices had little to do but sing recitative against it, though the passages in which Elsa described her dream

contain much that is beautiful, and were admirably sung by Mlle. Albani, yet did not awaken applause.

The restless character of the music and the absence of 'full closes' render it difficult for amateurs to know when they may applaud, and they—probably from fear of interrupting the singer—failed to bestow the plaudits which she justly merited.

This was frequently the case during the progress of the opera, and the effect on the singers must have been somewhat disheartening, Indeed a more cold and apathetic audience has seldom been seen: yet their enthusiastic applause at the end of each act was unbounded, and dissatisfaction was only once expressed in the shape of opposition to an 'encore' injudiciously demanded in an early part of the evening.

Nicolini as Lohengrin also sang well, but there was no warm applause till the end of the 'finale' which concludes the act:—

In this the tempest of sound was formidable, and Mlle. Albani fought bravely to make herself heard above the din—so bravely indeed, that it is certain a persistence in such efforts must have an injurious effect on her delightful but delicate voice.

Up to this point the general feeling was that the splendour of the setting and the story were more successful than the music, nor did the second act change that view, though Mlle. d'Angeri and M. Maurel as Ortrud and Telramund interpreted their depressingly long and tedious scene—shortened as it was—admirably. The third act, however, compensated for the music of the first two with the introduction, which was encored, the Bridal Chorus and the scene between Elsa and Lohengrin which 'awakened universal delight':—

Nothing can surpass the tenderness and grace of the music in this portion of the opera, nor can any praise be too great for the manner in which it was rendered by Mlle. Albani and Signor Nicolini, who throughout the opera fully maintained their high reputations by the beauty and dramatic power of their singing and acting.

The Times reported that *Lohengrin* was 'heard with satisfaction':—

That it was thoroughly understood and appreciated it would be rash to assert: but that a deep impression was created upon a majority of one of the largest audiences ever assembled within the walls of Covent-garden Theatre, may fairly be stated.

The audience included the Prince and Princess of Wales.

This critic too praised the settings, especially the first scene, which was 'one blaze of splendour', with one mundane qualification:—

It is difficult indeed to think how Henry the Fowler, after long marches, could have brought his followers to Antwerp in such glittering and superb condition.

He even admitted that Wagner was poetical, 'even in his musical treatment of the subjects he appropriates':—

We may question the soundness of his theories, we have often questioned it, and see no reason, even while acknowledging the genuine beauties that save *Lohengrin* and *Tannhäuser* (whatever may be urged against *Tristan and Isolde* and the Trilogy, hovering in the distance) from the charge of unceasing monotony. But what cannot fail to enlist sympathy is earnestness which carries him with more or less artistic self-contentment through every task he sets himself.

After the second performance *The Times* became more enthusiastic, pointing out how the introduction gains in importance and poetical significance when played in the opera-house, and going so far as to say that

to listen without being deeply impressed by certain passages, as for instance the duet between Lohengrin and Elsa after the bridal ceremony, and again the final scene when the 'Knight of the Swan' takes eternal leave of his disconsolate bride, argues in our opinion insensibility to the highest beauty of which musical expression is capable.

In a later issue of the same paper the influence of Wagner on Gounod is stressed, as exemplified by *Roméo et Juliette* especially in the final scene—'M. Gounod should compose another *Mireille*: and thereby quiet the apprehension of his warmest admirers. Fancy a Gallic Wagner!'

Tannhäuser was given exactly a year later all but two days, on Saturday, May 6, 1876, also at Covent Garden with as sumptuous settings as *Lohengrin*, and also in Italian, with Albani as Elisabeth, Carpi as Tannhäuser and Maurel as Wolfram. The *Observer* said it was obviously the work of a master mind, though the Wagnerites regarded it as uninspired, but thought the music varied between the eccentrically original, the tedious and the noble. The 'well-known overture' was encored, Albani and Maurel were excellent, especially in the Hymn and the 'Star of Eve', and 'judging from its reception last night, *Tannhäuser* is likely to prove even a greater success than *Lohengrin*'.

The *Morning Post*, which also drew attention to the fact that the model of the new National Opera House to be built on the Embankment was on view in Drury Lane Theatre—it could not know that operas would never be played in the future Scotland Yard—found it dreary and dull on the whole.

The professed followers of the school to which it belongs were in the theatre in full force, and showed a determination to be pleased, whatever might happen, and however the thing was done.

But there was no relief in

melodies which appear and give promise of pleasure, only to be cut off suddenly and crushed out by curious instrumentation, like spring buds nipped by an early frost and trodden under foot:—this is the general character of the music, whether given to the voices or to the instruments.

Nevertheless there are some wonderful fine ideas, taken from the point on which Wagner would place his hearers. Never once did the music suggest anything either commonplace or impertinent: never once, though wearied of its tediousness, was the mind sensible of any loss of dignity in the expression. All that could be wished was that there could have been more life and spirit in the performance, and that the subject should have had a little more human interest.

Influenced by the music, it is a matter of perfect indifference why and wherefore Tannhäuser prefers to sing the praises of love as taught to him by Venus herself rather than utter enconiums upon the purity of the passion as experienced by him in his relations with Elizabeth.

Wolfram's sentiments on the same theme of love, although approved by the assembly, are very prosy: the Pilgrim's hymns, in which heavenly love forms the motive, become somewhat tiresome upon repetition: and, were it not for the beauty of the character of Elizabeth and the strong chain of sympathy excited in her behalf, it is doubtful what the effect of the work could possibly be.

(No doubt some of the blame lay with Carpi as Tannhäuser):—

The stage direction in the very first scene says that he is to be discovered kneeling, with his head bent towards Venus, in rapture. This he carried out by being asleep when the scene opened, and he did not appear to recover from his somnolence the whole evening.

Albani's Elisabeth was even better than her Elsa, but one blot on the production was having a sixteenth-century hall for thirteenth-century action. It was to be hoped some cuts might be made so that the performance need not be so long—the first night it was not over till nearly one o'clock in the morning: 'It is only the most patient or the most enthusiastic that can endure four hours of Wagner.'

The Times regretted that the performance had not started till nine o'clock, but said it was a real success, and though Elisabeth was less grateful vocally than Elsa and not so dramatic, she was a worthy companion to Senta and Elsa:—

These are Wagner's women *par excellence*—Elisabeth perhaps the brightest and best because the most human and womanly of the three. They cannot be separated too carefully from the half-crazy Isolde or the questionable ladies of the Nibelungen, whose ways are by no means their ways.

A month after *Tannhäuser* Verdi's five-year-old *Aida* was produced at Covent Garden on June 22, 1876, before a distinguished audience, including the Prince and Princess of Wales, and the Princes Albert Ernest, George Frederick and Victor, and the Duke of Connaught. In the opinion of *The Times*, 'To the Prince of Wales the music of *Aida* may have awakened some remembrances of one of the episodes of his tour in the East: at all events he appeared to take a real interest in the performance.'

By now the tide had turned in Verdi's favour. *The Times* alludes to *Aida* as a new and important work 'by a dramatic composer, who for some thirty years has been one of the chief entertainers of our opera-going public'. At the same time it denies that there is any change in his style—'As for a leaning towards Wagner, there is not a trace of it. . . . Verdi knows better than to dive into unfathomable waters. He is, happily, still the Verdi of our long remembrance, our own Verdi in short, and may he continue to remain so.'

Not that all the score is good:—

We prefer the 'Miserere' in *Il Trovatore* to all the solemn music in *Aida*. . . . That the finale of the Triumph scene is very imposing in its way must be cheerfully conceded, but it is rather imposing as a combination of strident effects than anything else. The ballet music is quaint enough, but does not exhibit Verdi conspicuously as a master of what is called 'local colouring'. It is evidently intended for music in the Egyptian style, but leaves what the Egyptian style may actually be undecided.

In conclusion, *Aida* is an opera projected on a grand scale, and containing much that is excellent even for Verdi, but not an opera which Verdi's sincerest admirers would like to chronicle as Verdi's last and best.

Patti as Aida was excellent in three great duets: nothing was more impassioned than 'her acting, declamation, and singing', but her 'well-known features, by the way, were at first scarcely recognisable under their new complexion'.

The *Standard* thought the libretto, 'like the majority of those selected by Signor Verdi, gloomy and unexciting': but there was, however, 'a constant flow of melody, much of which cannot fail to delight, and some of the *ensembles* are worked up to a degree which Signor Verdi has rarely before attained'. 'Celeste Aida' was a 'graceful romance, prettily accompanied, though with perhaps an unnecessary introduction of cornet'. (At this time in London the cornet was heard in opera oftener than the trumpet: Shaw was one of the first to point out its shortcomings a few years later.) In the rich and varied Triumph scene

an unmerciful predominance of brass drowns the more delicate instruments, which we should find were employed judiciously enough, if we could only trace them out in the din and clatter. The omission of some of the noisiest would leave the finale quite as effective and make it much more agreeable.

The critic comments that

Madame Patti, with her face stained to a dark tint, dressed in robes of red, blue and gold, had a singular appearance, and it was soon made evident that she had not adopted the external guise of the Ethiopian slave.

Her voice was at its best, as was shown by the richness of tone with which her C in alt rang out above chorus and orchestra in the first *finale*. Perhaps, however, the most excellent incident of her performance was her rendering of the duet in the third act, where she demands her lover to fly.

The third act was the best.

Punch painted a lovely picture of the first night on July 1 suitably headed 'At the Opera':—

House crammed and brilliant. Temperature, ninety in the draughts. . . . House at first about a quarter full—no habitué, except the real opera-amateurs in the gallery, liking to be considered as excited on any operatic subject whatever, and the non-habitués, coming in late in the hope of being taken for habitués, but lamentably failing in their attempts to look as if they knew where their stalls were, and soon reduced to ask the man at the door.

In a serious moment *Punch* says, 'The mise-en-scène throughout is as splendid as anything yet seen at Covent Garden', though a Blasé Friend tells an Enthusiastic Young Gentleman, 'it is nothing to what it was in Cairo'. At Patti's first appearance a Habitué (with opera-glasses) says, 'Why the doose has Patti made herself so hideous? She's more like a Red Indian than an Egyptian.' Then The Royal Party arrives 'with the children in sailor costumes.

The Prince in the character of the Royal Paterfamilias . . . H.R.H. nods to the music, and keeps time with his book.'
In the first interval

Timid people are trying to find out how to pronounce Aida. . . . Bold people are calling it 'Ida'. . . People who know all about everything are setting everybody right and giving opinions generally. People who want to talk about it afterwards and have no ideas of their own on the subject, are getting as near the known musical critics, or musical celebrities, as possible, and picking up opinions to be retailed with additions, subsequently, as their own original notions.

During the second act the following dialogue takes place:—

Habitué (*much distressed*). It really *is* a pity that Patti has made herself such a red-brick-dust fright.
Facetious Party No.1. Yes! look here! (*points to book*). See what Amneris is saying about her (*reads*)

'Amneris (*fixedly looking towards Aida, Aside*).
Yon deadly pallor—her bosom panting.'

She's panting hard enough, but I'll be hanged if she could show any deadly pallor, unless someone would kindly empty a flour-bag over her. However, her singing is admirable.

At the end of the scene

there is a great recall, when, instead of taking it all to herself, Patti goes off, and returns, leading on Mlle. Gindele, whose hand she warmly shakes. Tremendous enthusiasm, evoked by this graceful act.

After a magnificent procession and allusions to the Ethiopian Serenaders and Massa Bones,

Enter Signor Graziani *as* Amonasro, King of Ethiopia, *and looking blacker than Othello or the above-mentioned Massa Bones.*
Facetious Person No. 2. (*struck by the fact of his colour*). I say, he's supposed to be Aida's father. He's as black as my hat, and she's as red as a brick wall. I say, this won't do, you know. (*Appeals to his Friend, who can't account for it himself, but suggests writing to Darwin on the subject.*)

The finale was splendid: 'Brass everywhere, voices nowhere'. Then came Act III, which is, as a Habitué says, 'a gem' . . . 'Late finish, but people stop to the end, and the verdict generally is success.'

Exactly two years later to the day—Saturday, June 22, 1878— Bizet's three-year-old *Carmen* was produced at Her Majesty's: this, too, was given in Italian. Writing of the original story by Mérimée, the *Whitehall Review* said that out of such material it was not dificult to construct an operatic plot. The chief wonder is that Verdi did not get hold of it before Bizet. If he had, we should certainly have been richer by another opera with a distressing end to a career of questionable conduct in the chief characters.

The gipsy melodies, the writer said, that Bizet had introduced

impart a flavour, if it may be so termed, to the opera—a flavour of musical garlic so to speak, which gives a special piquancy to the whole, and yet does not destroy the characteristic quality of the other materials.

He ends by saying that

the music of *Carmen* is good, that Minnie Hauk is irrepressibly delicious as Carmen, and that therefore, two Carmens being in the way, the sooner we command our coachman to drive over and hear, the better.

In the same issue of the *Whitehall Review* (June 22, 1878) there is an interesting comment on *Pinafore*, which had opened less than a month before: I print it here so that those who are interested in musical jig-saws can sort out the allusions and decide whether the attack was justified or merely malicious:—

Dr. Sullivan has produced a work displaying his clever knack of concentrating fragments of popular tunes into one entertainment, making them sufficiently recognisable to save the pain of thought, and sufficiently unlike their prototypes to win for himself credit for able originality.

The like peculiar musical humour of tacking on to a decent hymn-tune cleverly scored for a band the refrain of the popular nigger song of one's youth, which was one of the causes of the success of *The Sorcerer*, will also serve to secure patronage for the *Pinafore*.

(There are many intentionally reminiscent operatic touches in the Gilbert and Sullivan operas: are there any that were unintentional? Or was it intended as a musical joke, for instance, that 'The sun whose rays are all ablaze' in the *Mikado* recalled in no uncertain terms both the words and music of the Shepherd's dawn-song from Gounod's popular *Mireille*?)

On the day of the first performance the *Morning Post* announced that *Carmen* would begin at 8.15 precisely instead of at 8.30, which was the usual time of performance, and the day after printed a most glowing account, first praising the music for being full of character and originality:—

Of course here and there may be traced a passing likeness to some musical forms already known as having been first drawn by Gounod or Meyerbeer, but the resemblance is transient, and no more interferes with the claim to originality than the similarity of appearance among men destroys their claim to individuality. It is no small honour to the composer to find that he has not written a single weak bar in the whole of the music. From the joyous commencement in the prelude, the toreador melody, to the final note, all is pointed, poetical, and intensely dramatic.

Minnie Hauk's characterisation of Carmen the writer thought was

one of the most remarkable things seen upon the stage within the present decade. It is perhaps almost the first operatic character with any marked or especial individuality, and no one but an actress of particular genius could have created or sustained the part.

Campanini as José 'sang earnestly and with passion, and acted with more dramatic fire than it is his wont to exhibit before an English audience'.

Everything was excellent:—

Rarely has an opera been so well or so perfectly mounted or rehearsed with such care as to secure an almost faultless representation on the first night: rarely has such brilliant and dashing music been presented to an admiring audience from an unexpected source: and still more rarely has it been the good fortune of opera patrons to be delighted with the exhibition of such piquant and fascinating histrionic talent as shown by Mdlle. Minnie Hauk in the part of Carmen.

The *Observer* praised the skill of construction in the work:—

Although Carmen is an even less respectable personage than the heroine of *La Traviata*, the plot of the opera is not openly offensive. . . .

In the dramatic development of the plot room has been found for a number of effective incidents and situations, and the choruses are introduced in the most natural manner.

It is on Carmen herself that the weight of the opera falls. José, although he has plenty to sing, is a silly dupe, in whom little interest is felt: Escamillo is a conceited and brainless animal, and almost all the other personages are disreputable, except Micaela, of whom little is seen.

The heroine commands no respect and little sympathy, but the character has been so skilfully drawn, and the wilfulness of the gay coquette is so piquantly painted, that the spectator is too much fascinated to inquire whether he is justified in giving her his smiles and his applause.

The vocal music is difficult and

abounds in difficult intervals and changes of key, rendering the task of the singer more than usually onerous.

M. Bizet does not, however, wander from key to key—like some modern composers—in search of ideas, but because he has an abundance of ideas, and finds a certain mode of developing them congenial to his musical sense.

In listing the most successful numbers, however, the writer has to mention quite a dozen.

The Times was doubtful whether the original story was worth adapting, for though the librettists had done their best, there still was only one strikingly conspicuous character, the others being little better than abstractions—Don José was not greatly to be pitied, nor was there much of value in Escamillo,

of whom, though his only recommendation—so far as we can understand, is that, having vanquished bulls in the arena, he is proportionately muscular, our heroine has become passionately enamoured.

The music was full of local colour,

beginning with the first and not least charming—the 'Havanaise' ('Avanera') 'L'Amour est un oiseau rebelle' ('Amor misterioso' in the Italian version), borrowed, if we remember well, from Yradier's *Album des Chansons Espagnoles*, to which the composer has added orchestral accompaniments not less original than refined.

Minnie Hauk had wisely modelled her performance on that of the original—Galli-Marié (though Bizet had planned the part for the more sensitive singer Maric Roze,[1] who later toured England with the Carl Rosa Company and played both Carmen and Manon with great success—an interesting and more subtle reading of the character which might prove to be more exciting with bursts of unexpected and no longer controllable tempers than the more usual unchanging spitfire—after all, nobody willingly makes a pet of a snarling man-eating tigress, but it is very easy to think the animal lazily stretching in the sun to be merely a beautifully marked kitten—until the claws are bared).

The theatrical paper *The Touchstone, or the New Era* on June 29 saw some faults, but made a sure prophecy:—

Mdlle. Hauk left something to be desired in her singing, but, as an actress, fairly surpassed herself by her remarkable impersonation of the wayward and half-savage heroine. . . . The singing of Sgnr. Campanini was marred by a too throaty production of tone, but in his acting he displayed great spirit and intensity. In a short time, when the imperfections in the concerted music shall have been corrected, we have no doubt that *Carmen* will become a welcome addition to the great works of the lyric stage.

[1] Sutherland Edwards, *The Prima Donna*.

CHAPTER SEVEN

The Ring, Meistersinger, Tristan

ON May 5, 1882, *The Times* printed an interesting announcement:—

Richard Wagner's *Der Ring des Nibelungen*, a Festival Play for Four Nights. *First Cycle*, 5th, 6th, 8th, 9th May, 1882. *Director*, Mr. *Angelo Newmann*, who has been intrusted by Herr Richard Wagner with the sole right of its performance, and under whose management the brilliant renderings of this unique work were lately given at Berlin and other German cities with extraordinary success.

The conductor was to be 'Mr. *Anton Seidl* (according to Richard Wagner's own opinion, the best interpreter of his works)', with the orchestra of the Richard Wagner Theatre.

The performances took place at Her Majesty's (while Richter was at Drury Lane with a German opera season). The next morning, and for some days after, the professional critics had much to write about, though none were so adverse as the *Standard* which said that, though the greatness of the *Ring* had to be cordially admitted, it was 'a monument of industry and power—misdirected'. The article then went on to say that to listen to it would be 'a most fatiguing exercise', because of the

total absence of human interest, the gross contradictions and inconsistencies, the trivialities of the plot—to say nothing of its repulsive incidents—the introduction of childish dragons, bears, alligators, horses, real and pasteboard.

It also complains that the orchestra was not, as advertised, the same as at Bayreuth, and that it played in full view of the audience, not only with the desk-lamps showing, but with the chandeliers of the theatre turned on as well.

The scenery and dresses of *Rheingold*, the *Morning Post* said, were the same as had been used for the first Bayreuth production in 1876 and had been lent by the King of Bavaria. *The Times*, while admitting that the Rhinemaidens went about

singing their merry songs to a melody as sweet and wavey as the ripples of the transparent element in which they move, came back to its old attack on Wagner's vocal line:—

Singing Wagner's music is not easy at any time: but to sing it while suspended in elaborate bandages and literally floating through the air is to be handicapped somewhat severely.

The whole was not as good as at Bayreuth six years before, but Vogl was excellent as Loge (his original part), both as actor and singer (he was spontaneously applauded for his tale of 'Weiber, Wonne and Werth'),

and his admirable realisation of Loge's wilful and wayward nature is enhanced by a style of declamation and phrasing little short of perfect.

Scaria, the original Wotan, was dignified, but his sonorous voice was past its prime, Reicher-Kindermann, who had played Grim-gerde in the first Bayreuth cycle, was good as Fricka, while Scheper and Schlosser as Alberich and Mime were as fine as Vogl.

The least satisfactory feature of the performance was the orchestra, which, as regards beauty of tone and purity of intonation, was certainly not equal to the standard of our English players. The inferior quality of the instruments used accounts partly for this deficiency. On the other hand, the discretion with which the accompaniments were played was worthy of unqualified praise.

It was a triumphant success, the Prince of Wales with the Duke of Edinburgh (who used to play violin obbligatos for Christine Nilsson and Albani at public concerts) watching with 'unflagging interest. That interest will no doubt be even stronger tonight at the performance of the *Valkyrie*, when, instead of gods and giants, human beings will occupy the scene.'

The audience for *Die Walküre* was even more enthusiastic, said *The Times*, once bursting into spontaneous applause for Niemann in his original part of Siegmund. Although he was a 'born actor of genius', *The Times* critic said that he lacked

the finish of the Italian school, and his voice at no time was remarkable for sonorous beauty. But this intensity and truth of expression make up for want of physical charm, and that loveliest of Wagner's musical lyrics, 'Winterstürme wichen', was, if not perfectly sung, at least beautifully declaimed.

The love-duet with Mme. Sachse-Hofmeister as Sieglinde ('womanly grace and tenderness') was enthusiastically received. The Ride of the Valkyrie, which had often been heard in concerts, was most impressive on the stage. Mme. Vogl as 'Brynhild' was 'less heroic of stature and bearing' than Mme. Materna of Bayreuth, but sang with great spirit and artistic dignity. The orchestra was better than on the first night.

The *Morning Post*, which admired the scenery although there was gauze and not steam as in *Rheingold*, agreed that the orchestral ensemble was good, though the string tone was not equal to that of English players, but complained of the long waits between the acts before the 'customary fanfare instead of bell' called the audience back: but it said of the scene between Siegmund and his sister Sieglinde—'On the peculiarity of the construction of this scene it is undesirable here to make any comment'.

The *Standard* went further than that:—

The loathsome subject upon which the whole of *Die Walküre* is based altogether places it beyond the pale of human sympathy. . . . When the poem is full of the most revolting incidents, which are reiterated again and again, and dwelt on persistently by all the personages of the drama, what must be the effect of the music upon the hearer?

It ought never to have been licensed: admittedly the music is effective and ingenious, 'but the hateful nature of the story remains as an ineradicable and disgraceful blot'.[1]

The *Standard*—like many others since then—regretted the interminable scene between Wotan and Fricka, at the end of which Fricka, 'to the general relief, mounts her car and drives the rams over the bridge—that is to say, is pulled away, for the rams are all too plainly of the toy-shop breed'. Brünnhilde then argues with Siegmund,

while Sieglinde, who has come with her lover, but for whom there is no part in the dialogue, sits down and goes to sleep—a process in which she would in all likelihood have been anticipated by many of the audience, had they not been kept awake by the orchestra.

The fight with Hunding, which *The Times* had praised, was, said the *Standard*, 'probably the feeblest combat ever witnessed on the stage', while later 'in an orchestral storm of the most violent character Wotan vanishes, and so blessed peace falls upon the troubled theatre'. Incidentally, in the famous Ride of the Death-maidens 'little wooden hobby-horses are dragged across the back of the stage', while the first half of the last act is all 'blare and clatter. Put in plain words, at times the din is hideous'.

The morning of *Siegfried* Londoners read with horror of the Phoenix Park murders, but there was still room for full operatic notices: so the next day, after noting that Queen Victoria had sent congratulations to the Prince and Princess William of Prussia for the birth of Her Majesty's eldest great-grandson—later 'Little Willie', *The Times* published a full report on *Siegfried*.

It began by saying that the *Ring* was like a symphony:—

The *Rheingold* stands for the opening *allegro*, full of life and expectancy: the *Valkyrie*, with its sad story of love and death, is the mournful *adagio*: *Siegfried* represents the impetuous *scherzo*, and the *Dusk of the Gods* is the grand finale, showing the end of the old world and the dawning of a new.

To appreciate *Siegfried*, the *Times* said the audience had to become young again and 'accept in good faith the fancies and stories which charmed their childhood'. If they did not, they would

see little difference between the dragon, whose huge form is seen wriggling on the stage, and who sings through a speaking trumpet, and the fantastic creatures which every pantomime season brings forth.

Probably in ancient Greece they would have been

equally amused by Io appearing on the stage in the shape of a cow tortured by a gadfly, or if in Germany before Goethe was accepted among the classics, by the animals in the witch's kitchen in *Faust*.

Vogl was excellent as Siegfried, especially in the wander song and the sword song, which impressed the audience with the fresh charm of their melodies. The Waldweben or 'mysterious whirr of the forest', which at Bayreuth was one of the most charming features, was not well played in London, and though Wiegand 'roared right well' as the dragon, the death scene 'lost nothing by a strong touch of the grotesque which called forth a smile on many faces'.

The *Standard*, after stressing the point that its critiques were not set down in malice, but were written 'lest the immortal principles of music should be for a time obscured and abused by the pursuit of untenable theories', said that 'nothing that Herr Wagner has ever written for orchestra surpasses the sustained beauty of the forest music in the second act'. At the same time—

It must continue a matter of lasting amazement that the composer of this scene, the musician who could pour forth strains so purely melodious, should have wasted years in setting to music interminable themes so utterly unsuited to musical treatment.

The Erda scene was tedious, but the love-duet began beautifully, though when

the lovers grow rapturous, they grow noisy, and in portions of the duet the
chief idea conveyed is that the orchestra is striving to drown the singers' voices,
and that they will not permit anything of the sort.

At Bayreuth the orchestra was sunk, but in London 'the audience
is not thus protected, and the din which Herr Seidl encourages is
at times simply dreadful'.

The *Standard* is even more grandiloquently depressing on the
subject of *Götterdämmerung*, which, it says, 'has broken the faith
of many a Wagnerite':—

Gloom pervades it: only glimmerings of music, fitful and far between, sound
through the noise and monotony. The blare of brass is incessant, the drums
rattle and crash, and the cymbals add to the clatter. Herr Wagner is heard at
his wildest—and this terrible division of the Trilogy lasts for five weary hours.

The chorus of the Gibichungen 'proves beyond question that
there is something more intolerably unpleasant than even Wotan',
while

out of some five-and-forty personages which are seen in the course of the *Ring
des Nibelungen* one-and-forty perish in a more or less miserable, but rarely in an
unwelcome, manner, before the pleasurable moment is reached when the
curtain finally descends.

In London the Waltraute scene was omitted—luckily, said the
Standard critic—and at last came the scene where Brünnhilde
mounts horse and leaps into the flames:—

that is, she would have done so, but as a mere matter of fact she leads the horse
quietly from the stage, no doubt to the great relief of the animal, for the dreadful blare of the brass in front, the wild screaming of Brünnhilde . . . and the
blaze of the fire behind have naturally alarmed him.

The scenic ending is very feeble. A figure representing Brünnhilde is dragged
on a large wooden horse behind the funeral pile, and the curtain is finally drawn
after much red fire has been burnt. Once more the brass does its worst, and all
is over.

For a last word the *Standard* said: 'There are to be three more
cycles. The first seems to have made but little impression.'
    The Times gave the lie to this:—

Whatever the result of these performances for the position of Wagner's art
in this country may be, it is vain to deny that they have attracted public attention to a degree almost unprecedented.

This critic found *Götterdämmerung* more varied and dramatic than the rest, especially as Siegfried

is now a human being, full of the tenderness of love which breathes in the melody of his song. Note especially the beautiful effect of the 'turn', which conventional Italian embellishment seems to gain new significance in Wagner's melos.

The great triumph of the *Ring* was that of the Vogls:—

To Herr and Madame Vogl unqualified approbation is due for a characterisation of their respective parts which has seldom been equalled on the London stage. Not only had they mastered the difficulties of Wagner's music, but, what is more, they had realised the master's intentions in their fullness. No detail of dramatic *nuance* was neglected, no musical accent misplaced, and yet the entire conception, both of Siegfried and Brünnhilde, was marked by a breadth of purpose and a grandeur of style for which no praise can be too high.

The Times thought it impossible to overrate the importance of the performances for the development of dramatic music in this country:—

There were defects of detail, but the entire rendering was instinct with a spirit of artistic earnestness too rarely found on the operatic stage. There was here no striving for cheap effect, no shouting of high notes at the audience, no undue self-assertion on the part of the prominent singers. Everyone was intent only upon doing justice to the requirements of his part, and the result was a high standard of excellence sustained throughout.

At the end of the final performance of the cycle—

Herr Newmann was summoned to the Royal Box, where the Prince and Princess of Wales and other members of the Royal Family congratulated him on the success of the performance. The Prince of Wales remarked that he had seldom followed a work from beginning to end with such uninterrupted interest, and charged Herr Newmann with the expression of his satisfaction to the artists, and to Wagner, whose composition, his Royal Highness added, he had admired from his childhood.

Punch, however, came out on May 27 with some uncompromising and not unreasonable 'Wagner Waggeries', as the criticism was headed:—

Of course it is utterly bad taste to declare that we would far rather hear *The Flying Dutchman* or *Lohengrin* than the whole of the *Ring des Nibelungen*. After four nights of the *Ring*, with the *Ring* of it still in our ears—which makes us look and feel quite savage,—we deliberately say 'Never again with you, Wotan, Siegfried, and Co!'

It appears to our untutored and uncultivated taste that the *Ring*, taken as an 'all round' work, is just what might be expected from an impulsive musician after seeing a melodrama and a pantomine for the first time, and struck by the happy thought of combining the effects and setting them to music.

It is pointed out that the use of motives is not original: they occur in pantomime or ballet, for instance the Giant-motive in *Jack the Giant-Killer*.—'Nay, in a pantomine there is a recurring Motive, we fancy, for a policeman, and invariably a rum-tum-tum-tum-tiddly-iddly-iddly-iddly Motive for the entrance of Clown' (this, of course, was in the days of the Harlequinade) while in melodrama

the repetition in Act III of a strain that first occurs in Act I is so invariably recognised as a connecting link for a train of thought that on hearing it the spectator can positively say 'Here she is again!' or 'She's thinking of the parting with her lover in Act I.'

The Ring could easily have been given in three or four acts; anyway the vocal score was cut in performance: luckily the audience brightened up at anything like a tune or action and was always able to have a 'laugh at the Dragon's expense'.

After *The Ring* the production of *Meistersinger* at Drury Lane on May 30, 1882, came as a relaxation to the critics—even the *Standard*, which said that 'those who came to be pleased went away abundantly satisfied, and that those who came prepared to sneer, remained to approve and applaud'. It is true that this critic wondered, after the *Meistersinger*,

whether Wagner's innovations were worthy of the praise bestowed upon them, or whether the undeserved ridicule passed upon the pedantic school of German vocal music was fit to be considered as a representative phase of German humour.

but he did point out that *Meistersinger* was not to be taken for a Wagnerian opera in the usual sense:—

It is simply to be accepted as a genial and attractive piece of lyric workmanship. While freeing himself from the influence of hobgoblins, hippopotami, demons and spirits, Wagner had shown how possible it is to a man of his temperament to enter into an unassuming historic fable.

It would soon 'become the rage in operatic circles. There are but very few dull moments, and against them must be cited a veritable stream of melody—vocal and instrumental'. The final *volte-face* of this paper was: 'After the bombastic doctrines which have been associated with the name of Wagner, it is satisfactory to find an example of his work which will survive and endure tall talking.'

Nor was the *Standard* the only convert. On June 10 *Punch* wrote:—

As for the *Meistersinger*, the shock of hearing it for the first time is too much to make criticism possible till the listener has pulled himself together. *There are tunes in it.* THERE IS A WALTZ!! Hooray for Wagner Waltzing! 'His First Waltz,' companion to 'Weber's Last', which sounds as if Weber were a Shoemaker. Shall hear the *Meistersinger* again, as will many others.

A fortnight later *Punch* reported that this opera was the un-doubted success of the German opera season—'Here Richard is himself again': the objectionable gloomy *Ring* had been full of the lowest motives in every sense of the word, but the *Meistersinger*

is charming throughout. A simple and sufficiently interesting story illustrated by thoughtful, mirthful and delightful melody, which is never wearisome from first to last—and it is a long opera.

The Quintet would have been encored had Richter permitted, and there was only one blot—'The stage-management is weak', but the acting was excellent, especially Gura as Sachs: in fact 'No one fond of melodious opera, and no unbeliever in Wagner, should miss seeing his *Meistersinger*'.

Four days before this article, however, on June 20, 1882, *Tristan und Isolde* was given at Drury Lane, and then both *Punch* and the *Standard* had a chance once more to hit at vice and noise. According to *Punch*, this opera was 'the most wearisome thing we've sat out for some considerable time'—far rather 'a long, dull sermon in a stuffy church on an August afternoon' than one act of *Tristan*:—

taken as a whole, it is the embodiment of stupendous boredom, must be the verdict of all English Opera-goers who delight in the operas of Rossini, Mozart, Meyerbeer, Gounod, Verdi, Balfe, Wallace, Bizet and, we are not afraid to add, even in these days of aesthetic mysticism, art-vagueness, and higher cultchaw—Bellini.

At the opening the Knights and Attendants were like motion-less waxworks, till on showing any sign of singing a tune they were curtained off by the confidante, and after the strange pair had drunk the love-potion the stage-directions demand that they should behave in the most transpontine melodramatic fashion—(this can be checked by a glance at the score)—and at last they are locked in each other's arms, and this situation would be satisfactory if they had only one key between them, but as it seemed to our distracted ear, the lady shrieked spasmodically, while the gentleman growled, occasionally varying it with a shout. . . . This sort of music can never, in our lifetime, at least, thank goodness, become popular with the British public.

Wagner, said *Punch*, needs no vocalists, but only an orchestra, plot-books for the audience and tableaux vivants, because 'illustration is still necessary for the illiterate'; anyway 'singing and acting are thrown away on such vocal music and such tedious and unsavoury libretti'. Finally,

we don't mind hearing occasionally *The Flying Dutchman*, *The Meistersinger* (abbreviated) and selections from *Tannhäuser* and *Lohengrin*. Richard Wagner's operas will be remembered when the *Barbiere* and a few more trifles are forgotten, but not till then.

The *Standard* wrote that parts of the *Meistersinger*—for example, the apprentices—had been as 'sparkling and buoyant as if they had proceeded from the pen of Auber or Adolphe Adam', but not so *Tristan*, which, like the *Ring*, might have been better as a play. *Tristan* was certainly not moral—'The second act leaves a little—but not much—to the imagination.'

Taking it as a whole,

To those persons who were not previously saturated with the spirit of the Wagnerian lyric-drama last night's performance no doubt came as a revelation of all that is tawdry, artificial, and unnatural in art, while to the disciples of the master it appealed with the force of a revelation of the highest conceivable beauty.

There assuredly is some power in the elaborate love-duet in the second act, and the closing scene is not devoid of pathos: but against these isolated points of merit must be cited interminable quantities of tiresome declamation, and an insufferable amount of noise, turbulence, and striving after effect.

Richter conducted and the reception of the work 'was in every respect favourable'.

The *Morning Post* of June 21, which also had a leading article on the fact that the two-year-old Royal Victoria Coffee Hall was 'too improving' to be a success, though supported by Cardinal Manning, but that it would carry on (as it did, to turn into the Old Vic), said much the same as the *Standard* in other terms:—

Those who can appreciate Wagner's theories enjoyed a great treat. To others it was, perhaps, somewhat of a trial to have to sit out a long business under the impression that it was a musical entertainment, and to find so little that might be matched with previous experiences of the sort.

Those who were content to waive all consideration of the music and to enjoy the acting alone, and to submit to the influences which the orchestral sound produced upon the mind, were fascinated beyond expression.

Isolde's end, as played by Sucher, was such that 'few in the theatre could witness unmoved'.

The Times, which admired the great acting but found the music exacting for the singers, noted that *Tristan* completed all the Wagner works in the season at Drury Lane, 'a feat, by the way, which, we believe, is unprecedented even in Germany', its final comment on this latest production being:—

Whether a drama treating of unrelieved tragic passion in a style of commensurate severity will ever gain the popularity of such works as *Lohengrin* or *Die Meistersinger* must appear doubtful: but the value of a work of art cannot be measured by the degree of popular favour it is likely to find.

That last sentence is no doubt literally true, but I take leave to doubt if it is true in the sense meant by the writer: he is writing of operas—that is, musical works intended to be performed in a theatre, and though a painting or a poem can be valued according to the judgment of expert individuals, stage-works in the last result can only be judged by an audience—a crowd, in fact, which may or may not contain experts, but which certainly is in the theatre, hoping to be swayed, not by art, but by emotion of some kind, into tears, laughter or excitement. I do not say that a play or opera is good only *if* it is popular, though I believe that taken over the years this will be found to be true—*Hamlet* has lasted not because of its poetry (which may help to make it artistic but which the groundlings may not appreciate), but because of its exciting story (which makes it alive) and *Charley's Aunt* is certainly good of its kind. I only say that no play or opera can be of real value—however artistic—*unless* it appeals to audiences—which is one of the chief intentions of its author. It must in fact live by the invisible contact between stage and auditorium, not die between the covers of a book. If, as well as appealing to audiences, it is also well written, it will be all the better, as there will always be new beauties to be found in it: but there is a grave danger here—Mozart was such a brilliant musician by nature that we are inclined to forget that he intended to write and succeeded in writing intriguing entertainments. After all, he was glad when his tunes were whistled, and the whistler—who helped to make those tunes last—was never interested in the musical form of the tunes. Mozart could no more help writing in good style and with good technique, than the academic musician can be expected to stop noticing and admiring such skill, which is, after all, both his job and his pleasure, but no theatre can ever be filled solely by academic musicians—except at a Conference of Music Practitioners—and how often is a Conference carried away by enthusiasm?

[1] Many years ago when a German student maintained that true German opera was never as unmoral as Krenek's *Jonny Spielt Auf*, which was then notoriously popular, I queried the story of *Walküre*: the reply from the patriotic young enthusiast was 'Oh, I had not thought of that'.

CHAPTER EIGHT

Otello to Butterfly

During the six years that followed the great Wagner year of 1882 the only outstanding operas that were given their first London production were Ponchielli's *La Gioconda*, Delibes's *Lakmé*, Massenet's *Manon* and Bizet's *Pearl Fishers*. Then in 1889 Verdi's *Otello* was given at the Lyceum on July 5. By now he was accepted, so the critics had little to do but to assess the position of the work among Verdi's other operas and give opinions on the performance.

The *Morning Post* said:—

Without going to the length of admitting its superiority to the many other works Verdi has produced, the skill and genius of the composer in *Otello* may certainly be conceded. It is without question a most remarkable production, even if it does not possess those qualities which secure popularity.

Especially picked out for praise was Maurel as Iago, whose 'finely written solo', the Credo, was 'magnificently sung', and whose acting too 'may compare most favourably with some of the best representatives of the part on the dramatic stage'.

The *Standard* also praised Maurel 'with his striking intelligence', as well as Tamagno 'with his phenomenal voice' as Othello, while as Desdemona, 'if not an ideal Desdemona either in voice or appearance, Signorina Cataneo is, at any rate, superior to the artist who created the role'. The Kiss duet was fine, the deputation to Otello and Desdemona 'the prettiest episode in the opera', the Iago–Otello duet 'one of Verdi's finest inspirations and we could dwell on it with delight', the end of the third act was 'one of the most imposing ensembles ever written', while 'no composer has ever penned a more pitiful strain than that of the "Willow song"'. In fact it was 'a noble opera'.

Punch said the theatre was too small,

as Signor Tamagno's powerful voice would have filled one twice the size, and the orchestra was, in the opinion of those close to it, literally 'stunning'. *Otello* is the effect of Verdi con Verdid to Wagnerism.

There was not much tune, but good dramatic accompaniment and 'M. Maurel's acting generally excellent, though too much in it of the twopence coloured melodramatic style'. A great reception.

The Times, which, however, thought that only a few melodies were striking and that the Farewell was 'one of the few pages in the score which remind the hearer that he is listening to Verdi's music' (the *Morning Post* had found the second act Wagnerian), placed *Otello* as far above *Aida*, as *Aida* above *Traviata*.

For some time now the feeling had been growing that ingenious compositions full of interwoven themes and kaleidoscopic modulations had been rather too prominent in late years, and that there was a danger that simple melody as such had been swamped. So there was great relief when, on October 19, 1891, Mascagni's *Cavalleria Rusticana* was produced at the Shaftesbury Theatre on the opening night of a season run by Signor Lago, which was to include *The Secret Marriage*, *The Flying Dutchman*, *Cenerentola*, *Ernani*, etc.

As the *Telegraph* said, Mascagni might well prove to be the successor of old Verdi, idle Boito and dead Ponchielli: this new opera had a good book, a strong story and all the unities: 'As to the music, there is no very strong evidence that Mascagni possesses an original genius. But neither was there such evidence in the early works of Wagner'. He certainly was imitative, but while he 'says little particularly new, he delivers his message well'. He certainly knew how to write for effect and with melody, and in this probably lay the secret of his success.

Weary of musical mosaics, of constructive mazes through which the ordinary man needs a guide, the world, we cannot but think, is hungering for a great melodist, who shall wield the mightiest weapon of his art with the skill of a master and play upon the feelings by its most direct appeal.

In *Cavalleria Rusticana* the themes were excellent, the rhythms good and the harmonies modern. The cast was not outstanding, except for Francesco Vignas as Turiddu—'where has this gentleman been hiding from the sharp eyes of English managers?': Musiani's voice was 'neither strong nor steady', but her acting

sets the wronged Santuzza before us to the life. It is vigorous and picturesque, but quite natural, while her singing has moments of passion, in which one forgets defects of voice and is sensible only of admiration.

(How often in the nineteenth century the acting is regarded as of importance, even making up for lack of vocal technique, as here!)

The Times said that *Cavalleria* was 'a masterpiece of concentration—the quality which, of all others, is most essential in modern works, and no doubt that which has contributed chiefly to the wonderful success of the opera'. After all this was, the writer said, an age of short stories by Kipling and others.

The Intermezzo was encored and 'would have pleased more if the orchestra had been in perfect tune with the apology for an organ behind the scenes'. The Serenade also was encored, and by this means, 'and by the appearance of the singer before the curtain, the symmetry and illusion of the piece were, of course, destroyed'. Musiani was perfect as Santuzza, except for an 'almost perpetual tremolo', and 'Voi lo sapete, O Mamma' seemed to need more power of cantabile singing than she possessed, and, like most of the other numbers, 'it is remarkable less for actual melodic beauty than for a complete appropriateness to the situation and character'.

The most beautiful section of the work was the unaccompanied chorus, 'Regina Coeli',

the effect of which was not improved by the directions of the stage manager, which were last night plainly audible above the music. The female portion of the choir is the least satisfactory thing about the performance, for their voices are neither sweet nor fresh. . . .

This critic also bothered about the acting:

It is surely a mistake to allow the choristers to surround Santuzza in the *ensemble* of the hymn: she is excommunicated, and her neighbours must surely be aware of the fact. Where all is so marvellously convincing, a bit of conventionality, which would be accepted without hesitation elsewhere, cannot but be noticed.

Arditi conducted, but the orchestra was not with him. *Cavalleria* was preceded by *Crispino e la Comare* by the Ricci brothers, first seen in London in 1857: of this *The Times* said that the shortened version 'will probably prove quite enough for most musicians. The absurd antics of the buffo singers seem nowadays a little out of date.'

The *Morning Post* found in *Crispino* 'a certain charm that makes it ever welcome', and said that in *Cavalleria* there was scarcely a number that was uninteresting, but some were, of course, more attractive than others. The *Standard*, in an issue that reported Edison as having invented an underground electric line for trains, which was contradicted the next day by a claim that a Scotsman, John Gordon, had patented the idea two years before, hailed Mascagni as a melodist, with especial sympathy towards Bizet's methods. It was possible, however, that he was

somewhat too fond of abrupt contrasts of sonority—a *crescendo*, before it has reached its apparent climax, giving place to a *pianissimo*, for instance: but at a first hearing it must be admitted that these contrasts are extremely effective.

'No, no, Turiddu' was 'one of the gems of the opera—indeed, a number of unsurpassed charm. . . . It is worked to a climax with admirable dramatic power.' It was shocking of the conductor Arditi to repeat the Intermezzo—

indeed, the worst traditions of Italian opera were in several instances observed, the players destroying illusion by leaving the picture to come forward and bow, and forgetting their assumed characters to appear as mere vocalists.

The Brindisi was in fact sung three times.

The *Whitehall Review*, however, a few days later commented on the indignation of the musical critics at the encores:—

Of course it is impossible to defend the whole encore system, but it has grown so completely into a modern institution, particularly on the Italian stage, that it must, we suppose, be accepted. To such a pitch has it grown, that this very opera of Mascagni's, consisting of one act, suffices in an Italian theatre to fill up the entire evening, so numerous are the encores.

It was more reasonable to object to the 'inane' curtseying after the first act of modern comedies or dramas on the London stage. This critic anyway was pleased that here at last 'we have a modern opera which is not a mere echo of Wagner's least praiseworthy qualities, or a commonplace recollection of half a score of other compositions'.

In 1892 *Eugen Onegin* and Mascagni's *L'Amico Fritz* were introduced to London and *Cavalleria*'s twin, *Pagliacci*, was given at Covent Garden on May 19, 1893, with de Lucia as Canio, Ancona as Tonio and Melba as Nedda: it was preceded by Gounod's *Philémon et Baucis*, which had been first produced in Paris in 1860, but only given in London first in 1891.

The *Daily Telegraph* wrote that Leoncavallo was supposed to have founded his story on actual facts, in the manner of Zola:—

Whether that be true or not matters nothing: the great point is that the poet-musician discerned the signs of the times in regard to operatic libretti. We appear to have done for the present with legendary heroes and cloudy myths.

These personages are too far removed: they are not flesh of our flesh and bone of our bone. Nowadays the demand is for 'human documents'—for characters in tale and drama that are our kin, our exaggerated selves.

Mascagni did the same, and now 'opera has turned into a new course'. The music of *Pagliacci* bore a close resemblance to that of *Cavalleria*:

The music is Italian, with here and there a reminiscence of the modern French, and occasional orchestral effects which may be traced back to Wagner, or beyond him to Berlioz.

Melody has come back, but once more, in point of fact,

we have the statue on the stage and the pedestal in the orchestra, to uplift and sustain, but not to rival.

The critic gave a kind notice to Melba, who was never noted for her histrionic ability—'As Nedda, the erring wife, Madame Melba showed a marked dramatic advance. That she sang with fine effect needs no assurance'.

The *Morning Post* thought *Pagliacci* showed more maturity of treatment than *Cavalleria*, though it was less spontaneous in melodic invention:—

Although not denoting a striking individuality, it is instinct with life and is admirably adapted to the situations. We doubt whether any detached numbers will achieve the popularity that has been attained by certain extracts from *Cavalleria Rusticana*, but there can be no question as to the effect of the music, when heard in its proper place.

The only flaw in Leoncavallo's talented scoring was that he 'occasionally shows an undue fondness for strident brass effects'. The best thing in the opera was the Prologue, which was finely sung by Ancona, but, as the *Standard* reported, 'Unfortunately the ill-timed applause of the gallery before the end was reached did something to destroy the effect.' (It always does, but the fault is the composer's for having apparently brought the Prologue to an end too soon—just as he does with 'Vesti la giubba', though how he could have avoided it, especially in the latter case, without ending abruptly would puzzle any better composer.) 'Vesti la giubba' and the Balatella were encored, the audience had come to be pleased and were more than satisfied, and the performance ended at midnight.

The Times thought the avoidance of sentimentality most artistic, while the passion in the first act was less hysterical though not less forcible than in Mascagni's work, and after the disjointed snatches of melody in *Cavalleria*, the sustained numbers 'come as a most welcome relief'. There was some unconscious plagiarism—in the Balatella there were reminiscences of 'several operas beside the Wagnerian trilogy', and in the Nedda–Silvio duet there was an adaptation from the finale of Mendelssohn's Trio in D minor. The beautiful soliloquy at the end of the first act was spoilt 'not only by applause, but by an ill-timed lowering of the curtain'.

Melba was also praised here for her pantomime in the comedy on the little stage—'the singer's recent improvement as an actress stood her in good stead', but the scenery of the fit-up play was 'almost too well painted for such a company of players as that to which the characters belong: it failed to realise the stage direction of a "scena mal dipinta"'. Still, there was plenty to admire in the work, 'and those who have the best right to form an opinion will probably rate the new opera higher than either of Mascagni's'.

The only other outstanding production of 1893 was of Saint-Saëns's *Samson et Dalila* at Covent Garden, but in a concert version, so as not to offend religious susceptibilities and in English: but 1894 was an interesting year for London operagoers.

The first new production was of the first Puccini opera to be seen in town—*Manon Lescaut*, which was given at Covent Garden on Whitmonday, May 14. As the *Standard* said:—

It introduces a new composer of exceptional capacity, whose work, admirable as it is, has still richer promise in it. Signor Puccini possesses the gift of melody, is a master of orchestration, and has a rare comprehension of dramatic effect—the three essentials for an operatic composer. Last night he appeared with his singers after each act—and that more than once—to be on each occasion greeted with increased warmth.

The only adverse criticism might be that his music was characterised by 'its restlessness, its constant changes of rhythm and key, which are found here, as in the compositions of Signori Mascagni and Leoncavallo'.

The *Morning Post* started off by disliking the subject:—

Surely more than sufficient operatic honours had already been bestowed upon the fickle and unsympathetic heroine . . . and we regret that Signor Puccini should not have wedded his strains to a more attractive theme.

Massenet's version was better, but

Signor Puccini's music appears to us to fully deserve the praise that has been bestowed upon it. . . . The seeds of Wagnerian reforms have not fallen on barren ground. Puccini reveals himself in *Manon Lescaut* as a composer gifted with strong dramatic power, possessing an apparently innate feeling for stage effect, and considerable melodic expression. His score is exempt from the crudities and vulgarities from which certain Italian operas are not free. The instrumentation and general workmanship are excellent.

Most important, the opera is sincere.

The Times thought it a noble work full of atmosphere, 'as it is the fashion to call it'. The Havre prison scene, 'with its sustained emotional power and gradual working up to a strong climax, is by far the best in the work, though the merits of the score are not to be enumerated shortly'. The last act, which the *Morning Post* thought superfluous, *The Times* said was an anticlimax, for this final scene,

though it contains some really expressive music for the lovers, is decidedly too long, even with the slight omissions wisely made last night.

As a matter of fact, the sentimental parts of the work are the least convincing, apart from the procession scene in the third act: there is a sense of straining after effect, and here and there even of that hysterical mode of uttering, which becomes so wearisome in Mascagni's music.

The interpretation of the opera, 'though by no means superlatively good, was at least efficient'. Most of the singers, however, including Beduschi as Des Grieux and Olghina as Manon, had a constant tremolo and Sepelli, who conducted,

allowed the orchestra frequently to drown the singers.

The chorus has been greatly augmented by chosen singers from the Brussels and Milan opera-houses, and elsewhere: and it is safe to say that it is a great deal better than any chorus that has been heard in a London opera-house for many years. The tone is fine in quality and volume, and the refinements of certain passages unsurpassed.

The National Anthem was sung under Signor Mancinelli's direction, at the beginning of the evening, by the choristers, who were grouped round the bust of the Queen.

Five days later Covent Garden saw the first London production of Verdi's *Falstaff*, which had been first produced in Rome eight days after *Manon Lescaut* was produced in Turin in 1893. Verdi was now *persona grata* in London as an opera composer: the *Morning Post* admitted that now at last he had style—'Melody has not forsaken him, although the form in which it now presents itself differs essentially from that of former days.'

The Times called the work a masterpiece, and said it had an unequivocal success, but

it remains to be seen whether the subscribers and the fashionable world in public will care for an opera which, since it contains no dull moments, allows no opportunities for comfortable conversation during the music.

(It was like the early eighteenth century again with the fops and their small-talk.)

The *Standard* called *Falstaff* 'the ripest work of the most gifted living composer of opera', and said that 'as far as we are aware, not a single unfavourable criticism has been passed upon it':—

It is said that Signor Verdi laughed heartily as he penned the music of his most recent, though we trust not his last work, and the statement may be readily credited, for never were more humourous strains coupled with artistic workmanship of the highest class. The only defect we can find in the score of *Falstaff* is a plethora of tune. This may seem an unreasonable objection, but explanation is easy.

The explanation was that each fragment of tune was too short. The opera was received with cheers and applause.

Punch liked it, though the best scenes were without Falstaff, who only existed for the other characters, like a football: 'much of the music is delightful, but rarely catching', though the orchestra was full of fun—still Sullivan might have chosen the subject. It was incredible that so many friends could have been free for the hurriedly arranged meeting in the last scene complete with 'these very fairy dresses' all ready for use!

In June 1894 Massenet's two-year-old *Werther* was produced at Covent Garden, and on Boxing Day Humperdinck's year-old *Hansel and Gretel* was given at Daly's Theatre, preceded by the first performance in London of Mozart's hundred-and-twenty-six-year-old *Bastien and Bastienne*, both the last two being sung in English.

As the *Standard* said on December 27, 'Altogether last night will be memorable in annals of operatic history.' The criticisms, however, do not make such interesting reading: Humperdinck's music, the *Standard* said, was Wagnerian in the treatment of the themes and in its harmony, and Brahms-like in instrumentation, but folk-tune all the time: the vision of the angels was 'one of the

379

most beautiful and touching scenes ever produced on any stage', and naïvety was 'the most prominent and pleasing feature of the work. The very spirit of laughter-loving childhood and the ex-aggerative earnestness of youth seem to stream forth from the music.'

The *Daily Telegraph* found the 'simplicity and directness' of *Bastien* 'as graceful as a child', but wrote of *Hansel*:

The most serious question connected with the orchestral treatment of the child-ish story is whether—we halt just in time, and reserve the rest for a contentious season.

There was vehement applause at the end of the performance, which surprisingly was put on by George Edwardes of musical comedy fame.

In June 1895 the Saxe-Coburg Ducal Company gave the first London performance of Smetana's *The Bartered Bride* at Drury Lane, but though the music and the dancers were liked, it was not greatly appreciated as a whole, because—as the *Telegraph* said—not only was it done in German, but no translation was available. (The opera purists, of course, would have preferred it to have been sung in Czech, on Addison's satirical principle that even fewer would then have understood it.)

La Bohème was given for the first time in England on April 22, 1897, in Manchester by the Carl Rosa Company in English and the *Manchester Guardian* reported on it the next morning:—

Signor Puccini's new opera, about which so much interest has been excited, was produced last night for the first time in England before a large and brilliant audience, and we have not often had to record so successful a first performance.

English audiences as a rule are colder and less demonstrative than those of Italy, but last night the reception of the new work must have convinced the composer that his music was not less cordially appreciated in Manchester than it had been in Milan.

The construction of the opera allows for very few opportunities for respon-sive cheers in the course of an act, but more than once loud applause interfered with the continuity of the music, and once the audience insisted on the repetition of the elaborate concerted piece—

(that is the end of the second act).

At the end of every act, however, there were ringing cheers from all parts of the house, and the composer was compelled to make his bow more than a dozen times. Signor Puccini did not conduct the performance, though at one time it was thought he would do so. He had, however, directed all the final rehearsals, and had every reason to be gratified by the admirable efficient manner in which M. Jaquinot conducted his work.

The Times especially mentioned the final scene as being 'full of pathos, even though it suggests to some extent a similar scene in a vastly less interesting opera by Verdi'. (Does that imply that *Traviata* was losing its hold?) Some of the English, however, 'reads like absolute bathos. . . . Some passages in the lovely duet between Mimi and her lover are worthy of the "poet Bunn" at his worst'. It certainly was a successful evening:—

> The whole performance was marked from beginning to end by an enviable spirit and go, which is all too rare in English performances of emotional operas, and here the emotional element plays a very important part.

The article ends with fine praise for the composer:—

> Signor Puccini has proved to the hilt that all modern Italian composers are not entirely given up to the idea that 'fire and brimstone', as it were, are essential to the success of an opera. He has treated his subject with the delicacy, lightness, and power, and force of a master, and he has here attained to a height far above that which he reached in *Manon*, the only other one of his operas that has as yet been heard on an English stage.

In September 1897 his first opera *Le Villi* was given at Manchester, and then on October 2 the Carl Rosa production of *Bohème* opened at Covent Garden, when all parts of the house were packed, except for the pit—and the public were not aware that there was to be one.

The *Morning Post* was rather unenthusiastic when it said that Puccini's *Bohème*, 'if it will not perhaps greatly enhance his reputation, at any rate will not diminish it. The choice of the subject for operatic treatment can scarcely be considered a very happy one'. Murger's original work, the critic said, had been 'traced with a master hand', but as for the characters, 'once transplanted upon the operatic stage, they appear to lose their individualities, and are but pale reproductions of the originals. Then again the plot so essential a factor in an opera, is here of the slightest.'

The comment is made that Italian composers seem to love French stories:—

> If Signor Puccini would devote his attention to musically depicting a tale of his own country, if he would choose one in which the hero and heroine were of a different stamp to those of his former operas, one where the sentiments expressed were less superficial, he would doubtless himself rise to greater heights, and surpass his previous efforts.

Taking *La Bohème* as it is, and dismissing it as a musical realisation of Murger's book, there is much in the music that can be unreservedly admired. The composer possesses a copious flow of melody, his instrumentation is ever ingenious and often novel, whilst many of his harmonic effects show a desire that is to be encouraged, but to which is doubtless attributable to the presence of certain crude progressions that have no obvious 'raison d'être'.

The love scenes between Mimi and Rudolph are treated with great delicacy and refinement, while the lighter scenes are brimful of spirit and 'go'. An effective ensemble at the end of the second act was much applauded on Saturday, and the conductor, M. Claude Jaquinot, unwisely allowed it to be repeated. . . .

The 'mise en scène' was good. In the first act the light of the fire kindled by the four Bohemians was so powerful as to be almost blinding. This is a detail that might easily be seen to at the next performance.

1898, the year of W. G. Grace's Jubilee, produced a mountain of mouse at Covent Garden, *Henry VIII* by Saint-Saëns. As *The Times* said, *Samson and Delilah* would have been his first opera to be seen in London, 'had it not been for the present impossibility of obtaining the necessary permission to perform a work based on a biblical subject', but *Henry VIII*, the critic said, was a great success, being done in its original form, which even Paris had not seen—that is, without the ballet:—

Happily the ballet seemed not quite safe to bring out in London, since it taxes the imagination somewhat severely by presenting a troop of Highlanders dancing in Richmond Park to the strains of a number of English, Scotch, and Irish airs, many of which are little suitable for the dance.

The *Telegraph* said that Saint-Saëns's operas had for a long time been mocked at Covent Garden as not being European successes, like 'some of the catch-penny effusions of young Italy', the *Morning Post* hailed *Henry VIII* as 'a masterly achievement', and said that, though it was perhaps rather too conventional, it was 'one of the finest of modern operas', while the *Standard* thought it 'a work that deserves to endure'—though it might not—'The ways of the London public are apt to be capricious with respect to opera, and it is too rash to assume that *Henry VIII* will be anything more than a succès d'estime.'

In 1900, on July 12, *Tosca* was given at Covent Garden. The *Times* was especially struck by the end of the church scene, which

is one in which Meyerbeer would have delighted, but it is treated by Signor Puccini with far greater sincerity than Meyerbeer could ever command, and with a knowledge of effect at least equal to his.

The whole second act is extremely fine, and the scene between La Tosca and

Scarpia, while Cavaradossi is undergoing physical and the singer mental tortures, is carried on with masterly knowledge: throughout the music is individual,
in that it could have been written by no other hand than Puccini's, and characteristic, in that every note sung by the chief personages seems to belong to them
by natural right.

Ternina as Tosca was superb—it was the only non-Wagnerian
part that she sang at Covent Garden between 1900 and 1906, de
Lucia was a 'a very earnest lover, though he rather spares his
hearers the terrors of the torture chamber', and Scotti as Scarpia
'gives a finely thought out, though somewhat melodramatic,
picture of the malicious and passionate chief of the Roman police'.
The new scenery was painted from photographs of the actual
places, and in the last scene there was 'so much illusion that La
Tosca's suicidal leap from the parapet becomes quite horrible'.

Punch thought that 'to turn a successful modern acting play into
an opera is to court failure', still 'Puccini seems to have scored an
opera and a success', Ternina was vocally and dramatically excellent while the two leading men did their best:—

The opera, the public is informed, has been produced with great success in the
principal cities of Italy and South America, and as far as I am concerned, these
places are welcome to keep it to themselves as an opera. As music, there is much
I should like to hear again.

The *Morning Post* also questioned whether the play was suitable
as an opera subject, and thought that

Signor Scotti's appearance as Scarpia will scarcely increase the reputation he
has acquired in this country. The ferocity of the character was over-accentuated,
and there was a total absence of the diplomatic control and astuteness which
would pertain to the Chief of the Police in the year 1800.
    Of the minor characters special mention is due of M. Gilibert's personation
of the Sacristan, which was full of subtle touches of humour.

The *Daily Telegraph* was moved to a poetical dissertation on the
subject of melodrama in relation to opera, which certainly has
some foundation: 'It is curious to see how the grim and bloody
dramatic spirit which, for example, littered the Elizabethan stage
with corpses survives in the domain of opera'—for instance, the
writer said, in operas by Wagner or Verdi:—

Illustrative, for the most part, of primitive passions, and appealing as it does to
the lowest as well as the most powerful human feelings, that form of art must
needs be attended by blood. To this end the librettists call in the demons of

383

Jealousy and Revenge—ghastly shapes which, if there were no public taste for horrors, would at least be banished from the stage.

Now this is all very crude and elementary, as an adjunct to art. Moreover, it is very cheap. Nothing is easier than to commit a murder in a play, and dramatic murders, however manifestly achieved for sensational purposes, never fail to make their mark.

The author of *Tosca* turned this fact to account, He too called up the fiends of Jealousy and Revenge, made blood flow freely, and his characters to disappear amid lurid hues, as a red sun sinks in a stormy sky.

Nor is this all. In the person of Scarpia he lifted devilish wickedness to the position of arbiter of fate. That incredible villain, who wades in the waters of crime shoulder deep, is successful all along the line.

'Tis true that the knife of Tosca stops his career, but his plans work on and accomplish their purposes with the inexorableness of destiny. So we see the unwavering and inscrutable fate of Greek Drama intermixed with the lustful designs of a minister in the employ of a modern ruler.

The libretto was good, so was most of Act I, though much of Scarpia and Angelotti was 'unimpressive and even dull'. In the second act 'nothing more sinister has, we should say, been achieved in music' than Scarpia's love-song, and when he is murdered, 'one is not all ears, but all eyes'. The love-duet in the third act is the best thing in the work. But at last the curtain comes down, and 'only then did the audience shake off a nightmare that had possessed them'.

Another opera, more obviously connected with the French Revolution, Giordano's *Andrea Chenier*, was first produced in London in English in 1903 at the Camden Theatre, from which building so many studio performances of operas have been broadcast in recent years: it was given in Italian at Covent Garden two years later. In 1904 Massenet's *Hérodiade* and Cilea's *Adriana Lecouvreur* were given in London, and then on July 10, 1905, Covent Garden saw its first *Madama Butterfly* with Emmy Destinn in the name-part, Caruso as Pinkerton and Scotti as Sharpless.

The *Daily Telegraph*, after recalling that the original play by Belasco had been given in London some six years before with Evelyn Millard at the Duke of York's (which performance gave Puccini the idea), said that the opera was received with delighted applause, which was well justified:—

Madama Butterfly is not an epoch-making work. But its magic is full of that suavity and passion which Puccini most of all among the brethren of younger Italy has at command, and for such a favour in these barren operatic days we may well be grateful.

384

The critic placed it higher than *Bohème*, *Lescaut* or *Tosca*, which, 'with its ugly and unmusical subject, will never be among the cherished things of the lyric stage'. *Butterfly*, he said,

has the old qualities in profusion, and with them, we think, a further and deeper power of expression, and even more skilful mastery over the orchestra, and a heightened sense of what is beautiful in phrase, cadence and harmony.

It is mainly in the restraint and finish of his music that Puccini puts such as Mascagni and Leoncavallo to shame. Take *Cavalleria* and mark the banality of its scoring when set beside Puccini's best work. Measure the melodies of *Pagliacci* by those of *La Bohème* and *Madama Butterfly*, and their comparative poverty stands revealed.

After enumerating some of the beauties in the work he then deals with the performance and says:

The weight of the evening was upon Miss Destinn's shoulders, and hers was the chief triumph. Puccini might have written his music for this artist, so aptly did it suit her voice, and so brilliantly did she deliver it.

The *Morning Post* said all the cast were good, but was not quite so sure about the work itself, compared with *Manon Lescaut*, *Bohème* and *Tosca*:—

Whether *Madama Butterfly* is destined to be equally successful it is as yet too early to say. That it is extremely interesting and individual there can however be no question. . . .

At the same time there is a refreshing unconventionality about Signor Puccini's harmonic methods which cannot but appeal to one. In this respect he is, indeed, a master to himself. It must be added that over a richly embroidered harmonic 'parterre', brightened up by a variegated orchestral colouring, he has scattered some of those choice flowers of melody that only blossom under an Italian sun.

The overture, the critic thought, was like that to *The Bartered Bride*, the allusions to milk-punch and whisky sounded odd at Covent Garden, and why was 'America for ever' sung in English by Sharpless and 'Sir Francis Blummey Pinkerton, as he is quaintly named'? Butterfly's entry 'rather savours of the light opera stage', but the love duet, 'melodious, passionate, and quite in the right atmosphere', is Puccini at his best. In the second act, when Butterfly sees the ship, 'there are many interesting and dramatic moments in this scene, but it is far too long, and would undoubtedly gain in effect were it compressed'. The dawn was good but the climax was disappointing, Mrs. Pinkerton was unnecesary, and the two scenes of the last act 'strike one as being decidedly too much spun-out'.

The Times especially liked the love duet, the flower duet and the waiting for the ship—'the most beautiful section of the work, but all through it is a thing of very remarkable beauty, pathos, and charm'. The end, however, was 'almost too harrowing for ordinary susceptibilities', and Caruso came in for some criticism on the dramatic side:

Signor Caruso sang so well that his appearance was easily forgiven, but when he was not actually singing, some of the audience were moved to observe that he looked like an inspector of police in the first act.

Caruso certainly looks like a foreign policeman in the drawing of him and Scotti in *Punch* entitled 'Scotti-Viski', but *Punch* said that Destinn was 'operatically and artistically perfect' though not petite, she was 'destinn'd for the part' and 'we fancy this Butterfly will settle in the Garden'.

CHAPTER NINE

Samson and Delilah to Prince Igor

THE summer season at Covent Garden in 1909 opened on Monday, April 26—when the *Puritani* was being given at the Coronet Theatre, Notting Hill Gate—with the long-awaited first London stage-production of the now thirty-two-year-old *Samson et Dalila* in the presence of the seventy-six-year-old composer. Most of the music, was of course, well known from the concert-hall, and therefore, as the *Standard* said, except for the stage trappings and the French language 'all too long banished from the London operatic boards',

the proceedings last night were, for the most part, of a wholly familiar nature. There was the same brave array of empty boxes during the first act, the same regulation number of calls upon the fall of each curtain, and the same distracting confusion in the vestibule upon the conclusion of the performance.

Samson struck that critic as being better melodrama than opera, for although it was melodious, 'the work rarely, if ever, strikes the hearer as sincere or deeply felt'.

Kirkby Lunn, who sang Dalila, vocalised faultlessly and

cut a fine figure in her sumptuous dresses. It cannot, however, be said that she fully realised the seductive witchery and sinuous grace associated with the fair temptress.

Fontaine as Samson was 'more than convincing', but other soloists lacked

dramatic intuition. Indeed, in the absence of so many well-known singers this season it is difficult to resist the impression that the concert platform promises to become the happy hunting ground of unrequited effort and uncrowned genius.

The chorus, however, 'had evidently been carefully rehearsed. They displayed a more intelligent interest in the traffic of the stage than is often the case.' The general summing up was that 'in the light of modern developments *Samson et Dalila* is not good opera: but it unquestionably affords a pleasant evening's entertainment'.

The Times, however, thought the performance

a brilliant ending to a brilliant and beautiful day, in which spring and summer seemed to have joined hands to welcome back to London the birds of passage who form the majority of the box-holders at Covent Garden.

Unlike the *Standard*, *The Times* said that Dalila 'suits Mme. Kirkby Lunn to perfection, and the caressing quality of her beautiful voice, her skill as an actress, and her sound musicianship made her performance a thing of singular allurement'. On other hand,

M. Fontaine has neither a very commanding presence nor a very sonorous voice, such as are required for Samson: in the love-duet of the second act he was especially weak, and he was often out of tune.

The *Telegraph* agreed that it was a triumph for Kirby Lunn and that Fontaine was not good—'for some reason', the writer said, 'singers new to Covent Garden . . . force the voice': the performance was almost all superb. It was surprising to note that there were to be four other novelties in the season—*Louise*, *Pelléas et Mélisande*, d'Erlanger's *Tess* and Naylor's *Angelus*—while most welcomely Wotan, that 'unhappy god, seems to have been ejected, to all intents and purposes, from his once lofty pedestal as a social big-seasonable lion,' for there were to be only two *Ring* cycles.

The *Morning Post*, however, complicated things for future valuation of past singers by saying,

M. Fontaine . . . at once achieved success. His voice is rich and full in quality, he uses it well, and to his vocal equipment, which constitutes one of the best tenor voices of the robust order that has been heard in London for a long period, he adds great histrionic powers.

There was still more divergence of opinion over the first Richard Strauss opera to be seen in London—*Elektra*, which was produced in the first Beecham season at Covent Garden on Saturday, February 19, 1910, after a great gale in London. Beecham had indeed given the first London performance of Ethel Smyth's *Strandrecht* in English as *The Wreckers* at His Majesty's in the previous summer, but this was his first season of opera.

The production of *Elektra* was an event, said the *Standard*, second in importance to the first production of the *Ring* in England. The house was packed, and among the audience were the King and Queen, and with them the Prince and Princess of Prussia. It was, said the writer, amazing that it was given within twelve months of its first performance (this was only just untrue, for the world première was at Dresden on January 25, 1909).

This critic was obviously puzzled: 'Was *Elektra* an unqualified success? Well, that must be left to the judgment of the individual.

There was little question, however, as to the success of the evening.' The curtain-calls at the end were taken

to applause that was as spontaneous as it was genuine and heartwhole. How much of this applause was elicited by the music, and how much by Mr. Beecham's direction of it, it would be difficult to say: but at least it is certain that Covent Garden has never previously witnessed a scene of such unfettered enthusiasm.

The work was brilliant, though the spark of genius might be wanting: 'one thing, however, is certain: its discordance has been very grossly exaggerated'. There was one long crescendo,

culminating in a climax the like of which has never been achieved in terms of sound. And here again the highly imaginative accounts as to the nerve-destroying cacophony of the final scene have little foundation in fact.

The finest thing of the evening was the invocation to Agamemnon by Edyth Walker—'She is a splendid singer and an even better actress, a fact of which she gave eloquent proof during the long, trying waits which fell to her share'. Finally, '*Elektra* may not be great music in the sense that Wagner's music is great, but it is great drama—very great drama'.

The *Standard* did not find that the realistic touches in the score obtruded in any way. *The Times* thought otherwise: the dramatic music was essentially realistic—the flogging at the start, the procession of slaves and animals, Clytemnestra's haunted nights and physical symptoms—a horrible scene this, and the 'Glittering Jewels' theme. 'One thing is quite clear about Elektra', *The Times* critic said,

It will divide the opera-going public into two great classes, and the more deliberate remnant who recognise in it great merits and great defects will probably get their heads broken by both parties in the dispute.

According to German and American admirers,

it seems that we are allowed to think the music a little noisy, but we must admit that the tendency of the drama is a real advance . . . for the music we must express a bewilderment that is ready to pass into enthusiasm.

As for details of the music:—

What is called the 'Slippery Blood' motive in the music is the leading idea of the whole, and it certainly has been wonderfully realised by both dramatist and composer. The air is indeed so full of slaughter that by the time Aegisthus is seen flying about the Palace at the back of the scene, even the most bloodthirsty spectator must feel that he cannot care very much what happens—for tragedy has apparently found it necessary to cast off the buskin for the golosh.

Elektra's warning to her mother 'goes for very little' and the Recognition 'is almost tame'. The critic found Elektra's 'crazy dance of death the most sustained thing in the work', and her invocation of Agamemnon good for about sixteen bars and then merely sugary Bellini. Chrysothemis's desire for a natural life 'has beautiful passages', but the reverse was true of the horrible scene of the Queen's symptoms:—

Here the way in which the climax is treated is very powerful: and indeed nothing shows the skill of the composer better than his power of piling one kind of ungainliness on another in such a way as to produce a feeling of growing excitement—if sometimes of growing disgust.

The music for the entrance of Orestes had real dignity, and after the Recognition the beautiful sustained song

must command the admiration even of those who feel themselves degraded by the whole thing. The 'nameless dance' at the end, too, is certainly managed with masterly dexterity in the music, for it has the weird touch of insanity which is required to end the play in the mood of the beginning.

Edyth Walker was excellent as Elektra, while the Clytemnestra of Frau von Bahr-Mildenburg

is so vivid a picture of decadence that while she is on the stage it is possible to forget all about the music. She suggests a Late Roman empress rather than a Greek queen: her heavy-lidded eyes and her burden of gems, her ivory staff and her mad, almost drunken, gait must haunt every one who sees them.

Frances Rose succeeded well as Chrysothemis, Weidemann as Orestes sang impressively, but was too impassive in the Recognition scene—of course this was according to the authors, but surely he should be human,—while Mr. Beecham conducted finely and deserved great thanks.

Elektra was followed three days later by the first London performance of Delius's *Village Romeo and Juliet* in English, six days after that by the first performance on any stage of Debussy's 1884 'scène lyrique' *L'Enfant Prodigue* in French, and eight days after that a grand revival of Sullivan's one serious opera, *Ivanhoe*, first produced at the opening of the short-lived Royal English Opera-House in 1891 (now the Palace Theatre): in the Covent Garden revival the attack on the Castle was so alarmingly realistic, Sir

Thomas has told me, that quite a few of those engaged on the other side of the curtain jibbed at being concerned in it.

But such a programme, amazing as it was for a first Covent Garden venture and intriguing as it was to both artists and audience alike, was not enough for the conductor in one year, and so in May, as announced by Beerbohm Tree on the day *Elektra* opened, Mr. Beecham gave a season of opera at His Majesty's, reviving Stanford's *Shamus O'Brien* of 1896, Massenet's *Werther* of 1892 (1894 in London), *The Tales of Hoffmann* of 1881 (1907 in London), Mozart operas, and the first London production of Strauss's *Feuersnot* on July 7, all in English.

Even this was not enough, and so in the autumn the second Beecham season at Covent Garden took place with a programme that included revivals of *Fidelio* and *Don Giovanni*, the first London performance of d'Albert's seven-year-old *Tiefland* in English, and on December 8, 1910, the first London production of Strauss's five-year-old *Salome* in German.

It might have been thought that as the Lord Chamberlain had allowed a stage production of the Biblical *Samson* the year before, he might well allow Salome to dance on the stage, but the story from the Bible via Oscar Wilde was too much for him, and so the *Salome* by Strauss and Hofmannsthal had to be considerably modified for its first London production.

As the *Standard* said:—

Those who are called upon to discuss the version of *Salome* presented at Covent Garden last night, with the consent of the Lord Chamberlain, are placed in this dilemma—either they must judge the music in its relation to the revised text—in which case the dramatic, psychological, and social aspects of Strauss and Wilde's conceptions are almost wholly lost—or the characters on the stage must be regarded as saying one thing and meaning another.

Unfortunately Mrs. Grundy, as estimable a figure as Dr. Bowdler, is never influenced by ethics or aesthetics of art:

thus the famous passage,

'I want to kiss thy lips, Jochanaan',

becomes, in more polite, if scarcely synonymous phraseology,

'To death let me follow thee, Oh Prophet':

while, instead of apostrophising the head, Salome, among other things, merely enumerates her lover's physical virtues.

The five Jews, not even allowed to preserve their nationality, are by a sly touch of humour turned into five learned men, and all references to the Deity have been excised.

Technically, *Salome* is the logical outcome of the methods practised by Wagner, the critic said:—

Characterisation is suggested largely by thematic combination and deriva-tion, and much of this is at times so abstruse and heavily loaded that the eye detects it upon paper more easily than does the ear by sound. Melodically the score of *Salome* is richer than that of *Elektra*, of which in the final scene we are strongly reminded.

(This reads superficially as if *Salome* was a later work than *Elektra*, which of course was not the case.)

With the exception of the Prophet's music, the interest is none too well maintained up to the moment of the now famous Dance of the Seven Veils, which is not as rhythmically sensual as has been said. There is a lot of ugly music, as perhaps befits an ugly subject, and, needless to say, numerous realistic effects. . . . The apostrophe to the head is very tuneful, if not a little ordinary, though, as has been said, in this instance there is no head to apostrophise.

Of the cast the best were Aino Ackté as Salome, Clarence Whitehill as the Prophet and Maurice D'Oisly as Narraboth (the Page was Edna Thornton, the three Cappadocians were Robert Radford, Arthur Wynn and Charles Knowles, and the two soldiers Harry Dearth and Lewys James). The two fine instru-mental interludes were excellently played under Beecham:—'On both occasions the score seemed almost to speak'. Finally the article attacked the half-hearted censoring of the work:—

The action of the Lord Chamberlain in refusing to license *Salome* was as logical and easy to understand as was the attitude of the American public who insisted upon the withdrawal of the opera after one or two performances at most: but the present version is indefensible upon any but opportunistic grounds. It does justice to neither Wilde nor Strauss, to Mr. Beecham, nor his artists, and it will fail to satisfy purist, prude or prurient.

In America there had in fact been only one performance at the Metropolitan on January 22, 1907, with Fremstad as Salome, and, the *Telegraph* said, two at Chicago, which made Mary Garden 'a very angry Salome' when further performances were can-celled, as she had played it for Hammerstein many times at the Manhattan Opera House and elsewhere.

The London première was crowded, but the *Telegraph* critic was uncertain whether the cause was the banning of the original version, the name of Wilde, or 'the keen desire—save the mark!—

of the British public' to see a famous music-drama. Musically the work was a mixture, because Strauss at one moment

dazzles us by the gorgeous colour of his orchestra or enchants us by the sheer loveliness of the vocal music—as when Salome, kneeling, sings her long song to the head, or rather (anglicé) the blood, of John Baptist (anglicé, the Prophet) —at another repels us by the sheer hideousness of his expression.

Dramatically it was not as strong as *Elektra*, and there were weaknesses in the performance, thanks to the silly law which allowed a dancer

in one place of entertainment to execute her pirouettes and the rest in full possession of the head of John the Baptist, while in another, and that ostensibly of superior character, even the word 'head' is taboo, and, as a fact, is translated 'blood'.

(The dancer, who is wrongly described as pirouetting, was Maud Allan, whose performance was 'gruesomely parodied' at the Alhambra, as the *Play Pictorial* said—which also commented on 'the Pecksniffian policy' of banning the head at Covent Garden—

If we had an intelligent Minister of Fine Arts to keep an eye on our Art life, instead of a Lord Chamberlain and a London County Council, such absurd contradictions would not be evident.

The original play had already been given at two now forgotten London theatres in 1905 and 1906 and was again produced two months after the opera at the Royal Court Theatre.)

However, as the *Telegraph* said, to try to prevent Anglo-Saxons seeing the performance of a work famous elsewhere was 'to adopt the method of Mrs. Partington', who tried to sweep the sea out of her kitchen. The writer especially praised the Herod (Ernst Kraus) and the Salome:

Herod, at once sensual, neurotic—if so modern a term may be applied to so ancient a character—strong and weak, shifting and shifty, required for his right and proper presentment a singer of almost superhuman vigour, and in Mr. Kraus such a one is found. . . .

Madame Ackté, in spite of her tendency to overemphasis of gesticulation, was a superb and often seductive (and very serpentine) Salome, and nowhere more so than in the eviscerated climax, the scene with the tray, or dish, the music of which is so entrancingly beautiful, whatever the opinion may be of the merits of the situation (original or bowdlerised) that gives rise to it. . . .

It is said that only on rare occasions does Salome's interpreter actually perform the dance herself.[1] If this be so, then there goes all the more credit to

O   393

Madame Ackté, who danced with easy grace, great flexibility, and considerable charm. On the whole this artist from the far North easily surpassed last night any of her previous performances here, both vocally and histrionically.

Comparing the opera with *Elektra* the critic wrote:—

In spite of the bowdlerisation referred to, which makes what is only thought to be hideous in reality hideous, not to say also stupid, *Salome* is vastly less repellent, but more musical, and less gruesomely but more artistically fascinating, partly, no doubt, on account of the lusciousness and beauty of much of Salome's own music. It is a work of immense interest in its composer's development.

The Editor of *Punch*, Owen Seaman, went himself to the dress rehearsal of *Salome* and wrote a fascinating description which becomes vivid when 'Beecham's voice rang out "Where is the Prophet?"' Clarence Whitehill had insufficient light down in the cistern to see his score, so everything started again with Salome in a white blouse and a dark skirt. The argumentative Jews went wrong, and so were told by the conductor 'they must pay attention to the beat: this, in fact, being what the beat was there for': they then went through the passage correctly, though, as O.S. said, 'I confess that I noticed no difference, so terrible was the mêlée of jarring sounds'.

The executioner eventually went down into the cistern, and

during the awful interval that ensued the orchestra let itself go. There was one sound, painfully reiterated, like the chirrup of a sick hen, which, I think, came from some part of a violin which is usually left alone

there was also an instrument sounding 'between the click of muted bones and the smacking of fat cheeks'.

When the result of the execution was brought up dripping with red paint, Salome objected to the mess, and there was a hurried replanning and wiping of fingers, but the climax came when, on Herod's order to the soldiers to kill her, they were

mobilised a shade too soon. 'What in the name of —— are you doing?' said Mr. Beecham; 'I'm not half through the opera yet!' An overstatement, if pardonable.

But O.S. finished as follows:—

For those who propose to criticise this opera, no vocabulary could be too large or peculiar. I content myself with complimenting Mr. Beecham on the prodigies he performed with the bâton, and I gratefully hope that he will soon ask me to another dress rehearsal of an opera: one, for choice, in which Messrs. Strauss and Censor shall have again collaborated.

394

Three years later Strauss's *Rosenkavalier* opened the Beecham season at Covent Garden. The date given in Löwenberg (1st edition), January 1, 1913, is wrong,[2] for on that date the film of *The Miracle* with Humperdinck's music was being shown at Covent Garden. The date of the *Rosenkavalier* was January 29, 1913. It is interesting that for this season Beecham, always eager to make opera obtainable and palatable to more than the self-chosen few, insisted on a low rate of prices.

The *Telegraph* called the work

surely the wittiest opera that ever emanated from the brain of musician. Of the coruscating wit of the music there can be no two opinions.

(Here this critic was wrong.)

The stream of his music is as fluent as in any previous work, the characterisation at least as strong, and the veritable maze of sound, exquisite sound, too, that he is capable of producing from the orchestra, has never been better exemplified in any work than in the glorious music of the trio, for which, unhappily, one has to wait until well on in the third act. . . .

The subtleties of wit are not easily understood by a non-German, but the score is one 'that outwardly is so apparently simple and direct, and yet is one of the most complicated that have yet been produced in modern times'.

Hofmannsthal's libretto, though the jokes are rather long-winded, is far better than most opera-books, and the touches of immorality or suggestiveness will certainly not damn it. The performances were good:—

Nothing could have been more beautiful than the combined effect of stage demeanour and exquisite singing of Mesdames Margarete Siems, who played with fine dignity and sang magnificently as the Princess, and Eva van der Osten, a sheer delight as Oktavian one moment, as the quasi-serving-maid another. Nor have we often heard in German opera singing so beautiful as theirs, with that of Miss Dux, who played Sophie's part, in the magnificent trio already mentioned.

In fact singing by Germans was now better than it used to be and their diction was good. Beecham was the conductor, and,

as often before in his own seasons, he covered himself with glory by his wonderful alertness and grip: but he still persists in his old habit of dragging the tempo in passages that appear to him to call for depth of emotion.

The scenery of the third act was too beautiful for a hotel of by no means dubious reputation.

The Times, which pointed out that Siems and van der Osten were the original creators of their parts at Dresden in January 1911, while Knüpfer was the first Baron Ochs three months later in Berlin, said that at last Strauss had found here, and in *Ariadne auf Naxos* of 1912, eloquence of the human voice after exploiting the orchestra so long. The opera was too long, though some good cuts were made, but the farce and 'St. George's Hall' tricks—that is sudden materialisations as performed by the illusionists Maskelyne and Devant at that Hall—of the third act were weak, and indeed, apart from the fine lyricism of the trio, 'the versatility of Strauss, which never fails through two acts, is eventually baffled in the third'.

The *Morning Post* thought the story not worthy of Strauss's powers, and he

has not evolved any new manner for its illustration; neither has he acquired any new matter. With the exception of the valse measures, which naturally come without effort to one of Dr. Strauss's strong rhythmic feeling, the remainder of the material is familiar in his other works. It is the application that is altered, not the music itself. Heard in this connection the score suffers from mannerisms.

The arrival of the Rose-bearer in the second act is accompanied by strains 'that recall Salome or suggest the fine passion of Elektra', and in the Countess's soliloquy

there is beautiful music, but its real mood is that of Elektra when she recognises her brother. Evidently Dr. Strauss's true mission is to write serious dramatic music, and, unlike Wagner, he cannot venture with any degree of real success into a lighter vein: it must be the lightest or the heaviest—nothing between.

In fact there was not the advance anticipated.

The *Standard*, on the other hand, thought it was good, but 'old wine in new bottles'—borrowings from Mozart, Italy and Vienna past and present. There was a lack of distinction but brilliant tricks:

Of romance . . . there is little, of passion, next to none. Thus the love scenes as a whole hang fire. They contain some charming music, but it is much of a colour, and when it does not end where it began, an anti-climax is often the result.

In the final farce-scene there is thick paint and a babel of sound just as in *Elektra*. Hofmannsthal, too, thinks of 'multiplication of everything by ten as the quintessence of artistic achievement', though Strauss can lighten the longueurs. The complicated levée scene is charming: 'the whole thing is an amazingly complex web of sound, but everything comes through and comes off into the bargain.'

His romantic music is his weakest, but the Rose-scene twinkles like Clytemnestra's jewels, and the trio

is the talk of the opera. Musically, it reaches a higher plane than anything else in the work, always excepting the silver rose music, with which it does not compare either melodically or in point of colour and originality. Here one feels that things have come to an end, or should have, but there is another duet, and the little black boy is again pressed into service—rather lamely—for the final curtain.

The seasons of 1911, 1912 and 1913 were primarily devoted to the introduction of Diaghileff's Russian Ballet to London, apart from the inclusion of *Rosenkavalier* in 1913, when the first performance of *Petrouchka* was given: but in the summer of 1913 Beecham opened a season of Russian opera and ballet at Drury Lane on Tuesday, June 24, with Moussorgsky's *Boris Godounov* as altered by Rimsky-Korsakov, with Russian singers, costumes and scenery, but with Beecham's British orchestra. But the company, as the *Telegraph* said, only arrived the day before, and as the costumes, etc., were 'detained at dock almost up to the eleventh hour', there was no dress rehearsal. Sir Thomas has told me how he and everybody had to set to with paint and brushes to get the scenery ship-shape for the evening performance, which was conducted by Emile Cooper, a Russian, despite his name.

The *Telegraph* critic found the Hostess's song fascinating, the chorale in the coronation scene impressive, Varlaam's song boisterous and impulsive, and the scene of the children and the nurse charming, while in the title-part

with which his name has become identified both in Europe and America, Mr. Chaliapin, a basso of whose commanding gifts we have all heard, made his debut in this country and achieved, let us hasten to add, a striking success. His voice is of beautiful quality, and the artist's use of it is masterly: but over and above these recommendations Mr. Chaliapin possesses histrionic powers of a compelling order. His face, bearing, and manner in the part of the crime-haunted ruler were extraordinarily eloquent, as suggesting always a man obsessed by the memory of a hideous deed and torn by contrition.

The Times said that the intensely real performance was wonderful, and even the distressingly long pauses between the scenes and the ineptitude of an audience who would insist upon applauding as soon as the curtain fell and before the music was finished did not betray the sense of reality.

It is difficult to say how far Moussorgsky, how far the extraordinarily powerful acting of M. Chaliapin and the other principals, the fine singing, and natural action of the crowds, or the beauty of the scenery were responsible for the effect. They were all fused together in the total result.

In the gorgeous coronation scene several national melodies were used, and all through

the simple crudity of the music is the thing which impresses one most as far as Moussorgsky is concerned, and if Rimsky-Korsakov has polished the work to some extent he has certainly not deprived it of its directness.

The orchestra, however, had drowned the fine chorus in the coronation scene: 'The brass was constantly too noisy. Moussorgsky's orchestra should not, like Wagner's, direct, but merely suggest the development of the ideas which the stage pictures.'

The *Standard*, which especially liked the scene of Boris and the children, and thought the music best in all the choral scenes, said that Chaliapin's Boris

is a wonderfully dominating and arresting figure, and there is little question that the stage lost a really great actor when he threw in his lot with opera.

His voice is a singularly sympathetic one, and far more colourful and varied in expression than that of any bass—is it a bass, we wonder?—we have heard. There are a good many people who still put the singer before the song, and for such as these Chaliapin's advent should fill the gap caused by Caruso's departure.

The *Morning Post*, which recorded that the Poland scene was not performed, thought the production not as polished as the Russian ballets, but said that the chorus, Chaliapin, and the quaint scenery were fine:—

Taken altogether, the work shows immense prescience, but extraordinary crudity. Its interpretation is of decided strength, for the male voices are attractive, most of the basses being of exceptional character. The ladies' voices are more inclined to hardness and are much alike one another.

M. Chaliapin . . . has a voice of good range and of pleasing, though to English ears of by no means remarkable, quality. His acting, like that of the rest of the company, seems curiously unfinished and self-conscious. There was more distinction in his efforts than in those of any other member of the cast.

The night after *Boris* it was remarked that there was a far larger audience for the first reappearance of the Russian ballet with *Jeux*,

Pavilion and *Scheherazade* (with Nijinsky) than there had been for the first appearance of the Russian opera with Chaliapin.

In the first half of 1914, before the war broke out that was to overturn all the accepted and long-lasting habits, customs and conventions of Europe, there were two outstanding new productions of opera in London. The first was that of the thirty-two-year-old *Parsifal* at Covent Garden on Monday, February 2, in the presence of Queen Alexandra and a large audience, the gallery having waited twelve hours for their places.

The *Evening Standard and St. James's Gazette* printed an article signed 'G.H.', which said that *Parsifal* was not an opera but a music-drama, and as it depended so largely on a religious atmosphere—there was some offence taken at the inclusion of words from the Last Supper—

with the environment of a theatre the special atmosphere so obviously necessary cannot be suggested. Much of its significance is shorn of its mystic value. Much of it becomes theatrical which ought to be sublime and spiritual.

Apart from the 'peculiarly beautiful' music in the scenes of ritual or religious pageantry, it was no better than other operas by Wagner: the characters were 'of no very arresting interest':—

Gurnemanz is almost as tiresome as Wotan. Kundry . . . is more mythical than human. Parsifal himself is a vague, shadowy figure. . . unable to experience any true human emotion or realise any spiritual struggle.

The music was often 'of elegance and beauty, but at other times of a disappointing character'. The Prelude, the Flower Maidens and the Good Friday scene were better on the stage than in the concert hall, but were not Wagner at his best: the score 'has little of the richness of *Tristan*, the sensuous charm of the Venusberg scene in *Tannhäuser*, or the ethereal loveliness of *Lohengrin*'.

Bodansky conducted superbly, Knüpfer was 'memorable' as Gurnemanz, Hensel 'unequal' as Parsifal, Bender 'conspicuous' as Amfortas, while Eva van der Osten as Kundry was graphic, but not seductive in voice, though splendid in the declamatory passages.

The Times said that at the end of each act the applause was hushed and the doors were closed during each act. The moving panorama scenery during Parsifal's journey was 'one of Wagner's worst blunders in practical stage-craft' and the orchestra had to stop for seconds when it stuck. The Garden scene was far more brilliant at Covent Garden than at Bayreuth, and the Good Friday scene was better, but not so well lit, and 'on the larger stage one loses much of the intimacy of the action'.

Van der Osten, this critic said, had 'one of the most beautiful mezzo-soprano voices of modern times': her one fault as Kundry was that 'she was entirely too commanding, too big a creature to suggest seductive art'. The Love-feast of the Grail was 'intensely impressive', though the Knights sang flat—as they did also at the end, but when at last Parsifal raised the Grail it was an anticlimax both dramatically and musically. *The Times* ended by saying:— 'Even if we do not feel *Parsifal* to be Wagner's greatest work, its unique beauty and the loftiness of its standpoint are incontestable.'

In the *Morning Post* the criticism of the production, apart from saying much the same as the others except that the music was considered more highly inspired than any other of Wagner, included one comment that is well worthy of study both as regards the abilities of British artists of the day compared with the distinguished foreigners and also concerning the old argument as to whether the performance should be understood or not—sense or sound, in fact. Both these questions are still argued *ad nauseam* by people who believe the art of opera exists better in a vacuum of empty sounds with those who believe that sense can be compatible with beauty, and that our singers are not as a whole necessarily inferior to foreigners. Here is what the *Morning Post* critic wrote of the performance of *Parsifal*:—

Only in one essential has it failed in attaining perfection. Wagner himself expressed very strong views on the subject of his works being given in the language of the people before whom they were performed, and much would have been attained by giving attention to those views.

To making the first production in England of *Parsifal* entirely epoch-making the performance should have been given in English. The demands of the cast are of a nature that our means, limited though they be, could have met well, and there would have been no difficulty whatever in finding the suitable exponents.

Of course there is the important question of tradition, and since there are many of the Bayreuth singers in the cast it is to be presumed that it is well represented. But in a case of this kind the tradition is not so much one of interpretation as it is of attitude towards the spirit of the work—the spirit of Christian religion—which British artists could very well have been trusted to represent.

In the summer of 1914 there was another Beecham season of opera and ballet at Drury Lane, when *The Magic Flute*, and

Rimsky-Korsakov's *Nuit de Mai* and *Coq d'Or* were given, together with an exceptionally exciting performance on Monday, June 6 which combined the opera and the ballet—Borodin's *Prince Igor*, finished and edited by Rimsky-Korsakov and Glazounov.

In this opera, the *Morning Post* said:—

there is much less of the crudity of the other Russian national operas that have been seen in this country, and it is altogether a much more finished production. In many places the music has the perfection of workmanship to be found in Tchaikovsky... The whole opera is far superior to many of the others this company has mounted.

On the whole the style was more Western than in the other Russian operas, though some of it was typically Russian and Eastern—for instance, the scene in the camp,

though Igor's number in this scene is European almost to the point of being English.

Thus it will be seen that there are many contrasts of style in the opera, though no conflict, and it makes an entertainment that is is not difficult to prophesy will be extremely popular.

It was conducted by Leon Steinberg and produced by Alexander Sanine under the direction of Diaghileff with the dances arranged by Michel Fokine. The *Morning Post* critic said that 'clearly the dressing of scholarship added to Russian nationalism makes it more palatable'.

Paul Andreev was excellent as Igor, especially in the soliloquy, and Chaliapin sang the parts of both Galitsky and Konchak—the former being, as *The Times* said, 'a new kind of part for M. Chaliapin, for Galitsky is just a profligate'.

The sub-plot of the love of Igor's son for the daughter of the Polovtsy chief was omitted and the dances had been seen in London before—on June 30, 1913, but

set into the opera these dances have an even more thrilling effect than they can have alone.

One is amazed not only by the vitality of the thing, but by the extraordinary variety of types which the vitality can assume, just as one is amazed by seeing M. Chaliapin in one act as the careless Galitsky and in the next as the Khan Konchak, a man of thoroughly Eastern type.

His whole appearance as Konchak, the wonderful make-up of his face, his slow walk, swinging slightly from side to side, and the gestures of his hands seem to belong to a different civilisation.

The last act was 'exquisite', with the unaccompanied chorus of townsfolk at the start, though the duet between Igor and his wife was rather more conventional than most of the music—not that it mattered, for there was little interest in the principal characters. The reception was terrific:—

Though the opera lasted till close upon twelve o'clock, the audience would willingly have stayed longer to hear more of this amazing opera, and each scene aroused the greatest enthusiasm.

The *Standard* had much praise for the chorus—and indirectly the producer:—

Individually and collectively the chorus were as marvellous as ever. They never appear to look at the conductor or to take stock of what their neighbours are doing, and yet the ensemble is faultless, while the pictures they show us of national life are extraordinarily vivid and realistic.

Finally, the *Telegraph*, as well as welcoming the humour of *Igor* after the pessimism or melancholy of *Boris* and *Ivan the Terrible*, which had been produced in 1913 at Drury Lane—though it found some moments conventional (Vladimir's serenade, Igor's soliloquy) thought the music wonderful and the whole opera original and exciting, and well deserving the cheers that kept breaking through from the audience:—

It should be said here that the furore after the Polovtsienne dances and Kon-chak's great solo was of a kind quite unprecedented. Not only were Messrs. Fokine, Steinberg, and Sanine called, with Chaliapin, times impossible to count, but we did actually count no less than fifteen 'curtains', and for upwards of ten minutes a joyous pandemonium went on. Such a scene has not been witnessed in grand opera in the present generation.

It would not be true to say that with this production opera in England had come full circle, for no history—artistic or other-wise—moves in recurrent circles: but threads and echoes from the past are picked up from time to time, and here with *Igor*, that great combination of opera and ballet, we are reminded of Davenant's exciting musical plays with narrative dances, the apparently conductorless—and therefore freely emotional—per-formances by the best of the early eighteenth century Italian singers, the logic and sense that English enthusiasts had always begged for from Ben Jonson onwards, the value of popular en-thusiasm and so popular demand for the most lasting of what is good, and the inevitable truth that opera, like all arts, grows and flourishes, not under committees, but through the inspiration of the individual, whether as organiser or demonstrator—in the case of *Igor* and those magical four seasons between 1910 and 1914 through the personal enthusiasm and magnetism of Sir Thomas Beecham, who most surely has done more than any other single individual for opera in this country since the days of the first great enthusiast, Sir William Davenant.

[1] At the Metropolitan Bianca Froelich of the Corps de Ballet danced for Fremstad.
[2] The date is corrected in the second edition.

Bibliography

Apart from Pepys's *Diary*, the *Histories of Music* by Burney and Hawkins, all works by Professor Allardyce Nicoll and Professor Edward J. Dent, daily newspapers of the nineteenth century and Löwenberg's *Annals of Opera*, my chief books of reference have been the following:—

1656	W. Davenant	*The Siege of Rhodes.*
1657	W. Davenant	*The First Day's Entertainment.*
1658	W. Davenant	*The Cruelty of the Spaniards in Peru.*
1658		Public Intelligence, 1665–60.
1659	W. Davenant	*Sir Francis Drake.*
1661	W. Davenant	*Wit and Drollery.*
1663	Sir R. Stapleton	*The Slighted Maid.*
1664	Sir R. Stapleton	*The Stepmother.*
1673		The Works of Sir William Davenant.
1674	P.P.	*Ariadne.*
1675	Locke	The English Opera.
1675	T. Shadwell	*Psyche.*
1677	C. Davenant	*Circe.*
1687	L. Grabu	*Albion and Albanius.*
1692		The Works of Ben Jonson.
1701	John Dryden	Comedies, Tragedies and Operas.
1706	John Dennis	An Essay on the Operas.
1708	John Downes	Roscius Anglicanus.
1709	Anon.	A critical discourse upon Operas in England and a means proposed for their improvement.
	Anon.	A comparison between the French and Italian Music and Operas, translated from the French.
1709–11		The Tatler.
1711	Aaron Hill	Dedication and Preface to Rinaldo.
1712	Richard Estcourt	*Prunella.*
		The Spectator.
	J. Hughes	*Calypso.*
1719	Mrs. Aubert	*Harlequin Hydaspes.*
1720		The Theatre.
1721	Thomas D'Urfey	New Operas.
1723		Le Mercure.
	John Dennis	Remarks on *The Conscious Lover.*
1727	Anon.	Advice to the Composers and Performers of Vocal Music.
1728	Alexander Pope	The Dunciad.
1728	Roger North	Musical Grammarian.
	Niccolo Haym	*Tolomeo.*

[1720–34]		The London Journal.
	A Primcock	The Touchstone.
1729	Samuel Johnson of Cheshire	*Hurlothrumbo.*
	(Colley Cibber)	*The Rival Queens.*
1730	J. Ralph	*The Fashionable Lady.*
1731	A. Primcock	*The Taste of the Town.*
1732	Anon.	*Mr. Taste.*
1712–34	Francis Colman	MS. Opera register in British Museum. Add. MS. 11258.
1738	Anon.	*Pigeon-Pye* or *A King's Coronation.*
1740	Colley Cibber	An Apology for the Life of Colley Cibber.
1741	J. Ralph	The Champion.
1742	Pier Francesco Tosi	Observations on the Florid Song.
1747	Vanneschi	*Fetonte,* with A Discourse on Operas by S. Lockman.
1749	W. R. Chetwood	General History of the Stage.
1751	John Arbuthnot	Miscellaneous Works.
1752	Fred. Latreille	Playbills of London Theatres (1702–52). Add. MSS. 32,249–52 and 47,612–7.
1753	Aaron Hill	Works.
1755	Richard Steele	*The Conscious Lovers.*
1763	Anon.	A Fair Enquiry into the State of Opera in England.
1767	F. Algarotti	An Essay on the Opera.
1769	D. Webb	Observations on Correspondence, Poetry and Miscellaneous.
1773	J. Byrom	Miscellaneous Poems.
1775	Anon.	*Piramo e Tisbe.*
1777	M. Carey.	*Chrononhotonthologos.*
	C. Cibber	Dramatic Works.
1786–8	A. Pasquin	*Children of Thespis.*
1788		Dibdin's Musical Tour.
1814	A. Burgh	Anecdotes of Music.
1824	R. Edgecumbe	Musical Reminiscences.
1826		Reminiscences of Michael Kelly.
1828	J. Ebers	Seven Years of the King's Theatre.
	J. Nichols	Progresses, etc., of James I.
1834	W. Bingley	Musical Biography.
1838	G. Hogarth	Musical History, Biography and Criticism.
	G. Hogarth	Memoirs of the Musical Drama.
1845 (c.)	Michael Balfe	MS. note-books in B.M.
1848	T. Birch, D.D.	Court and Times of James I.
1851	G. Hogarth	Memoirs of the Opera.
1860	R. H. Whitelock	Memoirs of Bulstrode Whitelocke.
1863	Ellen Creathorne Clayton	Queens of Song.

1864	Benjamin Lumley	Reminiscences of the Opera.
1875	Charles Lamb Kenny	A Memoir of Michael William Balfe.
1881	B. Disraeli	Calamities.
1883	W. A. Barrett	Balfe: His Life and Work.
1886	H. Sutherland Edwards	Famous First Presentations.
1888	H. Sutherland Edwards	The Prima Donna.
1891	Horace Walpole	Letters (ed.).
1894–1912	J. Byrom, ed. A. Ward	Poems.
1896	Luigi Arditi	My Reminiscences.
1907	Ed. by F. J. Furnival	Rupert Laneham's Letter.
1908	Jeanette Marks	English Pastoral Drama.
1912, April		The Musical Times.
1912	W. J. Lawrence	Elizabethan Playhouse, 1st Series.
1912		The Musical Antiquary.
1913–4	W. H. Cummings	Lord Chamberlain and Opera in London.
1917		Shakespeare's England.
1917	R. Northcott	Francesco Algarotti.
1915, etc.		The Musical Quarterly.
1921	H. E. Rollins	Contribution to . . . Commonwealth Drama.
	H. E. Rollins	(Articles reprinted).
1922	Anon.	Anglia.
1923	Lily B. Campbell	Scenes and Machines on the English Stage during the Renaissance.
1923	H. E. Rollins	Cavalier and Puritan Ballads.
1926	Mary Susan Steele	Plays and Masques at Court during the Reigns of Elizabeth, James and Charles.
1927	Hazelton Spencer	Shakespeare Improved.
1927	Enid Welsford	The Court Masque.
1927–8		La Revue Musicale.
1928	Malcolm Elwin	The Playgoer's Handbook to Restoration Drama.
1932	E. Boswell	Restoration Court Stage.
1933	Herman Klein	The Golden Age of Opera.
1934	Montague Summers	The Restoration Theatre.
1942–3		Huntington Library Quarterly, VI.
1944	Sir Thomas Beecham, Bart.	A Mingled Chime.
1947	Sir Newman Flower	George Frideric Handel.

I. COMPOSERS AND CONDUCTORS

COMPOSERS

ADAM, Adolphe, 369
Albinoni, 171
Anfossi, 277
Ariosti, 222, 224–5, 228, 240 n.
Arne, Thomas Augustine, 255, 270, 277, 302
Arnold, Dr, 276–7, 280, 302, 313, 324
Arrigoni, Carlo, 259–60, 261 n.
Attwood, 298
Auber, 320, 321, 330, 337, 364

Bach, J. S., 270, 276–7, 279
Balfe, 324, 326–7, 328 n., 368
Banister, John, 76, 105, 129
Barnett, 324
Beethoven, 322–3, 351
Bellini, 320–1, 323–4, 329, 333, 336, 390
Benedict, 335
Beriot, De, 335
Berlioz, 376
Bertoni, 304
Bianchi, 280
Bishop, Henry, 286, 297–8, 300, 301–2,
    315, 320–3, 325
Bizet, 357–9, 360, 368, 372–5
Blow, Dr. John, 144–6
Boïeldieu, 330
Boito, 373
Bononcini, Giovanni, 165, 171, 177, 194,
    220, 222–6, 230, 232, 247, 251, 255–6
Bononcini, Marcantonio, 165
Borodin, 401
Brahms, 379
Buonaiuti, 284

Caldara, 284
Cambert, Robert, 104–5, 107, 109, 114,
    126 n., 137
Campion, 28–9
Cavalli, 146
Cherubini, 336
Chesterfield, Earl of, 218
Ciampi, 267
Cilea, 384
Cimarosa, 278, 280, 301–2, 336
Clayton, Thomas, 158–9, 169, 170, 189, 242
Cocchi, 268
Coleman, Dr. Charles, 52, 55
Contini, 177
Cooke, Captain Henry, 52, 55, 58, 93–6

Dalayrac, 278, 286
Debussy, 390
Delibes, 372
Delius, 390
Dibdin, Charles, 276–7
Didelot, 293

Donizetti, 321–2, 324–6, 329–30, 333, 335–6
Draghi, G. Baptista, 92–3, 98, 114, 116,
    127 n.

Eccles, John, 260
Erlanger, D', 388

Flotow, 330
Franceschini, 158

Gagliano, Marco da, 59 n.
Galliard, John Ernest, 208, 214, 259
Galuppi, 266, 267, 269
Gasparini, 171, 191, 206
Gazzaniga, 280
Geminiani, 259, 261 n.
Giles, Thomas, 29
Giordani, 303
Giordano, 384
Girardeau, Isabella, 194
Glazounov, 401
Gluck, 267, 276–7, 279–80, 305–6
Gounod, 330–1, 338–9, 340–1, 343–5, 347,
    350, 352, 358, 368, 375
Grabu, Louis, 104–5, 107–9, 114, 132,
    135–42, 146, 153, 171, 199
Greber, Giacomo, 160
Greene, Dr. Maurice, 225, 259
Grétry, 277
Guglielmi, 276

Halévy, 330
Handel, 157, 197–200, 211–12, 216–17,
    219–27, 232–5, 237, 240 n., 246–7, 250–
    65, 265–8, 277–9, 304, 311, 333–4
Hasse, 262, 264, 266, 303
Hawes, W., 313
Haydn, 311
Haym, Nicole, 163, 165, 176, 250
Horn, 298
Hudson, George, 52, 55
Hummel, 283
Humperdinck, 379, 395

Ives, Simon, 38

Jackson, William, 276–9

Krenek, 371 n.

Lampe, 254–5, 264
Lampugnani, 251, 266
Lanier, Nicholas, 32, 39
Lawes, Henry, 41, 52, 55, 71, 152
Lawes, William, 38–9, 41, 71
Leoncavallo, 375–7, 385

Linley, Thomas, 276–7
Locke, Mathew, 55, 71, 87 n., 90, 100, 114, 116–17, 127, 137, 148, 152, 158; re Psyche, 122–5
Loder, 324
Lully, 105, 144, 146, 153, 154 n., 279
Lupo, 29

Mancini, 195
Marazzoli, 49
Marschner, 320
Martin y Solar, 280
Mascagni, 373, 375–8
Massenet, 372, 379, 384, 391
Mayr, 301, 314
Mazzochi, 49
Mendelssohn, 377
Meyerbeer, 315–17, 319, 322, 325, 339, 347, 351, 358, 368, 382
Milton, John, the elder, 44
Mortellari, 304
Monsigny, 276–7
Moussorgsky, 397–8
Mozart, 276, 280, 283, 284–9, 292–4, 296–301, 304–5, 307–9, 311, 314, 320, 350–1, 368, 370–1, 379, 391, 396

Nasolini, 306
Naylor, 388

Offenbach, 351
Orlandini, 220

Paer, 283, 302
Paesiello, 276, 278–9, 280, 283, 298, 300, 302, 305
Panichi, Signora, 266
Pepusch, Dr. John Christopher, 171, 214, 259
Pergolesi, 267
Peri, 19–20, 59 n.
Pescetti, 264–5
Piccini, 276, 304
Ponchielli, 372–3
Porpora, 256–7, 259–60, 261 n., 262
Porta, 219
Predieri, 220
Puccini, 377–8, 380–2, 384–5
Purcell, Daniel, 157
Purcell, Henry, the younger, 32, 76, 100, 135, 137–51, 157–8, 179, 189, 197, 205, 213, 214 n., 263, 270, 277–8, 280; re music and words, 149–51

Quantz, re Faustina & Cuzzoni, 230–2

Radicati, Felice, 287
Rauzzini, 304
Reeve, 279
Reggio, 103
Ricci brothers, 374
Rimsky-Korsakov, 397–8, 401
Roseingrave, 219
Rossi, 294
Rossini, 298–9, 302, 310–11, 313, 316, 317, 320–1, 325, 330, 333, 336–7, 347 n., 350–1, 368

Sacchini, 279, 303–4
Saggione, Giuseppe, 164, 171
Saint-Saëns, 377, 382, 387
Sandoni, 233, 262
Scarlatti, Alessandro, 171–2, 176–7, 218–19, 254
Shield, 277, 302
Sidgeon (see Saggione).
Smetana, 380
Smith, 255
Smyth, 388
Spohr, 325
Spontini, 292, 320, 336
Stanford, 206, 391
Steffani, 171
Storace, 279–80, 302, 305
Strauss, Richard, 388, 391–7
Sullivan, 358, 379, 390

Tchaikovsky, 401
Thomas, Ambroise, 330, 347, 350
Thomson, 324

Veracini, 263, 267
Verdi, 327, 329–38, 341, 347, 355–6, 358, 368, 372–3, 378–9, 381, 383
Vinci, 225–47

Wagner, 53, 125, 342, 341–52, 355, 361–70, 372–3, 375–6, 379, 383, 389, 392, 396, 398–400
Wallace, 368
Weber, 133, 313–14, 320, 349–51
Weichsell, Carl, 279, 283–4, 299
Weichsell, Charles, 283
Whitelock, 38, 45
Winter, 314

Yradier, 360

CONDUCTORS

Arditi, 341, 349, 375

Kubelik, 191 n.

Beecham, 19, 328 n., 388–92, 394–5, 397, 400, 402–3
Bodansky, 399

Mancinelli, 378

Richter, 361, 368–9

Cooper, 393
Costa, 347

Seidl, 361, 365
Steinberg, 401–2

Jaquinot, 381–2

Weichsell, 283

II. MASQUES, OPERAS AND OTHER THEATRE ENTERTAINMENTS

MASQUES

Augurs, Masque of, 33
Blackness, Masque of, 23–4, 25, 40
Britannia Triumphans, 41
Chloridia, 16, 31, 34
Coelum Britannicum, 48 n.
Comus, 1634, 39, 52
Cruelty of the Spaniards in Peru, The, 60–9, 70, 72 n., 89, 97, 105, 117
Cupid and Death, 71
For the Honour of Wales, 32
Hymenaei, 1606, 25
Lethe, Masque of, 36 n.
Lovers made Men, 36 n.

Loves Triumph through Callipolis, 34
Luminalia, 41, 48 n.
Notte d'Amour, 31
Oberon, the Fairy Prince, 30
Pleasure reconciled to Virtue, 32
Solomon and the Queen of Sheba, 26–7
Temple of Love, The, 40
Tethys' Festival, 29–30
Triumph of Peace, 38–9, 42, 45, 71
Triumphs of the Prince d'Amour, The, 41
Twelfth Night Masque, 28–9
Vision of Delight, 31–2

OPERAS

Abu Hassan, 350
Acis and Galatea (scenes from), 253
Adelia, ossia La Figlia dell' Arciere, 325
Admeto, Re di Tessaglia, 228–9, 246, 250
Adolf and Clara (Adolphe et Clara, ou Les Deux Prisonniers), 286
Adriana Lecouvreur, 384
Adriano in Siria, 263
Africaine, L', 347
Agnese di Fitz-Henry, 302
Aida, 355–7, 373
Albion and Albanius, 132–44, 150, 242
Alceste, 280, 305
Alcina, 262
Alessandro, 227, 240 n.
Alessandro Severo, 265
Almahide, 194–5
Almaviva, o sia L'Inutile Precauzione (see Barber of Seville).
Amadigi di Gaula, 213, 219
Amadis, 144
Amanti Gelosi, Gli (see Jealous Lovers).
Ambleto, 191, 206
Amelia, 254
Amico Fritz, 375
Amore e Maesta, 220

Anato (Nabucodonosor), 333
Andrea Chenier, 384
Angelus, The, 388
Anna Bolena, 321
Antioco, 191, 206, 209
Aquilio, 225
Ariadne in Crete, 250, 257
Ariadne in Naxos, 256–7, 260–1
Ariane, 105, 107–14
Arianna e Teseo (see Ariadne in Naxos).
Ariodante, 262
Armida (Mortellari), 304
Armide (Lully), 146
Arminio, 212, 264
Arsace, 220
Arsinoe, Queen of Cyprus, 158–60, 163, 169, 174, 180, 189, 196, 242
Artaserse (Ariosti), 225
Artaserse (Hasse), 262, 303
Artaxerxes (Arne), 270, 302
Astarto, 220, 222
Astianatte, 230, 232
Atalanta, 264

Ballo in Maschera, 338
Barber of Seville (Bishop-Rossini), 300–1

Barber of Seville (Rossini), 276, 298–300, 302, 311, 317, 320, 369
Barbiere di Siviglia (Paesiello), 279–80, 302
Bartered Bride, The, 380, 385
Bastien et Bastienne, 379
Beatrice di Tenda, 324
Beggar's Opera, The, 234–9, 244, 247, 249–50, 253, 264, 292, 305
Berenice, 264
Black Huntsman of Bohemia, The, (Freischütz), 315
Bohème, La, 380–2
Bohemian Girl, The, 326–7, 328 n.
Bohémienne, La, 328 n.
Boris Godounov, 397–8, 402
Britannia, 255
British Enchanters, The, or No Magic Like Love, 164, 173
Buona Figliuola, La, 276, 280, 302, 304

Cadmus and Hermione, 144–6, 153–4
Caduta de' Giganti, La, 267
Caio Marzio Coriolano, 224
Calfurnia, 225
Camilla, Regina de Volsci, Il Trionfo di, 163–5, 169–77, 184, 190, 193, 214, 227–8, 235, 243–4, 250
Carmen, 357–60
Catone, 255
Cavalleria Rusticana, 373–7
Cenerentola, 302, 311, 373
Che Originali (Il Fanatico per la Musica), 302
Cherokee, The, 280
Children in the Wood, The, 246, 280
Chi Soffre, Speri, 49
Circassian Bride, The, 286
Circe, 129, 158
Ciro in Babilonia, o sia La Caduta di Baldassarre, 302
Ciro, or L'Odio e l'Amore, 222
Ciro Riconosciuto, 268
Clari, or The Maid of Milan, 302
Clearte, 213
Clemenza di Tito, La, 283–6, 289, 291, 294, 302, 309, 311
Clotilda, 177, 180, 182–3, 193
Comte Ory, Le, 320
Coq d'Or, Le, 401
Cosi fan Tutte, 287–8
Creso, Re di Lidia, 212
Crispino e la Comare, 374
Crispo, 223–4
Crociato in Egitto, Il, 315–20
Cyrus (see Ciro Riconosciuto).

Dafne, 19, 59 n.
Dario, Il, 225
Daughter of the Regiment, The, 330
Deidamia, 250, 266
Demetrio, 264
Demon of the Wolf's Glen and the Seven Charmed Bullets, The, (Freischütz), 315

Deserter, The, 276
Devil to Pay, The, 253
Didone Abbandonata (pasticcio), 278, 304
Didone Abbandonata (Sacchini), 303
Dido and Aeneas, 147–8, 154, 157–8, 227
Dioclesian, 148–50, 152, 213, 248
Don Carlos, 347
Don Ferdinando (Don Fernando), 260–1, 261 n.
Don Giovanni (Bishop–Mozart), 298
Don Giovanni (Mozart), 294–7, 311–12, 391
Don Giovanni Tenorio, 280
Don Juan (see Don Giovanni).
Don Pasquale, 325–6
Donna del Lago, La, 311
Dorinda, 211–12
Dragon of Wantley, The, 246, 264, 277
Due Foscari, I, 330
Duenna, The, 276
Dusk of the Gods, The, (see Götterdämmerung).

Elektra, 388–90, 393, 396
Elisir d'Amore, L', 324–6, 335
Elisabetta, Regina d'Inghilterra, 302, 311
Elphi Bey, or The Arab's Faith, 298
Elpidia, 225, 247
Enchanted Flute, The, (see Magic Flute).
Enfant Prodigue, L', 390
Ergasto (see Loves of Ergasto).
Erminia, 224
Ernani, 329–30, 333, 335–6, 373
Ernelinda, 191, 212
Eroe Cinese, L', 304
Esule di Roma, ossia Il Proscritto, L', 322
Eugen Onegin, 375
Euridice, 20
Ezio (Handel), 250
Ezio (pasticcio), 304

Fairy Queen, The, 152
Faithful Shepherd, The, 211–12
Falstaff, 378–9
Faramonso, 265
Farnace, 225
Faust (Gounod), 36 n., 338–47, 350
Faust (Spohr), 325
Fausta, 325
Favorita, La, 327
Fede Tradita e Vendicata, La (see Ernelinda).
Feuersnot, 391
Fidelio, 322–3, 391
Figaro (see Marriage of Figaro).
Filosofo di Campagna, Il, 269
Flauto Magico, Il (see Magic Flute).
Flavio, 225
Floridante, Il, 223
Flying Dutchman, The, 348–51, 366, 369, 373
Forza del Destino, La, 347
Fra Diavolo, 321
Frascatana, La, 302, 304
Freischütz, Der, 19, 125, 313–16, 323, 330

INDEX

Gare Generose, Le, 278
Gazza Ladra, La, 302, 310, 317, 325
Gemma di Vergy, 325
Giannina e Bernardone, 278
Gioconda, La, 372
Giulio Cesare in Egitto, 225–6, 278, 304
Giustino, 264
Götterdämmerung, 365–6
Griselda, 223–4, 246
Grove, The, or Love's Paradise, 157
Guillaume Tell, 320

Hamlet (see Ambleto).
Hamlet (Thomas), 347
Hansel and Gretel, 379–80
Haunted Tower, The, 279, 302, 305, 310
Henry VIII, 382
Hercules, 207
Hercules in Lidia, 49–50
Hermann, or The Broken Spear, 324
Herodiade, 384
History of Sir Francis Drake, 69–70, 72, 72 n., 89, 97
Hofer, the Tell of the Tyrol, 321
Holländer, Der (see Flying Dutchman).
House of Aspen, The, 324
Huguenots, Les, 325, 335, 339
Hydaspes (see Idaspe Fedele).

Idaspe Fedele, 195–7, 201–2, 207, 213
Ifigenia in Aulide, 262
Inez di Castro, 283
Inganno Felice, L', 302
Iphigénie en Tauride, 280, 306
Island Princess, The, 157
Isola del Piacere, L', 280
Issiphile, 262
Italiana in Algeri, L', 302, 311
Ivanhoé (Rossini), 320
Ivanhoe (Sullivan), 390–1
Ivan the Terrible, 402

Jealous Lovers, The, 268
Jessonda, 325
Jonny Spielt Auf, 371 n.

Katya Kabanova, 191 n.
King Arthur, 132, 150–2, 154, 164, 263, 270, 271

Lakmé, 372
Lancashire Witches, The, 132
Libertine, The, 158
Linda di Chamounix, 325
Lionel and Clarissa, 276
Lohengrin, 351–4, 366, 369, 399
Lombardi alla prima Crociata, I, 330
Lord of the Manor, The, 276
Louise, 388
Love in a Village, 270
Loves of Ergasto, The, 160–1
Love's Triumph, 167 n., 174–5, 181–2, 196

Lucia di Lammermoor, 325, 327, 333
Lucio Papirio, Dittatore, 254
Lucio Vero, Imperatore di Roma, 213, 228
Lucrezia Borgia, 325, 333
Luisa Miller, 335, 338

Macbeth, 100, 106 n.
Madama Butterfly, 384–6
Magic Flute, The, 19, 286, 288, 325, 400
Maid of Artois, The, 324
Maid of Judah, The (see Ivanhoé).
Maid of Milan, The (see Clari).
Maid of the Mill, The, 276, 280, 302
Manon, 372
Manon Lescaut, 377–8
Marriage of Figaro (Bishop–Mozart), 300–1
Marriage of Figaro (Mozart), 278, 292–4, 298, 304–5, 308, 311–12
Martha, 266, 330
Martyri, I, 335
Masaniello, 320
Masnadieri, I, 330, 333, 335
Matilde di Shabran, 302
Matrimonio Segreto, Il, 280, 302, 373
Médecin malgré lui, 341, 347 n.
Meistersinger, Die, 361, 367–9
Meridi e Selinunta, 266
Merlin, the British Enchanter, 263
Merope, 306
Midas, 275, 280
Mignon, 347, 350
Mikado, The, 358
Mireille, 347, 353, 358
Mosè in Egitto, 302
Mountain Sylph, The, 324
Muzio Scevola, 222

Nabuco (Nabucodonosor), 330, 335
Narciso, 219
Nero Infante, 188
Nina, o sia La Pazza per Amore (Paesiello), 280, 321
Nina, ou La Folle par Amour (Dalayrac), 278
Nino (see Nabuco).
Nonne Sanglante, La, 347 n.
Norma, 323, 335
No Song, No Supper, 279, 302
Nourjahad, 324
Nuit de Mai, 401
Numitore, 219–20

Oberon, 133, 320
Oca del Cairo, L', 350
Olandese Dannato, Il, (see Flying Dutchman).
Olimpiade, L', 304
Olimpia in Ebuda, 266
Olivo and Pasquale, 322
Opera of Operas, 255
Orazi ed i Curiazi, Gli, 301
Oreste, 262
Orfeo (Gluck), 276–7, 279

411

Orfeo (pasticcio), 263
Orlando, 255
Otello (Rossini), 311, 350
Otello (Verdi), 372–3
Ottone, Re di Germania, 224–5

Padlock, The, 276
Pagliacci, I, 375–7
Pan and Syrinx, 214
Parsifal, 399–400
Partenope, 251
Pastorella, La, 174
Pastor Fido, Il (see Faithful Shepherd).
Pearl Fishers, The, 372
Pelléas et Mélisande, 388
Périchole, La, 351
Philémon et Baucis, 341, 347 n., 375
Pietro l'Eremita, 302
Pinafore, 358
Pirata, Il, 320–1
Pirates, The, 279
Piu Fedel fra i Vassalli, Il (see Antioco).
Polifemo, 262
Polly, 219
Pomone, 126
Poor Soldier, The (The Shamrock), 302
Poro, Re dell' Indie, 250, 253
Prince Igor, 119, 401–2
Prophetess, The (see Dioclesian).
Psyche, 114–29, 137–8, 144, 147, 158, 291 n.
Puits d'Amour, Les, 326, 328 n.
Puritani di Scozia, I, 324, 387
Pyrrhus and Demetrius, 176–7, 183–4, 193, 213

Quinto Fabio, 304

Radamisto, 219–20, 249, 253
Rape of Proserpine, The, 229
Rheingold, 361–3
Ricardo Primo, Re d'Inghilterra, 234, 240 n.
Ricciardo e Zoraide, 302, 311, 317
Rigoletto, 331–6
Rinaldo (Handel), 198–201, 207, 212–13, 248
Rinaldo (Sacchini), 304
Ring des Nibelungen, Der, 361–8
Roberto d'Evereux, Conte d'Essex, 325
Robert the Devil, 322
Rodelinda, 225
Romeo and Juliet, 347, 353
Rosalinda, 267
Rosamond (Arne), 255
Rosamond (Clayton), 169–71
Rosenkavalier, Der, 292, 395–7
Rosina, 277

Salome, 391–4
Samson et Dalila, 377, 382, 387–8, 391
Sapho, 330–1, 341
Scipione (Handel), 227
Scipione Africano (Cavalli), 146

Scipione in Carthagine (Galuppi), 267
Scuola dei Maritati, La, 280
Secret Marriage, The (see Matrimonio Segreto).
Semele, 197
Semiramide, 302, 347 n.
Seraglio, Il, 320
Serse (see Xerxes).
Serva Padrona, La (Paesiello), 306
Serva Padrona, La (Pergolesi), 267, 277
Shamrock, The, 277
Shadow on the Wall, The, 324
Siege of Belgrade, The, 279, 305
Siege of Rhodes, The, 54–9, 61, 64, 69, 74–5, 92, 97, 101, 242
Siege of Rochelle, The, 324
Siegfried, 363–5
Siroe, 237, 240 n., 249, 264
Sonnambula, La, 320–3
Sorcerer, The, 358
Sosarme, Re di Media, 254
Spanish Barber, The, 276
State of Innocence and the Fall of Man, The, 131–2
Straniera, La, 323
Stravaganti, Gli, 276–7

Tales of Hoffman, The, 391
Tamerlano, 225
Tancredi, 302, 311, 317
Tannhäuser, 348, 350, 353–5, 369, 399
Telemachus, 254
Tempest, The (Dryden), 95–8, 117, 137–8
Tempest, The (Shadwell), 101–3, 106, 117, 122, 126 n., 127 n., 152–3, 157
Temple of Love, The, 164
Teraminta, 255
Terpsichore, 262
Teseo, 212
Tess, 388
Teuzzone, 240 n.
Thomas and Sally, 270
Thomyris, Queen of Scythia, 171–7, 196, 214, 216, 244, 250
Tiefland, 391
Tito Manlio, 213
Torquato Tasso, 325
Tosca, 382–5
Traviata, La, 337–8, 359, 373.
Trial by Jury, 351
Trionfo di Camilla (see Camilla).
Tristan und Isolde, 53, 192 n., 353, 361, 368–70, 399
Triumph of Love, The (see Love's Triumph), 167 n., 175
Trovatore, Il, 335–7, 341, 355
Turco in Italia, Il, 302, 311
Two Queens of Brentford, The, 222–3

Valkyrie, The (see Walkiire).
Vampyr, Der, 320
Venceslao, 213

INDEX

Vendetta di Nino, La, 280
Venus and Adonis, 144
Vêpres Siciliennes, Les, 338
Vespasiano, 225
Vestale, La, 292, 320
Village Romeo and Juliet, A., 390
Virgin Prophetess, The, 157

Walküre, Die, 362–3, 371 n.
Waterman, The, 276

Werther, 379, 391
Wonders in the Sun, or *The Kingdom of the Birds,* 164–5
Wreckers, The, 388

Xerxes, 165

Zauberflöte, Die (see *Magic Flute*).
Zelmira, 302
Zenobia, 303

ENTERTAINMENTS

Cruelty of the Spaniards in Peru, The (quasi revue), 60–9, 70, 72 n., 97, 105, 117
Figaro, ou les Noces du Comte Almaviva (Ballet), 292
First Day's Entertainment, The (quasi revue), 50–4, 56, 66
Gipsy, La (Ballet), 327
Gitana (Ballet), 327
Ildamor and Zulema (Ballet), 287
Jeux (Ballet), 398

Miracle, The (Film), 395
Pavilion (Ballet), 399
Peggy's Love (Ballet), 291, 293
Petrouchka (Ballet), 397
Playhouse to be let, The (Revue), 88–9
Scheherazade (Ballet), 399
Sweet and Low (Revue), 48 n.
Sylphide, La (Ballet), 323
Tamerlan and Bajazet (Ballet), 286
Tyrant Saracen and the Noble Moor, The (Show with horses), 288

PLAYS

Almanzor and Almahide, 99
Amphitryon, 149
Andromède, 99
Antony and Cleopatra (burlesque), 89
Appius and Virginia, 128 n.
As You Like it, 87 n., 267
Author's Farce, The, 251–2
Beaux' Stratagem, The, 173
Careless Husband, The, 206
Charley's Aunt, 370
Clandestine Marriage, The, 280
Conscious Lovers, The, 91, 224
Contre Temps, The, or *The Rival Queans,* 232–3
Coxcomb, The, 128 n.
Dear Brutus, 36 n.
Devil of a Wife, The, 145
Elfrida, 267
Empress of Morocco, The, 68
Fair Favourite, The, 41
Fashionable Lady, The, or *Harlequin's Opera,* 252
Faust, 364
Hamlet, 86, 370
Henry VIII, 90
Horace, 98
Hurlothrumbo, or *The Supernatural,* 252
Hyde Park, 128 n.
Indian Queen, The, 92
Just Italian, The, 37
Kind Keeper, The, or *Mr. Limberham,* 130
King Lear, 31, 165
Lady's Last Stake, The, 172

Lady's Triumph, The, 214
Life and Death of Common Sense, The, 263–4
Love for Money, or *The Boarding School,* 154 n.
Love in a Riddle, 251
Love in the Dark, 125
Macbeth, 37, 300, 316
Maid the Mistress, The, 175
Measure for Measure, 157
Metamorphosis, The, 158
Midsummer Night's Dream, A, 19, 152, 300
Miss Julie, 105
Mock-Tempest, The, 126
Oklahoma, 131
Othello, 37, 194, 300
Pasquin, 263
Pastor Fido, Il, 134
Phaedra and Hippolitus, 172
Prunella, 173–4
Psyche (Molière), 114–15
Psyche Debauched, 125
Rehearsal, The, 87 n., 100, 140, 173, 222
Richard III, 197
Rival Modes, The, 228
Rival Queans, The (see *The Contre Temps*).
Scarlet Pimpernel, The, 36 n.
Schoolboy, The, 206, 213
Sea-Voyage, The, or *The Storm,* 28
Sequel of Henry IV, The: with the Humours of Sir John Falstaff and Justice Shallow, 206
Sganarella, 89

Slighted Maid, The, 76–87, 90–1, 117, 119, 215 n.
Stepmother, The, 90–1
Storm, The (see *The Sea-voyage*).
Tale of a Tub, 35
Tempest, The, 21, 99
Tender Husband, The, 161–2

Theodosius, 146
Timon of Athens, 158
'Tis Pity She's a Whore, 128 n.
Troilus and Cressida, 85
Tunbridge Walks, 158
Wits, The, 37–8
Wives' Excuse, The, 153

III. SINGERS

Ackté, 392–4
Agujari, 276
Albani, 352–4, 362
Alboni, 347
Alda, 266
Ambrogetti, 295–9, 302
Ancona, 375–6
Andreer, Paul, 401
Angeri, D', 310, 312, 352
Angrisani, 298
Ansani, 304

Bahr-Mildenburg, 390
Baldassari, 220
Baldi, 247
Balfe, 325
Bannister, 305
Banti, 280, 303, 305, 306–8
Barbier, 244
Baroness, The, 163, 172, 174, 176–7
Baroni, Adriana, 49
Baroni, Leonora, 49
Beduschi, 378
Begnis, De, 312
Belloc, 312
Bender, 399
Bennet, 314
Berenstadt, 220, 246
Bernardi (*see* Senesino).
Berselli, 220
Bertinotti (Radicati), 287, 308
Billington, 278, 283–7, 289, 306
Bland, 305, 308
Bodoni (*see* Faustina).
Borgioli, Dino, 187
Boschi, 220, 246, 247
Bosio, 335
Boy, The (Holcombe), 165, 177
Braham, 285–6, 306

Caffarelli, 265
Campanini, 359, 360
Camporese, 297, 302, 309
Carestini, 259, 262
Carpi, 353–4
Caruso, 266, 384, 386
Cassani, 194

Catalani, 288, 290, 291–3–4, 304, 306–8, 311–12
Catoneo, 372
Cauvini, 287
Cauvini, Mme., 287
Chaliapin, 187, 397–9, 401–2
Cibber, 304
Colbran–Rossini, 312
Coleman, Edward, 54, 59
Coleman, Mrs. Edward, 54, 59
Collini, 287
Cook, 158, 176
Cooke, Captain Henry, 54
Corsi, 348
Crivelli, 295
Cross, 158, 169, 194
Crouch, 277–8, 304
Cuzzoni, 224–8, 230–1, 233–4, 236, 238, 247–8, 250, 261, 265

Dearth, 392
Dennis, 220
Destinn, 384–5–6
Dickens, 287, 292–3, 300–1, 308
Dotti, 247
Durastanti, 220, 222, 224–5

Elisi, 268–9
Epine, 158, 160, 167 n., 171, 174, 176–7, 194, 214

Farinelli, 261 n., 262–4, 269, 275, 279
Faure, 343–6
Faustina, 227, 230–1, 233–4, 236, 238, 246, 250, 265
Fenton, 235
Fodor, 298–9, 312
Foley (*see* Foli).
Foli, 348
Fontaine, 387–8
Frasi, 267
Fremstad, 392

Gabrielli, 303
Galerati, 220
Gallia, 164, 169
Galli-Marie, 360

Garcia, 298–9, 300, 308, 317
Garcia, Mlle (Malibran), 317–18
Garde, La, 220
Garden, 392
Gassier, 338–9, 340, 343, 345–6
Genoese, The, 50
Gillibert, 383
Gindele, 357
Giordani family, The, 268
Giuglini, 338–9, 343, 345, 347
Gordon, 220
Grassini, 306, 308
Graziani, 357
Griglietti, 285, 288, 290–1
Grimaldi (see Nicolini).
Grisi, 326, 347 n.
Grossi (see Siface).
Guadagni, 304
Gura, 368

Haitzinger, 323
Hauk, 358–9, 360
Hensel, 399
Holcombe (see The Boy).
Hughes, 158, 165, 169

Italian Lady, The, 153

Jacoby, 266
James, 392
Journet, 266

Kelly, 305
Knowles, 392
Knupfer, 396, 399
Kraus, 393

Lablache, 321, 326
Lanier, 32, 39
Lawrence, 194, 208
Leveridge, 158, 165, 244
Lind, 330
Lindsey, 158, 165, 194
Liston, 301
Locke, 59
Lovattini, 276, 304
Lucia, De, 375, 383
Lunn, 387–8

Malibran (Garcia), 317–18, 323–4
Manzoli, 275
Mara, 278, 304–6
Marchesi, Luigi, 305
Marchesi, Mme., 348
Marchesi, Salvatore, 348
Maria, Joanna, 164–5
Mario, 326, 332, 334–5, 347 n.
Materna, 362–3
Mattei, 268–9
Maurel, 352–4, 372–3
Melba, 348, 375–7
Mingotti, 268

Miolan-Carvalho, 342–3
Mountain, 287
Murska, De, 348–9, 350
Muscovita, The (see Panichi).
Musiani, 373–4

Naldi, 287–8, 292–3, 295, 297–9, 308
Nicolini, Ernest Nicholas, 352
Nicolini (Grimaldi), 176–7, 183–4, 186–7,
    193–5, 198, 201–2, 207, 209, 210–11, 213
Niemann, 362
Nilsson, 362

Oisly, D', 392
Olghina, 378

Pacchierotti, 303–5, 311
Paganini, The, 269
Paganini troupe, 268
Palmerini, 247
Panichi, 266
Pasta, 312, 315, 319, 321, 323
Patti, 355–7
Peretti, 270
Perotti, 348
Persiani, 325, 347 n.
Piccolomini, 337–8
Purcell, Henry, the elder, 59

Radford, 392
Ramondon, 165, 176
Reeves, 347
Reigher–Kindermann, 362
Rencia, 49–50
Righi, 285
Rinaldini, 348
Robinson, Anastasia, 220, 247
Robinson, Turner, 220
Romanzini (see Mrs. Bland).
Ronconi, 334, 347 n.
Rose, 390
Rovedino, 285
Roze, 360
Rubinelli, 304–5
Rubini, 321, 325

Sachse-Hofmeister, 362
Salvai, 220
Sandoni (see Cuzzoni).
Santley, 338, 341, 346–9
Scaria, 362
Scheper, 362
Schlosser, 362
Schröder–Devrient, 322–3
Scotti, 383–4, 386
Senesino, 216, 220, 225–7, 233–4, 246–8,
    250–1, 253, 257, 262
Sestini, 304
Sherrington, 347
Siems, 395–6
Siface (Grossi, Giovanni Francesco), 146
Smythson, 332

Sontag, 321
Spiletta, The, 269
Stephens, 301
Storace, Anna, 278–9, 304–5, 312
Strada, 259, 262
Sucher, 370

Tamagno, 372
Tamberlik, 330, 337, 343, 347
Tamburini, 325, 330, 347 n.
Tenducci, 270, 277
Ternina,383
Thornton, 392
Titiens, 338–9, 340–1, 343, 345, 347
Tofts, 158–60, 163, 165, 174, 176–8
Tosi, 153, 231
Tramezzani, 287–8, 290–3, 308
Turner, 165, 176

Urbani Valentino (see Valentini).

Valentini, 169, 172, 174–7, 181, 185, 194, 211
Van der Osten, 395–9, 400
Velluti, 315–16, 318
Viardot–Garcia, 330, 336–7
Vignas, 373
Vogl, 362, 364–5
Vogl, Mme, 362 365

Walker, 389–90
Weichsell (see Billington).
Weidemann, 390
Whitehall, 392, 394
Wigand, 364
Wynn, 392

IV. THEATRES AND OTHER PLACES FOR MASQUES, OPERAS, ETC.

Alhambra, 393
Apothecaries' Hall, 47
Banqueting House, Whitehall, 23, 41
Bartholomew Fair, 236
Bayreuth, 361–2, 364–5, 400
Blackfriars, 37, 43
Bridges St., 88, 98
Camden, 384
Cockpit (Drury Lane), 43, 47, 60, 69, 74, 89, 140
Cockpit (Whitehall), 43, 90
Covent Garden Opera House, 331, 337–8, 342, 344–7, 351, 353, 355–6, 375, 377–9, 381–91, 393, 395, 399–400
Covent Garden Theatre, 255, 262–4, 270, 275, 277, 287, 300, 315, 320, 322
Daly's, 379
Dorset Garden (see Duke's (Dorset Garden)).
Drury Lane (1) 43, 47, 70; (2) see Theatre Royal (2) and (3).
Dublin, 75
Duke's (Dorset Garden), 98, 100–2, 104–5, 110, 117, 121, 127 n., 128 n., 131–2, 148, 158, 162, 177, 326
Duke's (Lincoln's Inn Fields), 73–5, 86, 88, 90–2, 98, 100, 157, 162. Illustrated, 16.
English Opera House (see Lyceum).
Fortune, 68
Frankfurt Fair, 46
German (Leicester Square), 286
Goodman's Fields, 263
Hatton Garden, 95
Haymarket Little, 236, 254–5, 266
Her Majesty's, 298–361 (passim).

King's (Haymarket) (1) 220–65 (passim); (2) 267–324 (passim).
King's (Vere St.) (see Theatre Royal (1)).
Lincoln's Inn Fields (1) 47; (2) (see Duke's (Lincoln's Inn Fields); (3) 214, 216, 227–66 (passim).
Lindsey House, 147–8
London Hippodrome, 71
Lyceum, 313, 324, 338, 372
Merchant Taylors' Hall, 39
Metropolitan Opera House, 392, 403 n.
Middle Temple, 41
National Opera House, 354
Palace, 390
Phoenix, 43
Queen's (Haymarket), 160–219 (passim).
Red Bull, 65
Royal Amphitheatre, 315
Royal Court, 393
Royal English Opera House, 390
Royalty, 351
Rutland House, 47–8, 51, 54, 56–7, 64, 92
Sadler's Wells, 19, 163, 191, 263, 338
Salisbury Court, 74
Sanssouci (see German).
Shaftesbury, 373
Southwark Fair, 236
St. George's Hall, 396
St. John's (Clerkenwell), 47
Surrey, 315
Swan, 43
Théâtre Lyrique, 343
Theatre Royal (1) (Vere St.), 74–5; (2) (Bridges St.), 88, 91, 98, 100; (3) (Drury Lane), 103–402 (passim).
Vere St. (see Theatre Royal (1)).
Whitehall Palace, 107, 113–14

V. GENERAL INDEX

ACADÉMIE DES OPÉRAS (Académie Royale), 109, 146, 216
Academy of Ancient Music, 255, 259
Acrobats, 193–4
Addison, as librettist, 169–70; re Nicolini, 209; re sense in the theatre, 172, 198–207, 212, 380
Advice to the Composer, 229–30
Albion Blackamoor, The, rope-dancer, 65
Album des Chansons Espagnoles, 360
Algarotti, Count Francesco, 259; re opera, 270
Allan, Maude, dancer, 393
Alleyn, actor, 20
Anne, Queen, 176, 198, 213, 217, 238
Apology for his life, 173 (see Cibber).
Apuleius, 115
Arbuthnot, Dr. John, 218, 256; re opera, 238–9
Argyle, Duke of, re Beggar's Opera, 236
Aristotle, 243
Arkwright, Geoffrey, re Purcell's parentage, 59 n.
Arts Council, 324
Arundell, Dennis, re Bohemiam Girl, 328 n.; re "Fairest Isle", 154 n.; re Faust, 347 n.; re stage effects, 36 n.
Astley's horses, 288–9

Bacon, Roger, 47–8
Bacon, Sir Francis, Essay on masques, 34; finances masques, 31
Baker, Thomas, dramatist, 158
Ballet introduced to London, 214
Banister, flautist, 182
Barberini, Cardinal, gives opera, 49
Barbier, Jules, librettist, 341
Bardi, Count, and origin of opera, 19
Barry, Mrs., actress, 194
Bath, Earl of (see William Pulteney).
Baylis, Lilian, and opera, 19
Beaconsfield, Lord, 98
Beaumarchais, 276, 293
Beaumont and Fletcher, 98
Beecham opera seasons, 19, 388–403 (passim).
Beiblatt zur Anglia, 48 n.
Belasco, David, dramatist, 384
Bell, Sir Charles, re Grassini, 306
Bernini and opera, 49
Bertie, Peregrine, re French opera, 144–5
Bethnal Green Academy, 45–6, 49
Betterton, Thomas, actor, 148, 162, 194; as adaptor, 206; as producer, 118, 138–9, 152; importing French opera, 132; theatre-manager, 101
Betterton, Mrs., actress, 86
Beverley, W., designer, 342

Bingley, Robert Benson, Lord, 217
Blake, Admiral, 60
Blathwayte, Col., 218–19
Blenheim Palace, 162
Boileau, poet, 166
Book of Martyrs, 68
Bowdler, Dr., 391
Bracegirdle, Mrs., actress, 163
Brooke, Lord, 48 n.
Brotanek, Prof., re Luminalia, 48 n.
Brouncker, Lord, 92, 94
Bruce, James, 219
Buckingham, Duke of, dramatist, 87 n., 100, 140, 173
Bunn, Alfred, librettist, 326–7, 328 n., 381
Burgoyne, Lt.-Gen., dramatist, 276
Burke, Lady Dorothy, 227
Burke's Extinct Peerage, 211
Burlington, Countess of, pro Faustina, 231
Burlington, Richard Boyle, Earl of, 217, 219–20
Burlington Magazine, 55
Burney re Admeto, 228; re Almanide, 194; re Comparison, 208; re Cuzzoni, 230–1; re Ergasto, 161; re Faustina, 231; re Giardini, 268; re Manzoli, 215; re Muzio Scevola, 222; re Nicolini, 211; re opera decline, 264, 266, 276; re Paganina, 269; re Royal Academy, 223
Byrom, John, re Handel and Bononcini, 225–6, 251

Calamities and Quarrels of Authors, 98
Cambridge, Magic Flute, 19
Campbell, Lily B., 36
Campion, Thomas, masque-poet, 28–9
Cantate de Camera (Arrigoni), 261 n.
Capon, rope-dancer, 65
Cardigan, Earl of (see James Bruce).
Carew, Thomas, masque-poet, 48 n.
Carey, Henry, librettist, 254–5, 264; re London opera, 236
Carleton, Sir Dudley, re Masque of Blackness, 24
Carl Rosa Company, 360, 380–1
Caroline of Brunswick (Princess of Wales), 291 n.
Carré, Michel, librettist, 341
Carroll, Lewis, 291
Castrato singing, 49–50, 92, 94, 158, 185–6, 225, 263, 315, 317–19
Chapel Royal singers, 94, 103
Charles I, 34
Charles II, 52, 73, 114, 129, 135, 138; as musician, 74, 76, 100, 108, 120, 132, 136, 138, 142
Charles VI, Emperor, 261 n.

Charlotte (Princess of Wales), 291 n.
Charlotte, Queen, 293
Charterhouse Yard, 47, 66
Chatsworth art collection, 55
Chelsea, 146–8, 154 n.
Chetwynd, John, Viscount, 217
Children of Thespis, 277
Churchill, Charles, *re* opera, 270
Cibber, Colley, actor, 178, 194; as dramatist, 197, 206, 232; *re Dioclesian* and *King Arthur*, 152; *re Ergasto*, 160, 167 n.; *re* foreign artists' invasion, 169, 172–3, 189, 214, 265; *re* Lincoln's Inn Fields actors, 162; *re* Nicolini, 176; *re Pyrrhus*, 177; *re* sense in the theatre, 251; *re* Valentini, 169
Clarence, Duke of, 285
Clerkenwell, 65
Colman, Francis, *re Caio Marzio Coriolano*, 224; *re Faithful Shepherd* and *Dorinda*, 212; *re* Handel operas, 229, 254; *re Idaspe*, 213
Cobham, Lord, 237
Coke, Thomas, 219
Colman, George, dramatist, 211, 280
Commedia dell'Arte, 128 n.
Commonwealth and Restoration Stage, 45
Comparison of Operas, A, 180–8, 191, 208
Congreve and foreign artists, 162–3; as theatre-manager, 158, 160, 163; *re Ergasto*, 161; *re* sense in the theatre, 252; *re* words for music, 197
Corelli, 184
Cork, Earl of (*see* Burlington).
Corneille, 99, 114–15
Corseilles, designer, 41
Coryat, Tom, 48 n.
Cost of masques, 31, 39; of opera, 223, 250, 273–5; of scenery, etc., 115, 125, 152, 175; of singers, 162, 212, 265; of theatre, 100; of theatre company, 48, 91, 93, 98, 114, 152, 175–6; of theatre-seats, 98 n., 101
Court Masque, The, 48 n.
Cox, rope-dancer, 65
Crimean War, 336
Critical Discourse upon Operas in England, A, 180–92, 198
Cromwell, Oliver, 68; and entertainments, 45, 60, 62, 64, 68
Cromwell, Richard, and entertainments, 68, 70
Croza, 267
Crudities, 48 n.
Cumberland, Duke of, 267
Cummings, W. H., letter *re* Purcell parentage, 59 n.

Da capo, aria introduced to England, 130
Daniel, Samuel, masque-poet, 29
D'Arcy, Conyers, 217

Davenant, Charles, 101–2, 129
Davenant, Lady, 101
Davenant, Sir William, 37, 40–6, 60–4, 73, 101, 140, 144, 402–3; and music, 37, 94, 98; and orchestra, 56, 71; and stage effects, 92; First Day's Entertainment by, 50–4; masques by, 40–1; *Ode to Shakespeare*, 37; opera ambitions, 41–2, 51–2, 57, 60, 73; operas by, 60–73; plays by, 37–8, 41; *re* words for music, 57–8, 109; theatre aims, 41, 43, 47–8, 73, 75
Davis, Mary, actress, 144
de Gamerra, G., 288
de Grey, Lady, 19
Delaney, Mrs. (*see* Pendarves), 267
Delaware, Lady, *pro* Faustina, 231
Denmark, Prince George of, 176, 208
Dennis, John, against Italian opera, 165–9, 193, 214 n.; *re* theatre costs, 91
Dent, Edward J. (*passim*), 39, 216, 220, 222–3; and *Magic Flute*, 19; on origin of opera, 17; *re Beggar's Opera*, 235; *re* Davenant, 57; *re* Davenant opera, 42, 99; *re* "Fairest Isle", 154 n.; *re* national music, 205; *re* Psyche, 115, 117, 124–5; *re Slighted Maid*, 87 n.; *re* theatre orchestra, 56
De Quincey, *re* Grassini, 306
Des Hayes, dancer, 292
Designs by Inigo Jones, 48 n.
Deutsch, Otto (*Handel*), 240, 261 n.
De Vere, S. du C., trans. Vasari, 36
Devonshire, Duke of, art collection, 55
Diaghileff, 397, 401
Dialogues in masques, 28–9, 32, 39
Dialogues in plays, 37, 52, 96
Dictionary of National Biography, 217 sqq.
d'Israeli, Isaac, *re* Davenant, 98
Doggett, actor, 178, 194
Dormer, Brig.-Gen., James, 218
Dormer, Philip (*see* Chesterfield).
Dorset House, 74
Downes, actor, 74–5; *re* British Enchanters, 164; *re* Circe, 129; *re* Dioclesian, 148; *re Ergasto*, 160–1, 168 n.; *re* Lancashire Witches, 132; *re* Macbeth, 100; *re* Prophetess, 148; *re* Psyche, 114, 127 n., 128 n.; *re* Tempest, 101
Dryden, 92, 95, 97, 130, 144, 150, 153, 194, 196, 263, 267, 278, 318; and da capo aria, 130; attacks Duke's Theatre, 100, 103–4; *re* Davenant, 51, 99, 135; *re* French theatre, 105, 107, 202, 207; *re* Grabu, 135–6, 138; *re* opera, 134–8, 245; *re* origin of heroic plays, 52; *re* Purcell, 149, 151; *re Slighted Maid*, 85; *re* words for music, 58, 133–5, 151
Duffett, Thomas, dramatist, 126
Duke of York's servants, 74
Dulwich School, 20
Dunciad, The, 241
Duport, dancer, 292

D'Urfey, Thomas, author, 139, 141, 147, 164, 209; re Chelsea school, 154 n.; re opera, 222-3

Ebers, John, 315, 319
Edgar, Sir John, re sense in the theatre, 220-1
Edict of Nantes, 146
Edinburgh, Duke of, and music, 362
Edison, 374
Edwardes, George, 380
Edwards, Sutherland, re Carmen, 360 n.
Eighteenth Century Drama, 167 n., 168 n., 179 n., 240 n.
Elizabeth, Queen, 27
Elizabethan Playhouse, The, 42
Elssler, Fanny, dancer, 327
Endless Queries, pamphlet, 73
English Opera, The (see Psyche), 122
Essex, Countess of, 31
Essex, Robert, 2nd Earl of, 29
Essex, Robert, 3rd Earl of, 25
Estcourt, Richard, actor-author, re sense in the theatre, 173-4
Evelyn, diarist, re music, 98; re opera, 49-56, 71, 75, 94, 107; re rope-dancing, 65; re scenes, 92
Expostulation with Inigo Jones, 34-5

Fair enquiry into . . . operas in England, A, 270-5
Fairfax, Bryan, 217
Fassini, Sesto, 261 n.
Festival of Britain, 328 n.
Fielding re sense in theatre, 251-2, 263-4
First Night of Twelfth Night, The, 20
FitzHerbert, Mrs., 285
Flecknoe, Richard, re scenes, 91
Fletcher, 128 n.
Florence, Opera in, 17, 19, 49
Fokine, Michel, dancer, 401-2
Ford, 128 n.
Foundations of English Opera, 39, 42-56, 87 n., 115
Foxe, John, 68
Frankenstein, 327
Frederick Lewis, Prince of Wales, 225, 256
Frederick the Great, and music, 230
French Ambassador, Masque for, 32
French comedians, 89
French performers in England, 99, 101, 104-5, 110, 114, 127 n., 132, 144-6, 216
Froelich, Bianca, 403 n.

Garrard, George, re Masquing House, 41
Garrick, David, as actor, 268; as dramatist, 277, 280
Gay, John, 219, 244; as author, 236-7, 253; re foreign artists' invasion, 225
Gentileschi, Giulio, and opera, 74
George I and opera, 216-17

George II, 217, 233; for Handel, 225, 256, 262
George III, 287, 293
George IV (Prince Regent), 291 n.
Gerbier, Sir Balthazar, Academy of, 45-6
Gibbons, Grinling, decorator of Duke's Theatre, 100
Gibbon's Tennis Court, 47
Gielgud, Sir John, and stage effect, 36 n.
Gilbert and Sullivan, 358
Gildon, Charles, dramatist, 157
"God Save the King" at the opera, 287, 293
Goethe and Faust, 339, 341, 345, 364
Gondibert, poem by Davenant, 44
Gordon, John, inventor, 375
Gorges House School, 147
Gosnell, actress, 86
Grace, W. G., Jubilee of, 382
Granville, Mary (see Mrs. Delany), 227
Gray, Thomas, re opera, 267-9
Grove's Dictionary, 59
Guarini, dramatist, 134, 143 n.
Gulliver's Travels, 241
Gwynn, Nell, at opera, 103

Haines, Joe, actor, 126
Hamilton, Sir William, and opera, 283
Hammerstein, Oscar, and opera, 392
Hampton Court, 43
Handel (Dent), 223, 240 n.
Handel (Deutsch), 240 n.
Handel (Streatfeild), 261 n.
Handel Commemoration, 284
Harmony in an Uproar, pamphlet, 256-61
Harington, Sir John, re Solomon and Sheba masque, 26-7
Harris, actor, 101
Hawkins, re Duchess de Mazarin, 148; re Comparison, 208; re Royal Academy directors, 240 n.
Hay, Lord, and his masque, 32
Hayes, Lord, wedding masque, 28
Heidegger, John James (The Swiss Count), 171-3, 175, 177, 189, 212, 222, 232, 246, 252, 266
Henrietta Maria, Queen, and Davenant, 41, 44
Henry, Prince of Wales, 30
Herbert, Sir Henry, against Davenant, 60, 73
Heroic Plays, essay, 99
Hill, Aaron, re opera in English, 254; re stage effects, 197-8, 200
Histrio-Mastix: the Players' Scourge, 39
Hobbs, Mr., re composition, 44
Hofmannsthal, librettist, 391, 396
Hogarth, George, re Arsinoe, 160; re music and words, 204; re State of Innocence, 131
Hogarth, William, caricatures, 217, 279
Holderness, Earl of, 217
Hopkins, Father, and metrical Psalms, 139

Hotson, Leslie, 20, 65; re Davenant, 46–7, 73; re Gerbier, 45
Howard, Sir Robert, dramatist, 92
"How Daphne pays his debts", poem, 46–8
Hughes, John, re Italian opera, 159, 208–9, 277

Inns of Court masque, 38
Italian opera for London, 91–5, 129–30, 157 sqq., 169, 173, 175–280
Italian singers in London, 153, 158, 160–2, 169 sqq., 225, 267

James II, 108, 132, 139, 142–3, 146
Jenner's vaccination, 294
Jevon, Thomas, opera burlesque, 145–6
John Dory, ballad, 66
Johnson, Dr. Samuel, re opera, 276–7
Johnson, Samuel, of Cheshire, burlesque opera, 251; re Handel, 255–61
Jolly, George, actor, 46, 74–5, 95
Jones, Inigo, and effects, 25, 33–5, 37; and music, 29; attacked by Jonson, 26, 33–5; Covent Garden Church by, 217; Designer of Court masques, 24–41; in Italy, 24, 29, 31; Masques with, 24–5, 29–30, 34, 37, 40, 43; teacher of Webb, 55
Jonson, Ben, 27, 33, 41, 263; adopts sung dialogue, 30; attacked by Daniel, 29; attacks Jones, 26, 33–5; Expostulation, 34–5; Masques by, 23, 25–6, 30–4, 40; re lyrics, 116; re sense in theatre, 26, 31; stopped from writing masques, 34; Tale of a Tub, 35
Journal of a London Playgoer, 344–7

Kean, Edmund, actor, 316
Kent, Duke of, 285
Killegrew, Thomas, and opera, 91, 93–5, 98, 107; and orchestra, 57, 92, 111; and stage effects, 91; and theatre, 73–5, 88, 95, 114, 131
King's band, 76
King's Servants, The, 74, 88
Kipling, 374
Kip's map of Chelsea, 147
Kneller, 218

Lago, Signor, 373
Lansdowne, Granville, Lord, librettist, 164
Lawrence, W. J., re Ariane, 107, 113 n.; re Cadmus, 144–6; re Clotilda, 179 n.; re Davenant opera, 42; re Ergasto, 161; re Tempest, 106 n.
Lediard, Thomas, librettist, 255
Lee, dramatist, 263
Leicester Fields, 71
Leigh, actor, 139
Lennox, Duke of, in masque, 40
Letter to my Lord . . , A, pamphlet, re music, 266

Lewis, Monk, author, 341
Lighting effects, 24–5, 36, 102
Lindsey House, 147–8
Lisle, Thomas, tennis court of, 73–4
Lives of the Poets, 276
Loeillet, oboist, 182
Löwenberg re Astarto, 220; re Crociato, 327 n.; re Ergasto, 168 n.; re Freischütz, 327 n.; re Pastor Fido, 143 n.; re Psyche, 127 n.; re Rinaldo, 198; re Rosenkavalier, 395
Luttrell re Albion and Albanius, 143 n.

Manchester, Earl of, 175, 223
Mancini, Hortense (see Mazarin, Duchess de).
Manning, Cardinal, re Royal Victoria Hall, 369
Marlborough, Duchess of, 255–6
Marlborough, Duke of, 218
Maryborough, Lord, at opera, 318
Maskelyne and Devant, 396
Mason, 267–9
Masques and Triumphs, 34
Masques described, 23–36
Masques in plays, 21–2, 77–80, 96–8, 103
Masque in public, 39
Masquing-Houses built, 31, 41
Master of the King's Music, 105, 114
Master of the Revels, 46, 60, 73
Mattei, impresario, 270
Mazarin, Cardinal, 31, 107, 129; introduces opera to France, 44
Mazarin, Duchess de, 129–30, 146, 148
Mazzola, C., librettist, 284
McSwiney, Owen, 162, 173, 175, 178, 212
Medici, Duke Cosimo de', at masque, 31
Medici, Maria de', at masque, 20–1
Melodrama Italiano a Londra nella prima metà del settecento, Il, 261 n.
Memoirs of the Musical Drama, 160, 204
Mérimée, author, 357
Messiah, The, oratorio, 304
Metastasio, librettist, 266, 270, 284, 289
Middlesex, Lord, 266–7
Millard, Evelyn, actress, 384
Milton and Dryden, 131; Comus, 39; at opera, 49; saves Davenant, 44; son of composer, 44; verses to Baroni, 49
Molière, 89, 114–15, 341
Monconys, M. de, re scenes, 91
Monk, General, and entertainment, 73
Monmouth, Duke of, attacked, 138–9
Montford, rope-dancer, 65
Moralities, Scenery in, 20
Moray, Sir Robert, 92–3
Morley, Henry, re Faust, 344–7
Mosè in Egitto, oratorio (see also Pietro l'Eremita), 311

Motteux, librettist, 171, 174, 196–7
Mount-Edgcumbe, Earl of, re opera, 303–17
Muratori, Ludovico Antonio, historian, 227
Mürger, author, 381
Murray (see Moray).
Music adjunct to stage-effect, 29
Musical Reminiscences, 303
Mysteries, Scenery in, 20

Naples, King of, and music, 283
Napoleon, 292
Newcastle, Thomas Pelham-Holles, Duke of, 217–18
Newmann, Angelo, 361, 366
New Operas, 222
Newport, Rachel, re opera, 70
Nicholas of Fowey, 66
Nicoll, Allardyce, re Albion and Albanius, 143 n.; re Ariane, 113 n.; re Baroness, 164; re Beggar's Opera, 240 n.; re Clotilda, 179 n.; re Contre Temps, 232; re Davenant, 72 n.; re Dioclesian, 154 n.; re Ergasto, 168 n.; re lists of plays, 167 n.; re prologue to Tempest, 106 n.; re Psyche, 126 n.; re salaries, 168 n.; re Shakespeare scenery, 20; re theatre orchestra, 56–7
Nijinsky, dancer, 399
Nokes, actor, 139–40
North, Roger, re opera, 239–40
Northman, Mr., translator, 163, 165
Norwich puppets, 89

Observations on . . . music in London, 279
O'Hara, Col. James, 217
O'Hara, Kane, librettist, 275
Oldfield, Mrs., actress, 178, 194
Old Vic, 19, 369
Opera Arcade, Royal 298, illustrated frontispiece.
Opera dependent on public, 18
Opera of the Nobility, 256, 262, 264–5, 271–2
Opera, Origin of, 17
Opera, The, theatre (1) 66; (2) 74–5
Operatic jealousies, 158–9
Orange, Prince of, players, 46
Orchestra, Position of theatre-, 56–7, 92, 103
Ord, Bob, 225
Oriana madrigals, 44
Ottoboni, Cardinal, and opera, 175
Oxford, Harley, Earl of, 216

Paisible, flautist, 182
Paradise Lost, 131
Paris opera, 50
Patrons of opera, 18
Peadle, rope-dancer, 65
Pembroke, Lady, pro Cuzzoni, 231–2

Pendarves, Alexander, 227
Pepys, 127 n., 128 n.; re French comedians, 89; re Italian opera, 91–5; re natural sense in opera, 93–5, 204, 209; re perspective, 23; re Siege of Rhodes, 74–5; re Slighted Maid, 85–6; re Tempest, 97–8, 103; re theatre-orchestra, 92
Pereyra, Mlle. M. L., re Tempest, 154 n.
Periodicals:—
Blazing Comet, 25
Commonsense and Weekly Order, 319
Courier, 293–6, 324
Courier and Post, 319
Daily Telegraph, 373, 315–16, 380–5, 388, 392–5, 397, 402
Evening Standard and St. James's Gazette, 399
London Gazette, 154 n.
London Journal, 225, 232, 236–8
Manchester Guardian, 380
Mercure, 225
Morning Post, 381–3, 385, 388, 396, 398, 400–1
Musical Quarterly, 179 n., 227
News, 298–300, 314
Observer, 298–9, 314, 329–31, 334–7, 340–1, 351, 353–4, 359
Pictorial Times, 329
Punch, 351, 356–7, 366–9, 372–3, 379, 383, 394
Spectator, 198–209
Standard, 361, 363–5, 367–9, 372, 374–7, 379, 382, 387–9, 391–2, 396–8, 402
Sun, 292, 294–7, 301, 321, 331, 339–40, 344
Sunday Times, 319
Tatler, 193–4
Telescope, 319
Theatre, 220–1
Times, 283, 285, 288–90, 294, 296–301, 313–14, 316, 318–27, 330–1, 335–8, 341–3, 347–50, 352–3, 355–6, 360–6, 370, 373–4, 376–9, 381–3, 386–90, 396–9, 401–2
Times Literary Supplement, 113 n., 144
Touchstone or The New Era, The, 300
Whitehall Review, 357–8, 375
Perrin, Pierre, librettist, 105, 109–14
Perspective and Pepys, 23
Perspective glasses, 23
Perspective scenery, 23–4, 16 (illustrated)
Peru, ballad, 66–8
Philip V of Spain, 261 n.
Phillips, Mrs., dramatist, 98
Phoenix Park murders, 364
Planché, librettist, 133
Plays and Masques at Court, 36
Pope, Alexander, 218, 226; re Beggar's Opera, 236; re Italian opera, 241; re sense in the theatre, 212
Portland, Duke of, 217
Portugal, Ambassador of, at masque, 71

Pory, Mr., *re* Jonson's fall, 34
Povy, Mr., and perspective, 23
Preston, Lord, *re* opera, 132
Priest, Joseph or Josias, dancing-master, 100, 147–8, 152
Prima Donna, The, 360
"Primcock, A.", (*see* Ralph).
Prunières, M., *re Tempest,* 154 n.
Prussia, Prince and Princess William, 364
Prynne, William, against actors, 39–40, 44
Pulteney, William, 217
Puppets, 89, 175
"Purcell, Mrs.", *re* "Fairest Isle", 154 n.
Purcell's dialogues anticipated, 32
Purcell, Thomas, not composer's father, 59 n.
Puritans against the stage, 39, 44, 52–3, 65

Queen St., 66
Queensberry, Charles Douglas, Duke of, 219
Quinault, dramatist, 114–15

Rachel, actress, 336, 338
Raguenet, Abbé, on operas, 180–8, 208
Ralph, James, *re* opera, 241–50, 252, 264, 280
Rapin, historian, 243
Rathdowne, Baron of (*see* Chetwynd).
Recitative burlesqued, 37, 88–9, 100–1; in masques, 31–2, 39; in *Siege of Rhodes,* 58, 64, 75; introduced to England, 31–2, 35; possibly in Lord Hayes' masque, 29; technique, 185, 197, 209
Reresby, Sir John, *re* opera, 50
Restoration Drama, 56, 72 n.
Restoration Theatre, The, 103
Rich, Christopher, theatre-manager, 158–9, 163, 214; *anti* Italian opera, 161–2; *pro* novelties, 163, 165, 169, 173
Rich, John, theatre-manager, 214, 255; *pro* English tunes, 239, 259
Richardson, painter, 270
Richardson, Samuel, novelist, 276
Richmond, Frances, Duchess of, and Davenant, 40, 48 n.
Rinuccini, librettist, 59 n.
Riva, Abbate Giuseppe, *re* London opera, 226–7
Rochester, Earl of, poet, 173
Rolli, Paolo Antonio, librettist, 219–20, 236, 241, 266–7; satirised, 220–1, 260
Rollins, H. E., *re Peru,* 65
Rome, Opera in, 49
Rope-dancing, 61, 65–7, 162
Rosciad, The, 270
Rossi, librettist, 199, 207, 211
Rousseau, Jacques, designer, 146
Rowe, dramatist, 263
Royal Academy of Music (1674), 108, 114, (1718), 216–41, 246, 250

Royalty at Musical Entertainments:
Anne of Denmark, Queen (James I's consort), 23
Albert Ernest, Prince, 355
Alexandra, Queen, 388
Austria, Maria Maddalena, Archduchess of, 31
Bavaria, King of, 361
Bohemia, King and Queen of, 74; Queen of, 41
Caroline, Princess of Wales, 232
Caroline, Queen, 237, 256, 262
Charles I, 34, 37–8, 41
Charles II, 46, 144–5
Charlotte, Queen, 293
Christian IV of Denmark, 26–7
Connaught, Duke of, 355
Edward VII, 353, 355, 362, 366, 388
Elector Palatine, 31, 41
Elizabeth, Princess (Queen of Bohemia), 31, 41, 74
Ferdinand II, Emperor, 21
Ferdinand, Grand Duke of Tuscany, 20
Frederick Lewis, Prince of Wales, 264
George II, 237
George IV (Prince Regent), 285, 292
George Frederick, Prince, 355
Henri IV, 20–1
Henrietta Maria, Queen, 39–41
James I, 26–8, 30–2
Leopold, Emperor, 289
Mantua, Prince of, 21
Mary of Modena (James II's consort), 108, 143 n.
Poland, Prince of, 21
Prussia, Prince and Princess of, 388
Savoy, Princess of, 21
Saxe-Coburg, Duke of, 380
Victor, Prince, 355
Victoria, Queen, 325
Wales, Princess of (Caroline or Charlotte?), 287, 291 n.
Russian Ballet, 397–9
Rutland Papers, 144–5

Saggio sopra l'Opera in Musica, 270
St. Georges, Vernoy de, 327, 328 n.
Samson, oratorio, 304
Sanine, Alexander, producer, 401–2
Santa Cruz, Battle of, 60
Sardinian Ambassador, 285
Saxe-Coburg Ducal Company, 380
Scenery in Moralities and Mysteries, 20
Scenes and Machines on the English Stage, 36
Schikaneder, librettist, 288
Scotland Yard, 354
Seaman, Owen, *re Salome,* 394
Sense *v.* senses in the theatre, 26, 31, 53, 93, 95, 109, 133–8, 168–87, 193–4, 198–204, 207–8, 220–4, 229–30, 234, 238–40, 242–5, 251–4, 263–4
Serlio, Sebastian, on architecture, 24

INDEX

Settle, dramatist, 214
Shadwell, Thomas, dramatist, 76, 101–2, 114, 122, 131–2, 148, 157, 242; re *Psyche*, 115–17
Shaftesbury, Earl of, 139
Shakespeare, 20, 43, 95, 206, 252; adapted, 95–8, 100–6, 157, 197, 206, 267; and the Davenants, 37, 42; and music, 21, 30, 37, 206; and scenery, 21; ousted by music, 226, 252, 263
Shelley, Mary, authoress, 327 n.
Sheridan and opera, 276
Shirley, James, masque-poet, 38–9, 71, 128 n.
Siddons, Mrs., 294, 306–7
Simpson, re *Luminalia*, 48 n.
Smith, Edmund, dramatist, 172
Smith, actor, 139
Smyth, James Moore, dramatist, 228
Somerset, Duke of, and music, 150, 159
Somerset, Earl of, at a masque, 31
Sorace (*see* Storace).
Sorbières, M. de, re scenes, 91
South Sea Company, 216, 220–1
Spanish Succession, The, 261 n.
Spencer, rope-dancer, 65
Spiletta Company, The, 268
Sprat, Dr., re scenes, 91
Squire, Barclay, re Purcell's parentage, 59 n.
St. Andrée, dancing-master, 116, 127 n.
St. James's Palace, 129, 146
Stage effects, 25, 28, 33–6, 38, 40, 45, 49–50, 54–6, 60–4, 91–2, 157, 188, 197–8, 200, 274–5; aided by music, 29–30
Stair, John Dalrymple, Earl of, 218
Stanhope, General James, (Earl), 218
Stanhope, Lord (*see* Chesterfield).
Stanzani, librettist, 158
Stapylton, Sir Robert, dramatist, 76–87, 90
Steele, Mary Susan, 36
Steele, Sir Richard, re *Crispo* and *Griselda*, 224; re Italian opera, 161–2; re Nicolini, 194; re *Pyrrhus*, 193; re *Rinaldo*, 200; re sense in the theatre, 161–2, 193; re stage effects, 200
Stephenson, designer, 116
Sternhold, 139
Storace (Sorace), Stefano, 304
Streatfeild, 227, 261 n.
Strindberg, 105
Stuart, Charles
Studies in Philology, 65
Sultan Abdul Medjid, 337
Summers, Montague, 103; re *Ps*
Swedish Ambassador, 285
Swift, Dean, 218, 225–6, 237–8, 241, 262, 264
Swiney, Owen (*see* McSwiney).
Swiss Count, The (*see* Heidegger).

Taglioni, 327
Tasso, 199

Tate, Nahum, dramatist, 147
Terry, Fred and lighting effects, 36 n.
Theobald, Lewis, librettist, 214, 261 n.; re foreign artists' salaries, 229
Thurloe, Secretary, 60
Tickell, Thomas, re opera, 169–70; re Addison libretto, 170
Townshend, Aurelian, masque-poet, 34
Translation of libretti, Controversy of, 93–5, 105–6, 109, 134–5, 145, 153, 158–62, 164–7, 169–73, 190, 193–6, 202–5, 207–9, 212, 214–16, 220–1, 238–9, 242–3, 254, 274, 298
Tree, Beerbohm, announces opera-season, 391
Tudor, Lady Mary, in opera, 144
Tyrawley, Baron, 218

Underhill, Cave, actor, 140

Vanbrugh, Sir John, 162, 212, 218–19; as theatre-manager, 158, 160, 163; re opera costs, 212
Vaneschi, Abbé, as theatre-manager, 266, 268
Vasari's *Lives of the most eminent Painters*, 36 n.
Venice, First public opera-house, 21, 42; Opera in, 49–50; Playhouse in, 43
Vernon, re *Psyche*, 127 n.
Vestris, ballet-master, 287
Victoria, Queen, 364
Virgil, 199; ousted by music, 226

Wade, Major-General, 218
Wagner's early operas, 28 sqq.
Waldegrave, James, Earl of, 219
Walpole, Horace, re James O'Hara, 218; re Paganina, 269; re Panichi, 266
Walpole, Lady, pro Cuzzoni, 232
Walpole, Sir Robert, at *Beggar's Opera*, 235; pro Faustina, 231
Walpole Society, 55
Ward, A. W., re *Harmony in an Uproar*, 256
Webb, John, designer, 55–6
Webster, dramatist, 28 n.
Wellington, Duke of, at *Crociato*, 318
Welsford, Enid, re *Luminalia*, 48 n.
Westminster Abbey guide, 66
Westminster School Plays, 105
Westrup, Professor, re "Fairest Isle", 154 n.; re Purcell's parentage, 59 n.
Whitefriars Academy, 49
Whitehall, Masques in, 23, 40, 43; Offices in, burnt by masque-scenery, 33
Whitehead, rope-dancer, 65
Whitelock, Bulstrode, musical amateur, 38, 44; saves Davenant, 44
White's Club, re music, 226
Whitworth, Charles (baron), 218
Whitworth, Francis, 218

Wilcox, Ella Wheeler, 184
Wilde, Oscar, *Salome* by, 391–2
Wilks, actor, 178, 194
William III, 153 n., 158, 217
William and Mary, 146
Williams John, *re* stage-performers, 277–8
Wit and Mirth, or, *Pills to Purge Melancholy*, song-collection ,139, 164, 209

Wood, Anthony, *re* Rutland House performances, 64; *re* Sir Robert Stapylton, 76
Wren, Christopher, perspective instruments, 23; builds Dorset Garden Theatre, 98, 100

York, James, Duke of (*see* James II).

Zola, 375

PRINTED IN GREAT BRITAIN BY RICHARD CLAY AND COMPANY, LIMITED, BUNGAY, SUFFOLK